The Cambridge Companion to Schoenberg

Arnold Schoenberg – composer, theorist, teacher, painter, and one of the most important and controversial figures in twentieth-century music. This *Companion* presents engaging essays by leading scholars on the central works, writings, and ideas over Schoenberg's long life in Vienna, Berlin, and Los Angeles. Challenging monolithic views of the composer as an isolated elitist, the volume demonstrates that what has kept Schoenberg and his music interesting and provocative was his profound engagement with the musical traditions he inherited and transformed, with the broad range of musical and artistic developments during his lifetime he critiqued and incorporated, and with the fundamental cultural, social, and political disruptions through which he lived. The book provides introductions to his most important works, and to his groundbreaking innovations of the emancipation of the dissonance and composition with twelve tones. Chapters also examine Schoenberg's lasting influence on other twentieth- and twenty-first century composers and writers.

Jennifer Shaw is Professor and Head of the School of Arts at the University of New England, Australia.

Joseph Auner is Chair and Professor of Music at Tufts University.

D1616153

The Cambridge Companion to

SCHOENBERG

. . . .

EDITED BY
Jennifer Shaw and Joseph Auner

CAMBRIDGE
UNIVERSITY PRESS

WITHDRAWN

COLORADO COLLEGE LIBRARY
COLORADO SPRINGS, COLORADO

CAMBRIDGE UNIVERSITY PRESS
Cambridge, New York, Melbourne, Madrid, Cape Town, Singapore,
São Paulo, Delhi, Dubai, Tokyo

Cambridge University Press
The Edinburgh Building, Cambridge CB2 8RU, UK

Published in the United States of America by Cambridge University Press, New York

www.cambridge.org
Information on this title: www.cambridge.org/9780521690867

© Cambridge University Press 2010

This publication is in copyright. Subject to statutory exception
and to the provisions of relevant collective licensing agreements,
no reproduction of any part may take place without the written
permission of Cambridge University Press.

First published 2010

Printed in the United Kingdom at the University Press, Cambridge

A catalog record for this publication is available from the British Library

ISBN 978-0-521-87049-8 Hardback
ISBN 978-0-521-69086-7 Paperback

Cambridge University Press has no responsibility for the persistence or
accuracy of URLs for external or third-party internet websites referred to in
this publication, and does not guarantee that any content on such websites is,
or will remain, accurate or appropriate.

Contents

Contributors

Joseph Auner is Chair and Professor of Music at Tufts University. His research focuses on the Second Viennese School, Weimar Berlin, and music and technology. Publications include *A Schoenberg Reader* (Yale University Press, 2003), *Postmodern Music/Postmodern Thought*, ed. with Judy Lochhead (Routledge, 2001), and *Twentieth- and Twenty First-Century Music* (Norton, forthcoming).

Walter B. Bailey is Chair and Associate Professor of Musicology at Rice University's Shepherd School of Music. He is the author of *Programmatic Elements in the Works of Schoenberg* (UMI Research Press, 1984), co-author of *Radie Britain: A Bio-Bibliography* (Greenwood Press, 1990), and editor of *The Schoenberg Companion* (Greenwood Press, 1998). His article "Will Schoenberg Be a New York Fad?: The American Premiere of Schoenberg's String Quartet in D Minor" recently appeared in the journal *American Music* (Spring 2008).

Steven J. Cahn is Associate Professor of Music Theory at the University of Cincinnati, College-Conservatory of Music. His articles on Schoenberg appear in *Schoenberg and Words* (Garland, 2000), *Ostinato Rigore* (2001), *Schoenberg: Interpretationen Seiner Werke* (Laaber, 2002), the *Journal of the Arnold Schönberg Center* (2002 & 2003), and *Opera Quarterly* (2009). He has performed piano works of Schoenberg's in recital. He is currently leading an interdisciplinary group to incorporate neuroscience research on music into the Conservatory curriculum.

Joy H. Calico is Associate Professor of Musicology at Vanderbilt University's Blair School of Music. Her research focuses on music and cultural politics in the Cold War and on German opera. She is the author of *Brecht at the Opera* (University of California Press, 2008). Her current project on the European reception of Schoenberg's *A Survivor from Warsaw* in the 1950s is supported by the Howard Foundation and an ACLS Frederick Burkhardt Residential Fellowship for Recently Tenured Scholars.

Michael Cherlin is Professor of Theory and Composition at the University of Minnesota where he is also Founding Director of the Collaborative Arts Program. His book, *Schoenberg's Musical Imagination*, was published by Cambridge University Press in 2007. He is currently working on a book entitled *Varieties of Musical Irony*.

Craig De Wilde is Associate Professor and Deputy Director of the Yong Siew Toh Conservatory of Music, National University of Singapore. His research interests include nineteenth- and twentieth-century music, especially the works of Richard Strauss, as well as American and Australian jazz and popular music history. Recent publications have looked into the influence of the music business on artistic decisions in both art music and popular music traditions. In addition, his one-hour radio program, *The Resident Musicologist*, aired weekly for over ten years on ABC Radio 774AM in Melbourne.

Sabine Feisst is Associate Professor of Music History and Literature at Arizona State University. She specializes in the music of Arnold Schoenberg, exile studies, experimentalism, film music, and eco-criticism. Among her publications are the books *Der Begriff "Improvisation" in der neuen Music* (Studio Verlag, 1997) and *Arnold Schoenberg in America* (Oxford University Press, forthcoming).

Walter Frisch is the H. Harold Gumm/Harry and Albert von Tilzer Professor of Music at Columbia University, where he has taught since 1982. His research has focused on Austro-German music of the nineteenth and twentieth centuries. He is the author of *The Early Works of Arnold Schoenberg, 1893–1908* (University of California Press, 1993) and editor of *Schoenberg and His World* (Princeton University Press, 1999).

Ethan Haimo is Professor of Music at Bar-Ilan University and the University of Notre Dame. He is active as a composer and a theorist. His compositions include works for orchestra, chamber groups, choral works, and soloists. His theoretical writings include *Schoenberg's Serial Odyssey* (Oxford University Press, 1990), *Haydn's Symphonic Forms* (Oxford University Press, 1995), and *Schoenberg's Transformation of Musical Language* (Cambridge University Press, 2007). He has also written many research articles and reviews, with special emphasis on the music and ideas of Arnold Schoenberg.

Julian Johnson is Professor of Music at Royal Holloway, University of London. His research focuses on the idea of musical modernism from Beethoven to contemporary music. He is the author of four books, including *Webern and the Transformation of Nature* (Cambridge University Press, 1999) and *Mahler's Voices* (Oxford University Press, 2009).

Elizabeth L. Keathley is Associate Professor of Historical Musicology and Women's and Gender Studies at the University of North Carolina, Greensboro. Her scholarly work chiefly concerns musical modernism and its relationship to gender and ethnicity. She is currently writing a book on Arnold Schoenberg's female collaborators, and she is editing, with Marilyn McCoy, the correspondence of Alma Mahler and Arnold Schoenberg for Oxford University Press.

Richard Kurth is Professor of Music Theory and Director of the School of Music at the University of British Columbia. His work on analytical and interpretative approaches to the music of Schoenberg has appeared in *Music Theory Spectrum*, *Theory and Practice*, the *Journal of Music Theory*, the *Journal of the Arnold Schönberg Center*, and in *Schoenberg and Words: The Modernist Years*, eds. Charlotte Cross and Russell Berman (New York: Garland, 2000), and *Music of My Future: The Schoenberg String Quartets and Trio*, eds. Reinhold Brinkmann and Christoph Wolff (Cambridge, Mass.: Harvard, 2000).

Robert P. Morgan is Emeritus Professor of Music at Yale University. His most recent publications are "Chopin's Modular Forms" in *Variations on the Canon: Essays on Music from Bach to Boulez in Honor of Charles Rosen* (Rochester University Press, 2008) and, as editor, *Hearing and Knowing Music: Unpublished Essays of Edward T. Cone* (Princeton University Press, 2009). He is currently completing a book on Heinrich Schenker's ideology in relation to his theoretical development.

Severine Neff, the Eugene Falk Distinguished Professor in the Arts and Humanities at the University of North Carolina at Chapel Hill, is the Editor-in-Chief of *Music*

Theory Spectrum. Her publications include English and Chinese editions of Arnold Schoenberg's *The Musical Idea and the Logic, Technique and Art of Its Presentation*; co-authored with the late Patricia Carpenter (Columbia University Press 1995; Indiana University Press 2006; The Central Conservatory of Beijing 2009) and a Norton Critical Score of *Schoenberg's Second String Quartet in F# Minor, Op. 10.* She is currently at work on a volume of Schoenberg's writings about counterpoint for the collection *Schoenberg in Words* (Oxford University Press, forthcoming) of which she is General Editor with Sabine Feisst.

Jennifer Shaw is Professor and Head of the School of Arts at the University of New England, Australia. Her research focuses on the Second Viennese School, music copyright and moral rights, and performance studies. Recent publications include "Arnold Schoenberg and the Intertextuality of Composing and Performance," *Context* 26 (2006) and "'The Republic of the Mind': Politics, the Arts, and Ideas in Schoenberg's Post-War Projects," in *Music, Theatre and Politics in Germany, 1848 to the Third Reich*, ed. Nikolaus Bacht (Ashgate, 2006).

Richard Toop is Reader in Music at the Sydney Conservatorium (University of Sydney). His work deals mainly with European modernism since the Second World War. Publications include a Ligeti monograph, *Six Lectures from the Stockhausen Courses Kürten 2002*, and *Brian Ferneyhough – Collected Writings*, ed. with James Boros.

Peter Tregear is a Research Fellow of the University of Melbourne, and a former Fellow of Fitzwilliam College, Cambridge. Active as both a performer and academic, current research interests include a study of representations of urban culture in Weimar opera, and he has conducted several modern revivals of works from this period. A monograph on *Ernst Krenek and the Politics of Musical Style* (Scarecrow) is forthcoming.

Acknowledgements

We are enormously grateful to the outstanding group of scholars who have contributed their work to this *Cambridge Companion*. The dedication of those who study the music of Arnold Schoenberg is in itself an important facet of the historical legacy of this remarkable artist. All those who are involved with research, teaching, and performance of his music are deeply indebted to Nuria Schoenberg Nono, Ronald Schoenberg, and Lawrence Schoenberg for the unprecedented access they have provided to Schoenberg's vast archive, first through the Arnold Schoenberg Institute in Los Angeles, and since 1998 with the Arnold Schönberg Center in Vienna. Special thanks to Therese Muxeneder and Eike Fess at the Arnold Schönberg Center for their assistance at every stage.

This book would not have been possible without the tireless support and enthusiasm of Victoria Cooper at Cambridge University Press. We are also grateful to Rebecca Jones and to the entire production team at the Press. Many people have assisted us with all aspects of this project, above all Emily Hoyler and Marguerite Boland, who provided invaluable editorial and logistical support, including excellent work on the music examples. For other editorial help, we thank Jean Norman, Simon Powis and Allan DeSelby, as well as David Stallings for a crucial last-minute Finale intervention.

We are grateful to Lawrence Schoenberg and the Arnold Schönberg Center for permission to reproduce archival materials that appear throughout this book as well as the excerpts from the musical works. Except where noted below, score excerpts are based on those available in the *Arnold Schönberg Sämtliche Werke* (Mainz and Wien: B. Schott's Söhne and Universal Edition). Examples of the String Quartet in D Major are based on Arnold Schoenberg, *String Quartet in D major*, 1897, ed. Oliver W. Neighbour (London: Faber Music Limited, 1966). Example 15.1 is based on Arnold Schoenberg, *Zweite Kammersymphonie, Fassung für zwei Klaviere*, Op. 38B (Los Angeles: Belmont Music Publishers, 1973). Examples 4.1 a and b are reproduced from Arnold Schoenberg, *Structural Functions of Harmony*, ed. L. Stein (New York: W. W. Norton, 1969), 112–13. Examples 4.3 and 4.4 are reproduced from *Richard Wagner: Prelude and Transfiguration from Tristan und Isolde*, ed. R. Bailey (New York: W. W. Norton, 1985), 120. For the Richard Gerstl portrait of Schoenberg that graces the cover, we thank the Wien Museum.

This book was supported in part by a grant from the Tufts University Faculty Research Awards Committee.

Chronology of Schoenberg's life and works

The information given here is compiled from Marilyn McCoy's "A Schoenberg Chronology" in *Schoenberg and His World*, ed. W. Frisch; the timelines published in N. Nono-Schoenberg's *Arnold Schönberg 1874–1951: Lebensgeschichte in Begegnungen*; the work histories in G. Gruber, ed., *Arnold Schönberg: Interpretationen seiner Werke*; H. H. Stuckenschmidt, *Schoenberg: His Life, World, and Work*; and the biography given on the Arnold Schönberg Center website. The list includes all works with opus numbers, major works that were not given opus numbers, and the most significant fragments, including the date of premiere and performers when known. Titles in bold indicate year of completion. For a complete list of works and fragments consult the Arnold Schönberg Center website.

1874   Born September 13 in Vienna
1880   Enters elementary school (*Volkschule*)
1882   Earliest efforts in composition
1885   Enters secondary school (*Realschule*)
1889   Death of his father, Samuel
1890   After the completion of his fifth year, leaves school to work as an apprentice in a bank. His final report card from the 1889–1900 school year included classes in German, French, English, History, Mathematics, Zoology, Chemistry, Geometry, Free Drawing, Gymnastics, with grades ranging from Sufficient to Praiseworthy
1893   Composition lessons with Alexander von Zemlinsky

Many early songs, 1893–1900
Earliest extant completed work: "In hellen Träumen hab ich Dich oft geschaut" (In Clear Dreams I Oft Have Seen Thee)

1894   Three Piano Pieces

The song "Schilflied" wins composition prize

1895   Leaves bank, begins conducting workers' choruses
1896   Six Pieces for Piano Four Hands
1897   **String Quartet in D Major**, premiere in Vienna 1898, Fitzner Quartet

Works orchestrating and preparing piano-vocal scores for operettas

1898   **Two Songs, Op. 1**, premiere in Vienna, Eduard Gärtner

Conversion to Protestantism
Schoenberg takes his first pupil, Vilma von Webenau

1899   **Four Songs, Op. 2**, premiere of 1 and 2 in Vienna, Walter
          Pieau, Oskar Posa or Zemlinsky, piano

Begins Six Songs, Op. 3 (1899–1903)
Verklärte Nacht, **Op. 4**, premiere in Vienna 1902, Rosé Quartet

1900   Begins *Gurrelieder* (1900–03, 1911)

Friendship with Alma Schindler (who in 1902 marries Gustav Mahler)

1901   Moves to Berlin

Brettl-lieder (Cabaret Songs)
Conducts and arranges for Buntes Theater
Der Schildbürger (comic opera libretto)
Marries Mathilde von Zemlinsky

1902   Begins *Pelleas und Melisande*, Op. 5 (1902–03)

Birth of daughter Gertrud
Meets Richard Strauss

1903   Returns to Vienna

Completes ***Pelleas und Melisande*, Op. 5**, premiere in Vienna 1905, cond.
          Schoenberg
Completes **Six Songs, Op. 3**, premiere of 1–5 in Vienna 1907, Anton Moser,
          Zemlinsky, piano
Begins Eight Songs, Op. 6 (1903–05)
Begins Six Songs for Voice and Orchestra, Op. 8 (1903–05)
First scores published (Opp. 1–2, Dreililien Verlag, Berlin)
Awarded Liszt Stipend
Teaches in Schwarzwald School and privately (Egon Wellesz, Heinrich
          Jalowetz, Elsa Bienenfeld, and others)
Meets Gustav Mahler

1904   Begins String Quartet in D minor, Op. 7 (1904–05)

Society of Creative Musicians cofounded with Zemlinsky
Begins teaching Alban Berg and Anton Webern

1905   Completes **Eight Songs, Op. 6** (1903–05), premiere in Vienna
        1907, Theo Drill-Oridge, Arthur Preuss, Zemlinsky, piano

Completes **String Quartet No. 1 in D Minor, Op. 7** (1904–05), premiere
    in Vienna 1907, Rosé Quartet
Completes **Six Songs for Voice and Orchestra, Op. 8**, premiere in Prague
    1914, cond. Zemlinsky

1906   **Chamber Symphony No. 1, Op. 9**, premiere in Vienna 1907,
        Rosé Quartet with wind players from the Hofoper

Begins Second Chamber Symphony, Op. 38 (1906–39)
Birth of son Georg
Begins teaching Erwin Stein

1907   Begins String Quartet No. 2, Op. 10 (1907–08)

Two Ballads, Op. 12, premiere of No. 1 in Vienna 1920, Olga Bauer-
    Pilecka, Ernst Bachrich, piano
***Friede auf Erden*, Op. 13**, premiere of version with orchestra in Vienna
    1911, cond. Franz Schreker
Begins Two Songs, Op. 14 (1907–08)
Begins painting, meets Richard Gerstl

1908   Begins *The Book of the Hanging Gardens*, Op. 15 (1908–09)

Completes **Two Songs, Op. 14**, premiere in Vienna 1921, Erika Wagner,
    Ernst Bachrich, piano
Completes **String Quartet No. 2, Op. 10**, premiere in Vienna, Marie
    Gutheil-Schoder, Rosé Quartet
Marital crisis and death of Gerstl

1909   Completes ***The Book of the Hanging Gardens*, Op. 15**, pre-
        miere in Vienna 1910, Martha Winternitz-Dorda, Etta
        Werndorff, piano

***Three Pieces for Piano*, Op. 11**, premiere in Vienna 1910, Werndorff
***Five Orchestral Pieces*, Op. 16**, premiere in London 1912, cond. Henry
    Wood
***Erwartung*, Op. 17**, premiere in Prague 1924, cond. Zemlinsky
First essay published, "About Music Criticism"
Signs contract with Universal Edition
Begins teaching Josef Polnauer, Karl Linke

1910   Begins *Die glückliche Hand*, Op. 18 (1910–13)

Three Pieces for Chamber Orchestra, frag.
Begins *Harmonielehre* (1910–11)
First Exhibition of Paintings in Vienna
Adjunct teaching of harmony and counterpoint at the Academy of Music
    and Fine Arts

1911   Moves to Berlin

Completes **Gurrelieder**, premiere in Vienna 1913, cond. Schreker
Six Little Piano Pieces, Op. 19, premiere in Berlin, Louis Closson
Herzgewächse, Op. 20, premiere (?) in New York 1923, Eva Leoni, cond.
    Robert Schmitz
Figured-bass arrangements for the Monuments of Austrian Music
Teaches at Stern Conservatory (including Edward Clark)
Begins correspondence with Wassily Kandinsky; paintings and writings
    included in the *Blaue Reiter* (Blue Rider) Exhibition and *Almanac* (1912)

1912   **Pierrot lunaire, Op. 21**, premiered in Berlin, Albertine Zehme;
            subsequent tour in Germany and Austria

Seraphita, for Orchestra and Chorus, frag.
Conducts *Pelleas und Melisande* in Prague, Amsterdam, and St. Petersburg
Publication of *Arnold Schönberg*, essays in his honor by pupils and
    colleagues
Begins teaching Eduard Steuermann

1913   Completes **Die glückliche Hand, Op. 18**, premiere in Vienna
            1924, cond. Fritz Stiedry

Begins *Four Orchestral Songs*, Op. 22 (1913–16)
"Skandalkonzert" in Vienna, disruption of concert of works by Schoenberg,
    Berg, Webern, Mahler, Zemlinsky, shortly after triumphant premiere of
    Gurrelieder
American premiere of Five Pieces for Orchestra in Chicago, cond. Frederick
    Stock

1914   Begins Choral Symphony, frag. (1914–15)

Conducts Fives Pieces for Orchestra in London and Amsterdam

1915   Returns to Vienna

Conducts Beethoven's Ninth Symphony in Vienna
Begins text of *Die Jakobsleiter* (1915–16)
Writes poem "Totentanz der Prinzipien" (Death Dance of Principles)
First term of service in Austrian Army (1915–16), ends with medical release

1916   Completes **Four Orchestral Songs, Op. 22**, premiere in Frankfurt am Main 1932, Hertha Reinecke, cond. Hans Rosbaud

Works on Second Chamber Symphony; writes *Wendepunkt* melodrama
Die eiserne Brigade (The Iron Brigade), march for String Quartet and Piano, premiere at the barracks in Bruck an der Leitha where Schoenberg was serving

1917   Begins **Die Jakobsleiter**, frag. (1917–22) Second term of military service
1918   Moves to Viennese suburb of Mödling

Composition Seminar at Schwarzwald School, students include Fritz Heinrich Klein, Rudolf Kolisch, Paul Pisk, Karl Rankl, Erwin Ratz, Viktor Ullmann
Series of Ten Public Rehearsals of First Chamber Symphony
Founds Verein für musikalische Privataufführungen (The Society for Private Musical Performances)

1919   Teaches Josef Rufer, Rudolf Serkin, Hanns Eisler
1920   Begins Five Piano Pieces, Op. 23 (1920–23)

Begins *Serenade*, Op. 24 (1920–23)
First of 113 concerts of the Verein (1919–21)
Named president of International Mahler League

1921   Begins Suite for Piano, Op. 25 (1921–23)

Weihnachtsmusik, arrangement of Christmas Carols
Johann Strauss arrangements for the Verein
Schoenberg and his family asked to leave summer resort of Mattsee
Publication of Egon Wellesz, *Arnold Schönberg*

1922   Arrangements of two Choral Preludes by J. S Bach: "Komm, Gott, Schöpfer, heiliger Geist" and "Schmücke dich, O liebe Seele," premiere in New York, cond. Josef Stransky

Harmonielehre, Revised 3rd edn
Meets Francis Poulenc and Darius Milhaud

1923   Completes **Five Pieces for Piano, Op. 23**, premiere in Hamburg, Steuermann

Completes **Serenade, Op. 24**, premiere in Donaueschingen 1924, cond. Schoenberg

Completes **Suite for Piano Op. 25**, premiere in Vienna 1924, Steuermann
Begins Wind Quintet, Op. 26 (1923–24)
Meeting with his students to explain twelve-tone method
Correspondence with Josef Matthias Hauer about twelve-tone composition
Kandinsky asks him to join the Bauhaus; breaks with Kandinsky over anti-
   Semitic remarks
Death of Mathilde Schönberg, writes the poem "Requiem"
Teaches Roberto Gerhard

1924   Completes **Wind Quintet, Op. 26**, premiere in Vienna

Premieres of *Erwartung* in Prague and *Die glückliche Hand* in Vienna
50th birthday concerts
Marries Gertrud Kolisch
Meets Giacomo Puccini

1925   **Four Pieces for Mixed Chorus, Op. 27**, premiere unknown

***Three Satires* for Mixed Chorus, Op. 28**, premiere unknown
Orchestration of Johann Strauss, *Kaiserwalzer*, Op. 437
Begins Suite for Three Winds, Three Strings, and Piano, Op. 29 (1925–26)
Begins work on the first of many manifestations of the unfinished treatise
   on *The Musical Idea*
Conducts *Serenade* at International Society for Contemporary Music
   Festival in Venice
Named as Ferruccio Busoni's successor at the Prussian Academy of the Arts
   in Berlin

1926   Moves to Berlin

Completes **Suite, Op. 29**, premiere in Paris 1927, cond. Schoenberg
Begins Variations for Orchestra, Op. 31 (1926–28)
Begins play *Der biblische Weg* (The Biblical Way) (1926–27)
Universal publishes *Texte*, an anthology of libretti and literary writings
Teaches Gerhard, Walter Gronostay, Winfried Zillig, Rufer, Walter Goehr,
   Adolph Weiss
Honorary Member of Academy of Santa Cecilia, Rome

1927   **String Quartet No. 3, Op. 30**, premiere in Vienna, Kolisch
          Quartet

Completes *Der biblische Weg*, partially staged reading in Vienna 2001
Teaches Marc Blitzstein, Nikos Skalkottas
Festival of Schoenberg's works in Paris

1928 Completes **Variations for Orchestra, Op. 31**, premiere in Berlin, cond. Wilhelm Furtwängler

Begins *Von heute auf morgen* (From Today to Tomorrow), Op. 32 (1928–29)

Begins Piano Piece, Op. 33a (1928–29)

Begins Three Folk Songs for Mixed Chorus (1928–29)

Orchestration of J. S. Bach, Prelude and Fugue in E flat Major for Organ, premiere in Berlin 1929, cond. Furtwängler

Begins libretto of *Moses und Aron*

Six-month leave from the Prussian Academy for health reasons, spends time in France

1929 Completes ***Von heute auf morgen*, Op. 32**, premiere in Frankfurt am Main, cond. Wilhelm Steinberg

Completes **Piano Piece, Op. 33a**, premiere in Berlin 1931, Else Kraus

Completes **Three Folk Songs for Mixed Chorus**, premiere in Vienna, cond. Webern

Begins *Begleitungsmusik zu einer Lichtspielszene* (Accompaniment to a Film Scene), Op. 34 (1929–30)

Begins Six Pieces for Male Chorus, Op. 35 (1929–30)

Four German Folk Songs for Voice and Piano; Schoenberg arranged the first three in his Three Folk Songs Op. 49

Teaches Norbert von Hannenheim, Natalie Prawossudowitsch

1930 Completes ***Begleitungsmusik zu einer Lichtspielszene*, Op. 34**, premiere on Südwestfunk Radio in Frankfurt, cond. Rosbaud

Completes **Six Pieces for Male Chorus, Op. 35**, premiere in Hanau 1931, cond. Franz Schmitt

Begins *Moses und Aron*, frag. (1930–32)

Teaches Rudolf Goehr, Erich Schmid

1931 **Piano Piece, Op. 33b**, premiere in Frankfurt am Main 1949, Else Kraus

Conducts *Erwartung* in London for BBC

Extended leave from Prussian Academy for health reasons, in Switzerland and Spain

Radio lecture on Variations for Orchestra prior to Frankfurt performance, cond. Rosbaud

Teaches Henry Cowell, Hans Heinz Stuckenschmidt

1932   Begins Concerto for Cello and Orchestra after a Harpsichord
        Concerto by G. M. Monn (1932–33)

Radio lecture on Four Orchestral Songs, Op. 22 prior to premiere in
    Frankfurt, cond. Rosbaud
Birth of daughter Nuria

1933   Completes **Concerto for Cello and Orchestra after a
        Harpsichord Concerto by G. M. Monn**, premiere in London
        1935, Emanuel Feuermann, cond. Sir Thomas Beecham

Three Songs, Op. 48, published in 1952, premiere in Los Angeles 1950,
    Peter Page, Leonard Stein, piano
**Concerto for String Quartet and Orchestra after the Concerto Grosso,
    Op. 6, No. 7 by G. F. Handel**, premiere in Prague 1934, Kolisch Quartet,
    cond. Karl Jirák
Leaves Berlin, May 17, traveling first to France and then in October to New
    York
Jewish members denounced at a March meeting of the Prussian Academy;
    Schoenberg's contract cancelled in September
Explicit declaration of return to the Community of Israel, witnessed and
    signed, Paris 1933
Teaches at Malkin Conservatory in Boston and in New York; Lois Lautner is
    his first pupil in the USA

1934   **Suite for String Orchestra, G Major**, premiere in Los Angeles
        1935, cond. Otto Klemperer

Begins Violin Concerto, Op. 36 (1934–36)
Works on *The Musical Idea and the Logic, Technique, and Art of its
    Presentation*, frag. (1934–36, pub. 1995)
Princeton lecture on twelve-tone composition
Conducts *Pelleas und Melisande* in Boston
Moves to Hollywood, California
"Two speeches on the Jewish Situation," and other writings and activities
    concerning the Jewish cause

1935   Summer composition seminar at the University of Southern
        California

Teaches John Cage, Leonard Stein, Gerald Strang, Oscar Levant, and
    Hollywood film composers Alfred Newman, David Raksin
Meets Charlie Chaplin

1936   Completes **Violin Concerto, Op. 36**, premiere in Philadelphia
        1940, Louis Krasner, cond. Leopold Stokowski

String Quartet No. 4, Op. 37, premiere in Los Angeles 1937, Kolisch
    Quartet
Professor of Music at University of California at Los Angeles
Begins work on *Preliminary Exercises in Counterpoint* (1936–50, pub. 1963)
Teaches Dika Newlin, Clara Steuermann
Meets George Gershwin

1937   Orchestrates **Brahms Piano Quartet in G Minor, Op. 25**,
        premiere in Los Angeles 1938, cond. Klemperer

Begins work on *Fundamentals of Musical Composition* (1937–48, pub.
    1967)
Kolisch Quartet performs the Four String Quartets at UCLA
Publication of the book of essays *Schoenberg*, ed. Merle Armitage
Birth of son Ronald

1938   ***Kol Nidre*, Op. 39**, premiere in Los Angeles, cond. Schoenberg

Teaches Leon Kirchner

1939   Completes **Second Chamber Symphony, Op. 38**, premiere in
        New York 1940, cond. Stiedry

Teaches Klemperer

1940   Columbia recording of *Pierrot lunaire*, cond. Schoenberg

Teaches Earl Kim

1941   ***Variations on a Recitative for Organ*, Op. 40**, premiere in
        New York 1944, Carl Weinrich

Birth of son Lawrence
Schoenberg, Gertrud, and Nuria become American citizens

1942   ***Ode to Napoleon Buonaparte*, Op. 41**, premiere in New York
        1944, Mack Harrell, cond. Artur Rodzinsky

Piano Concerto, Op. 42, premiere in New York 1944, Steuermann, cond.
    Leopold Stokowski
Teaches Patricia Carpenter
Leonard Stein becomes his teaching assistant
Models for Beginners in Composition

1943   **Theme and Variations for Wind Orchestra Op. 43a,** (arr. for
          Orchestra Op. 43b), premiere of Op. 43b in Boston 1944, cond.
          Serge Koussevitzky

Teaches Lou Harrison

1944   Works on *Die Jakobsleiter*

Retires from UCLA

1945   **Prelude to *Genesis*, Op. 44,** premiere in Los Angeles, cond.
          Werner Janssen

Rejected for Guggenheim Fellowship
Begins work on *Structural Functions of Harmony* (1945–48; pub. 1954)

1946   **String Trio, Op. 45,** premiere in Cambridge, MA. 1947, mem-
          bers of the Walden String Quartet

Suffers heart attack

1947   ***A Survivor from Warsaw*, Op. 46,** premiere in Albuquerque,
          New Mexico 1948, Sherman Smith, cond. Kurt Frederick

Award of Merit for Distinguished Achievement, American Academy of
     Arts and Sciences
Teaches Richard Hoffmann

1948   **Three Folk Songs for Mixed Chorus, Op. 49,** premiere
          unknown

Completes *Structural Functions of Harmony*
Dr. Faustus controversy with Thomas Mann

1949   ***Phantasy for Violin with Piano Accompaniment*, Op. 47,**
          premiere in Los Angeles, Adolph Koldofsky, Leonard Stein,
          piano

***Dreimal tausend Jahre*, Op. 50a,** premiere in Sweden, cond. Eric
     Ericson
***Israel Exists Again*,** premiere in Hamburg 1958, cond. Rosbaud
Named Honorary Citizen of the City of Vienna
"Notes on the Four String Quartets" and Program Notes on *Pelleas und
     Melisande* and First Chamber Symphony

1950   ***Psalm 130 De Profundis*, Op. 50b,** premiere in Cologne 1954,
          cond. Bernhard Zimmermann

Moderner Psalm, Nr. 1, Op. 50c (frag.), one of a set of texts in "Psalms, Prayers and Other Conversations with God," premiere in Cologne 1956, cond. Nino Sanzogno

Publication of *Style and Idea*

Program Notes on *Verklärte Nacht*

1951   Named honorary president of Israel Music Academy

Premiere of "Dance round the Golden Calf" from *Moses und Aron* in Darmstadt, cond. Hermann Scherchen

Dies July 13 in Los Angeles

1 Introduction

JENNIFER SHAW AND JOSEPH AUNER

This Cambridge Companion provides an introduction to the central works, writings, and ideas of Arnold Schoenberg (1874–1951). Few would challenge the contention that Schoenberg is one of the most important figures in twentieth-century music, though whether his ultimate achievement or influence is for good or ill is still hotly debated. There are those champions who regard as essential his works, theories, and signature ideas such as "the emancipation of the dissonance," and "composition with twelve tones related only to one another," just as there are numerous critics who would cite precisely the same evidence to argue that Schoenberg is responsible for having led music astray.

No doubt many readers will take up this volume with some measure of trepidation; for concertgoers, students, and musicians, the name Schoenberg can still carry a certain negative charge. And while the music of other early modernist twentieth-century composers who have preceded Schoenberg into the ranks of the Cambridge Companions – including Debussy, Bartók, Stravinsky, and even Schoenberg's pupil Alban Berg – could be regarded as having achieved something of a state of artistic normalcy, Schoenberg's music for many remains beyond the pale. It is not our purpose here to bring Schoenberg in from the cold or to make him more accessible by showing that the alleged difficulty, obscurity, fractiousness, and even unlovability of his music are mistaken. On the contrary, much of his music – indeed almost all of his creative output, be it theoretical, literary, or in the visual arts – could be characterized to some degree as oppositional, critical, and unafraid of provoking discomfort. He began his *Theory of Harmony* specifically by challenging what he characterized as "comfort as a philosophy of life," with its pursuit of the "least possible commotion," arguing instead that "only activity, movement is productive."[1]

But this passage also points in turn to what has been much less understood, namely the degree to which Schoenberg's contrarian impulse was driven by what was ultimately a productive intent, aimed at reforming, rebuilding, extending, and ameliorating all aspects of musical life. Reductive and monolithic views of Schoenberg have obscured the range of issues, problems, and developments with which he sought to intervene over the course of a long life that spanned late nineteenth-century Vienna, Berlin of the Weimar Republic, and Los Angeles émigré culture from the 1930s to the early 1950s. Yet it is our contention, as demonstrated by many of the essays in this collection, that what has kept Schoenberg and his music interesting, provocative, and problematic for well over a century is precisely his profound engagement with the musical traditions he inherited and transformed, with the broad range of musical and artistic developments during his lifetime he critiqued and incorporated, and with the fundamental cultural, social, and political disruptions through which he lived. The evidence of this engagement can be found in the pages of his scores, his published writings, and through the vast archive of his correspondence, library, sketches, writings, and paintings that he collected and cataloged throughout his life, much of which is now available through the Arnold Schönberg Center in Vienna to anyone with an internet connection.

That such a case still needs to be made a hundred years after Schoenberg first confronted audiences with his musical "air from another planet," as evoked by the text for the last movement of his String Quartet No. 2 from 1908, can be attributed to many factors, but perhaps most directly to the composer's own self-presentation. In 1911 Schoenberg published a rather rude aphorism that would seem to sum up his problematic position in the musical life not only of that period, but for much of the century that would follow:

> The artist never has a relationship with the world, but rather always
> against it; he turns his back on it, just as it deserves. But his most fervent wish
> is to be so independent, that he can proudly call out to it: Elemia, Elem-ia![2]

Here we have a distillation of many of the characteristics that have shaped the reception of Schoenberg's music and thought: a self-imposed isolation, a disdain for an uncomprehending public, and a seemingly intentional difficulty and obscurity that even if unraveled turns out to be something unpleasant. Indeed, the mysterious final word "Elemia" appears in no dictionary, but is a reference to the German acronym "L. m. i. A.," which could be translated, somewhat delicately, as "Kiss my ass."

And of course, many audiences, critics, and other composers have been more than ready to return the insult. Richard Strauss's remark in a letter to Alma Mahler from the time of the aphorism, "I believe that it would be better for him to be shoveling snow than scrawling on music paper," sets the tone for a hundred years of critics who have repeatedly proclaimed Schoenberg's incompetence, irrelevance, and misguidedness.[3] Indeed, if on no other account, Schoenberg's continuing relevance is demonstrated by the rivers of ink spilt by those who have sought, once and for all, to prove his irrelevance. But Schoenberg's advocates, too, have often accepted his claims of isolation. For Theodor Adorno, the degree to which he heard Schoenberg's works as severing "the last communication with the listener" and becoming a music into which "no social function falls," is a measure of its ultimate authenticity.[4] Adorno's very influential interpretation of Schoenberg's music as "the surviving message of despair from the shipwrecked" resonates more broadly with accounts of modernism in general that emphasize its quest for autonomy, its break from everyday life, and its "adversary stance" to bourgeois culture.[5]

But it is ironic that Schoenberg's antisocial aphorism appeared in a very visible place in the *Gutmann Concert Calendar*, published by the noted impresario Emil Gutmann, who was responsible for the 1910 premiere of Mahler's Eighth Symphony and who played an important role in the commission of *Pierrot lunaire* by the actress-singer Albertine Zehme and the subsequent extensive tour of the work. Schoenberg mentions Gutmann in a 1912 diary entry describing a concert of Ferruccio Busoni's music that gives a vivid sense of his active engagement in the rich musical life of Berlin:

> made the acquaintance of [Serge] Koussevitzky. Gutmann dragged me to him. He wants to perform *Pelleas* in Petersburg and Moscow next year. Would be very nice. Hopefully. At least this year foreign countries are starting to take some rather keen interest in me. In two weeks, says K. they will do my IInd Quartet in Petersburg … Went to Heidelberger Restaurant with Gutmann, [Emil] Hertzka, [Anton] Webern, and [Edward] Clark after the concert. Gutmann in very high spirits. But is supposed to have sworn (!!) to perform the *Gurrelieder* in the fall. We shall see. Hertzka beamed![6]

Reading this rather dizzying display of name-dropping (including a famous conductor, Schoenberg's publisher, and two of his students), it will come as less of a surprise that Schoenberg planned an autobiography to be entitled "Life-Story in Encounters" that would "present all persons with whom I have been in contact, in so far as their relationship to me is of some interest."[7] The list of names he assembled counts more than 250, in such categories as "Performers," "Musicians, Painters, Poets, Writers," "Publishers," and "My Friendships"; surprisingly, in light of Schoenberg's reputation for irascibility, there are only two censorious categories: "Thieves" and "Rascals," with only eight names between them. For a composer who is often interpreted from the perspective of the character of the isolated, misunderstood prophet Moses seeking purity in the wasteland, as depicted in his opera *Moses und Aron*, Schoenberg's encounters could populate a small town. Among the musicians, painters, poets, and writers he includes on this list are Gustav Mahler, Alexander Zemlinsky, Richard Strauss, Max Reger, Hans Pfitzner, Ferruccio Busoni, Max Schillings, Paul Hindemith, Franz Schreker, Ernst Krenek, Ernst Toch,

Igor Stravinsky, Darius Milhaud, Maurice Ravel, Arthur Honegger, Charles Koechlin, Heinrich Schenker, Leopold Godowski, Franz Lehár, Alfredo Casella, Gian Francesco Malipiero, Ernest Bloch, Eusebius Mandyczewski, Artur Schnabel, Anton Bruckner, Pablo Casals, Erich Korngold, Fritz Kreisler, Oskar Kokoschka, Jascha Heifetz, Carl Moll, Gustav Klimt, Adolf Loos, Wassily Kandinsky, Max Liebermann, Thomas Mann, Heinrich Mann, Franz Werfel, Peter Altenberg, Karl Kraus, Richard Dehmel, Arthur Schnitzler, Hugo Hofmannsthal, and many others.

Many of the chapters in this book deal with Schoenberg's intensive encounters with these and other figures, including the chapters by Jennifer Shaw, who provides an overview of finished and unfinished collaborative works from throughout his life, Craig De Wilde on Schoenberg's interactions with Strauss, Elizabeth Keathley on Schoenberg's productive partnership with Marie Pappenheim for the opera *Erwartung*, Op. 17, Richard Kurth, who considers Albertine Zehme's influence on the vocal writing in *Pierrot lunaire*, and Joy Calico who discusses Schoenberg's complex relationship with his student Hanns Eisler.

Schoenberg's most profound and long-lasting encounters, as Calico argues, were through his many students in Europe and the United States. In addition to his direct involvement with a large number of students, Schoenberg also published many articles and books concerning the theory and practice of teaching, and still more of his teaching materials have been published posthumously. Through his direct impact, and even more through the teaching activities of his students, including influential performers, conductors, administrators, and teachers, the impact of his ideas and music has been vast, including on many universities in North America and the United Kingdom, such as the University of Southern California, University of California, Los Angeles, Black Mountain College, North Carolina, the Tanglewood Music Center in Massachusetts, New York's New School, and Morley College, London, and stretching from the Darmstadt International Summer Courses for New Music, Berlin's University of Arts, North German Broadcasting in Hamburg, the BBC, Covent Garden, Australia's Elizabethan Trust Orchestra, Hammer Films in London, and the film industry in Hollywood.

As the list cited above makes clear, Schoenberg's encounters were by no means limited to musicians, but included many leading artists and intellectuals in Germany and Austria. His closest contacts among painters were Oskar Kokoschka, Wassily Kandinsky, and Richard Gerstl, whose portrait of Schoenberg appears on the cover of this book, but he had dealings with many others including Carl Moll (1861–1945), the stepfather of Alma Mahler and a Secessionist painter in the circle around Gustav Klimt. A keen inventor and designer of card games, board games, and small machines (such as his own bookbinding machine), Schoenberg also painted and drew throughout his life. His most intensive activity as a painter coincided with the years of his pursuit of an ideal of direct and intuitive emotional expression, 1908–12, when his comparative lack of technical training as a painter seems to have permitted a kind of spontaneity that he struggled to achieve in his composition. The first one-man exhibition of his works took place in 1910 at the Heller Bookshop in Vienna, and the following year his paintings were included in the first of Kandinsky's *Blue Rider* exhibitions. Contemporary accounts of Schoenberg frequently mentioned his paintings along with his musical works. Hundreds of his paintings and drawings survive, including many self-portraits, "visions," and "gazes" (ranging from the more explicitly expressionistic self-portraits to nearly abstract works), portraits (mostly of family and acquaintances), caricatures, landscapes, stage settings, and still-life compositions.[8]

The intensity of Schoenberg's encounter with Kandinsky is evident in its impact on both artists. Kandinsky, Franz Marc, and others in Kandinsky's Berlin circle attended an all-Schoenberg concert in Munich on January 2, 1911 at which Schoenberg's Op. 11 piano pieces were performed, as well as a number of his tonal songs and his two string quartets. Schoenberg did not attend, but Gutmann, who had organized the concert, told him that it had been "A great and loud success . . . there was some opposition following the piano pieces, but these really need to be heard more than once to be understood."[9] In fact, it seems there was loud applause after the songs and a mixture of applause and hissing after the Op. 11 pieces. This was a concert of contrasts. One of the songs performed was Schoenberg's "Erwartung" (Expectation), Op. 2, No. 1 (1899), a setting for vocal soloist and pianist of a text by one of Schoenberg's favorite poets, Richard Dehmel. Schoenberg's Op. 2 is highly effective and, to his Viennese audiences, reasonably familiar territory. Schoenberg's profound engagement with the German lied tradition is explored in the chapter on the songs by Walter Frisch, as well as in Richard Kurth's discussion of *Pierrot lunaire* and its allusions to Schumann's *Dichterliebe* and other songs. In contrast, the Op. 11 piano pieces, which Schoenberg composed in February 1909, were heard as radically new works. As Ethan Haimo charts in his chapter, this was only one of a series of works from these years in which Schoenberg tested the limits of comprehensibility. For Kandinsky and Marc, it was the Op. 11 piano pieces that made the strongest impression. After the concert, Marc wrote to a colleague, "Can you imagine a music in which tonality is completely suspended? I was constantly reminded of Kandinsky's large *Composition*, which also permits no trace of tonality . . . and also of

Kandinsky's 'jumping spots' on hearing this music, which allows each tone to stand on its own (a kind of white canvas between the spots of color!)."[10]

Kandinsky's response was even more direct. He first made two sketches of the concert, both of which depict the grand piano dominating the space with the audience members crowded around it. He then turned this into his painting entitled *Impression III: Concert* where the details have become more abstract; the dramatic effect of the music translated by Kandinsky into blocks, columns, and streaks of color. Kandinsky, who had not yet met Schoenberg, wrote to him after the concert that their radical ideas about music and color shared much in common: "The independent progress through their own destinies, the independent life of the individual voices in your compositions, is exactly what I am trying to find in my paintings."[11]

This began an important artistic friendship and collaboration that lasted into the early 1920s. The relationship with Kandinsky is also taken up in Julian Johnson's chapter on *Herzgewächse*, Op. 20 (Heart's Foliage), a brief work for voice and chamber ensemble from 1912, first published in Kandinsky's *Blue Rider Almanac*. Johnson discusses the song in terms of a "seismic change in the geology of modernism" evident in the emergence of a metaphysical dimension that is so fundamental to Schoenberg's development in the years 1908–23, between the break with tonality and the twelve-tone works. Richard Kurth's chapter on Schoenberg's unfinished opera *Moses und Aron* similarly emphasizes Schoenberg's willingness to test the limits of comprehensibility as a way to point toward an otherwise unrepresentable metaphysical dimension.

These contrasting styles of Romantic and radical composition, sometimes within the same work, combined with sharply divided responses from audiences and critics to those works, form the background not only to the composer's activities and development but also to strong reactions to performances of his music that continue today. A particularly important work in Schoenberg's development was his First Chamber Symphony, Op. 9, composed in 1906 and premiered in Vienna the following year. Its rich and complex harmonic language, although tonal, is at the very edge of tonality; Robert Morgan's chapter delves into theoretical issues around what Schoenberg described as "fluctuating tonality" in the context of analyses of two songs from the Eight Songs, Op. 6 completed just before he began work on the Chamber Symphony. Schoenberg never stopped composing tonal music, and, as Severine Neff shows in her study of his Second Chamber Symphony, Op. 38, started right after the first, but not completed until 1939, he was stimulated by the challenge of reconciling tonality with his later compositional approaches.

Characteristic of Schoenberg's compulsion to engage with and transform whatever genre he encountered, the Chamber Symphony is not really a symphony as his audiences would have understood the Beethovian model of a large-scale, multi-movement work (in fact Schoenberg never completed a full symphony, although he began plans for two during his life). Yet neither was it conceived on the typically more modest scale of a chamber work, but as a work for a small symphony – as in the sense of instruments (in this case fifteen of them) sounding together – with a focus on the kinds of solo textures usually found in chamber music. In other words, there are inherent tensions both in the hybrid genre Schoenberg chose to write and in his harmonic language – and these tensions are played out in all aspects of the piece, through its complex rhythmic writing, its network of solo instrumental lines, doublings and dense *tutti* parts, and its very broad range of dynamics, registers, and expression. Although written as a one-movement work, Schoenberg himself marked five sections in the score as Sonata-Allegro, Scherzo, Elaboration, Adagio, and Recapitulation and Finale, and while there are some extreme demands made of the players, this is a reasonably accessible piece for audiences to listen to: themes and motives do return (although rarely is anything repeated in exactly the same way) and, especially in the Adagio, there are some exquisitely beautiful solos.

Throughout his life the chamber music tradition offered a particularly fertile resource, as Michael Cherlin discusses in his chapter on the very popular *Verklärte Nacht* (Transfigured Night) for string sextet of 1899 and other chamber music for strings. He was also active in writing choral music, including his 1907 a cappella chorus *Friede auf Erden* (Peace on Earth) which premiered (in a version with a small string ensemble) in Vienna in 1911, conducted by Franz Schreker. One of his most popular works is *Gurrelieder* (Songs of Gurre), a dramatic cantata that he began in 1900, completed in 1911 and which premiered (also under Schreker's direction) to great popular and critical acclaim in 1913 – and which, like the First Chamber Symphony, continues to receive mainstream performances today.

In writing for the huge choruses that fill the stage with *Gurrelieder*, Schoenberg could draw on his own experience conducting and composing for several suburban workers' choirs, which began shortly after leaving his job as a bank clerk in 1895 and continued through his first move to Berlin in 1901.[12] In Berlin Schoenberg became involved in another activity difficult to reconcile with the image of the isolated, elitist Schoenberg. From December 1901 until July 1902 he worked as music director of the famous *Überbrettl* Cabaret in Berlin, one of the many artistic cabarets aimed at the fashionable urban intelligentsia. In addition to writing his own cabaret lieder, a large part of his job there had been to make arrangements of existing songs (mainly about alcohol and sex!). In fact, Schoenberg made arrangements of his own and others' compositions throughout his career and, in particular, he spent a good part of his military service during the 1914–18 war arranging patriotic songs and marches for Austrian military bands. Schoenberg's experience of the war was directly linked to his compositional output. In a short note that appeared in a Berlin newspaper in 1916 about a proposed performance of an expanded orchestral version of the First Chamber Symphony it was announced that:

> Arnold Schoenberg, the most modern of the modern composers has been conscripted into the army reserves in Austria. At this time Schoenberg's most recent, still unfinished symphony, was supposed to have had its premiere in Prague under Alexander Zemlinsky. The premiere did not take place at the behest of the composer. In a letter to Zemlinsky, Schoenberg indicated that he would like to postpone the premiere until after the War. He would not want during the War to be the reason for new attacks and hostilities, as could well result from this symphony. When peace again comes, he will no longer steer clear of such attacks – peacetime for him shall again be wartime.[13]

This newspaper report points to Schoenberg's increasing interest in the public dimension of his music during the war years. That he would have postponed the work with an eye toward what the audience's response might have been – or even proposed that as an excuse – marks a significant change from his pre-war aesthetic when he accepted and embraced the fact that his music would only be appreciated by limited circles of like-minded listeners.

The war itself undoubtedly had a significant impact on how Schoenberg saw his social role. His experience of military service (for even men in their forties like Schoenberg were called up for compulsory military service for the Austro-Hungarian forces during World War I) is most directly evident in the jovial chamber work *Die eiserne Brigade* (The Iron Brigade), a march and trio for piano quintet which he wrote in August 1916 for an evening party for recruits at the Bruck an der Leithe military school. By using trumpet signals and other music based on the military drills familiar to all Austro-Hungarian army recruits, Schoenberg took pains to make music that would be readily comprehensible to its intended audience. Attention to Schoenberg's new concern for the audience can clarify the function of such projects as the Verein für Musikalische Privataufführungen (Society for Private Musical Performances), which presented over one hundred concerts over the three years it operated in Vienna (1919–21), with Schoenberg as president and many of his current and former students as members. While the "private" aspect is often emphasized, its purposes were to build the audience for modern music and reform concert life by challenging the power of critics, eliminating what was identified in the prospectus as the "corrupting influence of publicity," and to avoid the disruptions that had accompanied many performances.[14]

Schoenberg's relationship to the public is also bound up with the origins of the twelve-tone method, as is made clear in the history of the massive Choral Symphony that he began in 1914 just before the outbreak of the war. It is in the fragmentary sketches for this work that Schoenberg first used a twelve-tone row and explored ways to generate material by using inversions, retrogrades, and other twelve-tone techniques. In a letter to Alma Mahler he described his vision of a work which was to include seven movements, an orchestra of 300, and a chorus of at least 2,000:

> It is now my intention after a long time to once again write a large work. A kind of symphony. I have already felt it; I can see it already, now perhaps this summer it will come to something. For a long time I have been yearning for a style for large forms. My most recent development has denied this to me. Now I feel it again and I believe it will be something completely new, more than that, something that will say a great deal. There will be choirs and solo voices; that is certainly nothing new. Today that is already allowed to us. But what I can feel of the content (this is not yet completely clear to me) is perhaps new in our time: here I will manage to give personal things an objective, general form, behind which the author as person may withdraw.[15]

In light of the subsequent history of twelve-tone composition – in particular its adoption and transformation by composers like Pierre Boulez, Karlheinz Stockhausen, and Milton Babbitt after World War II – it is common to characterize twelve-tone composition as the quintessential elitist, insider art. Thus it is striking that it was in a large-scale public work like the Choral Symphony that Schoenberg first systematically pursued the new ways of thinking that led to the development of the twelve-tone method. Moreover, in contrast to an image of twelve-tone music as cerebral and abstract, the sketches for the Symphony indicate that Schoenberg's new compositional tools were closely linked to the eclectic selection of texts he had chosen, and to his ideas about spirituality, death, transcendence, and immortality.[16] The linkage between such metaphysical concerns, the twelve-tone method, and Schoenberg's central concept of the "Idea" (*Gedanke*) is the subject of Joseph Auner's chapter on Schoenberg's row tables. During 1917–18, while his Choral Symphony evolved into his oratorio *Die Jakobsleiter* (Jacob's Ladder), Schoenberg wrestled with defining the idea of comprehensibility in an unfinished theoretical work entitled *Coherence, Counterpoint, Instrumentation, Instruction in Form*, a major focus of which is on techniques the composer must use "if the author addresses himself to many listeners or to those of limited capacity."[17] By April 1923 Schoenberg had completed three works that chart the transition from what he called "working with tones of the motive," to the first twelve-tone pieces, the five Piano Pieces Op. 23, the Serenade Op. 24 for chamber ensemble and baritone, and the Suite for Piano Op. 25.

In the postwar years, Schoenberg's often critical engagement with the many new trends was shaped by what he perceived as his obligation to reinforce and extend the influence of German music. Between 1918 and 1922 Schoenberg arranged popular tonal pieces, some in the style of his cabaret songs, for teaching purposes and for the benefit of the Society for Private Musical Performances as well as for his own family's entertainment. He also agreed to a request from Josef Stransky, conductor of the New York Philharmonic Orchestra, to orchestrate two of Bach's chorale preludes. The first of these Schoenberg completed in April 1922, the second in June 1922, and the New York Philharmonic performed them on November 7 that year. In both arrangements Schoenberg extensively modified Bach's scores, not just by means of contrasts of register, articulation, timbre, and tone doublings, but also by the addition of harmonic tones and new contrapuntal lines. In both pieces the changes primarily emphasize motivic coherence, even to the extent, as scholars have discussed, of creating motivic connections that, in Bach's original settings, were "not at all present."[18] Schoenberg's decision to arrange organ chorale preludes by Bach rather than any of his own works – tonal or free-atonal – must have been guided both by his desire to reclaim Germany's superior place in music, as he had claimed in his 1919 *Guidelines* for the new Ministry of the Arts, but also to emphasize his own connections to the German musical tradition.[19]

The image of Schoenberg as the isolated prophet with his back turned to the world was further established by the post-World-War-II avant-garde who sought a music free from tradition, as Richard Toop discusses in Chapter 18. There has been a related emphasis in discussions of Schoenberg's works from the 1920s and 1930s of twelve-tone works such as the Third String Quartet, Op. 30 (1927), the Variations for Orchestra, Op. 31 (1928), and his opera *Moses und Aron*. But as Peter Tregear discusses in his chapter on Schoenberg's "opera of the times" *Von heute auf morgen* (From Today to Tomorrow) and other works, there is plentiful evidence of Schoenberg's engagement with the latest developments in the works of the younger generation, including Kurt Weill, Paul Hindemith, and Ernst Krenek, with their connections to popular music, contemporary life, and the impact of film and radio.

Once the National Socialists' policies came into effect in 1933, Schoenberg, who had been a target of anti-Semitism from the early 1920s, fled Berlin with his family to Paris, where his reconversion from Lutheranism to Judaism was formally witnessed by the painter Marc

Chagall. As Steven Cahn discusses, Schoenberg's formal reentry into the Jewish community must be understood as part of a long personal journey for the composer as well as in the context of the complexities of German–Jewish history. From France he sailed to New York, finally settling with his family a year later in Los Angeles. Unlike many émigrés in their sixties who struggled to create new lives in their adopted countries, for Schoenberg the experience of moving to the United States – while often challenging and mystifying – also proved liberating. As he told an audience in Hollywood in 1934, "I . . . came from one country into another where neither dust nor better food is rationed and where I am allowed to go on my feet, where my head can be held erect, where kindness and cheerfulness is dominating, and where to live is a joy, and to be an expatriate of another country is the grace of God. I was driven *into* Paradise!"[20] He desperately needed to settle in and lead a "normal life" – and, personally, he achieved this, with an extensive photographic record from the time documenting his relative material success, his passion for games and time for recreation, especially involving tennis, and his deep affection for his three young children. Professionally, he yearned for the success other émigrés to Los Angeles had achieved in making the transition to Hollywood's film music culture, but, apart from one well-known and disastrous encounter with MGM, this was not to be.

Yet his new country – of which he became a citizen on April 11, 1941 – proved surprisingly receptive to his music, as Sabine Feisst documents. The United States also gave him the freedom to comment, both in written documents and through his music – on injustices and atrocities that he suspected the Nazis were committing under cover of war. The most famous of these wartime documents, his *Survivor from Warsaw*, Schoenberg composed after the war in 1947 in response to accounts he had heard of the Warsaw Ghetto uprising in 1943. Less well known is his setting of Lord Byron's 1814 poem "Ode to Napoleon Buonaparte", which Schoenberg wrote in 1942 for Reciter, Piano, and String Quartet. In a version for string orchestra, the work was premiered on November 23, 1944 by the New York Philharmonic, conducted by Artur Rodzinski with Mack Harrell in the speaking role and Schoenberg's former student and member of the Viennese Society for Private Musical Performances, Eduard Steuermann, at the piano. As Schoenberg later explained, the *Ode*'s origins were pragmatic, emotional, and didactic:

> The League of Composers had ([in]1942) asked me to write a piece of chamber music for their concert season. It should employ only a limited number of instruments. I had at once the idea that this piece must not ignore the agitation aroused in mankind against the crimes that provoke this war. I remembered Mozart's *Marriage of Figaro*, supporting repeal of the *jus*

primae noctis, Schiller's *Wilhelm Tell*, Goethe's *Egmont*, Beethoven's *Eroica*,
and [his] *Wellington's Victory*, and I knew it was the moral duty of the
intelligentsia to take a stand against tyranny.
But this was only my secondary motive. I had long speculated about the more
profound meaning of the Nazi philosophy. There was one element that puzzled
me extremely: the relationship of the valueless individual being's life in respect to
the totality of the community, or its representative: the queen or the *Führer*.[21]

Byron's bitter ode was written two years after Napoleon's failed attempt to
invade Russia; Schoenberg's just a couple of months after Hitler's likewise
unsuccessful push on the eastern front. This is an overtly dramatic work in
which Schoenberg was adamant in his performing directions for the piece
that the words must be comprehensible: the singer must declaim but very
musically and rhythmically. Schoenberg was in fact adamant that *all* his
works should be performed in the language of their audiences, so that they
could be understood: in this instance he made a German translation of
Byron's text, no doubt for his own benefit, but also, one suspects, for
performances that he hoped would happen in Germany and Austria in the
future – a remote hope in 1942. The musical language, too, although
twelve-tone, is also comprehensible, with much direct word-painting. In
this piece the music is a backdrop to the message, but that backdrop
includes several coded messages of its own – at Byron's line "The earth-
quake voice of Victory," Schoenberg refers to the rhythm of the opening
motive of Beethoven's Fifth Symphony, which, from January 1941, had
been strongly associated with the Allies' ubiquitous "V for Victory"
campaign; and, at the very end of the piece, the final, unexpected E flat
major chord must be a reference to Beethoven's E flat "Eroica" symphony –
itself originally dedicated by Beethoven to Napoleon. Even though this is a
twelve-tone piece, this is hardly the work of an intellectual "constructionist," a label Schoenberg disputed throughout his life. It is clearly dependant
on tonal music's grammar, vocabulary, and phrasing; the music is very
much a response or reaction to the text rather than a straightforward
setting of it. Walter Bailey's chapter on the Piano Concerto similarly
presents that piece as a work intended to communicate to his new
American audience; a work that shows Schoenberg's lifelong engagement
with the challenges of reconciling the "Heart and Brain in Music."

It is our hope that this Cambridge Companion will be useful to those
who wish to begin their own encounter with Schoenberg, a complex man,
profoundly interested in music and the arts, as well as in politics and
religion, and committed to maintaining a strong connection to tradition at
the same time as he explored and celebrated the new.

Schoenberg's early years

2 Schoenberg's lieder

WALTER FRISCH

Schoenberg found his artistic voice largely through the composition of lieder or art songs, which also mark important nodal points in his creative development. (See Table 2.1 for an overview of his lieder.) Close to thirty songs, all published posthumously, survive from Schoenberg's formative years through about 1900. They show him grappling with basic issues of structure and expression in an idiom that owes much to Schumann and Brahms, and something to Hugo Wolf. Of his first eight published opuses, composed between 1898 and 1905, five consist of lieder (Opp. 1, 2, 3, 6, and 8, the latter for orchestra). In this period Schoenberg also completed most of *Gurrelieder*, initially a song cycle with piano that evolved into the colossal cantata marking the climax of his tonal period.

Across these works we can trace a growing command of a Wagnerian and post-Wagnerian musico-poetic rhetoric. The cabaret songs or *Brettl-lieder* from 1901 hone a more popular, satiric tone that was to play a role in Schoenberg's later works, especially *Pierrot lunaire*. In the songs based in the poetry of Stefan George from 1907 to 1908, including the cycle *The Book of the Hanging Gardens*, Op. 15, Schoenberg plunges beyond the limits of conventional tonality and form. The Orchestral Songs, Op. 22, of 1913–16, mark the end of Schoenberg's free atonal period. The Three Songs, Op. 48, the only ones to use the twelve-tone method, are Schoenberg's very last compositions before he left Germany in the spring of 1933.

That Schoenberg would have found the lied a congenial genre is not surprising. Since 1800 it had been the quintessential form of *Hausmusik* in Austro-German culture, where almost every middle- and upper-class house possessed a piano, and many family members could play and sing. The lied fulfilled what a number of writers have identified in the nineteenth-century German-speaking musical world as a growing dependency on words to enhance musical understanding. The rise of program music was one manifestation of this trend. The lied from Schubert through Mahler was another; it brought two fundamental aspects of German culture – instrumental music and lyric poetry – together into a genre that was greater than the sum of its parts. That Schoenberg understood this potential of the lied is clear from his well-known essay of 1912, "The Relationship to the Text,"

Table 2.1 *Schoenberg's Lieder*

Opus Number	Title/ Contents	Date of Composition	Date of First Publication*	Poets
–	(over 30 Lieder)	1893–*c*.1900	1987–88	Christen, Dehmel, Geibel, Goethe, Gold, Greif, Heyse, Hofmannsthal, Lenau, Lingg, Pfau, Redwitz, Reinick, Vrchlicky, Wackernagel, Zedlitz
1	Zwei Gesänge	1898	1903	Levetzow
2	Vier Lieder	1899–1900	1903	Dehmel, Schlaf
–	*Gurrelieder*	1900–11	1913, 1920	Jacobsen
–	*Brettl-lieder*	1901	1969–70	Bierbaum, Colly, Falke, Hochstetter, Salus, Schickaneder, Wedekind
3	Sechs Lieder	1900–03	1904	*Knaben Wunderhorn*, Dehmel, Jacobsen, Keller, Lingg
6	Acht Lieder	1903–05	1907	Conradi, Dehmel, J. Hart, Keller, Mackay, Nietzsche, Remer
8	Sechs Lieder (with orchestra)	1903–05	1913	*Knaben Wunderhorn*, H. Hart, Petrarch
12	Zwei Balladen	1907	1920	Amman, Klemperer
14	Zwei Lieder	1907–08	1911, 1920	George, Henckell
15	Fünfzehn Gedichte	1908–09	1914	George
20	*Herzgewächse*	1911	1912, 1920	Maeterlinck
22	Vier Lieder	1913–16	1917	Dowson, Rilke
48	Drei Lieder	1933	1952	Haringer

* All Lieder have been published in Arnold Schönberg, *Sämtliche Werke*, Abtheilung I, Reihe A, Bände 1 and 2 (ed. Josef Rufer and Christian Martin Schmidt)

where he argues that an art song is an organic work, in which the "outward correspondence between music and text," which involves aspects of declamation and tempo, is far less important than the more ineffable "inward" correspondence.[1]

Throughout the later nineteenth century lieder increasingly formed a core of concert and recital repertory, thanks in part to the advocacy of professional singers such as Julius Stockhausen, Gustav Walter, and Lilli Lehmann. By the 1880s thousands of lieder were being issued by publishing houses, a trend that began to subside only after World War I. Works by Brahms, Wolf, Mahler, Richard Strauss, Zemlinsky, Reger, and Pfitzner represent only the most visible crest of this vast wave of song.[2] *Liederabende* or song recitals were ever more frequent events in these years in the Austro-German realm. Between 1900 and 1914 in Berlin alone there were some twenty such recitals each week, and they were generally sold out.[3]

Schoenberg participated in this thriving culture of the lied. After about 1900 his own songs were premiered or performed by important artists at numerous recitals in Vienna. Some of these were all-Schoenberg events; others were concerts that mixed genres and composers. Figure 2.1

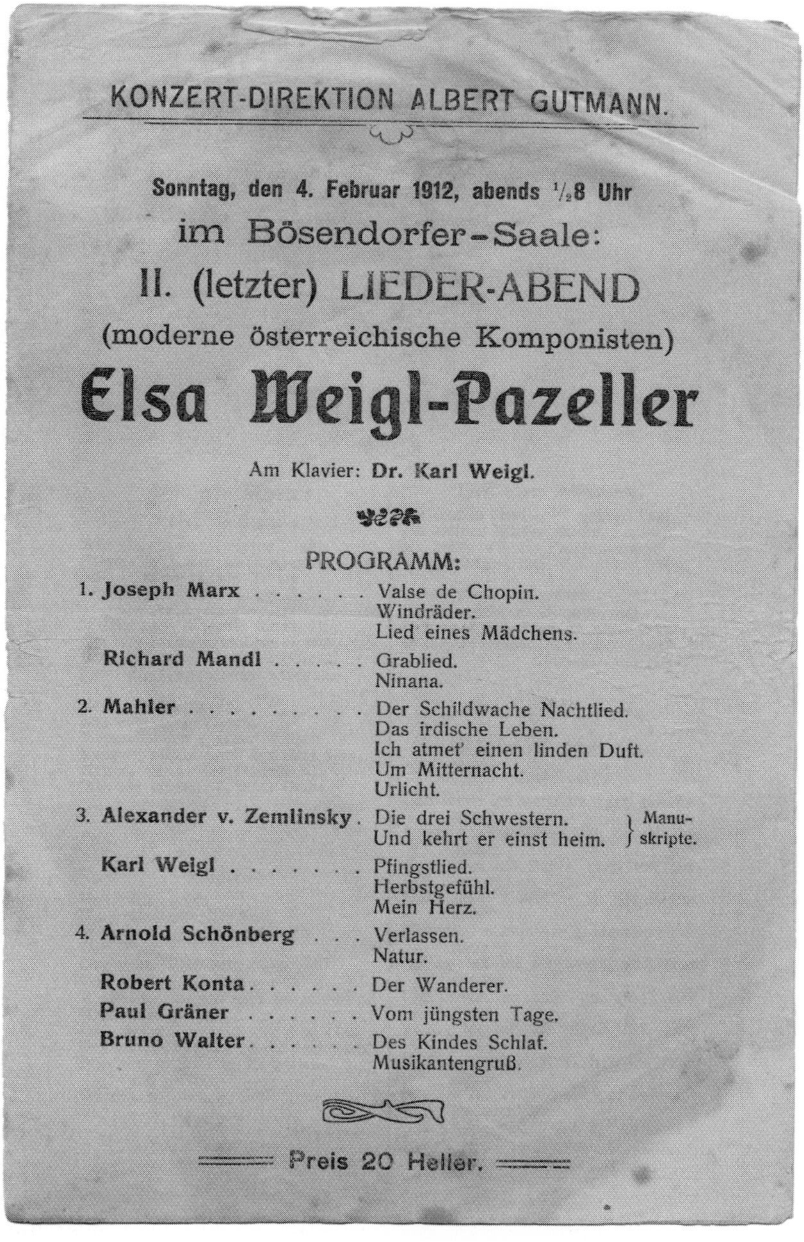

KONZERT-DIREKTION ALBERT GUTMANN.

Sonntag, den 4. Februar 1912, abends ½8 Uhr
im Bösendorfer-Saale:
II. (letzter) LIEDER-ABEND
(moderne österreichische Komponisten)

Elsa Weigl-Pazeller

Am Klavier: **Dr. Karl Weigl.**

PROGRAMM:

1. **Joseph Marx**	Valse de Chopin. Windräder. Lied eines Mädchens.
Richard Mandl	Grablied. Ninana.
2. **Mahler**	Der Schildwache Nachtlied. Das irdische Leben. Ich atmet' einen linden Duft. Um Mitternacht. Urlicht.
3. **Alexander v. Zemlinsky** .	Die drei Schwestern. Und kehrt er einst heim. } Manu-skripte.
Karl Weigl	Pfingstlied. Herbstgefühl. Mein Herz.
4. **Arnold Schönberg** . . .	Verlassen. Natur.
Robert Konta	Der Wanderer.
Paul Gräner	Vom jüngsten Tage.
Bruno Walter	Des Kindes Schlaf. Musikantengruß.

Preis 20 Heller.

Figure 2.1 Program for Lieder Recital, February 4, 1912, Bösendorfer-Saal, Vienna. Arnold Schönberg Center

reproduces a characteristic program from the Bösendorfer-Saal in February 1912, in which Schoenberg lieder from Op. 6 and Op. 8 (the latter in Webern's piano arrangement) are included among songs from prominent contemporary composers.[4] Figure 2.2 represents a more specialized Schoenberg-Mahler program of 1915, which, along with the

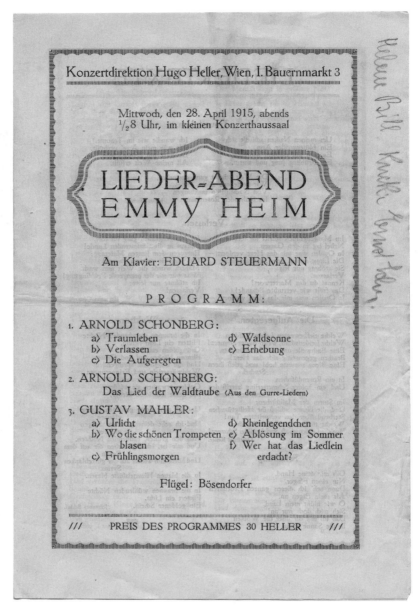

Figure 2.2 Program for Lieder Recital, April 28, 1915, Konzerthaus, Vienna. Arnold Schönberg Center

soprano Emmy Heim, featured the principal pianist of the younger composer's circle, Eduard Steuermann. Like many of his works, Schoenberg's lieder may not have been much appreciated by critics and audiences in Austria and Germany at the end of the nineteenth century. But there is no question that they were heard and noticed.

The songs through 1905

After youthful works in which he tended to set lyric poetry by relatively minor figures (such as Ludwig Pfau), Schoenberg reached a Janus-faced moment in 1897. Two of the songs from this year, "Mädchenlied" and "Waldesnacht," are set to texts by Paul Heyse (1830–1914), a prominent poet who had attracted the musical attention of both Brahms and Wolf. These poems represent elegant examples, respectively, of the *volkston* (folk tone) and the *Stimmungslyrik* (or "mood" poetry, usually based on descriptions of love or nature). Schoenberg rose to the occasion with songs that show real mastery of the Brahms style.

In the same year, however, Schoenberg began to leave that world behind with his discovery of the modernist poet Richard Dehmel (1863–1920). The two Dehmel songs of 1897, "Mädchenfrühling" and "Nicht doch!," were to be the first of over twenty settings of this poet across the next eight years. In a letter written to Dehmel in 1912, Schoenberg confessed, "Your poems have had a decisive influence on my development as a composer. They were what first made me try to find a new tone in the lyrical mood."[5] Dehmel, one of the leading poets of the post-Heyse generation, infused his verse with naturalism, impressionism, and overt eroticism. In "Mädchenfrühling" the arrival of spring is developed as a metaphor for the emergence of feelings of love and sexuality. Schoenberg responds with a song that attains a new level of formal and harmonic fluidity, dominated by the half-diminished seventh chord (the "Tristan" chord in a different voicing), which undermines or replaces traditional tonic-dominant relationships.

The Two Lieder, Op. 1, composed in 1898, were the first works of Schoenberg to be published and the first songs to be heard in public. They were performed in Vienna in the year of composition by the baritone Eduard Gärtner and were issued by the Berlin firm of Dreililien Verlag in October 1903, dedicated (as was Op. 2) to "my friend and teacher Alexander von Zemlinsky." Schoenberg had studied composition with Zemlinsky in 1896–97; they became brothers-in-law in 1901 when he married Zemlinsky's sister Mathilde. The contrast of Op. 1 with Schoenberg's earlier songs is extreme. The Op. 1 pair, almost mini-cantatas, are expansive settings exemplifying what has been called *Begriffspoesie* (conceptual or philosophical poetry) by the Viennese writer Karl von Levetzow. In musical style and affect the songs show some affinity with Brahms's Four Serious Songs, Op. 121, written only two years earlier, in 1896. The vocal part is wide-ranging, and orchestral effects in the piano part at times strain against the medium.

In the Four Songs of Op. 2, the first three of which can be dated firmly to 1899, Schoenberg returns to the realm of the *Stimmungslyrik* as boldly

Example 2.1 Schoenberg, "Erwartung," Op. 2, No. 1

reinterpreted by his favorite poet of the time, Dehmel. Once again Dehmel fired Schoenberg's musical imagination to new heights, especially in the song Schoenberg placed at the head of the set, "Erwartung," which brings together the influences of Brahms, Wolf, Wagner, and Strauss into a style that is recognizably his own. Dehmel's poem, a symbolist vision of a man awaiting a tryst, is filled with color words describing the various physical phenomena (sea-green pond, opal ring, a woman's white hand). Schoenberg in turn creates a kind of "color" chord, a five-note sonority which acts as a source of much of the harmonic activity in the song and which in alternation with the tonic forms what Schoenberg would later call a *Grundgestalt*, or basic shape (Example 2.1).

Between 1900 and 1903 Schoenberg was occupied largely with the composition of *Gurrelieder* and the *Brettl-lieder*. He also moved from Vienna to Berlin to take up a position offered to him at the Überbrettl, the first German cabaret based on the Parisian model of a counter-cultural venue where young artists would present songs and sketches of social criticism or satire. In the *Gurrelieder*, especially the orchestral versions, the rich, chromatic language of the Op. 2 songs and of the great Dehmel-inspired instrumental work of 1899, *Verklärte Nacht*, Op. 4, is enhanced by a more distinctly contrapuntal style and expansive approach to form. All but one of the *Brettl-lieder* are settings of poems that appeared in the collection *Deutsche-Chansons (Brettl-lieder)* in 1900. ("Brett" means plank or board, and has the connotation of the stage, as in the English phrase "the boards.") Schoenberg shows an impressive command of the chatty, racy cabaret singing-speaking style (but does not use *Sprechstimme*), although the piano accompaniments are often far more elaborate than is characteristic for the idiom.

The Eight Songs of Op. 6, composed between 1903 and 1905, mark another key moment in the development of Schoenberg's expressive and structural powers. Some were written just prior to, concurrently with, or after the First Quartet, Op. 7, and they share that work's intensity of counterpoint and the prominence of what Schoenberg would later call "vagrant" harmonies – harmonies not clearly attached to any key. "Verlassen" (Forsaken), Op. 6, No. 4, was composed in December 1903 to a text by a leading modernist German poet, Hermann Conradi. In it, the protagonist reports "moaning" (*stöhnt*) the title word and feeling very out of sorts with the beautiful spring day dawning around him.

The basic material of the song consists not of a single theme or motive, but a contrapuntal complex comprising three different figures (marked a, b, c), which are recombined and inverted among the two hands of the piano and the voice part (Example 2.2). The emphasis on counterpoint, on the greater independence of lines, works to weaken traditional tonal syntax and increase the complexity of Schoenberg's harmonic language. The tonic of the song, E flat minor, is articulated by the left hand on the downbeats, but is otherwise obscured by the pervasive chromaticism, which becomes more structural than ornamental. Thus, the vocal part begins on F flat, which is ostensibly a half-step neighbor or appoggiatura to the tonic, but in fact moves right through the tonic note, to outline a striking D7 chord. This sonority is a truly vagrant harmony that bears no clear relationship to E flat minor and certainly does not function as a dominant of G minor. Somewhat like the "color" chord in "Erwartung," it consists primarily of neighbor notes to the tonic, plus one chord tone (F sharp or G flat). Ostensibly a dissonance, in the tonal world of "Verlassen" it sounds logical and almost stable.

The Six Orchestral Songs, Op. 8, date from the same time frame as Op. 6, 1903–05. The immediate impetus for their composition is not clear,

Example 2.2 Schoenberg, "Verlassen," Op. 6, No. 4

but in them Schoenberg was following a path of orchestral song well established by Mahler and Strauss. Dreililien Verlag, the publisher of Schoenberg's early, smaller-scale opuses, balked at taking on such a massive score (as they did when refusing Schoenberg's earlier symphonic poem *Pelleas und Melisande*). The Op. 8 songs were not to appear in full score until 1913, from Universal; they received their premiere in 1914 under the baton of Zemlinsky in Prague. The Op. 8 set was not conceived as a cycle, and the poetic selection is something of a miscellany – one text by the contemporary naturalist Heinrich Hart, two from the early Romantic collection (beloved by Mahler) *Des Knaben Wunderhorn*, and three German translations of Petrarch sonnets. The songs share with Op. 6 and with *Gurrelieder* an advanced harmonic language and a richness of counterpoint. The first two Petrarch settings, "Nie ward ich, Herrin müd" (I have never grown tired, Lady) and "Voll jener Süße" (Full of that sweetness), the longest in the set, are also perhaps the most impressive. The beginning of "Nie ward ich" contains a freely inverted canon between bass line and voice, to which the middle part adds a repeated chromatic motive. As in "Verlassen," the parts are reshuffled in the later reprise of this material. "Voll jener Süße" was cited by Schoenberg in his *Theory of Harmony* as an example of "fluctuating" (*schwebende*) tonality: clear triads are avoided throughout most of the song, and the principal tonic D flat is shadowed by and frequently juxtaposed with B major.

The George songs

Between the fall of 1905 and the spring of 1907, Schoenberg's engagement with lieder composition became less intense. The Two Ballads of Op. 12, from March to April 1907, represent something of a sport among his works. In early 1906 the Berlin journal *Woche* had called for "a revitalization of German ballad poetry" and later that year published a special issue with a number of newly submitted ballads, announcing a competition for musical settings. Schoenberg, whose financial situation was precarious at the time, decided to enter the competition and selected four poems, of which he completed settings of only two, "Jane Grey" (the poem was entitled "Lady Jane") by Heinrich Amman and "Der verlorene Haufen" by Viktor Klemperer.

In musical style, the Op. 12 ballads (which did not win the contest) continue on the path of Op. 6. The real turning point for Schoenberg came, by his own admission, later in 1907, when he began an intensive eighteen-month engagement with the poetry of Stefan George. George (1868–1933) was something of a cult figure who set himself up as a prophet or high priest of art separated from the real world. His circle of acolytes became known as the George-Kreis. Strongly influenced by French symbolism, but also tending in the direction of nascent German expressionism, George shunned the naturalism popular among his literary contemporaries. His strongly confessional poems, which are often addressed to his real-life muse Ida Coblenz or his young male lover Maximin Kronberger, stress personal loneliness or sadness – or genuine anguish.

Schoenberg's first settings of George, from the late fall of 1907, included the song "Ich darf nicht dankend," which appeared in Op. 14, and initial work on the final two movements of the Second String Quartet, Op. 10, set to the poems "Litanei" and "Entrückung." In March 1908, as he completed the quartet, Schoenberg began work on the songs that were to form *The Book of the Hanging Gardens* cycle, which was finished in February 1909. "I was inspired by the poems of Stefan George, the German poet, to compose music to some of his poems," Schoenberg recalled in later years. "And, surprisingly, without any expectation on my part, these songs showed a style quite different from what I had written before . . . New sounds were produced, a new kind of melody appeared, a new approach to expression of moods and characters was discovered."[6] In the program accompanying the premiere of *The Book of the Hanging Gardens*, Schoenberg characterized this moment even more dramatically: "I am conscious of having broken through every restriction of a bygone aesthetic . . . I am being urged in this direction . . . I am obeying an inner compulsion, which is stronger than my education."[7]

For *The Book of the Hanging Gardens*, arguably the greatest German song cycle since Schubert and Schumann, Schoenberg chose fifteen poems from a collection by George that traces the erotic fantasies, memories, and, ultimately, disappointment, of a young Babylonian prince. The lush imagery of the garden forms the backdrop for the prince's powerful feelings, as in the second poem:

> Hain in diesen paradiesen
> Wechselt ab mit blutenwiesen
> Hallen ˙ buntbemalten fliesen.
> Schlanker störche schnäbel kräuseln
> Teiche die von fischen schillern ˙
> Vögel-reihen matten scheines
> Auf den schiefen firsten trillern
> Und die goldnen binsen säuseln –
> Doch mein traum verfolgt nur eines.

> [Groves in these paradises alternate with fields of flowers, halls, gaily colored flagstones. Beaks of slender storks ripple, ponds shimmering with fishes, faintly gleaming rows of birds trill on the sloping ridges, and the golden rushes rustle. Yet my dream pursues only one goal.]

(translation by the author)

Example 2.3 Schoenberg, *The Book of the Hanging Gardens*, Op. 15, No. 2

George cultivated a style of typography that uses lower-case letters except at the beginning of lines, special punctuation marks (as after "Hallen" and "schillern"), and even certain fonts that became known as *Georgeschrift*. This poem, like all in the cycle, uses a regular metrical scheme – here trochaic tetrameter – and there is also a distinct if less predictable pattern of rhymes. In his setting Schoenberg tends to obscure these features (Example 2.3). The opening pair of lines is set in a recitative-like style over a sustained chord. The harmonic language hovers on and beyond the edges of tonality in a way that seems at once intuitive and completely logical. Although the initial chord has a distinct flavor of D minor (one of Schoenberg's favorite keys in his early tonal works, as in the First Quartet, *Verklärte Nacht*, and *Pelleas und Melisande*), the added C sharp makes it into what Brian Simms has called a "triadic tetrachord" characteristic of Schoenberg's early atonal period.[8] When the bass changes to E flat at the end of the second measure, the chord hints at still another identity, based on whole tones. At the cadence to "fliesen" in m. 5, Schoenberg provides a genuinely tonal cadence to B major, complete with a full triad and a very traditional appoggiatura resolution from A sharp to B. The extraordinary fluidity of the harmonic language in the *Hanging Gardens* cycle is the perfect musical analogue not to the formal structure of George's poetry, but to its imagery and syntax, which obscure conventional meaning through a profusion of adjectival descriptions of natural phenomena.

Herzgewächse and the Orchestral Songs, Op. 22

The creative energy unleashed by Schoenberg's encounter with George's poetry flowed over into the masterpieces of the atonal period, composed between 1909 and 1916, including the Three Piano Pieces, Op. 11; the Five Orchestral Pieces, Op. 16; the monodrama *Erwartung*, Op. 17; the short "drama with music" *Die glückliche Hand*, Op. 18; the Six Little Piano Pieces, Op. 19; the song with chamber ensemble *Herzgewächse*, Op. 20; *Pierrot lunaire*, Op. 21; and the Four Orchestral Songs, Op. 22. The momentum foundered only as Schoenberg began to draft his most ambitious work until then, the unfinished oratorio *Die Jakobsleiter*, in 1917. The human voice obviously plays a large role in this series of works. Schoenberg found that having a text to set could help give form in the new universe of free atonality, where traditional period structure and harmonic progressions were suspended. More than this, the vocal works of this period serve as confirmation of what Schoenberg would articulate in his essay "The Relationship to the Text" of 1912, as discussed above. There Schoenberg seems to uphold a view of songs as absolute music free of extramusical associations. But he is also really suggesting that in the best songs or vocal music, text and music relate to each other not in a superficial, mimetic way, but on a deeper, more organic level.

The essay was written for Kandinsky and Marc's *Blue Rider Almanac*, one of the great documents of German expressionism, and it was accompanied by a facsimile of the score of *Herzgewächse* (Foliage of the Heart), a thirty-measure song for voice, harmonium, celesta, and harp, which Schoenberg wrote in early December 1911 expressly for inclusion in the publication. The text is a free translation of a poem by Maurice Maeterlinck, the symbolist poet who was much admired by Kandinsky and his circle and whose *Pelléas et Mélisande* had formed the source for Schoenberg's symphonic poem in 1903. The style of the poem bears resemblance to George's *Hanging Gardens* verse, where an anguished soul seems isolated, even trapped, within a luxuriant natural environment, although here the setting is a hothouse, not a real garden.

The musical style of *Herzgewächse* represents something of a breakthrough for Schoenberg. (It is a pity this work, which is seldom performed because of its brevity and unusual scoring, is not better known.) As Wolfgang Ruf has perceptively pointed out, in other vocal works of this free atonal period, including *Die glückliche Hand* and *Pierrot lunaire*, song tends to be approximated to speech and thus in a sense "de-musicalized." In the concluding segment of *Herzgewächse*, by contrast, "language is musicalized."[9] The vocal part becomes highly melismatic; in the final measures its rhythm is broadened and to some degree regularized in

Example 2.4 Schoenberg, *Herzgewächse*, Op. 20

quarter notes as the voice floats up to its ethereal high F, then drops over two octaves to its cadence (Example 2.4).

The Four Orchestral Songs, the final works of Schoenberg's free atonal period, also represent the last large-scale work that Schoenberg was to complete before the creative hiatus of the years 1916–20, which was to end with the first of the Op. 23 Piano Pieces. The first of the songs completed was "Seraphita," set to a text by the English poet Ernest Dowson as translated by Stefan George. "Seraphita" is a surviving trace, along with a one-page fragment of a work for orchestra and chorus from 1912 with the same title, of Schoenberg's quest to compose a massive, multi-evening stage work based on Balzac's *Séraphita*, a novel of 1835 which had featured the religious-philosophical ideas of Emanuel Swedenborg. (Schoenberg would recast the project in the unfinished oratorio *Jakobsleiter*.) Swedenborg's ideas about a gradual progression of mankind to the state of angels were similar to those of Theosophy and Anthroposophy, contemporary movements in spiritual philosophy and mysticism to which Schoenberg was attracted at this time. Dowson's sonnet has little overtly to do with this complex of ideas, but Ruf has argued that together with the three Rilke poems that make up the other songs, Schoenberg created for the Op. 22 cycle a kind of Swedenborgian trajectory: "being develops in the three realms of the natural, spiritual, and heavenly, and mankind can and should advance through all three stages of creation."[10]

The scoring of the four songs deviates from the broad dimensions of Mahler, Strauss, and the earlier Schoenberg. In the first, which is also the longest, Schoenberg deploys a large orchestra in a distinctive fashion: the string complement lacks violas; the only woodwinds are clarinets; and the only brass are trumpets, trombones, and bass tuba. In the remaining three songs, Schoenberg employs a more chamber-like setting, featuring more profiled individual instrumental voices. There is a certain symmetry in the cycle in that brass instruments appear only in the outer songs, "Seraphita" and "Vorgefühl," which also share certain motivic shapes, poetic imagery (the storm), and orchestral figures.

The Op. 22 songs are the only atonal works to which Schoenberg himself devoted an extended analysis, in his well-known Frankfurt radio address of 1932.[11] In this talk, directed at a general public, the composer emphasizes how his intuitive, instinctive sense of "form" and "logic" guided him through this period of composition, and how music theory always lags behind current practice. He explains that traditional structural analysis cannot account for what happens in the songs, and he goes on to stress how, especially in "Seraphita," to which he devotes the most attention, logic and unity are provided by means of motivic variation. The components of a basic three-note figure (F–G flat–A in its initial appearance) are transposed, inverted, retrograded, and reordered throughout the song. Even though Schoenberg is analyzing "Seraphita" from a vantage point well on the other side of his development of the twelve-tone method, the techniques of Op. 22 represent an important precursor of that technique.

Three Songs, Op. 48

Schoenberg composed the Three Songs, Op. 48, in February 1933 in Berlin, where he was in his eighth year as Professor of Composition at the Prussian Academy of the Arts. They were the last compositions he would complete in Germany. Hitler had come to power in January, and in March the Academy's president declared that "Jewish influences" had to be eliminated. Schoenberg voluntarily submitted his resignation, and soon thereafter he and his family departed for Paris in what was to be a permanent exile. Perhaps in the crush of events, the songs seem to have been forgotten by Schoenberg. In 1948 the American music publisher Bomart (later Boelke-Bomart) learned about the songs and contacted Schoenberg about publishing them. They were part of a group of Schoenberg works that Bomart would issue, including *Kol Nidre*, Op. 39, the String Trio, Op. 45, and *A Survivor from Warsaw*, Op. 46.

The texts for Op. 48 are by Jakob Haringer (1898–1948), a relatively minor poet and writer on the edges of the Expressionist movement, with whom Schoenberg had at least a fleeting acquaintance in 1932. Adorno disparaged Haringer's poetry as "a mixture of Verlaine and infantilism."[12] Indeed, the three poems selected by Schoenberg are not at the level of the verse he set in the early atonal period; in some ways they are a throwback to the more sentimental *Stimmungslyrik* of the later nineteenth century.

The poems trace an emotional trajectory from optimism in "Sommermüd" (Summer Weariness), in which God and nature are praised, to a much darker outlook in "Tot" (Dead) and "Mädchenlied" (Maiden's Song). The stars and faith of the first poem are rendered powerless in the last one to help the maiden's "poor heart": "Dem hilft kein Stern, kein Gebet" (No star, no prayer can help it).

The Op. 48 songs were composed with Schoenberg's mature twelve-tone technique. Row forms are divided into three- or four-note segments that are treated not only horizontally but vertically, as harmonic entities (trichords or tetrachords). The songs of Op. 48 display another aspect of Schoenberg's later twelve-tone technique, hexachordal combinatoriality, whereby the first six-note segment of the row will be identical in pitch content to the second segment of another row form at certain levels of transposition or inversion, thus allowing for the aggregate of all twelve pitches to be presented simultaneously in the vertical and horizontal dimensions. The deployment of the row forms in Op. 48 is also closely linked with the poetic structure. Schoenberg divides "Sommermüd" into three strophe-like segments and a postlude. In each segment, the alternation of pitch content between two row forms (P^0 and I^5) corresponds with the design of the poem, in which contrasting sentiments are presented in an antithetical style.[13]

Schoenberg's choice of texts often bore a relation to his current life situation (as when the George poems of 1907–08 captured his feelings about the affair of Schoenberg's wife with the painter Richard Gerstl). Although we should be wary of making too direct an association, it seems more than likely that the worsening political and cultural climate in Berlin in the winter and spring of 1933 contributed to Schoenberg's selection of these Haringer poems.

It is probably a coincidence that what was to be Schoenberg's last song, "Mädchenlied," shares its title with three others in his oeuvre. This title was not unusual in German lyric poetry or lieder of the nineteenth and early twentieth centuries. Yet, like Brahms, returning at the end of his career to a folk poem that had inspired his Op. 1, and commenting to a friend that "the serpent bites his tail," there is a suggestive symmetry in Schoenberg's choice. The earliest of Schoenberg's "Mädchenlied" songs dates from before 1896 and uses a Geibel text in an innocent *volkston* about how the absence of the girl's lover spoils the world around her. The Haringer poem Schoenberg selected in 1933 is much less naive. No lover is mentioned, just sadness, despair, and thoughts of suicide.

By 1933 the Austro-German culture that supported the composition, performance, and publication of lieder had virtually dissolved. There was little place for the Op. 48 songs, or for Schoenberg's other works, in the world created by the Nazis. But Schoenberg's personal story was not to conclude in the gloomy tone of the maiden, and perhaps that is why – at least at an unconscious level – the Haringer songs were put in a drawer or a trunk as Schoenberg and his family took off for the new world, a new life, and a new phase of his compositional career.

3 Schoenberg and the tradition of chamber music for strings

MICHAEL CHERLIN

Chamber music was as central to Schoenberg's life's work as it had been for the great Viennese composers before him: Haydn, Mozart, Beethoven, Schubert, and the central model of Schoenberg's youth – Brahms. While a significant proportion of Schoenberg's chamber works was composed for idiosyncratic ensembles (including *Herzgewächse*, Op. 20; *Pierrot lunaire*, Op. 21; *Serenade*, Op. 24; *Suite*, Op. 29; and *Ode to Napoleon*, Op. 41), it is through the chamber music for strings that Schoenberg most directly engages, continues, and transforms a tradition that was at the very core of his self-identity as a composer. Moreover, the genre of the string quartet in particular continued to develop in extraordinary ways throughout the second half of the twentieth century on into our own time. The string quartets of the Second Viennese School – Schoenberg, Berg, and Webern – along with those of Bela Bartók were the chief inspiration for these remarkable developments.

Schoenberg's chamber music for strings consists of seven works, the String Quartet in D major (1897), the string sextet *Verklärte Nacht*, Op. 4, the four string quartets with opus numbers (Opp. 7, 10, 30, 37), and the String Trio, Op. 45. In addition to the sextet, quartets, and trio, there is the *Phantasy* for violin and piano, Op. 47. (Schoenberg also composed a Scherzo for String Quartet, originally the second movement for the 1897 String Quartet in D major).[1] The chamber music for strings spans nearly fifty years, including all of Schoenberg's compositional periods: the early tonal music inspired principally by Brahms; the highly chromatic tonality of his first maturity; the contextual "atonality" of his second period; the twelve-tone music from the Weimar years; and the late twelve-tone music composed after his emigration to the United States. This chapter will concentrate on Schoenberg's first two chamber works for strings, the String Quartet of 1897 and the string sextet *Verklärte Nacht*. Despite the vast changes in Schoenberg's compositional language, the later works are genetically related to the earlier ones and through them to the larger tradition from which Schoenberg springs.

String Quartet in D major, 1897

Although preceded by other works for string quartet, including a quartet in C major composed in 1894, the String Quartet in D major is the earliest of Schoenberg's large-scale compositions still extant. Schoenberg felt strongly enough about the piece (and his newfound homeland, America) to deposit its manuscript and a set of parts in the Library of Congress. Its Viennese premiere on December 20, 1898 was the first significant public performance of a work by Schoenberg.[2] In a review of the concert, the eminent Viennese critic and champion of Brahms's music, Eduard Hanslick, remarked, "It seems that a new Mozart is growing up in Vienna."[3] Yet the work has more than historical interest and deserves to be performed and studied more widely than it is.

Although the influence of Brahms is most pervasive, the opening motive of the first movement and the rondo subject of the finale are reminiscent of Dvořák, a similarity that is quite surprising given Schoenberg's later development as a composer. While the sonata form of the first movement is to be expected, what is remarkable about the form, if not without precursors, is that there is no cadence on the tonic (D major) until the very end of the movement, after the recapitulation, in the coda. Example 3.1 analyzes the first violin part for the opening phrase, a musical sentence ending on an F sharp major chord, which functions as the dominant of the relative B minor.[4] Although the sunny diatonicism of the opening will not be found in Schoenberg's later works, there are a number of features even within the first phrase that remain hallmarks of Schoenberg's ever-changing compositional language.

The rhythmic impulse of the opening gesture, labeled *a* in the example, drives upward to the accented B, scale degree 6 in D. The first three notes are heard as an anacrusis, while the accented B has the quality of a downbeat, misplaced in the notation. The motive, labeled *a'*, is slightly modified and transposed upward, landing on F sharp, with a displaced accent as before. The accented notes forecast the later progress of the movement: B minor, primarily expressed through its dominant F sharp,

Example 3.1 String Quartet in D, I, mm. 1–12, with motivic analysis

will be the key of the subordinate theme. The pitches from the tail of *a'*, in a rhythm derived from the incipit of *a* (or *a'*), form the next motivic cell, labeled *frag. a'*. This functions to shift the perceived accent so that it arrives perceptually a half note beat "too soon," coinciding with the written downbeat of m. 3. The upward gestures of *a*-derived material are then complemented by the downward thrust of *b* and *b'*. The pitches of *b* develop out of the *a'* pitches in retrograde, while the original rhythm is modified by subdividing the internal quarter notes into eighth notes. Continuing the downward motion, *b'* then terminates on the B half note at the downbeat of m. 6, the first harmonized moment in the passage, an arrival on G major, IV of D. From this point there are two competing hearings of the rhythmic subdivisions. A weaker hearing would group measures 5–6, 7–8, and 9–12 (with the last extending the phrase by prolonging F sharp, V/vi). A more imaginative hearing continues the anacrustic motives, all derived from *a*, labeled *c* and so forth. The rhythmic language might have been inspired by any number of composers in the Viennese tradition; the crosscurrents within and against the written meter will remain an aspect of Schoenberg's mature style, through all of his stylistic periods.[5] The opening as seed idea for all that follows exemplifies Schoenberg's concept of *Grundgestalt* – the "basic shape" that contains both conflict and cohesion, and functions as a seminal idea for an entire musical composition.[6]

The extended musical sentence that follows (from m. 13 until m. 38, not shown in the example) begins in B minor, takes a decidedly Brahmsian turn, developing the motives that we have already heard and visiting some fairly remote harmonies, including A minor and C major, before cadencing once again on F sharp, the dominant of B. The subordinate theme begins at m. 39. Its first sentence is shown in Example 3.2.

The subordinate theme is a beautiful *dolce*, much more Brahmsian than the first theme. Its most basic harmonies are F sharp (V of B minor) and its dominant, C sharp. The accompanimental figures derive from the *c* variant in the first group, and the principal line, in the first violin, is arguably developed out of the incipit for the original *a* motive. After the third iteration of the three-note head motive, Schoenberg expands and develops the motive into a four-note figure, beginning with the *sf* B of m. 41. This time, the perceived downbeat does not shift, but the groupings change so that each four-note motive straddles the measure. Although the sentence is an eight-measure structure, there is no feeling of squareness. The voice leading within the passage is sure-handed and exquisite. At the outset, contrary motion in the outer voices – E to F sharp in the violin and G to F sharp in the cello (paralleled by B to A sharp in the second violin, with C sharp as an escape tone) – adds poignancy to the principal line's

Example 3.2 String Quartet in D, I, mm. 39–46

ascent. Among other deft moves, the delayed arrivals of the C sharp applied dominant, through the viola figures in mm. 41 and 42, and then more emphatically through the embellishing 6/4 through m. 44 into m. 45, show Schoenberg's mastery of chromatic harmony.

The figure in the cello that closes m. 46 (the final measure of Example 3.2) voice-leads directly into the next sentence, beginning with the theme in the cello. As in the first theme, the second sentence is more developed than the first; a cadence on B major is hinted at, and avoided (at m. 54), as the sentence continues into another half-cadence on F sharp at m. 64. This sets up the closing section of the exposition, which is composed of two closing themes, the first a sentence comprising m. 65 through the downbeat of m. 79, and the second overlapping with the end of the first and spinning out until the end of the exposition at m. 96.

Whereas the sentence structures of both the principal and subordinate themes began with motives one measure in duration (the *a* motive in the first theme, and the first ligature in the second theme), both closing sentences begin with ideas that are four measures in duration. In the second closing theme this comprises measures 79–82, with the modified reiteration of the idea in measures 83–6. The result is a sense of expansive relaxation (an *Entspannung* in German terminology), which coincides with the closing area. This is complemented by the downward drift of the closing theme, in contrast to the upward thrust that opens both the first and second themes,

Example 3.3 String Quartet in D, I mm. 165–72

and by the slow-moving harmonies particularly characteristic of the second closing theme. The transference of the cello F sharp, mm. 79–82, to the high F sharp of the first violin, mm. 83–6, is a brilliant touch, as the harmony moves from F sharp to B minor, with the principal line adjusted accordingly. By placing the arrival of B minor within the initial part of the sentence, Schoenberg is able to compose a significant arrival of the local tonic without placing it as a terminal cadence. He then shifts to B major to initiate a circle of fifths (which go beyond the excerpt in Example 3.2), moving through E and then A to effect the return to D major as the exposition is repeated. The avoidance of a cadence on the local tonic within the close of the exposition will function in a similar way within the recapitulation to avoid a cadence on D major. Before we examine that passage, the beginning of the recapitulation deserves some commentary. The passage is shown in Example 3.3.

At the outset of the recapitulation, Schoenberg uses a technique that is common in Brahms's recapitulations. He brings the first theme back in a manner that takes us well into the theme before we recognize it as recapitulatory. (Some striking examples of the technique in Brahms include the String Quartet in C minor, Op. 51/1; the Piano Quintet in C minor, Op. 60; and the String Quintet in G major, Op. 111.) The end of the development is based on sequential variants of the *a* motive from the principal theme. With the *ritardando* of m. 165, the motive, targeting B flat, is handed off from the cello to the viola. At m. 167, the motive returns to the cello, now at its original level, but supporting a B minor seventh harmony. The cello moves from *a* to *a'* as in the original, but instead of progressing to the fragmented version of *a'* as before, the *a-a'* sequence is reiterated at the octave. It is only with the *ff* downbeat of m. 171 and that which follows (derived from mm. 3–4) that we recognize that we are in the midst of the recapitulation, an intuition confirmed as the music continues. The play of retrospective reassessments of where we have been (and where we are going) is a crucial aspect of Brahms's compositional practice, and it will remain central to Schoenberg's development through-out his career.[7]

The second closing theme of the exposition returns in m. 237. The passage is essentially a transposition of the original, so that D minor arrives at m. 241, and we move to the parallel major at m. 245. The tonic has arrived, but without a definitive cadence. As the sentence continues, the motive targets B flat (mm. 250–3), recollecting the move that precipi-tated the recapitulation and anticipating a more global significance that we will address in due course. The sentence and the recapitulation end with the fermata in m. 254, another half-cadence. It is only within the coda space, beginning with the affirmative repetition of the opening, that the tonic is finally confirmed by a cadence. Similar procedures will be part of Schoenberg's language throughout his first maturity in works such as *Pelleas und Melisande*, the First String Quartet, Op. 7, and the Chamber Symphony, Op. 9.

The second movement of the 1897 quartet was the last to be composed, as a substitute for the original Scherzo.[8] It is a lovely *grazioso* in F sharp minor, clearly indebted to Brahms. In contrast to the first movement, where sentence structures abound and parallel periods are not to be found, the slow movement begins with a parallel period. The principal line is in the viola, the antecedent moving from tonic to F sharp to the relative A major in m. 4. The consequent phrase begins as before, but moves to a half-cadence on the dominant at m. 9. The phrase is then extended, reiterating the dominant at m. 11. The accompanying figuration in the first violin is somewhat reminiscent of Brahmsian technique as well; however, Schoenberg shows a coloristic flair not found in Brahms. The score indicates that the figures are to be played *sul ponticello*, giving them a ghostly quality not typical of Brahms: "Diese Figuren durchaus leise, leicht und zurücktretend; am Steg zu spielen" (Play these figures at the bridge, soft, light, and held back throughout). The overall form of the movement is an ABA structure with an added coda. The beautiful figuration in the coda anticipates some of the textures associated with "Verklärung" (trans-figuration) in *Verklärte Nacht*.

Example 3.4 String Quartet in D, III, mm. 1–8

The third movement of the 1897 quartet is a theme and variations. The theme is shown in Example 3.4. I have added some analytic notation, indicating the basic implied harmonies, fleshed out in the variations, and the phrase structure, two periods, with both consequent phrases ending on the B flat minor tonic.

Although not without interest, the theme and variations movement does not show the genius of the first two movements. Schoenberg evidently felt ambivalent about the length of the variation movement, having cut two variations when the parts were copied.[9] Despite Schoenberg's obvious attempt to create interest within the theme's somewhat enigmatic cello line, the resulting phrases are rather square: two musical periods, 2+2 bars each. The variations are well wrought, following the typical pattern of variations, each with its own characteristic figuration. Yet the overall result is more like a student exercise (an A+ exercise, but an exercise nonetheless).

Of particular interest, however, is the role of the variation movement within the global structure of the whole quartet. The theme and variations movement is in B flat minor; with the return of D major in the finale, the overall key plan of the quartet is D major to F sharp minor to B flat minor to D major. The underlying augmented arpeggio exemplifies the principle of inversional balance: F sharp lies a major third above D, while B flat lies a major third below. As we shall see, the same key centers will play a major role in the form of *Verklärte Nacht*. Inversional balance would turn out to be one of the most basic and highly ramified of Schoenberg's compositional strategies, one that transcends his various musical periods and remains central throughout his career.[10]

The finale for the quartet is a rondo-sonata form in D major. The obvious function of the opening is to retransition from the closing B flat minor of the third movement into the global tonic of D major. The move from B flat to D (voice-leading B flat to A) is recurrent in the movement, happening for the last time just five bars before the end. The sunny diatonicism of the first theme of the first movement returns with the rondo subject. The affirmation of diatonicism is a deeply engrained strategy of the common practice period, particularly evident in Beethoven (think of the Fifth or Ninth Symphonies for example), but with roots in Mozart and Haydn as well. In Schoenberg's practice, this kind of affirmative diatonicism is found only in the early works – *Gurrelieder* is the last major work to end on an unequivocal and affirmative tonic. The subordinate theme, anticipated at m. 53 and begun in earnest at m. 55, once again takes on a Brahmsian flavor, although the texture is more simple than one is likely to find in Brahms. Example 3.5 shows its first appearance, at the (minor) dominant level.

Apart from the minor inflection, the theme comprises a fairly normative period: the antecedent phrase terminates after four bars on a half-cadence (m. 58) and the extended consequent cadences on the local tonic, a minor, overlapping with the beginning of its second statement (m. 65). Schoenberg cleverly brings in A major (in mm. 60, 61, and 62); however, it functions not as local tonic, but rather as the applied dominant of D minor (iv of A). All of this is adjusted at the recapitulation of the theme (beginning at m. 175) so that D minor (now parallel to D major) functions as tonic. The melody has a gypsy-like quality, so typical of many of Brahms's themes. As with all of the lyrical themes in the quartet, the subordinate theme of the finale shows Schoenberg's superb gifts as a melodist.

Verklärte Nacht

While the String Quartet of 1897 is the first of Schoenberg's works worthy of continued performance, *Verklärte Nacht* constitutes Schoenberg's first incontrovertible masterwork. Barely two short years separate the 1897 quartet from *Verklärte Nacht*, yet in many respects the works are worlds apart.[11] Under the tutelage of Alexander Zemlinsky, Schoenberg had come to terms with

Example 3.5 String Quartet in D, IV, mm. 55–65

Wagner, and it is the dialectic between Schoenberg's assimilation of Brahms and newfound possibilities derived from Wagner's practice that principally inform the innovations of *Verklärte Nacht*. Schoenberg wrote:

> I had been a Brahmsian when I met Zemlinsky. His love embraced both Brahms and Wagner and soon thereafter I became an equally confirmed addict. No wonder that the music I composed at that time mirrored the influence of both these masters, to which a flavour of Liszt, Bruckner, and perhaps also Hugo Wolf was added. This is why in my *Verklärte Nacht* the thematic construction is based on Wagnerian "model and sequence" above a roving harmony on the one hand, and on Brahms' technique of developing variation – as I call it – on the other.[12]

Schoenberg's contrapuntal imagination had made great strides. The extraordinary command of contrapuntal technique that would run as a thread throughout Schoenberg's career is foreshadowed in the 1897 quartet, but it is central and essential to the achievement of *Verklärte Nacht*. There can be no doubt that Wagner's leitmotivic developments had had a profound impact on Schoenberg. Working in conjunction with Schoenberg's augmenting contrapuntal imagination is a newfound sophistication in his large-scale formal conception. The sense of musical form is remarkably freed up and this works in conjunction with an extraordinary capacity for musical narrative that allows Schoenberg to take inspiration from poetry, another recurrent thread in Schoenberg's musical thought. In choosing to write a string sextet, Schoenberg might have been inspired by the two superb sextets by Brahms, but his solution for writing a sextet is far removed from Brahmsian composition.

Verklärte Nacht is in one continuous movement, the first of a series of works that explore the formal and dramatic possibilities of embedding multiple movements (or large formal sections) within a larger, unified, and continuous structure. The large-scale single movement works that embed smaller structures are *Verklärte Nacht, Pelleas und Melisande*, the First String Quartet, Op. 7, and the Chamber Symphony, Op. 9, all from Schoenberg's first maturity. Toward the end of his life, Schoenberg returned to the idea with the String Trio and the *Phantasy* for violin and piano. The fact that commentators have disagreed as to how to characterize the form of *Verklärte Nacht* indicates how elusive that form is.[13] My own understanding of the form has much in common with the double sonata suggested by Richard Swift, but there are also significant points of departure.[14] Figure 3.1 shows an outline of the formal design as I interpret it.

The figure is mostly self-explanatory, but a few words of clarification are needed. The parenthetical title that I give to Part Two, "Verklärung" (transfiguration) is taken from Schoenberg's title, and from the Richard Dehmel poem that inspired the work. My interpretation of Part Two is informed by the underlying narrative for the work, and by the notion that recapitulation in the classical sense would be impossible given that narrative. Thus, the second exposition stands in lieu of a recapitulation that would be normative after the development in a sonata form. The formal key scheme, by my understanding, is based on a large-scale development of Schoenbergian inversional balance. Both principal themes are set in the tonic D: D minor in the first part and D major in the second part. The second themes balance about D, B flat, a major third below in the first part and F sharp, a major third above in the second part. These three, inversional balanced keys are identical to those across the movements in the 1897 quartet. The keys preceding the recapitulation at m. 341 also inversionally balance about the tonic, E flat minor at m. 266 (also

PART ONE (Exposition)

First Theme Group
1a. mm. 1–29: Sentence in D minor
1b. mm. 29–49: Sentence in D minor (without tonic closure)
Second Theme
mm. 50–99: B♭ minor (vi in D minor)
Closing Theme
mm. 100–32: begins in E major (V/V in D minor)

Development
Part One
mm. 132–69 (harmonically unstable, introduces new characteristic material and develops
    motives from the Second Theme and 1b)
Part Two
mm. 169–87 (develops Closing Theme and 1b)
Retransition
mm. 198–228: ends in E♭ minor (develops 1a)

PART TWO (Verklärung)

Second Exposition (in lieu of a Recapitulation of Part I)

Post-Verklärung First Theme
mm. 229–48: D major (without tonic closure); counterpoint remembers 1b
Post-Verklärung Second Theme Group
2a. mm. 249–65: F♯ major
2b. mm. 266–76: begins in E♭ minor (without closure); remembers 1a
Post-Verklärung Closing Theme
mm. 277–94: begins in D♭ major (without closure)

Post-Verklärung Development
Part one
mm. 294–320: begins in F, ends with implied D; develops 1b, Closing Theme of Part One and
    Closing Theme of Part Two
Part two
mm. 320–41: functions as close for Second Development and Retransition; begins in Db,
    ending dovetails with return of D major; introduces new theme, develops 1b and post-
    Verklärung Closing Theme.

Recapitulation
Post-Verklärung First Theme
mm. 341–69: D major; remembers Closing Theme of Part One
Post-Verklärung Second Theme Group
mm. 370–90: D major (without closure); counterpoint remembers 1a
Coda
mm. 391–418: D major (with strong tonic closure); remembers 1a and brings post-Verklärung 2a
to D major tonic closure

Figure 3. 1. *Verklärte Nacht*: Outline of the Form

heard at the end of the retransition concluding Part One) and D flat major at
m. 277 and again at m. 320, respectively a minor second above and below the
tonic. The sole exception to this scheme is the closing theme of Part One. It is
set in E major (which I interpret as V/V in D minor or D major) and its
reciprocal key would be C major or C minor (IV/IV or iv/iv in D minor or D
major).

Richard Dehmel's thirty-six line poem can easily be paraphrased: a man
and a woman walk alone in the moonlight; the woman tells the man that she
is carrying a child, not his, but conceived by a stranger ("einem fremden

Beginning m. 1: "Promenading in a park," [Theme 1a]
Continuing through m. 15 and following, through m. 22 and following: "in a clear, cold
  moonlight night," [1a continued]
Beginning m. 34: "the woman confesses a tragedy to the man in a dramatic outburst."
  [within Theme 1b]
Beginning m. 50: "She had married a man whom she did not love. She was unhappy and
  lonely in this marriage," [Second Theme]
Beginning m. 75: "but forced herself to remain faithful," [Second Theme continued]
Beginning m. 105: "and finally obeying the maternal instinct, she is now with child from a
  man she does not love . . ." [Closing Theme of the first exposition]
Beginning m. 137: ". . . her self-accusation of her great sin." [within the Development]
Beginning m. 202: "In desperation she now walks beside the man with whom she has fallen
  in love, fearing his verdict will destroy her." [Retransition]
Beginning m. 225: "But the voice of the man speaks, a man whose generosity is as sublime
  as his love." [end of Retransition into post-Verklärung First Theme]
Beginning m. 249: "Harmonics adorned by muted runs express the beauty of the moonlight."
  [introduction to post-Verklärung Second Theme]
Beginning m. 255: "a secondary theme is introduced . . . This section reflects the mood of
  the man. . . 'the child you bear must not be a burden to your soul.'" [post-Verklärung
  Second Theme]
Beginning m. 279: ". . . a new theme . . . expressing the 'warmth that flows from one of us into
  the other.'" [post-Verklärung Closing Theme]
Beginning m. 320: ". . . this warmth 'will transfigure your child,' so as to become 'my own.'"
  [part two of post-Verklärung Development]
(Without musical example): "A long coda section concludes the work. Its material consists
  of themes from the preceding parts, all of them modified anew, so as to glorify the miracles
  of nature that have changed this night of tragedy into a transfigured night." [my Coda
  begins at m. 391, but it is possible that Schoenberg thought of all of the music characterized
  as Recapitulation in my analysis (mm. 341–91) as part of a larger Coda to the whole; it is
  also possible that Schoenberg simply does not mention the recapitulation in his notes]

Figure 3.2. Summary of Schoenberg's program notes of August 26, 1950

Mann"), before she met the man she is now with; they continue walking as the
man replies: "the universe glistens ('das Weltall schimmert!') enveloping all, it
will transfigure the strange child ('Die wird das fremde Kind verklären') and
you will bear the child for me"; they embrace and continue to walk through
the bright night. In the composer's program notes, written late in life for a
recording of the work, Schoenberg assigns specific imagery to musical passages (evidently misremembering some aspects of the poem).[15] I summarize
these in Figure 3.2, correlating Schoenberg's program notes with the formal
design of Figure 3.1 within the square brackets.

Example 3.6 shows the opening six bars of *Verklärte Nacht*, followed by an
ellipsis leading into the end of the first sentence, Theme 1a in Figure 3.1. The
principal motive, depicting the opening image of the poem, is well grounded
in the tonic harmony. Its scalar descent of a minor sixth begins on B flat, in
what will turn out to be the key of the second theme group. We recall the
similar emphasis of B natural in the motive that opens the 1897 quartet (there
the final, accented note of the head motive). The end of the sentence overlaps
with the beginning of the second theme in the first group (as in Figure 3.1),
terminating with an arrival on D.

The beginning and end of the second theme of the group, 1b in
Figure 3.1, is shown in Example 3.7. The music is markedly more

Example 3.6 *Verklärte Nacht*, mm. 1–6 and 26–9

turbulent than in the first sentence and its intensity increases as it quickly approaches its climax at m. 34, the music that Schoenberg characterized as the moment where the woman tells the man of the child that she carries. As before, the theme is a sentence grounded in D minor, although this time the final resolution is avoided. One vividly hears this as the dominant in m. 45, prepared by a cadential 6/4, does not come to tonic closure in m. 46. Instead, the diminished chord over an F sharp bass hurdles us into the short bridge that prepares the second theme area at m. 50.

The second theme group begins at m. 50, continuing until it leads directly into the closing theme area beginning at m. 100. The theme beginning at m. 50 is the one characterized by Schoenberg as the place where the woman describes her unhappy marriage (a description that misremembers the "fremden Mann" of Dehmel's poem). In that this theme is given considerable weight during the exposition, it is remarkable that it is not recollected within Part Two (although commensurate or even augmented weight is given to its substitute, the post-Verklärung second theme group). It is unique among the first part themes in this respect.

Example 3.7 *Verklärte Nacht*, mm. 29–36 and 41–9

The beginning of the closing section (m. 100) broadens the rhythms and prepares the arrival of E major through its dominant. The music takes on an elegiac quality as the broad melody unfolds over the dominant pedal. The main part of the closing section begins at m. 105. The music, marked *etwas ruhiger* (somewhat more peaceful or quiet), continues the expansive feel of the closing section, the sustained E-B pedal contributing to the effect. In contrast to the sentence structures that have composed the themes up until this point, the phrase structure is an expanded period (the antecedent ending with a half cadence in m. 114, the consequent never reaching closure, and dovetailing with the beginning of the development that follows).

Example 3.8 *Verklärte Nacht*, mm. 132–9

Example 3.8 shows the beginning of the development section. The E bass that opens the development recalls but does not resolve the tonic of the closing section. The episode that begins at m. 135 is an extraordinary development of the music from m. 34. The accented notes in the second violin (also played pizzicato, at the octave, in the second viola) are derived from the melody at m. 34 (Schoenberg's "the woman confesses a tragedy to the man in a dramatic outburst"). The extended harmonies of the sextuplet figures work in pairs, with each initiating harmony moving to the next in stepwise motion. The melodic fragment derived from m. 34 terminates with the second violin G natural half way through m. 136. The bottom falls out, as the eighth-note triplets cascade downward, each a

6/3 chord, first moving through an augmented arpeggio and then targeting the bass motion D flat to C into m. 137. This arrival works in conflict with the bass motion in the second cello from the beginning of the passage into m. 137, a small-scale inversional balance, E to D to E flat. The E flat initiates an emphatic outburst of the head motive from the same theme (1b) whose climax had just been more elusively recalled in the sextuplet figuration. With the upbeat to m. 138, a new theme arrives in the first violin. Marked *wild, leidenschaftlich* (turbulent, passionate), this is the theme that Schoenberg characterized in his notes as "her self-accusation of her great sin." The extraordinary energy of this passage, with the driving descent of the violin complemented by the rising pizzicato figure in the viola, is unlike anything that we have heard before.

The turbulence of the development section continues; the listener does not need Schoenberg's program notes to recognize that it portrays some sort of crisis. After experiencing such a crisis, it is psychologically impossible to go back to where we were before. The feasibility of a recapitulation in the classical sense has been ruled out. Theme 1a has been notably absent throughout the extended development, but it returns strikingly in the passage that I characterize as the retransition. Because we cannot go back, this retransition will lead to something else, and that is "Verklärung" and all of Part Two. The troubled return of the opening motive is shown in Example 3.9.

The motive, in the second violin and first cello, is shortened from its original six-note descent to five notes, now spanning a diminished fifth, E flat to A, and terminating on a D flat augmented chord, as the harmony wavers back and forth from G diminished to D flat augmented. We recall Schoenberg's program note for the passage: "In desperation she now walks beside the man with whom she has fallen in love, fearing his verdict will destroy her." The 1a motive is developed over the following bars, and finally liquidated as we approach the beginning of Part Two. The final

Example 3.9 *Verklärte Nacht*, mm. 201–5

Example 3.10 *Verklärte Nacht*, mm. 222–37

measures of that liquidation and the beginning of Part Two are shown in
Example 3.10.

   The retransition ends in E flat minor, which is then pared down to its
dominant, B flat. The B flat then voice-leads into A natural within the
stunning D major chord at m. 229, the moment of Verklärung. The theme
proper begins with the upbeat to m. 231, composing a three-measure idea
that embellishes a plagal cadence, with the melodic notes comprising little
more than a D major arpeggio. A short extension, mm. 234–5, embellishes
a cadence to F sharp major, anticipating the key area of the second post-
Verklärung theme. And then the music starts to spin out sequences

Example 3.11 *Verklärte Nacht*, mm. 251–4

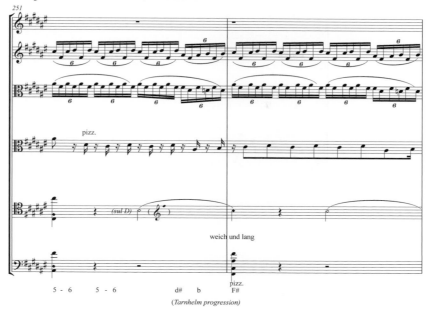

derived from m. 232 accompanied by recollections of theme 1b – the woman's "tragedy" has been transfigured. The second Verklärung theme, along with its reprise in the coda, constitutes the most sublime passage in the whole work: Schoenberg's portrayal of the transfigured moonlight. The beginning of the passage is shown in Example 3.11.

This magical theme stands in lieu of the B flat minor theme from the first half ("she was unhappy and lonely"), and as it develops, its figuration can be understood to be a transformation of the earlier motives. The example notes that Wagner's "Tarnhelm" progression is embedded in the figuration. In Wagner's *Ring des Nibelungen*, this is the motive that

Example 3.12 *Verklärte Nacht*, mm. 337–45

signified the magical helmet that caused one to become invisible. Here things not perceived before become clear – Schoenberg has inverted Wagner's meaning in his depiction of the transfigured moonlight.[16]

The last musical example shows the music that leads into the recapitulation of the D major theme at m. 341 (Example 3.12). At the outset of Part Two of the final development section (m. 320), Schoenberg introduces the final new theme of the work. It is a broad, soaring theme, designed to bring the whole development to a climax, which dovetails with the recapitulation of the D major theme (the post-Verklärung first theme). That theme reaches its *fff* climax at m. 337, the first measure of Example 3.12, a climax that is sustained over the next four measures. In m. 340 the development theme begins to decrescendo as the first cello crescendos into the restatement of the D major theme. The effect is that the D major theme emerges out of the development without being set off by a preliminary D major chord as it was in m. 229. It is only at m. 343 that the D major chord arrives. As in the first movement of the 1897 quartet, the recapitulation is Brahmsian: it is upon us before we are fully aware of its presence. Recollections from the first part of the work return, beginning with the recollection of the closing theme from Part One in m. 345. The moonlight theme returns at m. 370, with a recollection of theme 1a in the counterpoint. However, Schoenberg withholds the shimmering sixteenth notes that had so magically accompanied the theme. He saves that for the very end. The coda, beginning at m. 391, continues to recollect fragments from Part One and Part Two. The work finally comes to a close with a glorious recapitulation of the moonlight theme, now with its shimmering sixteenth-note accompaniment and in the tonic key of D major.

The late chamber music for strings

We will close this chapter with some brief remarks about three important late chamber works for strings dating from Schoenberg's years in America: the Fourth String Quartet, Op. 37; the String Trio, Op. 45; and the *Phantasy* for violin and piano, Op. 47. All three intensify a dialectical tension that was always integral to Schoenberg's musical imagination: the innovative and the reminiscent sit side by side, and Schoenberg remains true to a specifically Viennese tradition of composing, while being arguably the most innovative composer of the first half of the twentieth century.

The Fourth String Quartet, Op. 37, was begun on April 27 and completed on June 26, 1936. The Kolisch Quartet premiered the work in Los Angeles on January 8, 1937. Following what had become Schoenberg's normative procedure for his twelve-tone works, the entire quartet is based on transformations of a single tone row: <D, C sharp, A, B flat, F, E flat, E, C, A flat, G, F sharp, B> in its opening formulation (first movement, mm. 1–5, violin I). In some aspects, apart from the D major quartet of 1897, the Fourth Quartet is the most conservative of Schoenberg's quartets. The overall four movement design harkens back to classical models, and the forms of the individual movements are reminiscent of tonal forms as well: the first and third movements mimic aspects of sonata form, the second movement combines aspects of a scherzo with a sonata-like development section, and the finale is a rondo. I have argued elsewhere that Schoenberg not so much abandons tonality as he represses it, and while the Fourth Quartet is a remarkable example of Schoenberg's "classical" twelve-tone technique, the attentive listener cannot help but hearing tonal implications that rise and submerge again and again in the musical surface.[17] In an analogous way, the rhythmic language of the piece often reminds the listener of tonal rhythms, although the work's elastic musical gestures violate the notated meter more often than not. Capturing the often subtle and erratic flow of Schoenberg's rhythmic language is a major challenge for performers.[18]

The first movement has the energy and rhythmic drive typical of first movement sonatas. The movement features quirky, asymmetrical phrases, abrupt shifts in texture and affect, and rhythmic crosscurrents in the polyphony of musical gestures. Some of its most striking passages remind us of Schoenberg's remarkable gifts as a musical colorist. The transition from the first theme group to the subordinate group (mm. 63–5) provides one example of this aspect of Schoenberg's craft often overlooked in discussions about the composer. The second movement is for the most part an easy-going (marked *comodo* in the score) parody of Viennese dance forms. The music here continues the lineage of *Pierrot lunaire*, and some of Schoenberg's works during the Weimar years. The crowning achievement of the Fourth Quartet is its sublime slow movement. The movement begins with the work's tone row, transposed to begin on C, and very uncharacteristically stated as unison in all four parts. In fact, this statement, along with its inverted recapitulation, comprises the only two times in the entire quartet where its source row is heard unadorned by contrapuntal combinations. The music has a recitative-like or even chant-like quality, reminiscent of the instrumental recitatives in Beethoven's late string quartets. At its recapitulation (m. 664), the "chant" is heard with rhythms and unison preserved, but now with inverted pitch interval. The plasticity of musical ideas, the expressive lyricism and mystery of the movement, place it among the great achievements in the literature for string quartet. The rondo finale for Op. 37 is another compositional tour de force, with remarkable shifts of mood, musical texture, and timbre, and no shortage of whimsy, a quality often lacking in Schoenberg's musical palette.

The String Trio, Op. 45, was commissioned along with several other compositions by Harvard University for a symposium on music criticism that would eventually take place in May 1947. Schoenberg began composing the work in June of 1946, but he radically reimagined the piece after suffering a nearly fatal heart attack on August 2, 1946. The Trio was principally composed during Schoenberg's period of convalescence, August 20 through September 23, 1946, and Schoenberg told his students and friends that the work depicted his near-death experience.[19] The String Trio is one of Schoenberg's greatest masterworks, comparable to the highest achievements by any composer before or since. Composed in a single movement that incorporates smaller movements within it, the Trio in this respect returns to procedures characteristic of Schoenberg's first period and works that include *Verklärte Nacht* and the First String Quartet.

The twelve-tone rows that are foundational for the work notably depart from Schoenberg's usual practice where a single twelve-tone row would function as the source idea for the entire piece. The Trio is composed of five basic sections, each of which is notated in the score: Part 1; First Episode (m. 52); Part 2 (m. 133); Second Episode (m. 180); Part 3 (m. 208). Parts 1, 2, and 3 are generated by transformations of an eighteen-note series, the final six notes being a reordering of the first six: <D, B flat, E flat, A, E, C sharp> + >B, G sharp, F sharp, G, F, C< + <E, D, B flat, A, C sharp, D sharp>. In contrast, the two "episodes" are composed out of transformations of a twelve-tone series whose first hexachord is identical with the source for Parts 1–3, with the second hexachord being a reordering of the consequent: >D, B flat, E flat, A, E, C sharp< + <F sharp, F, A flat, B, G, C>. Typical of Schoenberg's late style, the tone rows are deployed in very free and highly inventive ways throughout.

One of the most striking attributes of the Trio is its fractured musical rhetoric, no doubt inspired by the sometimes anguished and sometimes drifting and fragmentary self-awareness of Schoenberg's convalescence. The piece begins with an intensely strident passage that intensifies before it eventually breaks off into silence (notated as fermata over the bar line at the end of m. 44). The music that immediately follows is in stunning contrast: soft, mysterious tremolos, ethereal chords played *sul ponticello*, and an enigmatic single pizzicato played *forte* (Schoenberg told students that the pizzicato depicted an injection into his heart). This music segues into the first episode, and the first touches of lyricism that will emerge and break off in varying sized fragments as the work continues. Eventually music that is evocative of a Viennese waltz begins to emerge (as early as m. 86), and the continuing emergence and breaking off of waltz-like fragments remains salient for the remainder of the work. The waltz fragments provide the most stable and the most sublime music in the Trio.

In using waltz evocations in this way, Schoenberg taps into and further develops a long tradition in Viennese composition. In classical Viennese composition, Haydn, Mozart, and even Beethoven, the dance movement had typically been the least stormy and the least introspective movement. In the Romantic period it had often taken on a darker aspect, the dance becoming a *danse macabre*, an ironic mockery of what it once had been – examples include the third movements of Mahler's second and seventh symphonies as well as dark invocations of the waltz in earlier Schoenberg, for example the "Valse de Chopin" in *Pierrot lunaire*. In the Trio, the waltz fragments clearly depict memories elicited by the approach of death, but death, not achieved in that Schoenberg came back to compose the work, has taken on a benign and welcomed aspect.

The *Phantasy* for solo violin and piano accompaniment, Op. 47, was Schoenberg's final piece of chamber music. Composed during March of 1949, it was premiered in Los Angeles on Schoenberg's seventy-fifth birthday, September 13, 1949. The *Phantasy* is a highly condensed work, under ten minutes in total duration. Like the Trio before it, the *Phantasy* incorporates a multi-movement design into its single movement structure. Here the sections are evocative of the four movements of a classical multi-movement sonata form (as in a classical symphony, string quartet, and so on): a sonata-allegro, a three-part slow movement (beginning at m. 34), a scherzo (beginning at m. 85), and a finale (at m. 135). Schoenberg continues to loosen up his approach toward twelve-tone technique: the violin plays an ordered twelve-tone series whose second hexachord is an inversion of the first; in contrast, the subordinate piano part – completed a week after the violin part was fully composed – uses the same hexachordal source material, but here it is freely ordered.

As with the String Trio, the *Phantasy* is a highly evocative piece, summoning up ghosts of Schoenberg's precursors: hints of Haydn, Mozart, Liszt, and Mahler, as well as faint echoes of a Viennese waltz, all contribute to the uncanny effect of this miniature gem.

4 Two early Schoenberg songs: monotonality, multitonality, and *schwebende Tonalität*

ROBERT P. MORGAN

Arnold Schoenberg is so closely associated with the development of atonality and the twelve-tone system that his earlier tonal music, which is sizeable (Schoenberg was in his mid-thirties when he broke with tonality), tends to be considered primarily in relation to his later work. Even Schoenberg himself leaned toward this interpretation in his writings; and recent theoretical and analytical work has also seen the early work primarily in evolutionary terms, especially in relation to traditional tonality. This has produced valuable insights, but it has also downplayed the degree to which much of Schoenberg's tonal music maintains common-practice conventions.

The idea that Schoenberg's more advanced tonal compositions fundamentally undermine these conventions fits neatly with recent efforts to expand the general concept of tonality to include more varied and ambiguous types. But it has also fostered the development of analytical concepts that, however useful in themselves, do not necessarily apply to all chromatic music of the pre-atonal period. In this chapter I argue that one such concept, multitonality, leads to incorrect and exaggerated readings of some of Schoenberg's most original tonal compositions.

I

One of the leading figures in recent endeavors to enlarge the concept of tonality has been Robert Bailey, who in a number of articles has advanced the idea that late chromatic tonal works are no longer necessarily monotonal: rather than adhering to a single tonic, they are multitonal, having what he calls a "tonic complex" in which two or more keys compete for priority. Bailey's influence has been widespread and serves as the primary reference point for the most comprehensive publication to date delineating a theory of extended chromatic tonality.[1]

Bailey's work is linked to a long theoretical tradition concerned with expanding tonality beyond its traditional confines. In the first years of the nineteenth century, Georg Vogler introduced the idea of harmonic *Mehrdeutigkeit*, arguing that chords may have multiple meanings implying more than one key; and shortly thereafter Gottfried Weber extended the idea into non-harmonic areas. Subsequently F. J. Fétis divided tonality into four historical "orders," the last, the *ordre omnitonique*, representing tonality's "final stage" and encompassing all possible chords including those based upon enharmonic equivalence. By the middle of the nineteenth century Karl Friedrich Weitzmann, the author of monographs on the augmented triad and diminished seventh chord, penned a rejoinder to his critics entitled *Neue Harmonielehre im Streit mit der alten* (A New Theory of Harmony in Conflict with the Old), in which he not only referred to both "harmonische Mehrdeutigkeit" and "Ungewissheit über die Tonart" (tonal uncertainty), but maintained that in principle any chord could be followed by any other. By the turn of the twentieth century, efforts to explain broadening tonal practices in late nineteenth-century music had produced both relatively conservative responses – Karl Mayrberger's explanation of Wagnerian harmony from a diatonic, scale-derived basis – and progressive ones, such as Georg Cappelen's chord-derived conception of a single key embracing all twelve chromatic notes.[2]

By far the most influential earlier theorist for recent ideas about expanded tonality, however, especially the double-tonic idea, was Arnold Schoenberg. It is thus instructive to examine the Austrian composer's theoretical writings in light of the views of such recent tonal revisionists as Bailey and his follower Christopher Lewis, whose work raises the question of the appropriateness of bringing the double-tonic idea indiscriminately to bear on late tonal music. In particular, Lewis has applied it to two of Schoenberg's own early tonal songs, "Traumleben" and "Lockung" (Op. 6, Nos. 1 and 7), works that are extremely chromatic and, standing on the edges of tonality, are not only interesting in their own right but useful tests for evaluating the dual-tonic idea.

It is clear that in his *Harmonielehre*, Schoenberg offered the basis for a more nuanced approach to expanded tonality. His well-known concept of *schwebende Tonalität*, or "fluctuating tonality," which he first presented there, offers many suggestive hints, even if failing to provide a succinct definition of the phenomenon.[3] Schoenberg, in fact, states that *schwebende Tonalität* does not lend itself to easy generalization or being "readily illustrated in short phrases." He nevertheless identifies several instances in Beethoven, Schumann, Mahler, Wagner, Bruckner, and Wolf, though only two are actually discussed, and these only briefly: the first movement of Beethoven's String Quartet in E minor, Op. 59, No. 2, which "begins in a sort of C major which, however, keeps reaching over toward E minor"; and Wagner's *Tristan* Prelude, whose tonic is "scarcely sounded in the whole piece," "always expressed in circuitous ways," and "constantly avoided by means of deceptive cadences."

There is one work, however, that receives a somewhat more detailed discussion, Schoenberg's own "Lockung" (1905). It expresses "an E flat major tonality without once in the course of the piece giving an E flat major triad in such a way that one could regard it as a pure tonic." Indeed, "the one time [the tonic] does appear, it has a tendency, at least, toward the subdominant." Though that is basically all that Schoenberg offers, he does add that if one studies this song, along with his orchestral song "Voll jener Süsse," Op. 8, No. 5 (which "wavers principally between D flat and B major"), "one will know what I mean [by *schwebende Tonalität*]." He also provides the following more general description:

> If the key is to fluctuate, it will have to be established somewhere. But not too firmly; it should be loose enough to yield. Therefore it is advantageous to select two keys that have some chords in common, for example the Neapolitan sixth or the augmented six-five chord. C major and Db major or A minor and Bb major are pairs of keys so related. If we add the relative minor keys, by fluctuating between C minor and A minor, Db major and Bb minor, then new relations appear: A minor and Db major, C major and Bb minor; the dominant of Bb minor is the augmented six-five chord of A minor, etc. It is evident that vagrant chords will play a leading role here: diminished and augmented seventh chords, Neapolitan sixth, augmented triad.[4]

Though Schoenberg acknowledges that *schwebende Tonalität* is too elusive to pin down precisely, his remarks do indicate that it depends upon one of two possible conditions: either the tonic is implied without being explicitly stated, or the harmonic motion is "suspended" uncertainly between two keys sharing common chords.

Schoenberg returned to *schwebende Tonalität* some forty years later in the chapter on "Extended Tonality" in his *Structural Functions of Harmony*, where once again he takes "Lockung" as his prime example. This time he provides a Roman numeral analysis of mm. 1–23 and mm. 42–5, and gives four brief examples illustrating how dominant ninth chords in the song are transformed through elaboration and substitution.[5] His complete example is reprinted as Example 4.1. Noting that the tonic E flat is consistently in competition with the submediant C, Schoenberg observes:

> Perhaps the most interesting feature of this song, as mentioned in my *Harmonielehre*, is that the tonic, Eb, does not appear throughout the whole piece; I call this "schwebende Tonalität" (suspended tonality). Many parts of the song must be analyzed in the submediant. The contrasting modulatory section, mm. 32–41, uses for a retransition [i.e. modulation back], the segment mm. 5–10 in mm. 42–7. This is analyzed in e) in the submediant and subtonic. It begins (in m. 42) and ends (45–6) at the same chords as mm. 5 and 8–9 respectively. The fine point is that this similarity is produced in spite of the transposition of the melody a half-step higher (mm. 42–4). Accordingly all degrees are one step higher.[6]

Example 4.1 Schoenberg's analytical example for "Lockung," Op. 6, No. 7. Schoenberg, *Structural Functions of Harmony*, ed. L. Stein (New York: W. W. Norton, 1969), 112–13

Example 4.1 (cont.)

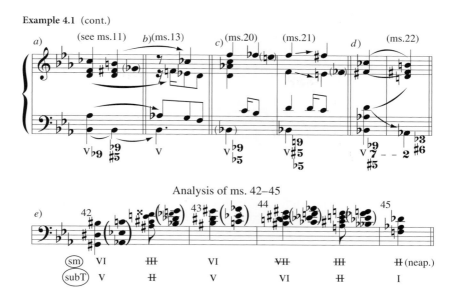

Analysis of ms. 42–45

Schoenberg's Roman numeral analysis may seem to suggest that two keys – C minor and E flat major – are simultaneously expressed in "Lockung", and that the tonal motion might ultimately tip in either direction; but it seems clear that he did not have anything in mind resembling a "dual-tonic complex." Neither *Harmonielehre* nor *Structural Functions* ever refers to "equal" tonics: E flat alone is the principal center.

It is not surprising, however, that Schoenberg's theoretical ideas were adapted by subsequent analysts and applied to a variety of late tonal works, including his own. His conception of a more flexible, contextually defined, and directionally ambivalent tonality offered a useful new way of thinking about chromatic compositions of the late nineteenth and early twentieth centuries. Difficulties result, however, when his generalized comments are hardened into a rigid theoretical principle – namely the dual-tonic complex. Of course tonic pairings do sometimes occur, producing pieces that retain tonal ambiguity until the end, when one key is chosen as final tonic; but such cases are, in my view, rare, at least in shorter pieces.[7]

The analytical problem is illustrated by "Lockung" itself. Example 4.2 provides a monotonal analysis constructed along Schenkerian lines (though only in general conception and notation, not in many basic assumptions). The song's AABA form, along with significant subdivisions, is indicated above the analysis, and measures are given below, with those beginning formal units circled. For purposes of clarity, enharmonic spellings are used at certain points in the graph and registers are occasionally simplified. The analysis indicates that the overall tonal motion is controlled primarily by a prolongation of B flat as dominant of E flat. True, this B flat is significantly

Example 4.2 Analytical Graph of Schoenberg: "Lockung," Op. 6, No. 7

elaborated by secondary dominant prolongations, of C minor in the first two A sections and of B natural (= C flat) major in the B section. But since all three A sections are directed toward V of E flat, with the last resolving to the tonic, the song as a whole asserts only one key: all significant linear and harmonic motions ultimately unfold a single tonality. Moreover, E flat is the *only* possible key, a point supported by the close correlation between this key and the song's formal layout.

II

Though I will return to "Lockung" later, I now want to turn to two articles that have played seminal roles in developing the dual-tonic idea. The first is Bailey's own groundbreaking essay on *Tristan*, in which he first formulated at some length his new "principle of later nineteenth-century chromatic tonality."[8] Bailey cites several compositional developments that influenced its emergence: free modal mixture, structural chromatic voice-leading, chord substitution in semitone-related progressions, cadential progressions other than V–I (especially iv–I), and directional symmetry in standard two-chord progressions (IV–I becoming "equivalent" to I–V, for example).

Though Bailey's new tonal principle does not completely do away with traditional tonal functions, it fundamentally transforms their meaning by locating them within a system of third relationships. As the following passage explains, the traditional tonic–dominant axis gives way:

> to a new system with polarities based on the interval of a third. For any given tonic, there are four possible thirds – the minor and major third above, and the minor and major thirds below. Extension beyond these particular thirds in either direction can be accomplished in two different ways. The first possibility is to progress on to V (in the upward direction) or to IV (in the lower direction):

Example 4.3

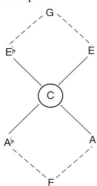

> In this case, the tonality based on V frequently *functions* not as the dominant but rather as the III of III. Similarly, the tonality based on IV often *functions* not as the subdominant but rather as the VI of VI.

> The alternative is to work only an axis of thirds of the same quality (major or minor), perhaps even to the point of making a complete circle of major or minor thirds:[9]

Example 4.4

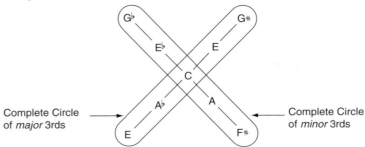

Complete Circle
of *major* 3rds

Complete Circle
of *minor* 3rds

Though Bailey says nothing about the limitations of his new tonal system, it obviously applies only to certain works of the chromatic tonal repertory; it does not represent a "common practice" in any sense comparable to functional tonality. Nevertheless, one can understand why its emphasis on third motion encouraged a more emphatic formulation of the multiple tonic idea: unlike fifth motion, motion by thirds is traditionally understood as directionally neutral, with neither of its two components necessarily being functionally prior. But this still leaves open the basic question: has fifth centricity, as Bailey maintains, really been usurped in most chromatic music?

An answer obviously depends on how particular pieces are organized. And since Bailey chooses as his main example Wagner's *Tristan und Isolde*, in particular the Prelude and Transfiguration, and refers to it as "the first work to present these new relationships systematically," it provides a useful starting point. Although, significantly, Bailey does not himself ascribe a double-tonic function to the Prelude, considering it to be basically in A, he does say that "the entire first act" of the opera has an "A/C complex . . . as the controlling tonic" and that the Prelude "establish[es] the close duality between A and C." Indeed, the Prelude's first two phrases, directed toward the dominants of those keys, already adumbrate this duality and its ending "prepares the eventual shift of emphasis to C" for the opening of Act I.

Though this in itself seems unproblematic, Lewis, in an article following up on his former teacher, extends the tonic-complex idea to encompass the *Tristan* Prelude itself: "We understand [the Prelude's] essential tonal issue [to be] the pairing of the tonics A and C," a "background progression . . . reflected in the musical texture from the opening measures." Further, "an analysis that reduces one of the implied tonics to the role of a decorative element will misrepresent the background duality."[10]

Although I do not want to dwell on *Tristan* here, a word about the Prelude's tonal organization may be useful. First, the functions of the two keys A and C are hierarchically distinct from one another. In addition, the conflict between them participates in a more richly detailed tonal structure than a dual-tonic conception can accommodate. In the Prelude's very first section (mm. 1–17), A is already clearly prior. The two sequential opening phrases mentioned by both Bailey and Lewis, though directed toward V of A and C, are followed by a third, directed toward V of E; and this goal is prolonged three times as long as the previous two. Its V, moreover, "resolves" back to V7 of A, which then moves to F major (VI) at the Prelude's first major tonal arrival, a deceptive cadence articulating its first tonal-melodic segment as a comprehensive unit in A. A's centrality becomes even more evident when the dominant E returns to initiate the long climactic section (mm. 63–73), where it appears at its beginning (mm. 63–70) and again at its end (m. 73), delineating another extended V prolongation. Other contrasting keys are also significant. E major appears off and on throughout, and in many respects is as important as C; and D minor and E flat minor are also prominent. To reduce the "essential tonal issue" to a single pair of tonics, then, is to rob the music of its tonal richness, for which all keys – A, C, E, D, and E flat – are critical. Nevertheless, only one is primary. Until the final modulation, for example, the supposed paired C major appears exclusively "in transition," associated solely with internal segments located within larger formal units centered on other pitches.[11]

III

Lewis's over-reliance on the double-tonic complex becomes even more evident when his article addresses its main concern: the tonal music of Schoenberg. "Lockung," which not surprisingly once again provides a central example, is now said to be "structured around a primary complex of Eb and C, with an extended diversion to B (Cb)." Although there is no question of the importance of these keys (or of B's relative subordination to the other two), C and E flat cannot be taken as equally primary. Lewis seems to be misled by a false assumption: that "post-Wagnerian" tonal music "differs from … earlier [tonal music] not only in its effects and vocabulary, but in the very essence of its conception." Thus, "in this music apparent surface details become so important in foreshadowing and creating certain aspects of the tonal relationships … that they become, in effect, another dimension of the background itself."[12] Melodic embellishment, in other words, is considered equally important to its harmonic support – even though traditionally such embellishment has always been taken as surface manipulation of a more fundamental harmonic base. If this claim were true, then chromatic and diatonic tonality would indeed be fundamentally different; but virtually all triadically based tonal music, including "Lockung" (as the graph reveals), preserves unmistakable hierarchical distinctions between harmony and voice leading.

Lewis makes a number of convincing and useful observations about the non-harmonic, or "motivic," aspects of "Lockung," which, considered purely from that perspective, point to the significance of the song's two other keys. But here these are combined with harmonies that define a pervasive E flat tonic. Lewis even acknowledges that the melodic passages he has in mind "serve simply to decorate the dominant of E flat," but then incorrectly infers that, since a second key is motivically suggested, both keys are actually present simultaneously, one melodic and one harmonic, and are thus equal in importance. The mere melodic reference to a foreign key, even when carried out as consistently as here, does not make that key essential – a point supported by the presence of numerous comparable simultaneous references in common-practice music.

Thus even though Schoenberg is correct in saying that "Lockung" has two areas – E flat and C – that compete with one another, this does not mean that these keys perform analogous functions. Returning to Example 4.2, the analysis shows that the E flat-defining harmonic goals coincide with the endings of the three A sections; and the contrasting B major segment closes with a deceptive cadence to vi of B, which is then reinterpreted enharmonically as IV of E flat when A returns. The C minor prolongations that begin the first two A sections are undeniably important (they even support the structural top voice g"); but they are ultimately incorporated into motion directed toward V of E flat, and are thus separate from the song's most significant formal goals.[13]

This does not mean that there are no conflicts and ambiguities in "Lockung". It is significant that all the A phrases begin away from the tonic, so that they must all work their way toward it, producing a more continuous formal-tonal type (increasingly common in nineteenth-century music).[14] This feature causes Schoenberg (as noted) to view mm. 42–7 as a retransition despite the return of opening melodic material, some of it at pitch. It also explains why "pivot" chords, all but one redirecting motion toward E flat, play such a prominent role (see the boxed chords below the analysis).[15]

The relatively unstable harmonic-linear structure (see Footnote 13) joins the skittish quality of the vocal and piano writing to reflect the sardonically playful cat-and-mouse imagery of Kurt Aram's text. The top voice especially contributes: until its final note (m. 60f), the structural g" is associated solely with C minor's dominant (mm. 4–6, 19, 51–3) rather than with E flat; and even when finally joined with E flat harmony at the end (mm. 60–65), it sounds only while the accompaniment continues to prolong the dominant, its tonic support withheld until the voice has dropped out. Since the only previous E flat triad (mm. 50–51) is joined with D flat (as Schoenberg notes), stable support is denied until the final measure; and there it is only implied. This helps account for the song's text-related instability, its evocation of motion despite the static top voice.

The first two A sections of "Lockung" do exemplify one meaning of *schwebende Tonalität*: after being "suspended" between two keys, tonality is clarified as the music achieves its formal goals. All but one belong to this type (the exception being the finale of Schumann's Piano Quintet) and are thus ultimately monotonal. Of course all the pieces mentioned by Schoenberg have well-established secondary key areas, played off against the tonic (for example, the extensive C major passages within the E minor of Beethoven's Op. 59, No. 2/i). But so do all classical sonata forms. The main difference would seem to be that in *schwebende Tonalität* the most important keys, in addition to being third or second (rather than fifth) related, are played off against one another *within*, rather than between, formal units.

IV

Lewis's analysis of a second Schoenberg song, "Traumleben," published in the same collection as "Lockung" but composed two years earlier (1903), provides a different but equally instructive example. Here, however, monotonality is even more pronounced: despite extensive chromaticism, the song hardly strays from E major. Yet Lewis again finds a "background and foreground exploitation of a double-tonic complex," in this case E and F.[16] He is right to recognize the significance of F, which influences many details and strongly colors the whole. But it hardly competes for primacy as a key. Thus when the vocal line arpeggiates an (enharmonically spelled) F major triad in m. 2, it is harmonized within an unambiguous E context; and even when this figure returns in the reprise, harmonized in F major (m. 22f), that key appears only fleetingly.

The larger tonal orientation is again clarified if one considers the overall form: ABA' plus Postlude. Example 4.5, another quasi-Schenkerian two-level monotonal graph (in which the two Postlude levels are placed side by side to save space), indicates that each A section has two phrases, designated a and b; and that the B section opens with a varied repetition of b, so that it appears to be a variant of A, but whose end is then tonally deflected and followed by a new extension c. The overall tonal structure closely conforms. All four A units cadence on E: mm. 4, 9, 25, and 31; and though phrase b in the B section is redirected to a C dominant seventh (m. 14), its extension c – and thus close – returns to yet another E chord, this time with lowered seventh (m. 19).

Though Lewis states that the function of the voice's enharmonically spelled F major triad in m. 2 "is clearly to announce the other member of

Example 4.5 Analytical Graph of Schoenberg: "Traumleben," Op. 6, No. 1

the complex," F is undeniably subordinate. The m. 2 line, for example, is subsumed within a tonic-oriented progression, V4/2–I6–aug.6th–V/V–V7–I (mm. 1–4), within which it helps to form the aug.6th–V/V portion (consistent with its spelling). Moreover, there is no hint of F as a key during the entire first section. Following this E progression in phrase a, the first b unit also asserts E: vii6/5–I in mm. 6–7, followed by a plagal continuation with mixture, IVb7–I, in mm. 8–9. Consistent with traditional models, the B section is less stable. Though its first phrase begins like its predecessor, repeating the vii6/5–I in mm. 11–12, it then moves (more tentatively) toward Cb7, suggesting a shift toward F (as Lewis feels). But that possibility is undermined when the chord first alternates ambiguously with an A dominant seventh (resembling the IV chord of m. 8), and then becomes an augmented sixth leading to V of E (m. 18), which continues sequentially to IV before closing on E (as V7 of IV) in m. 19.

This entire B section is unusual by any standard, not least because it begins and ends with an E chord. It brings us, moreover, over halfway through the song without a tonicization of F, despite the pitch's melodic prominence. (F provides, for example, the highest note of a recurring piano figure heard in mm. 4 and 9 (later in mm. 25 and 31), each time calling forth an E–F bass response.) This emphasis no doubt suggested Schoenberg's reharmonization of the first phrase in F major at mm. 21–3. But as noted, this new orientation is fleeting, and it is ambiguous: the F chord is in 6/4 position and approached circuitously following the arrival on E7 in m. 19. The ambiguity of both this E and F allows the return to E major in mm. 24–5 (by way of another C7) to sound like a convincing resolution instead of a mere redundancy. Unlike the previous E and F chords, the E chord at m. 25 is essentially a pure triad in root position; and its cadence recalls features of cadential progressions from the first A section (compare mm. 24–5 with mm. 3–4 and 8–9).

F returns again at the song's climax (m. 29), again briefly tonicized, but only as a momentary Neapolitan that cadences safely back on E two measures later. Indeed, the E orientation is especially strong from m. 25 on: I (m. 25)–VII6/5 (m. 27)–I (m. 28)–IV (m. 29)–I (m. 31). F is again prominent in the Postlude, but only melodically, elaborating the tonic E in mm. 32 and 34. With so much E emphasis, even the C6 chord in m. 34, preceding the final elaborating F chord, sounds less like a tonicizing dominant than a tonic substitute.[17]

Despite its prominent coloring of the tonic, then, F behaves according to common-practice norms. What is most striking, in fact, is the extraordinary emphasis on the tonic in "Traumleben." All six cadences, closing each of the four A subphrases, the B section, and the Postlude, end on E chords. Indeed, it is difficult to think of a comparably chromatic tonal composition with so much tonic saturation.

Schoenberg's surprising decision to return to E with a lowered seventh at m. 19, at the end of the middle section, is, I believe, part of his plan for reinterpreting the opening voice phrase in F major at m. 22. The cadence on E7 brings the following F tonality (mm. 21–3) into immediate association with the tonic pitch; and though the E in m. 19 is not a tonic, it creates a strong bond with the E cadence at the next arrival, m. 25, even anticipating its plagal character.

But why does Schoenberg emphasize the tonic in such a persistent manner? One answer may be that it offers a way to compensate, through concrete tonic emphasis, for the almost complete absence of functional V–I cadential progressions (there are none after m. 4, though internal ones appear in mm. 7, 12, and 28). Even at this stage Schoenberg is inclined to substitute contextual associations for conventional ones, above all at cadential points.

Yet despite their apparent overabundance, the tonic cadences in "Traumleben" never sound formulaic. Of the six main cadences on E, only the first has a traditional dominant-tonic progression; the others are all plagal, using a form of IV–I (mm. 8–9 and 18–19), bVI–I (mm. 24–25 and 30–31), or bII–I (mm. 34–5). In addition, the cadences are linked by motivic correspondences: all but those at mm. 19 and 31 have syncopated rhythms in the penultimate measure; and all conclude on the downbeat with unaltered root-position tonic chords with third or fifth in the top voice, avoiding the tonic as a linear goal.[18] The four with G sharp in the soprano share additional features: this note is approached by an at least partly chromatic rising line in the piano (at times doubled by voice) and, except for the cadence at m. 4, the final G sharp is preceded by F double sharp (spelled G natural), duplicating a chromatic relation first heard in the tenor voice of the piano in m. 3. This produces a contextually established, key-defining "norm" that, far more than a competing key, accounts for the special character of the tonality of "Traumleben."[19]

V

Toward the end of Lewis's article, he quotes Schoenberg's *Harmonielehre* at length to support the double-tonic idea.[20] All but two of his quotes are taken from the section considered at the beginning of this chapter, where we have seen that Schoenberg does not claim that "Lockung" – much less "Traumleben" – has two equal tonics. The final two are taken from an earlier chapter, on modulation, and give the last two of four modulatory "functions" listed by Schoenberg.[21] The first (Schoenberg's third) deals with "suspended tonality": "From the outset the tonic does not appear unequivocally," which allows "the victory to go to one of the rivals." Even if this suggests the possibility of two equal tonics, whether that actually occurs will depend upon where, and how consistently, the goal tonic appears. And the E flat goal in "Lockung" is evident early on (by the end of the first A section) and its primacy remains unchallenged, while the tonic of "Traumleben" is never in question from the beginning. The final quote states: "The harmony is nowhere disposed to allow a tonic to assert its authority. Structures are created whose laws do not seem to issue from a central source (*Zentrum*); at least this central source is not a *single* fundamental tone." This is admittedly suggestive, seeming to support the double tonic idea; but it seems to apply more to atonal music (also discussed in *Harmonielehre*) than tonal music. In that light, Schoenberg's four modulatory maxims are, significantly, not offered to explain particular examples (there are none) but to make a more abstract point about grades of modulatory practice, no doubt with the intention of supporting his own recent turn toward atonality.

Finally, regarding the analytical graphs of "Lockung" and "Traumleben," whereas in the former middleground prolongations of C minor (through its dominant) are evident, the latter reveals no significant F prolongations at all. Does this mean that the prevalent F-natural features of "Traumleben" must simply be ignored? Obviously not. But graphs such as these, focused on larger tonal organization, are ill-suited to reveal features that, whatever their prominence otherwise, are largely played out on the music's surface. The importance of F natural as an associational feature has little impact on the larger syntax; and it is thus better left to other kinds of graphs or to verbal analysis. This limitation is unavoidable, since no analysis can be fully comprehensive. And what is finally most distinctive tonally about "Traumleben" is how weakly F (or any other subordinate key) is articulated as an independent area. Paradoxically, the song is "progressive" – a favored Schoenbergian word – precisely because, as if in denial of its chromaticism, it clings so desperately to its tonal moorings.

5 Arnold Schoenberg and Richard Strauss

CRAIG DE WILDE

The pairing of the names of Richard Strauss (1864–1949) with Arnold Schoenberg is not one that comes readily to mind, certainly not for Schoenberg scholars in any event. Critical commentaries on their music rarely find much common ground when comparing the musical styles of these two diverse composers. Strauss's place in music history is often seen as one of the last viable vestiges of the so-called New German School, taking up the Lisztian-Wagnerian notion of *Musik als Ausdruck* (music as expression), where the poetic idea was the basis for the structure of a work, rather than basing this structure on pre-existing or otherwise inherited musical forms.[1] In the first decade of the twentieth century, Strauss was considered at the very forefront of musical innovation, utilizing some of the most advanced compositional techniques of the day.[2] His work is identified by brilliant orchestration, daring harmonic treatment, and expansive musical expression. Indeed at the very moment when it looked as if the degree of chromatic extension and tonal uncertainty would propel Strauss's music into the very next stage of atonal musical expression, he ultimately stopped short of a total break from tonality. While both the operas *Salome* (1905) and *Elektra* (1908) signaled a headlong rush from extreme chromatic instability into atonality, *Der Rosenkavalier* (1910) was much more conventional, not only in its formal operatic conception but in its tonal clarity, set against a libretto which recounts a bittersweet love story rather than a deeply intense psychological drama.

What is most striking in this context is the fact that Schoenberg himself was going through his own compositional crisis in the years between 1908 and 1910. Works such as the Second String Quartet, Op. 10 (1908) and *The Book of the Hanging Gardens*, Op. 15 (1908–09) take the next step towards the so-called "emancipation of dissonance," whereby dissonance no longer seeks justification through tonal resolution. In the works that followed, including the Three Pieces for Piano, Op. 11 (1909) and the Five Orchestral Pieces, Op. 16 (1909), dissonance is treated with complete independence through the disintegration of functional harmony. It is precisely the divergent paths taken by these two composers at this time that signal what was to be the ever-widening division of their respective musical styles.

Schoenberg would have first become aware of Strauss's music in Vienna, having at least heard the tone poems performed there. It was during Schoenberg's stay in Berlin beginning in December 1901, when the two composers resided in the same city, that the opportunity for a meeting arose. In November 1898 Strauss had replaced Felix Weingartner as First Conductor of the Berlin Royal Opera in the Unter den Linden. At or near this time, Strauss met the writer Ernst von Wolzogen, beginning a collaboration that culminated in Wolzogen writing the libretto to Strauss's second opera *Feuersnot* (premiered in Dresden in November 1901). Schoenberg came to Berlin in part to begin work with Wolzogen, so it is probable that the writer provided the young composer with an introduction to the older musician.

The first of the extant correspondence between Strauss and Schoenberg is noted in Stuckenschmidt's biography of Schoenberg as a postcard dated April 15, 1902, in which Strauss responds to an earlier letter (now lost) inviting Schoenberg to meet him at his home "every day from three until four."[3] As noted by Stuckenschmidt, the contact was likely continued directly between the two composers immediately after this time, with the unfortunate consequence from a historical point of view that no letters or postcards exist for the three-month period that followed. Schoenberg moved to Augsburger Straße in late 1902, placing him within about three kilometers of Strauss's address in Charlottenburg and close enough to encourage regular face-to-face contact.

The website for the Arnold Schönberg Center in Vienna lists a total of twenty extant items between Strauss and Schoenberg in the correspondence, dating between April 15, 1902 and November 27, 1928, and with the majority sent between 1902 and 1909.[4] The letters during this seven-year period in particular display a closeness and genuine affection between the two composers, with Strauss assisting his younger contemporary with his professional career. In the next letter of July 19, 1902, Strauss writes that he will support Schoenberg's application as a music theory instructor at the Stern Conservatory in Berlin, mentioning that he will personally contact the director, Gustav Holländer, if required. The Conservatory was founded in 1850 initially as the Berlin Conservatory, and was one of the first private institutes for higher music education in Europe. Holländer (1855–1915), a violinist with a background as a performer, teacher, and composer in both Cologne and Berlin, assumed the Directorship of the Conservatory from 1895 until his death.

Strauss also mentions how he is looking forward to seeing Schoenberg's score to *Pelleas und Melisande* once it is completed. It was probably Strauss who drew Schoenberg's attention to Maurice Maeterlinck's five-act drama in the first place, initially suggesting it as ideal for adaptation as an opera libretto. Instead, Schoenberg composed the work as a one-movement symphonic poem between April 1902 and February 1903, publishing it as Opus 5.[5] This work shows a close resemblance to late nineteenth-century orchestral writing; indeed in many respects the work displays the mature extremes of German Romanticism. Its uninterrupted single movement is divided into four parts, alluding to the four separate movements of a symphony (with an opening movement, Scherzo, Adagio, and Finale), thus continuing the legacy of the great symphonic poems of Strauss, with a massive orchestral setting and a literal programmatic context. The premiere, conducted by Schoenberg on January 25, 1905, was greeted with much controversy. A famous quote from one critic suggested that Schoenberg be placed into an insane asylum, with music paper kept well out of his reach![6] It is difficult today to see what was so controversial about the work, considering its shifting tonal harmonies were a far cry from the emancipation of dissonance conceived in the works composed a mere three years later.

By late 1902 Strauss employed Schoenberg to assist in copying out the parts to Strauss's massive choral cantata *Taillefer*, Op. 52. Three letters (dated September 15, November 6, and November 25, 1902) refer to Schoenberg collecting the score from Strauss at various times to complete the job. Schoenberg had much to keep him busy. Strauss's sixteen-minute work includes three vocal soloists, an eight-part choir, and an orchestra consisting of 145 performers, including ninety strings, nine timpani and drums, eight horns, and six trumpets. Schoenberg's orchestration for *Pelleas and Melisande* is similar to that of *Taillefer*, which is interesting considering he was copying Strauss's parts at the same time as he was writing his own work.[7] *Taillefer* was commissioned for the Centenary Jubilee celebration of Heidelberg University, and was inspired by a setting of Ludwig Uhland's ballad of the same name, commemorating the Norman Conquest and the heroic role of Duke William's favorite minstrel.

In a letter dated December 5, 1902, Strauss makes good on his earlier promise to Schoenberg. It is in this letter where we first see the extent to which Strauss was supporting the younger composer's professional career:

Dear Herr Schoenberg,
    Today I saw Direktor Holländer [from the Stern Conservatory in Berlin]: he sincerely promised to take you on. He will arrange a small class for you now (so that at least you can call yourself a teacher at the Stern Conservatory.) But from 1 January onwards he hopes to give you a larger class: he also has copying work for you . . . If you are really in need, write a request for support to me as the President of the General German Musical Society: I could tide you over the worst patch with 50 marks. So good luck! Best greetings from Richard Strauss.[8]

This letter now shows Strauss acting as a true mentor to Schoenberg. There is no doubt that Strauss should take much of the credit for obtaining this teaching position for Schoenberg, as it would have likely been impossible for the younger composer to have secured the position on his own without the support of his famous colleague. In addition, one popular image of Strauss as a materialistic penny-pincher is certainly dispelled here, with his offer of both professional as well as monetary support for Schoenberg.[9]

As can be expected at this stage, Strauss was also working behind the scenes to secure financial support for Schoenberg. Strauss lobbied on Schoenberg's behalf for a Liszt Foundation scholarship – a bequest made to the General German Musical Society by Countess Hohenlohe, daughter of Franz Liszt's mistress, the heiress Countess Carolyne Sayn-Wittgenstein.[10] The trustees of the scholarship were Strauss and his good friend, the German composer Max von Schillings (1868–1933). Intended to support the careers of composers and pianists, ultimately Schoenberg was to receive the scholarship twice, thanks in large part to Strauss's support. Strauss's letter to Schillings on December 18, 1902 makes clear his opinion of Schoenberg:

> I have recommended a man who lives in the most dire poverty and is very talented, to be given urgently a scholarship of 1000 marks a year for some years. Please support me and write a splendid testimonial for him. You will find that his works, if a bit overcharged at the moment, show great talent and gifts.[11]

The next letter of significance, dated September 10, 1903, shows the level of importance Schoenberg had assigned to his relationship with Strauss. Schoenberg informs Strauss that he is planning to remain in Vienna in the hope of finding work with the then newly established publisher Universal Edition.[12] The letter ends with the following heartfelt sentiments:

> So I must say goodbye to you for a long time. I would like to take this opportunity to thank you, honoured master, once again for all the help you have given me at a sacrifice to yourself in the most sincere manner. I will not forget this for the whole of my life and will always be thankful to you for it – If I ask you to keep a good memory of me, I hope you will forget the great amount of trouble that I have caused you.
>
> I ask you to give my best regards to Frau Strauss and remain, again with thanks, yours very sincerely, Arnold Schönberg.[13]

There is a brief exchange between the two composers in February 1905 shortly after the premieres of Strauss's *Sinfonia Domestica* in November 1904 and Schoenberg's *Pelleas und Melisande* in January 1905. There is some general discussion of possible performance opportunities for each composer, but nothing definite at this stage. There follows a break in contact for over a year and a half until August 31, 1906, when Schoenberg writes a long letter to Strauss, asking again about possible performance opportunities for his works. Schoenberg suggests his *Pelleas und Melisande*, the Six Orchestral Songs, Op. 8, and the recently completed Chamber Symphony No. 1, Op. 9, as possibilities for Strauss's concerts with the Vienna Philharmonic. Strauss answers by saying he is only conducting two concerts in the current season and therefore "couldn't introduce any novelties,"[14] but if Schoenberg were willing to leave the first performances of the latter two works until the summer of 1907, Strauss would once again take a look at them. Schoenberg sent a reply lamenting the fact that he was having difficulties in interesting conductors in performing his music in general, and communicates a general impatience in having to wait too long for premiere performances of his music. Ultimately Schoenberg managed to have the Chamber Symphony premiered in February 1907 in Vienna, and the Orchestral Songs seven years later in Prague; the latter conducted by Alexander Zemlinsky.

In May 1908 the ever-hopeful Schoenberg again asked Strauss about premiering his music, but Strauss replied that the program for 1908/1909 was already decided. Strauss does request that Schoenberg send "a few (not too long) pieces to have a look at and would be very happy if I could find something among them that I could perform to the Berlin Opera House public, which unfortunately is madly conservative, without too great a risk." Schoenberg apparently acted quickly and sent some music to Strauss, including a copy of the Chamber Symphony. On September 27, 1908 Strauss replied that he had read the works with great interest, but that since they would not be suitable with the "bad acoustics" of the Berlin Opera House, he would consider an alternative series to program the works.

A flurry of letters between July and September 1909 brought the situation to a head. On July 14, Schoenberg describes to Strauss a series of short, one- to three-minute orchestral pieces he is composing that should be well suited for a premiere by the Berlin Philharmonic. At the time of the letter, Schoenberg states that three pieces are completed, with a fourth to be added in a few days and the further possibility of one or two more.[15] As cited by Stuckenschmidt, Schoenberg is referring to what ultimately became the Five Orchestral Pieces, Op. 16. Strauss answers Schoenberg's letter on July 22, from his home in Garmisch to say that, while the current performance schedule was already complete, he would be very interested in seeing the score of Schoenberg's new work. Schoenberg sent the score of the now four completed pieces with his letter

of July 28, stating that a "cheerful" fifth piece was soon to be finished. He
ends the letter lamenting the fact that he has had much difficulty in Vienna
with securing performances of his works; indeed he exclaims that, at age
35, he has had only one single orchestral performance![16] He asks further
for Strauss's help in general, stating that if such an esteemed musician as
Strauss were to perform his work, the benefit to Schoenberg's compositional career would be invaluable.

In August the Viennese publisher Universal Edition expressed an
interest in the Five Orchestral Pieces. Schoenberg writes to Strauss to
ask that the scores be returned, and further states that if Strauss were to
perform the works, it would very much help with future negotiations with
the publisher. It is not difficult to understand then that Strauss's response
of September 2 was a crushing blow to Schoenberg:

> I am very sorry to have to send your scores back to you without a promise of
> performance. You know I am glad to help people and I also have courage.
> But your pieces are such daring experiments in context and sound that for
> the moment I dare not introduce them to the more than conservative Berlin
> public.[17]

In all fairness, it should not come as a surprise that the older and more
experienced composer/conductor was reluctant to program the Five
Orchestral Pieces. Even Schoenberg himself underscores the newness of
his compositional approach in these pieces in his letter of July 14:

> I believe that this time it is really impossible to hear the music from the score.
> It would almost be necessary to perform it "with blind judgement." I expect a
> great deal of it, especially as regards sound and mood. For it is these that the
> pieces are about – certainly not symphonic, they are the absolute opposite of
> this, there is no architecture and no build-up. Just a colourful, uninterrupted
> variation of colours, rhythms and moods.[18]

Clearly, a Berlin Philharmonic audience more accustomed to traditional
symphonic repertoire would be highly challenged by this work, particularly a composition by a virtually unknown composer at that stage. The
bane of any music director's existence is the careful balancing act that
must be maintained between challenging artistic innovation on the
one hand and rationalist economic viability on the other, whether artists
like it or not! The Five Orchestral Pieces would have certainly tested those
limits.

An interesting comparison can be made between the relationships
Schoenberg maintained with Strauss during this period, and the one
with the Italian composer and pianist Ferruccio Busoni (1866–1924). In
a similar way to the Schoenberg/Strauss relationship, the differences
between the compositional styles of Schoenberg and Busoni suggest few

points of agreement. Their correspondence consists of thirty-eight letters exchanged between the two composers between 1903 and 1919. Busoni, as Schoenberg, had also lived in Berlin since 1901, and the latter would most likely have been aware of Busoni's concerts there. Schoenberg first wrote to Busoni prior to May 1903 (this letter is lost), apparently requesting Busoni to perform one of his works. The date suggests that this work was probably *Pelleas und Melisande*, as it would correspond to letters written by Schoenberg to Strauss and others during this time requesting possible performance opportunities. Busoni's response on May 14, 1903 is cordial and clever:

> Your letter has pleased and interested me and made me very curious to see your score. So I would be grateful if you would send me the manuscript. Perhaps it will be my lot, as a new Siegfried, to step through the circle of fire which makes your work unapproachable and to wake it from the sleep of the unperformed.[19]

While obviously Busoni did not perform Schoenberg's work, Stuckenschmidt does note that Schoenberg's name did appear on the next orchestral concert conducted by Busoni, which took place on November 5, 1903. Here Schoenberg's orchestration of the Syrian Dances by Heinrich Schenker (1868–1935) was given its first performance.

In his article on the Schoenberg/Busoni relationship, Daniel Raessler provides an outline of the correspondence between the two composers as found in the letters as well as other sources, including brief essays, references in letters to others, and diary entries.[20] Raessler reinforces the comment that there is little obvious artistic connection between Schoenberg and Busoni other than the fact that each was involved with a search for a new mode of musical expression, and as such Busoni might be more sympathetic than others to the musical innovations of Schoenberg – hence the explanation for Schoenberg contacting Busoni initially in 1903.[21] It is easy to see the connection here as with Strauss, since the latter was also considered by many to be the *enfant terrible* of German Romantic music at the turn of the twentieth century.

From July 7, 1909 until July 18, 1910, there is a total of seventeen letters involving extensive discussion and analysis by Busoni and Schoenberg of Schoenberg's *Klavierstück*, Op. 11, No. 2 (1909). Schoenberg's initial letter of July 7, 1909 is a request to Busoni as to whether he might be interested in performing his new work. There then follows an extensive series of detailed discussions between the two composers, where Schoenberg is explaining and attempting to justify his compositional approach in the work, while Busoni is critical of what he sees as imperfections in the music as well as lamenting the impossible demands imposed on both the pianist and the instrument. Typical of the exchange is the passage that follows from a letter Busoni wrote to Schoenberg on July 26, 1909:

> I have received your pieces and the letter with them. Both testify to a person who thinks and feels, which I have already recognised in you . . . However, my impression as a pianist is different; I cannot get away from this, perhaps because of my education or because of my onesidedness as a specialist. – The first doubts about your music "as piano pieces" arose because of the small span of the writing in the circumference of time and space. The piano is a short-breathed instrument and one can't help it enough. However, I will work through the pieces again until they really get into my blood – and then perhaps I will think differently.[22]

In a letter from August 2, 1909 Schoenberg replied:

> I have given considerable thought to your objections to my piano style and come to the conclusion that in a certain respect you are absolutely correct . . . Nevertheless, I believe that I may say it does not appear to me as though this deficiency is one that is grounded in the essence of the music. It is, indeed, clear that always when some new ability is achieved, old priorities must fall. And so it also appears to me that with music that is based on so rapid a harmonic consumption, the breadth of the phrase must be just as unusual as it can be common in the broader disposition of the chords. To create decorations and ornaments through chord displacement can be done with ease only when the chord has sufficient length. But, as I see it, the piano phrase is more dependent upon the development of successive chordal elements than upon their simultaneity, that it must result in the phrase losing some of its lustre and splendour.[23]

We do not find this level of musical analysis and candid commentary in the Schoenberg/Strauss correspondence. While Strauss clearly admired Schoenberg's work and attempted to support his career with professional references and even monetary support when it was needed, he does not appear to have engaged himself as directly with Schoenberg's music as did Busoni. In addition, Strauss's professional stature at this stage was more advanced than Busoni's, so it stands to reason that Schoenberg was often more interested in the professional advantage Strauss's support and endorsement would provide his music, rather than being interested in his critical comments about the music itself.

The Schoenberg/Busoni correspondence also includes similar appeals by Schoenberg for financial assistance during difficult times, in spite of the fact that, after 1910, Schoenberg's fame began to increase dramatically, particularly after his successful negotiations with Universal Edition in October 1909 to purchase the rights to Schoenberg's works composed since 1903, as well as the right to his future compositions for the next ten years. Busoni, as Strauss, was also willing to introduce Schoenberg to influential professionals and patrons of the arts where appropriate, and to support his applications for performances and funding opportunities when requested.

For all intents and purposes, the close correspondence between Strauss and Schoenberg ended in 1909. There is a very brief exchange of letters in September 1911, with Schoenberg stating his intention of visiting Strauss in Garmisch and Strauss inviting him to do so. There is no record that this meeting took place. Nevertheless, even as late as 1911, Schoenberg, in his *Harmonielehre*, cites Strauss as "a great master of our time" and mentions him in the book more frequently than any other composer.[24]

As an appropriate final chapter to the relationship, Schoenberg came to the aid of Strauss in 1946, just at the time when Strauss's activities during the Nazi era – in particular questions about his level of support for the Nazi regime – were being scrutinized. This level of speculation was not without foundation. In November 1933 Strauss was installed as President of the Reich's Music Chamber, one of the seven so-called Chambers of Culture instituted by Josef Goebbels.[25] It is clear that Strauss saw the main goal of this organization as the general improvement of musical life in Germany, particularly with regard to the protection of copyright and other legal rights for composers, as well as issues including the fostering of music education and the promotion of performances of German music. Although Strauss held this position for less than two years, until July 1935, the fact that he maintained such a high profile in the Chamber of Culture during this time, as well as participating in other major events, such as composing and conducting the Olympic Hymn for the Opening Ceremonies at the 1936 Summer Olympics in Berlin, suggested the possibility of a close relationship between Strauss and the political heavy-weights of the Nazi Party. In addition, the fact that musicians such as Strauss and the conductor/composer Wilhelm Furtwängler remained in Germany throughout the war years, at a time when other musicians either fled the regime or met with far less fortunate fates, raised further suspicions regarding their moral and political allegiances. Michael Kennedy discusses the question of Strauss and the Third Reich in depth in his 1999 biography of Strauss, and within this discussion includes Schoenberg's comments regarding the question of Strauss's involvement with the Nazis. Beginning by stating that he is "not a friend of Richard Strauss," Schoenberg nevertheless writes:

> I do not believe that he was a Nazi, just as little as W[ilhelm] Furtwängler. They were both *Deutsch-Nationale* (Nationalistic Germans), they both loved Germany, German culture and art, landscape, language and its citizens, their co-nationals. They both will raise their glass if a toast is brought to Germany "*Hoch Deutschland*" and though they estimate French and Italian music and paintings highly, they consider everything German as superior.[26]

It is obvious that any musical aesthetic relationship between Schoenberg and Strauss was long since past at this stage, as indeed had been the case since Schoenberg's 1914 letter refusing the invitation to write for Strauss's fiftieth birthday, where he stated "[Strauss] is no longer of the slightest artistic interest to me."[27] Nevertheless, this division was not so extreme as to prevent Schoenberg from defending Strauss some thirty-two years later. For Strauss's part, he clearly had a genuine admiration for Schoenberg, even if he was not sympathetic with his musical direction after 1912. The mere fact that Strauss, when appointed as a trustee to the Mahler Foundation in 1911, continued to support Schoenberg by recommending on three separate occasions that Schoenberg be awarded 3,000 kronen, is clear evidence of the continued regard Strauss had for his younger contemporary.

Relationships are often complex affairs that have the uncanny ability to change radically over time, and the relationship in question here is certainly no different in that regard. It is also true that this change is always going to be inevitable when it revolves around two such lofty artistic temperaments as Strauss and Schoenberg. Yet there is a reaffirming sense one gets when examining the circumstances surrounding the relationship between these two composers. Despite their artistic differences, there is a strong bond clearly displayed here. Perhaps it is due to the fact that two successful artists who shared some commonalities in their life experience – goals, challenges, successes, and failures – came together with a shared sense of purpose. In our volatile and highly competitive world, it is rare when two great minds can parallel, but it is even more remarkable when they intersect, even if only for a moment.

Schoenberg, modernism, and modernity

6 Interpreting *Erwartung*: collaborative process and early reception

ELIZABETH L. KEATHLEY

In 1909 Arnold Schoenberg completed his first work for the stage, the monodrama *Erwartung* (Expectation), Op. 17, on a text by Dr. Marie Pappenheim (1882–1966), a recent graduate of the University of Vienna medical school. Composed immediately following his Five Orchestral Pieces, Op. 16, *Erwartung* figures among Schoenberg's early atonal works and stands as one of the most notable achievements of musical modernism. It was here, it is widely held, that Schoenberg attained his goal of unmediated emotional expression through music, attested by his rapid composition and the apparent lack of thematic repetition over the half-hour course of the work. In spite of the vicissitudes of its performance history, *Erwartung*'s spike in popularity in the 1990s demonstrates the emotional appeal and contemporary relevance of both its music and text.

The plot of the monodrama concerns a nameless Woman who has waited for her lover to visit and now seeks him. She traverses a dark, frightening forest, eventually finding his dead body near the house of another woman. The Woman experiences a wide range of emotions, including horror, jealousy, rage, forgiveness, and despair, finally leaving open the question of whether or how she can continue without her lover. The verbal and visual details of Pappenheim's libretto and Schoenberg's sensitive musical rendering of the text invest this simple plot with psychological depth and emotional salience.

With few exceptions, recent interpretations of *Erwartung* view it as a slice of Schoenberg biography or a Freudian portrait of female hysteria. Such interpretations discount the authorial role of the librettist, generate misunderstandings about the composer's creative processes, and invest authority in Freud's problematic theories of hysteria and gender. They also point toward a need to reconsider the roles of gender, women, and feminism in the production and consumption of Schoenberg's works and of modernist music more generally. This chapter will contest the prevailing psychoanalytic interpretation of *Erwartung* and show that Marie Pappenheim exercised considerable control in the writing and revision of the libretto: Schoenberg's composition complements rather than diminishes her authorial claims. Finally, I will argue that an interpretation of *Erwartung* as women's allegorical journey toward self-determination is consistent with both Pappenheim's political sentiments and the goals of contemporaneous Viennese feminist movements.

Erwartung's early reception

The view of *Erwartung* as a depiction of female madness or hysteria has become nearly canonic, invoked by such insightful and diverse scholars as Adorno (1949), Willi Reich (1971), Schorske (1981), McClary (1991), and Albright (2000).[1] Few commentators have taken into account Pappenheim's aesthetic and political aims, while the operatic tradition of the "demented diva" informs others. Most tenaciously, Freud's presence in Schoenberg's cultural milieu has driven several scholars' interpretations, which take apparent validation from the fact that Marie Pappenheim shares her surname with Bertha Pappenheim, the real "Anna O" of Freud and Breuer's *Studies on Hysteria*.[2] The hysteria interpretation overwhelms the authors' deliberate open-endedness in Robert Lepage's 1992 Canadian Opera production of *Erwartung*: a psychiatrist onstage suggests the entire story is a hallucination, and the Woman ultimately finds herself in a straightjacket.

Although a psychoanalytic reading of *Erwartung* may be interesting and productive, there are several reasons to question why the "hysteria" interpretation should be the preferred or default reading of *Erwartung*: such (psycho)analyses of the monodrama are based on the questionable assumptions that knowledge of Freudian psychoanalysis necessarily constitutes agreement with Freud's theories of hysteria, and that vernacular understandings of psychoanalysis are sufficient to sustain an analogy between *Erwartung* and clinical hysteria "according to Freud." There is no evidence that the authors or early audiences regarded the Woman as hysterical in that sense.

Schoenberg's only published statements about *Erwartung* are gender neutral and do not suggest pathology. In 1930 he wrote that his goal in *Erwartung* was "to represent in *slow motion* everything that happens during a single second of maximum spiritual excitement."[3] Moreover, Schoenberg rejected the gendered inferences drawn by the music critic Paul Bekker in 1924. Bekker had asserted that, like Wagner's operas, *Erwartung* represents "a music of womankind, of sounds representing erotic feelings . . . a music of liberation, transformation, and redemption." Schoenberg's marginal annotation responds:

> Not at all . . . What does *Erwartung* have to do with redemption? The
> woman may have been wrong in her fearful states of mind, or not (this is not

clear, but, all the same, there are only fearful imaginings and these become manifest). She is not at all redeemed by them.[4]

Although the Woman's perceptions may not be real, Schoenberg does not attribute them to madness.

Delayed by a world war and perceived performance difficulties, *Erwartung* received its premiere thirteen years after its composition at a modern music festival in Prague, with the Vienna Opera star Marie Gutheil-Schoder singing the role of the Woman and Alexander Zemlinsky conducting. Greeted enthusiastically by the Prague audience, the monodrama also received overwhelmingly positive press reviews. The approving tone of critic Max Unger is typical:

> "Die Erwartung" is an unusual work in every respect; it is a stage genre by itself. In anguish about her lover, a woman wanders about in search of him driven by fear and longing, only to find him at the edge of the forest murdered by a rival for his love . . .
>
> Maria Gutheil-Schoder portrayed the only dramatic role with a most powerful range of emotional changes and extraordinary virtuosity of the special type of Schönberg's Sprachgesang . . . Long ovations rewarded the composer and the performers.[5]

Other reviews comment on the emotionally moving qualities of the music, its close connection to the text, and its overall coherence. For example, the reviewer of the *Montagsblatt Prag* wrote:

> The heart-wrenching persuasiveness with which the music makes these emotional processes come to life is the result of a creative ability which deserves our utmost admiration and which has no equal in modern music. But it is not the uncompromising boldness of Schönberg's music which . . . makes it come across as something unique, strong in character and profound: from this music flows such inner warmth and glowing passion, so much awareness of tender nuances of nature and emotions, such creative power . . . Every measure of *Erwartung* . . . is a testimony to the fact that the music does not develop randomly, but rather develops according to an inner law[.][6]

And Adolf Aber wrote for the *Leipziger neuste Nachrichten*:

> The close connection with the scene is also strictly maintained through the music, which fuses in a wonderfully successful way the sounds of the night forest with the dark emotional experiences of the woman as they are given musical expression . . . Only a Schönberg has the ability to transform into music even the most tender, innermost feelings of the human heart with all its nuances and changes at every single moment . . . The presentation . . . was a triumph for . . . [Gutheil-Schoder], who gave proof that it was wrong to push this Schönberg work aside for years as "impossible to perform."[7]

Although many of the critics stated that Pappenheim's libretto was based upon Schoenberg's idea, which she disputed, most early reviews made no suggestion of poor literary quality or lack of coherence. Erich Müller's review in the *Dresdener Anzeiger* represents a minority opinion, and provides the unique reference to hysteria among reviews of the premiere. Significantly, Müller uses "hysteria" not as a clinical term, but rather as a term of feminine derogation to describe an incoherent libretto by a woman poet:

> The arrangement of the [Woman's] accusations [against her lover] by Pappenheim was in no way able to satisfy literary claims. It is incoherent, almost hysterical . . . crying and calling.[8]

Most reviewers, for example "F. A.," sympathized with the Woman's internal struggle:

> Essential . . . is the process in the soul, which runs through all stages of emotion from a restless apprehension of the unknown to visionary ecstasy. In between the hurrying uncertainty, courageous decision, tender longing, painful outcry at the sight of the dead man . . . there is comfort in remembering shared experiences and gentle forgiveness. Dr Maria Pappenheim, though no poetess by profession yet extraordinarily poetically gifted, has put all of this into concise words of a most moving intensity with great sensitivity to Schönberg's line of ideas.[9]

Critics stressed *Erwartung*'s accessibility and viewed the monodrama as a harbinger of the future of opera, as this example from the *Arbeiterzeitung* shows:

> Schönberg saturated this text with a music that is quite new. But the powerful experience is forced upon the listeners with such intensity that they are deeply moved, even sensing that this first attempt is important for the future of opera composition . . . Through totally new combinations of instruments new sounds of a hitherto unheard beauty are created . . . The gradual lyrical ebbing after the climax is an architectural wonder where the intensity of expression increases even as the volume decreases. Every measure is filled with a richness of thought and musically alive.[10]

By any measure, *Erwartung*'s premiere was successful, although Pappenheim did not receive the credit she was due, and Schoenberg's music was greeted with amazed admiration. Any suggestion of clinical hysteria was far from anyone's understanding of this plot.

The German premiere in Wiesbaden four years later met with popular success but mixed press reviews; the Berlin premiere at the Kroll-Oper in 1930, still applauded by audiences, was marked by a critical reception redolent of anti-modernist sentiment. *Erwartung* and *Die glückliche Hand*, which made its Berlin premiere on the same program, were labeled "totally exhausted . . . cacophonic mischief . . . neurasthenic," "inept products of an isolated creator," "inorganic, synthetically-produced music . . . meaningless" and completely lacking in "both healthy ethical power and imagination," "two atonal monsters" from which "the public turned away, shuddering."[11] "These are abortions of an overheated imagination . . . degeneration," declared one review.[12] Some reviewers took the opportunity to condemn Schoenberg's twelve-tone method of composition (irrelevant to these works), to praise, in contrast, Pfitzner's *Palestrina*, to advocate for a "popular music practice" vis-à-vis the putative "l'art pour l'art" attitude of modernists, or to condemn the modernist inclinations of conductor Otto Klemperer and the Kroll-Oper, which was, in fact, shut down the following year.[13] One reviewer made a veiled reference to Hebrew, and thus to Schoenberg's Jewishness, in describing the "incomprehensibility" of *Die glückliche Hand*, whose libretto "can be read either from the beginning or from the end."[14]

These pejorative reviews of the music and texts of *Erwartung* and *Die glückliche Hand* do not merely register a change of musical taste; rather, terminology such as "healthy ethical power" and "degeneration," as well as some of the musical preferences critics expressed, suggest their alignment with the anti-modernist aesthetics of the growing National Socialist movement.

Nora Pisling-Boas's mixed review was unusual in its sympathy with *Erwartung*'s premise, her recognition of Pappenheim's authorial role, and her attention to gender:

> Schönberg wants to show here, in the poetic work of the monodrama "Erwartung" by Marie Pappenheim, what happens in the emotional life of a person – in this case, a woman – at a moment of utmost tension, during the most extreme and most intense experience of an affect – what affect can equal the pain of expectation which is familiar to all sensitive and insensitive persons?![15]

H. H. Stuckenschmidt, later Schoenberg's biographer, wrote the only unmixed positive review of the program, and his is the only review to mention hysteria, not in a pejorative way, as with Dr. Müller in 1924, but also not as a clinical term:

> Using a work by Marie Pappenheim, Schönberg describes the feelings of a woman who is searching for her lover at night in the forest . . . Fear, anticipation, pain, despair, rage toward another woman overlap, rage unrestrained and hysterically against each other.
> With tremendous sureness Schönberg found the musical form for this text, which is psychologically exaggerated and constantly in a sphere of emotional high tension . . . Though quite abstract, it is illustrative in a higher sense, that is, fits itself perfectly to the soul emotions of the text.[16]

Most of the reviews of the Kroll-Oper premiere had little to say about Pappenheim's libretto, perhaps because they saved their bitterest invective for *Die glückliche Hand*, but one review in the *Deutsche Allgemeine Zeitung* labeled *Erwartung* "an example of unquestionably 'feminine' poetry," cautioning that one "should not analyze the text too critically," as though a woman's literary work could not stand up to scrutiny.[17] Two reviews observed that *Erwartung* was a psychological study, pairing internal with external events. They were less kind to *Die glückliche Hand*: "If the monodrama [*Erwartung*] is concerned with psychological matters, then this work [*Die glückliche Hand*] apparently is pathological in nature, and can only have a revolting effect."[18] None of these reviews labeled *Erwartung*'s Woman "mad" – that epithet was reserved for Schoenberg himself.[19]

Erwartung and postwar neo-Freudianism

The Nazi regime suppressed Schoenberg's music as degenerate, and *Erwartung* was not staged again until after World War II. Following the war, psychoanalytic interpretations of the monodrama began to appear, evidently originating with Adorno's assertion that *Erwartung*'s Woman:

> is consigned to music in the very same way as a patient is to analysis. The admission of hatred and desire, jealousy and forgiveness, and – beyond all this – the entire symbolism of the unconscious is wrung from her; it is only in the moment that the heroine becomes insane that the music recalls its right to utter a consoling protest.[20]

Subsequently, the Zurich premiere in 1949 elicited reviews naming *Erwartung* a "musical transposition of a psychoanalytic dream transcription,"[21] or linking it with Schoenberg's "expressionist" painting and "modern psychology."[22] Citing the liner notes of Robert Craft's 1960 recording, Willi Reich's 1971 Schoenberg biography pointed up "the resemblances between the woman's ejaculatory and often incomplete remarks and the things said by patients during psychoanalysis."[23]

By the time of the US premiere in 1951 (Dorothy Dow, soprano; Dimitri Mitropoulos conducting the New York Philharmonic) the nexus of *Erwartung*, Expressionism, and hysteria seems to have been cemented, as this *New York Times* review suggests:

> [I]f [Dorothy Dow] did not give the part the hysterical, neurotic intensity it should probably have, it could be because Miss Dow is too healthy for that sort of thing. No one can pick up the orientation implicit in this work during a sojourn in Europe; it has to be in the blood, and Miss Dow, happily for her, is from Texas.[24]

To summarize, the reception of *Erwartung* has been subject to the vicissitudes of political and intellectual trends, and the interpretation of the work as depicting a woman's hysteria is a late overlay with no demonstrated basis in the historical origins or early reception of the work. In the process of Freudianizing *Erwartung*, Pappenheim's authorship has been erased, and her Woman has been pathologized. Not coincidentally, Freudian psychology enjoyed a surge of popularity following World War II, particularly in the United States, when terms like "hysteria," "repression," and "penis envy" became part of everyday discourse, and neo-Freudian theory became a mainstay of the campaign to redomesticate women who had spent the war years working in traditionally male professions. The dictum "anatomy is destiny" informed the social sciences and popular culture, and women who were unhappy with their new, more "feminine" roles were sent to psychoanalysis for reprogramming.[25]

It is doubtful that Pappenheim would have embraced Freud's problematic theories of hysteria and gender, which were, in fact, contested by his own colleagues: Breuer, the actual analyst of Anna O., rejected Freud's insistence on the sexual origins of hysteria, and Adler split from Freud in 1911 over similar issues of sex and psychopathology. In Freud's view, it was women's passivity that predisposed them to hysteria,[26] but Pappenheim clearly questioned the binary division of active man/passive woman.[27] Moreover, Pappenheim's professional experience and social activism were inconsistent with Freud's advocacy of a sexual division of labor and his opinion that women's demands for social justice were motivated solely by penis envy. If *Erwartung* were to portray female hysteria according to Freud's theories of its etiology, the Woman would experience both a relatively recent sexual precipitant (trauma) and a preconditioning infantile sexual experience or fantasy, such as seduction by her father. She would begin and *remain* passive, expressing her neuroses as somatic symptoms (paralysis or involuntary movement), rather than acting. That, however, is not the libretto that Pappenheim wrote. Rather, the Woman's emotional outpourings constitute an "energetic reaction" to a highly charged event, precisely the type of response that would, according to Freud, discharge the affect and prevent conversion of the trauma into hysterical symptoms.[28] Thus, *Erwartung*'s Woman may be "hysterical" in some colloquial, non-clinical sense – the sense frequently used to discredit women who display discomforting levels of emotion – but not according to Freud.

Erwartung's collaborative authorship

The conventional account of *Erwartung*'s creation has Pappenheim surrender the manuscript libretto to Schoenberg, who modifies it freely to

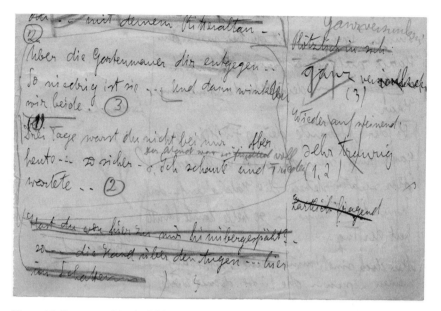

Figure 6.1 *Erwartung*, Ms. draft libretto, ASC archive no. 2415, demonstrating some of Pappenheim and Schoenberg's interactions in revising *Erwartung*. Arnold Schönberg Center

forge his own narrative, but the documents do not support this version of events.[29] The bottom layer of the manuscript draft libretto is entirely in Pappenheim's hand, with emendations by both the librettist and the composer, and Schoenberg drew his initial musical sketches into this source. In addition, three other sources – a typescript libretto, evidently prepared by a typist at Universal Edition;[30] an autograph reduced score; and an autograph fair copy – document the collaborative interactions between Schoenberg and Pappenheim, demonstrating that the librettist exerted considerable influence over the final form of the work. Correspondence between the two collaborators is short on specifics, yet it supports rather than contradicts a collaborative creative process.[31]

A portion of a page from the manuscript draft libretto demonstrates some of the authors' interactions (See Figure 6.1). The plot events on this page transpire after the woman has discovered her lover's dead body and immediately before her dramatic cry, "No, it's not true . . . how can you be dead?" Passages were deleted above and below the circled text, and these show characteristic marks the two collaborators used throughout the manuscript to demarcate text they considered deleting, relocating, or changing. For example, Pappenheim used question marks and parentheses (in black ink), as around the text at the bottom of the page, "Hast du von hier zu mir hinübergespäht?" (Have you watched me from here?). Schoenberg's marks include corner brackets (in red pencil), visible at the end of the passage above the circled text. Most deletions in the draft libretto share these features: there are marks by Pappenheim, marks by Schoenberg, and the material is crossed out more than once, suggesting that the authors discussed and agreed upon emendations.

It is also evident that Pappenheim did not passively accept all of Schoenberg's revisions, but rather modified them or in some cases restored the original text. For example, in the second part of the circled text, Schoenberg penciled in, "Der Abend war so friedlich" (The evening was so peaceful), Pappenheim's words relocated from another page. In response to Schoenberg's amendment, Pappenheim crossed out the adjective "friedlich," and wrote "voll Frieden" (full of peace), apparently an aesthetic choice. Pappenheim's revised wording appears on the fair copy over the top of an erasure; thus Schoenberg evidently first inscribed "friedlich" into the manuscript, then changed it to conform to Pappenheim's revision.

Schoenberg used Arabic numerals to signal a reordering of the sung text, and the numerals in the right-hand column show Pappenheim's effort to match up the stage directions to Schoenberg's new ordering. The changes in this section delay the Woman's questioning attitude until a later scene in which she begins to deduce her lover's infidelity; the emotional rhythm of this portion of the drama changes to this: first, self-pity – "Drei Tage warst du nicht bei mir" (For three days you weren't with me); then reminiscence – "Über den Gartenmauer dir entgegen" (Over the garden wall toward you); then crisis – "How can you be dead?" (on the following manuscript page). These changes of dramatic pacing do not alter the character of the Woman or the trajectory of Pappenheim's narrative.

A Roman numeral VI appears (in blue pencil) to the right of the reordered passage: it is one of fourteen such numerals that appear throughout the manuscript in places where significant modifications of the original text were executed or contemplated. These numerals constitute an important piece of evidence for Pappenheim and Schoenberg's collaboration, although the key to their definitive meaning is not extant. Logically, the numerals relate to a list of some sort, very likely a list accompanying a letter that, according to Dika Newlin, Schoenberg sent to Pappenheim, waiting for a reply before he could finish the composition of the reduced score.[32] Moreover, it is likely that a "separate piece of paper" bearing the "last revisions," about which Pappenheim wrote to Schoenberg on a postcard of September 9, 1909, included her responses to this list of questions.[33] On September 11, 1909 Pappenheim sent the revised manuscript libretto to Schoenberg, perhaps with the "last revisions" keyed to the Roman numerals,[34] and he completed and signed the reduced score the following day, September 12. Schoenberg's care to

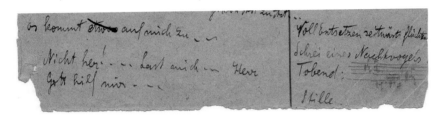

Figure 6.2 *Erwartung*, Ms. draft libretto, ASC archive no. 2403, Scene II, mm. 77–8: *Schrei eines Nachtvogels* (Cry of a night bird). Arnold Schönberg Center

Example 6.1 Transcription of Nachtvogel sketch, Figure 6.2

consult Pappenheim on proposed revisions and to await her response before completing the score clearly contradicts the standard narrative of *Erwartung*'s creation.

The manuscript draft libretto bears nearly all of Schoenberg's musical sketches for *Erwartung*, each inscribed near the text the sketch expresses musically; thus, as early reviews noted, Schoenberg's music is closely knit to Pappenheim's text. The sketches include suspense-building ostinati; a climactic vocal/orchestral arrival; austere, sustained harmonies depicting the desolate opening of Scene IV; and a verbal indication for a painterly effect to suggest dripping blood (harp with paper strips).

Figure 6.2 shows a portion of a manuscript page with Schoenberg's musical sketch added below Pappenheim's indication, "Schrei eines Nachtvogels" (cry of a night bird). At this point in Scene II, the Woman senses that she is under assault from the creatures of the forest; she feels something crawling on her hands and face, then hears rustling overhead.

Schoenberg's sketch effects the stylized "cry" through dissonant half-step harmonies and appoggiaturas (Example 6.1). In the full score the cry is realized as a figure in oboes and clarinets passed only one sixteenth note later to trumpets, then bassoons, and descending in register with each "ragged" attack (Example 6.2). Pappenheim's "cry" and Schoenberg's musical translation make the Woman's frightening journey more palpable for the audience, helping us to hear and feel what she hears and feels.

The autograph sources make clear that Schoenberg responded creatively to Pappenheim's specific verbal indications, and that, far from appropriating her narrative to create his own, the composer largely agreed with the librettist on the content and interpretation of their collaborative work.

Example 6.2 *Erwartung*, Scene II, mm. 77–8. Realization of Example 6.1 sketch in published score, Universal Edition 13612 (copyright 1923, renewed 1950)

Pappenheim's politics and Viennese feminism: rereading *Erwartung*

If Marie Pappenheim's authorial voice remained intact throughout the collaborative process of revision, we must ask what *Erwartung* meant to *her*. Pappenheim was an educated professional from a family of professional women and she entered the University of Vienna medical school only two years after it opened its doors to women. She was also a social activist, participating, for example, in the Conference for the Fight against White Slavery (that is, female sex slavery), and a political radical, joining the Austrian Communist Party – the only party advocating absolute gender equality – shortly after World War I, where she held several leadership positions, including chair of the Women's Committee.[35] While the mainstream of feminist activity in Vienna in the early part of the twentieth century was bourgeois in its origins and aims, Pappenheim's actions reflect goals across the feminist spectrum.[36] For example, in 1928 she co-founded with Wilhelm and Annie Reich the Socialist Society for Sexual Reform and Sexual Research, an organization with a Marxist perspective on the common feminist goal of sex education. Pappenheim's sex reform work and published critique of abortion laws led to her arrest in 1934. Pappenheim regarded Engels's *The Origins of the Family, Private Property and the State* (1884) – the "Urtext" of Marxist feminism – to be second only to *Capital* as a foundational text of Marxist-Leninism.[37]

Like other *fin-de-siècle* feminist literature, Pappenheim's literary works before and after *Erwartung* address contemporaneous gender issues, such as unwed motherhood, as well as modernist themes, such as alienation, and they experiment with modernist literary techniques, such as narrative fragmentation and internal monologue.[38] Imaginative literature was crucial to such *fin-de-siècle* Viennese feminists as Rosa Mayreder, the most significant feminist theorist of her milieu. In her 1905 collection of essays, *A Survey of the Woman Problem*, Mayreder set forth ethical and psychological goals for women because, she contended, economic and legal parity were not sufficient to guarantee women's personal freedom unless women were able to "transcend the norms of average femininity," to become self-determining subjects.[39] In her growth toward self-determination, women must pass through a transitional stage laden with conflict between their increasing awareness of self and "the demands of sexuality."[40] This conflicted, transitional stage is the substance of *Erwartung*.

Erwartung's trajectory from passive dependency, through painful experiences to a state of heightened self-knowledge, informed by a "recognition of the contingency and uncertainty of experience" and "counterposed to the deceptive mythology of romance," describes a genre that feminist literary critics have called a "feminist *Bildungsroman*."[41] *Erwartung*'s Woman begins her journey as a stereotype of femininity, passive and emotionally dependent, but she exceeds "the norms of femininity" by undertaking physical and emotional risks when she decides to seek her lover. She struggles with nostalgia and romantic longing, which tempt her to return to her state of dependency, and she persists in questioning and truth-seeking in the face of horror and distress.

Pappenheim linked the Woman's fluctuating emotional states – bravery and resolve alternating with fear and retreat into reminiscence – to repeated, gender-laden verbal and visual images of "the path" and "the garden," and these also structure the musical ebb and flow of the monodrama: decisive declamation alternates with vocal lyricism, supported by *espressivo* orchestral accompaniments and delicate timbres. Like much twentieth-century feminist fiction, *Erwartung* has no definitive conclusion, nor does its music resolve, but the Woman finally achieves awareness of her*self* as utterly alone in a world without meaning except what she imparts to it. This flicker of insight opens up the possibility for an independent and meaningful existence.

Many musical and textual details support a reading of *Erwartung* in terms of contemporaneous feminist thought. Indeed, such an interpretation is intuitive when we take the librettist's viewpoint into account, while the "hysteria" interpretation is only plausible when Pappenheim's voice is occluded, when we deny the collaborative nature of the work. Although we habitually think of Freud, Kraus, and other famous men as constituting the cultural context of Schoenberg's Vienna, Rosa Mayreder, Marie Pappenheim, and many other significant women were also constituents of that culture, exerting influence on the ways music and other arts were created and understood.

7 The rise and fall of radical athematicism

ETHAN HAIMO

In a famous letter from early August 1909, Arnold Schoenberg wrote to Ferruccio Busoni, describing his credo of composition. For our purposes, the key passage is:

> I strive for: complete liberation from all forms
> from all symbols
> of cohesion and
> of logic.
>   Thus:
> away with "motivic working out."
> Away with harmony as
> cement or bricks of a building.
> Harmony is *expression*
> and nothing else.
>   Then:
> Away with Pathos!
> Away with protracted ten-ton scores, from erected or constructed
> towers, rocks and other massive claptrap.
> My music must be
> *brief.*
> Concise! In two notes: not built, but *"expressed."*[1]

Schoenberg's rapturous and poetic description of his compositional philosophy is a remarkably precise portrayal of his compositions, beginning with the third movement of the Three Pieces for Piano, Op. 11 (completed August 7, 1909). Beginning in August 1909, there is indeed "liberation from all forms" and from "symbols of cohesion and logic." There is no "motivic working out," no "harmony as cement or bricks of a building," no "ten-ton scores," no "erected or constructed towers," and Schoenberg's works have become significantly shorter than before (and in the Three Pieces for Chamber Orchestra of 1910 would become shorter still).

At the same time, essential aspects of the compositional philosophy described in this letter are completely incompatible with the compositions that Schoenberg had written only days earlier. If one were pressed to name the single most prominent compositional feature of the compositions that immediately preceded the letter to Busoni (the first two movements of

Example 7.1 Principal themes of Op. 11, No. 1

Example 7.2 Return of "A" theme in Op. 11, No. 1, mm. 9–11

Op. 11 and Nos. 1–4 of the Five Orchestral Pieces, Op. 16), it would have to be "motivic working out," arguably some of the most careful, pervasive, and thorough motivic working out there ever was. "Symbols of cohesion and logic" do not merely litter the landscape of those works; they are the landscape of those works. There is no liberation from form; to the contrary, their forms are invariably simple and clear, with even an ABA' making an appearance (in Op. 16, No. 3). Yet, in a matter of days Schoenberg had turned his back on all of this, initiating a period that was characterized by the complete absence of thematic repetition in his compositions – a compositional approach we shall refer to as "radical athematicism."

In this chapter I focus on this strange and fascinating period in Schoenberg's career. When and why did Schoenberg adopt this compositional approach? What were its artistic goals? And when and why did he abandon it?

We need only examine the thematic structure of the compositions that preceded the change in artistic direction to appreciate how different Schoenberg's radically athematic compositions were from their immediate predecessors. In February 1909 Schoenberg wrote Op. 11, No. 1; Example 7.1 presents its four principal themes. These themes make their first appearance toward the beginning of the composition: A in mm. 1–3, B in mm. 4–5, C in m. 12, and D in m. 13.

Although they never return in completely literal form, each of the themes comes back at least once later in the composition. For example, easily recognizable versions of A return no fewer than nine times: in mm. 9–11, 17–18, 26–7, 34–5, 36–7, 46–7, 50–2, 53–4, and 60–1. As can be seen in Example 7.2, the second statement of A (in mm. 9–11) differs in many particulars from the initial statement. But although it is not identical to the initial statement, we recognize it as a varied restatement of theme A because of the identical rhythm and the (mostly) identical contour.

Even when the principal themes are absent, the musical surface virtually always consists of readily recognizable variations of the motives of those themes. As a result, there is hardly a measure in the composition that does not include either an explicit statement of at least one of the four themes or a transformation of their motives. Given the modest dimensions of the composition (sixty-four measures), the limited number of its themes (four), and the multiple appearances of those themes (nine times for A alone), one might well regard Op. 11, No. 1 as one the most thematically and motivically concise compositions ever written.

If we were to distill from these analytical observations the essence of Schoenberg's attitude toward thematic and motivic structure in Op. 11, No. 1, we would conclude that he operates according to two basic maxims: 1) every theme that appears at the beginning of the composition must reappear at least one more time in the composition in a recognizable – though frequently varied – form; 2) virtually everything else must be a transformation of the component motives of those themes.

After he completed Op. 11, No. 1 (February 1909) but before he wrote the letter to Busoni (August 1909), Schoenberg completed five more compositions: Op. 11, No. 2, and Op. 16, Nos. 1–4. All five of these compositions hew faithfully to the two maxims that governed his treatment of themes and motives in Op. 11, No. 1.

By contrast, the first composition that Schoenberg completed following the letter to Busoni seems to come from another planet. Example 7.3 presents the first three measures of Op. 11, No. 3.

The piece begins with a vigorous and densely polyphonic passage (mm. 1–2) in which the bass line, in octaves, and the alto line (beginning C sharp-D sharp) take on leading roles. By m. 3, however, the original texture has changed. At the end of m. 2 the right hand launches into a new format and rhythm: a single line in thirty-second notes that includes a literal repetition (marked "y"). The bass line also changes its character, though a little later than the right hand. In the first two measures the left hand had concentrated almost exclusively on a single rhythmic motive (marked "x"); there are four instances of this motive in the first two measures. After completing the last of those (end of m. 2 to the downbeat of m. 3), the left hand turns mostly to block chords. Therefore, we have a solid basis for identifying two fairly distinct (though slightly overlapping) phrases: an opening phrase that closes on the downbeat of m. 3 (in the left hand) and a subsequent phrase that begins on the upbeat to m. 3 (in the right hand).

Example 7.3 Op. 11, No. 3, mm. 1–3

We find similar relationships in the next section of the work (see Example 7.4). Much like the beginning three measures, we can readily parse the surface into phrases: this time there are four short, but clearly distinct mini-phrases (mm. 3–5; 5–6; 6–7; 7), the first of which itself subdivides into two sub-phrases. Each of the four phrases has enough internal consistency to be considered a distinct and coherent entity. Each one also contrasts with the phrases on either side so as to be considered as separate from them, an impression that is reinforced by the rests and the changes in tempo. But the four phrases of mm. 3–7 join together to form a

Example 7.4 Op. 11, No. 3, mm. 4–7

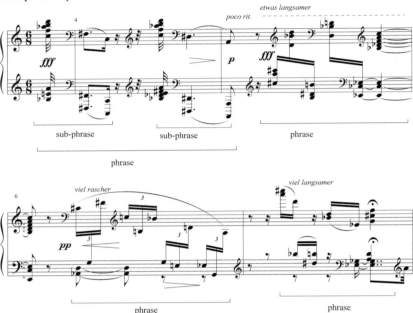

coherent unit. In turn, that means that the first seven measures of the work fall into two clear, and mutually contrasting, sections: mm. 1–3 and mm. 4–7.

Up to this point, this is not that much different than what happened in a work like the first of the Five Orchestral Pieces, Op. 16, which also began with a succession of contrasting phrases. What sets Op. 11, No. 3 so totally apart from its predecessors – what makes it a work of radical athematicism – is its lack of any return to prior material. Instead of placing a limit on the expository section, Schoenberg continues on to more phrases or groups of phrases that introduce still more new ideas. The ideas of mm. 1–7 do not give way temporarily to other ideas; they give way permanently to those ideas, which – in turn – have their own fleeting moment on center stage only to disappear forever. Subsequent passages may have slight similarities with prior passages (for example, m. 21 resembles mm. 1–3), but the correspondences are always vague and indistinct.

Nothing like this had ever occurred before in Schoenberg's music. Although there had been a wide variety of approaches to theme and motive in Schoenberg's previous works, every single piece before Op. 11, No. 3 treated thematic and motivic return as a *sine qua non* of musical structure. Schoenberg's sudden abandonment of the principles of thematic and motivic return is as surprising as it is unprecedented. Only

Table 7.1 *Chronology of Schoenberg's radically athematic works*

Piece for Piano, Op. 11, No. 3 (completed August 7, 1909)
Orchestral Piece, Op. 16, No. 5 (completed August 11, 1909)
Erwartung, Op. 17 (August 27 to September 12, 1909)
Three Pieces for Chamber Orchestra (February 1910)
Six Pieces for Piano, Op. 19 (February 19, 1911 for Nos. 1–5; June 17, 1911, for No. 6)
Herzgewächse, Op. 20 (December 5–9, 1911)

eight years later (1917) Schoenberg would write that the "artistic exploitation of *coherence* aims at *comprehensibility*" and that "coherence is based on repetition."[2] The compositions written before August 1909 and after 1912 are consistent with that aesthetic stance. Clearly, however, Op. 11, No. 3 and the other radically athematic works do not subscribe to those core aesthetic principles.

Something else of great import is also missing from Op. 11, No. 3 and the other radically athematic pieces. In the compositions that preceded the letter to Busoni, there was a clear emphasis on learned compositional techniques: canons, inversions, imitation, augmentation, diminution, and invertible counterpoint. In Op. 11, No. 3, however, those devices vanish, utterly and completely, not only between phrases (as would necessarily be the case given the lack of thematic return) but even within phrases. In short, it appears as if there was a fundamental change in compositional direction that took place beginning with Op. 11, No. 3. This work (and the contemporaneous fifth movement of Op. 16) marks the beginning of radical athematicism in Schoenberg's works.

We are fortunate that the chronology is detailed enough for us to know precisely when this transformation took place (see Table 7.1). It occurred after Schoenberg wrote the Orchestral Piece, Op. 16, No. 4, but before he began writing the Piece for Piano, Op. 11, No. 3, and the Orchestral Piece, Op. 16, No. 5. Schoenberg finished the draft of Op. 16, No. 4 on July 17, 1909 and completed the fair copy the next day. He finished Op. 11, No. 3 on August 7, 1909. Schoenberg then turned back to Op. 16 and completed the fifth piece. There is no date of completion on the draft of Op. 16, No. 5 itself, but Schoenberg did date the fair copy August 11, 1909, only four days after completing Op. 11, No. 3.

Therefore it is possible to state with a good deal of certainty when radical athematicism began. Sometime in the three-week period between July 18, 1909 (the date of completion of Op. 16, No. 4) and August 7, 1909 (the date of completion of Op. 11, No. 3) Schoenberg turned his back on much of what hitherto had been near and dear to his heart. Never – before or after – did two adjacent works of Schoenberg demonstrate such a stark contrast in compositional approach.

COLORADO COLLEGE LIBRARY
COLORADO SPRINGS, COLORADO

What happened? What could possibly have brought this sudden abandonment of what we have every reason to believe had been Schoenberg's core artistic principles? The record is very nearly silent. In his writings Schoenberg barely discusses this change at all. His surviving letters also give us no clue. Given the absence of hard evidence, the impetus for Schoenberg's sudden change in artistic direction may never be known with utter certainty. However, I believe a fairly strong circumstantial case can be built for what prompted this sea change in aesthetic attitudes.

In 1949, the one time Schoenberg discussed this radical change in aesthetic approach, he said the following:

> In fact, I myself and my pupils Anton von Webern and Alban Berg and even Alois Hába believed that now music could renounce motivic features and remain coherent and comprehensible nevertheless.[3]

It is telling that when Schoenberg looked back at this period, he mentions his students. Clearly, however, Schoenberg's memory was at least partially faulty, because Hába cannot have played any role in these events. In 1909 Alois Hába was only sixteen years old and was in school at the teachers' training institute of Kromeriz where he remained until 1912. Berg is also likely to have played little or no role in this aesthetic transformation. As of 1909, Berg's works were still noticeably more traditional than Schoenberg's.

Anton Webern is another story. Webern began studying with Schoenberg in 1904 and by 1908 had finished his formal studies. The last two works he wrote under Schoenberg's direct supervision were the *Passacaglia*, Op. 1 and *Entflieht auf leichten Kähnen*, Op. 2, both completed in 1908. Neither of these works would have threatened Schoenberg's position as the leader of the modernist movement. But tellingly, as soon as he left Schoenberg's tutelage, Webern's works quickly became much more radical: in some of his George songs from 1908–09 (ten of which eventually appeared as Opp. 3 and 4) Webern abandoned key signatures and referential tonics. Nevertheless, Schoenberg's own George songs (Op. 15) were at least as radical and, from what we know of the chronology, preceded Webern's.

That is not the case with Webern's next important work. During the spring of 1909, Webern wrote his Five Pieces for String Quartet, Op. 5. In terms of their harmonic language, dynamic range, formal freedom, and exploitation of instrumental color, these pieces were at least as radical as anything Schoenberg had done to date. If one were inclined to think in these terms (and it is crystal clear that both Webern and Schoenberg were inclined to think in precisely these terms) the stunning brevity of these works – the second piece is only thirteen measures long – could have led to the conclusion that it was Webern, and not Schoenberg, who should be regarded as the most radical of the radicals. Although Schoenberg's works had become steadily shorter ever since his abandonment of programmatic forms, his compositions until then could not compare to the shorter-than-aphoristic length of the five pieces of Webern's Op. 5. So, too, were Webern's treatment of theme and motive equally as radical. Indeed, given the avoidance of anything like motivic or thematic return, some of the movements of Webern's Op. 5 (for example, No. 2) could stake a claim to being the first radically thematic compositions written.

Could Schoenberg have been concerned that Webern was about to supplant him as the leader of the avant-garde? Did he worry that his position was about to be challenged by a former student?[4]

Although concerns of this sort may seem meaningless to us, it is clear that Schoenberg and Webern cared very much about issues like priority and the leadership of the avant-garde. There is ample evidence that there was considerable rivalry between Schoenberg and Webern about precisely this issue. Although Webern was almost pathologically dependent on Schoenberg, he continually sought to surge ahead as the leader of the avant-garde, often to Schoenberg's annoyance and anger. As a result, there are a number of places in his writings where Schoenberg sparred with Webern about who did what first. Schoenberg even revisited the events of the summer of 1909 and attempted to claim priority for the composition of small forms. In the earliest such comment, in an essay revealingly entitled "The Young and I" (1923), Schoenberg claimed to be the inventor of the tiny musical form: "To most of them I am an architect – a drawer of bold (if old-fashioned) bows – even though it was the small form which I was the first to compose in our time."[5]

A decade later (in 1932) Schoenberg wrote a collection of fragmentary notes entitled "Priority." Although he was mostly concerned to establish that he and not Hauer was the inventor of twelve-tone music, he also had a bone to pick with Webern:

> Cowell told me about Webern, went into raptures about him, and said that he had seen things from the year 1907 that were supposedly already very interesting. (Why? Webern must have shown these to him specifically, for they are not among what is published; he is therefore still conducting this underground battle of falsehoods against me!) I have long since established that Webern must have simply backdated these compositions. At that time, every person in our circle knew this series of events: how Webern was breathing down my neck, and scarcely after I had written a piece he wrote a similar one; how he carried out ideas, plans, and intentions that I had expressed in order to get ahead of me![6]

Similarly, in 1951, upon hearing that Webern had claimed to be the originator of *Klangfarbenmelodie*, Schoenberg fumed:

> Anyone who knows me at all knows that this is not true. It is known that I should not have hesitated to name Webern, had his music stimulated me to invent this expression. One thing is certain: even had it been Webern's idea, he would not have told it to me. He kept secret everything "new" he had tried in his compositions. I, on the other hand, immediately and exhaustively explained to him each of my new ideas (with the exception of the method of composition with twelve tones – that I long kept secret, because, as I said to Erwin Stein, Webern immediately uses everything I do, plan or say, so that – I remember my words – "By now I haven't the slightest idea who I am."[7]

Schoenberg then goes on to focus in on precisely the period in question and raises the issue of who really had priority in the composition of extremely short compositions:

> On each of these occasions I then had the pleasure of finding him highly enthusiastic, but failed to realize that he would write music of this kind sooner than I would.
>
> It was like that when I had just completed the first two of the Three Piano Pieces, Op. 11. I showed him them and told him that I was planning a cycle (which I never wrote), among which would be a very short piece, consisting of only a few chords. This he found surprising, and it was obviously the cause of his extremely short compositions.[8]

From all of this the following is clear: we have a possible impetus (a radical new work by Webern), a plausible motivation (rivalry for the leadership of the avant-garde and credit for priority of innovations), and a feasible chronology (Webern's Op. 5 precedes Op. 11, No. 3). But is there any evidence that Schoenberg was aware of the radical character of Webern's Op. 5 before he began to compose his own Op. 11, No. 3?

We do know that before he began Op. 11, No. 3 Schoenberg was aware that Webern had completed a string quartet. On June 16, 1909 Webern wrote to Schoenberg from his father's country estate, Preglhof, telling him that he had completed a string quartet. Webern even told Schoenberg that "all the pieces are short." He offered to send Schoenberg a copy of the score, "If I am not able to see you for some time, I would very much like to send my quartet to you."[9]

But did he? Did Schoenberg see Webern's quartet before he began work on the Piece for Piano, Op. 11, No. 3 or the Piece for Orchestra, Op. 16, No. 5? When we reconstruct the events of that summer, we find that it is quite likely that Schoenberg saw Webern's quartet at exactly the right time.

In July 1909 Webern was suddenly called to Innsbruck to take a job as an emergency replacement assistant conductor for a theater. Upon arriving in Innsbruck, he found that he hated the work, hated the repertoire, and hated his superior. After writing a desperate letter to Schoenberg on July 25, 1909, he precipitously quit the job and went running home to his father's estate at Preglhof. From there he wrote Schoenberg again on July 28, 1909, telling him what he had just done.

Webern's next letter to Schoenberg is not until August 20, 1909, and it was not clear what Webern did or where he was during the intervening weeks. Did he simply remain at his father's estate? But if so, why didn't he write Schoenberg again, particularly given the emotional upheavals he was going through?

Documentary evidence has come to light that shows that Webern did not have to write because, by July 31, 1909, Webern had gone to Steinakirchen and saw Schoenberg in person. The evidence is a postcard of that date to Alban Berg from Max Oppenheimer mailed from Steinakirchen (Österreichische Nationalbibliothek, Musiksammlung, Fonds 21 Berg) and it is co-signed, not only by Schoenberg, but also by none other than Anton Webern.

This demonstrates that Webern was in Steinakirchen at exactly the right time. And it is difficult to imagine that he made the journey to Steinakirchen without taking his new string quartet along. It should be remembered that in his letter of June 16, 1909 Webern had said that he wanted to send Schoenberg a copy of the quartet, if he would not see him for some time. Since it is now known that Webern visited Schoenberg in late July 1909, he did have the opportunity to show Schoenberg the quartet.

It is clear, therefore, that Webern's arrival, undoubtedly with the string quartet in hand, happened only days before Schoenberg wrote an impassioned and poetic letter to Busoni, a letter that provides a good description, not of Schoenberg's works – at least not yet – but a spectacularly accurate description of many details of Webern's Op. 5.

Given this background, can it be coincidental that only days after these events, Schoenberg began writing compositions that made a dramatic break with his own past? With no apparent warning Schoenberg abandoned motivic repetition, motivically based form, and learned compositional devices.[10]

The chronology of events suggests that there was a powerful motivation for this sudden turn of events. There can be little doubt that Webern brought his new quartet with him when he went to Steinakirchen in late July. There can be little doubt that Schoenberg looked at this quartet and immediately realized its implications – suddenly he was facing an aggressive challenge to his leadership of the avant-garde. There can also be little doubt that it was this sudden and unexpected confrontation that was the proximate cause for Schoenberg's sudden breaking free of ties to the past and the sudden radicalization of his music. We might like to think that important decisions regarding aesthetic direction and philosophy are made with calm deliberation. The evidence suggests that Schoenberg's sudden turn to radical athematicism may have resulted less from careful reflection than from a sudden burst of emotion sparked by a former student's unexpected challenge to Schoenberg's leadership of the modernist movement.

Schoenberg's sudden adoption of radical athematicism in August 1909 is particularly striking because it constituted such a forceful and abrupt break with his past. But it is almost equally striking that this period in Schoenberg's career was so short. There are very few compositions that can be described as radically athematic, namely those works listed in Table 7.1: Op. 11, No. 3; Op. 16, No. 5; *Erwartung*, Op. 17; the Three Pieces for Chamber Orchestra (1910); Op. 19; and Op. 20. This list suggests that, roughly speaking, radical athematicism lasted from August 1909 to approximately the end of 1911. But the evidence also suggests that Schoenberg quickly retreated from the extreme position he had adopted so suddenly in August 1909.

Possibly the first sign of Schoenberg's wavering commitment to the idea of radical athematicism came around February 1910, when Schoenberg worked on the Three Pieces for Chamber Orchestra. The first two pieces are tiny (twelve and seven measures, respectively). They are prototypical representatives of the style: there is no thematic return, no "motivic working out," no "symbols of cohesion and of logic," and, of course, they are "Concise! In two notes: not built, but '*expressed*.'"

But the third piece was left incomplete at only eight measures (with the manuscript written in ink, no less). One can scarcely imagine that there was much more to write, yet probably only a few measures away from the end, Schoenberg abandoned the work, perhaps an indication that he was losing interest in this approach to composition.

Admittedly, this evidence is far from unequivocal: Schoenberg left many compositions incomplete and it might be a mistake to read too much into this example. More persuasive evidence that Schoenberg was growing disenchanted with radical athematicism emerges the following year (1911) with the Six Pieces for Piano, Op. 19.

Some of these pieces are as radically thematic as anything else Schoenberg wrote: there is no repetition, no motivic return, no motivic working out, and there are no learned devices. And in their tiny dimensions (three of the pieces last but nine measures each), Schoenberg again challenged Webern for brevity.

But in the fourth piece Schoenberg reintroduced the concept of varied return to his compositions (see Example 7.5). The thematic idea that

Example 7.5 Op. 19, No. 4, mm. 1–2, m. 10

the opening theme:

varied return (m. 10)

occurs in the first measure returns an octave lower in varied form in
m. 10 – roughly speaking it is also a diminution. Two other passages
(mm. 3 and 7) are also clear transformations of the opening theme.
Altogether, these passages constitute a significant proportion of the total
piece. Less than two years after his letter to Busoni, "symbols of cohesion
and of logic" and "motivic working out" have returned to Schoenberg's
music.

So, too, in the second piece the recurring dyad G B acts as a motive, the
point of departure and arrival. And in the final piece (written four months
later than the first five pieces), the opening trichord (A–F sharp–B) acts as
a harmonic motive, lasting throughout the first pair of phrases (mm. 1–4),
returning at the beginning of the next phrase (mm. 4–5) and returning for
the final phrase of the work (m. 9). Once again, harmony is functioning as
"cement."

But nowhere is Schoenberg's waning commitment to the ideals of
radical athematicism clearer than in the opera *Die glückliche Hand*.
Schoenberg finished the libretto in June 1910 and had begun work on
the score by September of that year. Given the aesthetic of radical athematicism and its belief in direct, unmediated expression, one might have
expected Schoenberg to write this composition quickly, much as he did
with *Erwartung* (which was composed in a little more than two weeks).
Instead, the composition of *Die glückliche Hand* sprawled out over a
period of three years.

It seems likely that Schoenberg began *Die glückliche Hand* intending it
to be much like *Erwartung* in compositional approach. Like its predecessor, *Die glückliche Hand* was to avoid thematic return, motivic working
out, learned devices, and anything approaching a traditional formal
structure. And from what can be reconstructed from the earliest levels of

Die glückliche Hand, that is exactly how Schoenberg began the work. But unlike *Erwartung*, Schoenberg could not complete *Die glückliche Hand* in an uninterrupted frenzy of inspiration. Instead, at some point – we don't know precisely when – he stopped work on it.

When Schoenberg returned to work on *Die glückliche Hand* (in 1912 or 1913), the intuitive aesthetic was clearly crumbling. As Joseph Auner has documented, when Schoenberg came back to this composition, he introduced ideas that had not been part of the work in its beginning stages: "intricate counterpoint, thematic recurrences, and a clear formal design."[11] Not exactly the stuff of which intuition is made. Radical athematicism was in its death throes.

The structure of *Pierrot lunaire* also lends support to the notion that Schoenberg lost interest in radical athematicism around 1912. *Pierrot lunaire* (written between March and July 1912) is a work that is torn between the intuitive aesthetic and more traditional notions of motivic and formal structure. Some of the individual melodramas (for example, "Der kranke Mond") are as extreme in their forswearing of motivic recurrence as any piece Schoenberg ever wrote. In other melodramas there are ostinati ("Mondestrunken"), an extended retrograde ("Der Mondfleck"), a passacaglia ("Nacht"), and there is even an interlude (between the thirteenth and fourteenth melodramas) that is a reprise of part of an earlier number ("Der kranke Mond").

By 1913 radical athematicism had run its course in Schoenberg's music. It is perhaps not a coincidence that the end of radical athematicism marks the point at which Schoenberg made the first explorations into what became the serial idea.

The first step toward the twelve-tone serial idea came in sketches for the Scherzo of Schoenberg's projected but never completed Symphony (1914–15), a work that, if completed, might well have dwarfed the largest of Mahler's symphonies in both duration and number of musicians required for its execution. In the Scherzo, for the first time, Schoenberg constructs a twelve-tone theme and experiments with various proto-serial techniques.

One can scarcely imagine a more complete rejection of principles of radical athematicism, as laid out in the letter to Busoni, than the Scherzo of 1914. The Scherzo was to be part of an enormous composition (a "protracted ten-ton score") in a traditional form (the very antithesis of the "complete liberation from all forms"). The sketches show a plethora of experiments with compositional devices ("symbols of cohesion and of logic") and with invariants ("motivic working out"), and in the continuity draft Schoenberg shows clear signs of using "harmony as cement or bricks of a building." With the Scherzo of 1914 and with the twelve-tone period that followed, Schoenberg completely turned his back on radical athematicism and everything that it stood for.

Seen from the perspective of Schoenberg's entire career, therefore, radical athematicism is a perplexing and mysterious detour. With the exception of this brief period, all of Schoenberg's music treats thematic and motivic return as an indispensable component of musical structure. But during the period of radical athematicism – and only during that period – Schoenberg wrote music that was "not built, but *'expressed.'*"

8 Schoenberg, modernism, and metaphysics

JULIAN JOHNSON

Metaphysics

Herzgewächse, Op. 20 (Heart's Foliage) has to be one of the most extraordinary works in Schoenberg's extraordinary output. Only thirty measures long and lasting little over three minutes in performance, it is the most diminutive of all the works to which Schoenberg gave an individual opus number. Composed in just a few days in 1911 (December 5–9), the score was reproduced in facsimile in the 1912 almanac of *Der Blaue Reiter*, though there is no record of a performance before 1923. Scored for an ensemble of soprano, celesta, harmonium, and harp, its setting of a short poem by Maurice Maeterlinck (translated by Stefan George), requires a voice of extreme agility which is frequently taken above a high c''' and which, four bars before the end, climaxes (*pppp*) on a high f'''.

The poem constructs a melancholic and languorous world through the imagery of tangled plant forms. Only the pale and fragile lily reaches upwards with its "mystical white prayer." Sensuous, erotic, and spiritual at the same time, Maeterlinck's poem recalls Wagner's "Im Treibhaus," the third of the *Wesendonck-lieder* and thus part of the sketching process for *Tristan und Isolde*.[1] Both songs use the claustrophobic imagery of winding foliage as a metaphor for spiritual malaise, but also to express an intense longing for release – a metaphor thematized in Schoenberg's *Das Buch der Hängenden Gärten*, Op. 15 (The Book of the Hanging Gardens), to texts by Stefan George, completed in March 1909.

Herzgewächse is usually described as falling into three parts.[2] A section of freely accompanied recitative (mm. 1–15), gives way to an arioso marked by a clear quarter note pulse (mm. 16–19), and then to a cantilena section deploying the ornamental character and high register of coloratura writing (mm. 20–30). As Wolfgang Ruf observes, this tripartite division creates a "discrepancy of textual and musical structure."[3] But the sudden change that marks the introduction of the image of the lily (m. 16) creates a binary division which *is* congruent with the structure of the poem; decadent melancholy here gives way to fragile ascent. This is clearly marked by the soprano's even quarter notes rising steadily from a low B flat to a high C. The binary division, I suggest, is the most basic, but the differentiated four-measure section of mm. 16–19 is also highly significant. It functions as a musical threshold, a transformational axis for the whole piece, from a declamatory style in low register (spiritual malaise) to a lyrical style in the highest register (release through prayer). At the same time, the motivic density of the first half of the song here gives way to coloristic and melismatic proliferation in the second.[4] Ruf refers to this moment (m. 16) as an "expressive ascent towards breakthrough."[5]

The brevity, scoring, and technical difficulties of *Herzgewächse* have discounted it as a central work for either performers or scholars. But this diminutive song not only foregrounds the central compositional category of the threshold, it also represents a threshold in Schoenberg's work. To use a different metaphor, to which I will return later, this piece marks the site of a major fault line and one that runs far deeper and wider than the ambit of Schoenberg's own music. It is, rather, a central feature of the musical geology underlying the shift from Romanticism to Modernism. While *Herzgewächse* alone might seem to be a rather insignificant crack in the surface of musical style, it is one that becomes magnified in Schoenberg's (largely uncompleted) compositional projects over the ensuing twelve years. The most sustained eruption of the subterranean force it registers is undoubtedly the unfinished fragment of *Die Jakobsleiter* (Jacob's Ladder), but the oratorio, like all the works of this period, can itself be viewed as part of a larger, ongoing project.

My focus here is not the purely technical aspects of stylistic change; Schoenberg's "path to the new music," through athematicism, atonality, the dissolution of traditional forms, and so on, has been told plenty of times before. My interest is rather what we might learn of the cultural and historical fault line of which *Herzgewächse* and its related works are audible and visible signs. My contention is that this fault line has to do, above all, with the working out of a definitive metaphysical thread in European thought. Moreover, since metaphysics turns out to be a defining element for one branch of aesthetic Modernism, this in turn might require us to rethink the usual disjunctions between Romanticism and Modernism.

Wolfgang Ruf points to the "experimental character" of *Herzgewächse* that accounts for its solitary and singular nature.[6] I suggest, however, that this piece foregrounds elements that are axiomatic to Schoenberg's work as a whole. Other chapters give an account of the works of the Expressionist period (*c.*1908–23) but I want to draw out both the extent to which the same metaphysical concern underlies all of these works, and how it is manifest in distinct and recurrent technical devices. The eruption of a metaphysical dimension in Schoenberg's work has been much discussed.[7] For decades, largely excised from dominant technical accounts of his music, it has more recently become a familiar topic. For some, it offers a counterbalance to the idea of Schoenberg as detached constructor, a way of connecting his music to ideas of the spiritual, intuitive, and mysterious that might give the lie to readings of Modernism as cold, objective, and scientific. One unwelcome consequence, however, is that Schoenberg's turn to metaphysics is sometimes read simply as a colorful phase of his biography and thus reduced merely to an idiosyncratic set of personal beliefs and influences.

Few accounts of Schoenberg's life and work during this period omit to mention the usual catalog of such influences – Richard Dehmel, Stefan George, Maurice Maeterlinck, August Strindberg, Balzac's *Séraphita* (and thereby Emanuel Swedenborg), Rudolf Steiner, and Wassily Kandinsky (to name only the central figures). But to talk of influences is always superficial. The simultaneity of interest in the metaphysical and occult testifies to the manifestation of a cultural, rather than merely personal, idea. My argument is that this "colorful phase" is the personal and individual manifestation of a much broader cultural process that breaks the surface in Schoenberg's music just as, in a related but quite distinct way, it does simultaneously in the work of Kandinsky.[8] In other words, what happens in Schoenberg's music has to do with the working-out of tensions in the modern European mind. Specifically, as we shall see, it represents a critical development of German Idealism in the context of the modern world but, crucially, one performed in the realm of art rather than that of philosophy.

The metaphysical concerns of Schoenberg's music are often signaled outwardly by the texts he chose to set and by those he wrote himself. The text for *Die Jakobsleiter*, written between 1915 and 1917, draws on a diverse range of literary, religious, and philosophical texts, and represents a compendium of current ideas. By the same token, Schoenberg's own libretto for *Die glückliche Hand* (The Lucky Hand), first drafted in 1910, thematizes the nature of his own creative and spiritual journey, expressing at one and the same time the frustration inherent in trying to realize the unattainable and to find worldly form for unworldly thoughts. The presence of a metaphysical topic is also signaled clearly by certain musical devices. The most immediate of these is the use of a distinctive kind of instrumentation that Schoenberg and Webern took directly from Mahler. Ideas of the heavenly, the angelic, and a paradisial landscape are denoted in Mahler by a group that includes harp, celesta, glockenspiel, cowbells, harmonium, mandolin, and triangle. The luminosity of high bell sounds is sometimes enhanced by the use of sustained string harmonics.[9] Webern takes this celestial ensemble of Mahler's and foregrounds it in many of his orchestral works, most famously perhaps in the third of his Five Pieces for Orchestra, Op. 10.[10] More often than not, both Mahler and Webern associate this ensemble with the use of a solo violin, deployed lyrically in its upper register. The number and specificity of examples of this topic make clear its function of denoting an angelic voice. In some cases it is used with an actual soprano voice; at other times it stands in for the voice.[11] In *Herzgewächse*, the high soprano is itself transposed into the "angelic" register; in the closing section of *Die Jakobsleiter* the wordless voice of The Soul (indebted to the vocal part of *Herzgewächse*) is used in conjunction with the high solo violin.

Thresholds

While instrumentation is a signifier of metaphysical presence or vision, often underwritten by Schoenberg's choice of texts, it is through the structural function of the threshold that metaphysics has its most powerful effect on Schoenberg's music at this time, because in this way it becomes internalized as musical form. The arresting transformation midway through *Herzgewächse* functions like a hyper-condensed version of the Mahlerian threshold (consider the "Grosse Appell" in the finale of the Second Symphony, for example). Adorno discusses the Mahlerian threshold under the idea of *Suspension* – in other words, a holding-up of the surrounding narrative process by an episode that composes out the idea of a *senza tempo*.[12] In Mahler, as in Webern and Schoenberg, the threshold denotes the suspension of a linear progress of musical time and its displacement by an exploration of musical space. The metaphysical aspect of this is frequently underlined by text and/or use of clear musical topics that reference ideas of celestial landscape or angelic presence. The idea is famously thematized in Act 1 of Wagner's *Parsifal*, in Gurnemanz's line "You see, my son, here time becomes space," these being the last words heard before the beginning of the Transformation Music during which the scene changes from the external world of nature to the interior of the Castle of the Grail, a representation of the spiritualization of nature that anticipates the move toward abstraction a generation later.

This concern with the threshold between two worlds explains the recurrent fascination, of Schoenberg and others, with Balzac's mystical novel *Séraphita*, which is in turn indebted to the thought of Emanuel Swedenborg. *Séraphita* is concerned not simply with the idea of the angelic (itself a threshold between man and God), but rather with the liminal state between a mortal and an angelic being. The novel explores the relationship between the angelic Séraphita-Séraphitus (whose gender shifts in response to the person he/she is with, an androgynous element that resurfaces elsewhere in Schoenberg)[13] and two humans, Minna and Wilfred. Its final chapter, "The Assumption," foregrounds the tension between the two worlds as Séraphita, unable to live any longer in the mortal world, gives up her earthly form. This moment is explicitly also a threshold to a new language:

> The last hymn was not uttered in words, nor expressed by gestures, nor by any of the signs which serve men as a means of communicating their thoughts, but as the soul speaks to itself; for at the moment when Séraphita was revealed in her true nature, her ideas were no longer enslaved to human language.[14]

Metaphysics is defined by a basic duality. In the Kantian system, the existence of a world known through our senses (the world of phenomena) implies a world that is *not* known in such a way, but is transcendent to empirical knowledge (the noumenal world). In other words, the basis of a philosophical metaphysics is precisely the non-congruence of aspects of reality to our systems of knowledge. The noumenal is defined negatively, as that which lies outside the empirically verifiable. The proposition of metaphysics is thus a critical one: it asserts the limits of knowledge. This self-critique of philosophy becomes, in Romanticism and Modernism, a self-critique of representation. Similarly, Schoenberg's self-critique of musical language is powerfully shaped by an awareness of the inadequacy of language – specifically, of the inadequacy of a musical language modeled on the representation of human emotions when challenged at the threshold of a fully spiritual reality.

It is for this reason that *Séraphita* assumed such importance for Schoenberg in the years between 1911 and 1914.[15] Both *Die glückliche Hand* and *Die Jakobsleiter* underline Schoenberg's view that the artist was also a kind of threshold, an intermediary in touch with two worlds at once, an idea with its roots in Wagner's reading of Schopenhauer by which the composer is understood as a "clairvoyant." This view is thematized in Schoenberg's "Vorgefühl," Op. 22, No. 4, and by the character of "The Chosen One" in *Die Jakobsleiter*. Such an idea brings us closer to how Schoenberg's Modernism is bound up with metaphysics. It makes sense (as has often been observed) of why *Die Jakobsleiter* was left unfinished at the very point that the soul flies from the body towards God, of why *Moses und Aron* is left unscored after the close of Act 2 with Moses's cry of despair, "Oh word, thou word that I lack!," and why the late choral work, *Moderner Psalm*, Op. 50c, breaks off at the line "And yet we pray."[16] It fulfills what Hegel predicted in his notorious "death of art" thesis – not that art would literally come to an end, but that its material would become inadequate to its content.[17] Schoenberg's entire career might be understood as a wrestling with this idea.[18]

Outwardly, Schoenberg progressed no further with a setting of Balzac's *Séraphita* than a single-page, thirteen-bar sketch that sets the first sentence of the final chapter ("The Assumption").[19] Dated December 27, 1912, this sketch appeared just three weeks after the composition of *Herzgewächse*, with its similarly angelic concerns and sound-world.[20] The final chapter of *Séraphita* foregrounds many of the ideas that were key to Schoenberg at this time, that he shared with Kandinsky, and which found their way into his creative work as theosophical themes. In Séraphita's parting speech she refers to the series of levels by which the soul attains purity by a specific reference to Jacob's ladder.[21] Evident also is the doctrine of reincarnation that figures prominently in Schoenberg's libretto, the notion that one must live countless times in order to gradually ascend the stages of this mystical ladder.[22] Séraphita sets out the progression of levels by which one moves to God, the last of which is prayer. "To pray," she says, "you must be refined in the furnace to the purity of a diamond."[23] Unsurprisingly, there are a number of similarities between Schoenberg's sketch for *Séraphita* and parts of *Die Jakobsleiter* by which it was later subsumed.[24]

But there are also important points of contact between Balzac's text and Schoenberg's thinking on musical and theatrical techniques, as is clear in the following extract:

> Light gave birth to melody, and melody to light; colors were both light and melody; motion was number endowed by the Word; in short, everything was at once sonorous, diaphanous, and mobile; so that, everything existing in everything else, extension knew no limits, and the angels could traverse it everywhere to the utmost depths of the infinite.[25]

The interrelation of light and melody, the subject of an intense exchange with Kandinsky, was explored most obviously in Schoenberg's work in the orchestral movement "Farben" (Op. 16, No. 3) and in the detailed lighting directions for *Die glückliche Hand*. The idea of motion as number shaped by the Idea might be said to underlie the thinking behind the twelve-tone method, a means by which Schoenberg and his pupils sought to realize musically the "equivalence of musical space," and a state of "everything existing in everything else." The exceeding of limits (an "angelic" state of being) is at first explored in a literal way in Schoenberg's music – the crossing of boundaries of harmonic grammar, pushing registral extremes, exceeding the received vocabulary of instrumental combinations and sonorities; *Herzgewächse* might serve, in miniature, to illustrate all three. But this exceeding of literal limits is later transmuted into the abstractions of twelve-tone music. For Schoenberg, as for Webern, the change from free atonality to twelve-tone composition was itself a threshold moment, as if, after working intuitively in the dark, they had suddenly broken through to the abstract order that had been sought all along. For them, this was not just a technical breakthrough but a spiritual one; its abstract objectivity represented the transcendence of a merely subjective desire, the release, one might argue, longed for equally by Tristan and Amfortas.

Die Jakobsleiter, despite remaining an incomplete fragment, is Schoenberg's most sustained and single-minded exploration of the idea of the threshold.[26] As its title suggests, it thematizes the notion of a liminal space by means of the reference to Jacob's dream-vision of a staircase joining heaven to earth, which the angels ascend and descend between the two (Genesis 28: 10–17). That this work, more than any other, anticipates Schoenberg's development of the twelve-tone method underlines the inseparability of his technical and metaphysical projects.[27] The opening lines of the oratorio, sung by Gabriel, announce the radically different nature of the new musical space ("Whether to the right or the left, forwards or backwards") and the opening bars deploy Schoenberg's basic hexachord both linearly (as a marching figure in the bass and cello part) and vertically (as a chord in the wind). But it is in the closing section of the fragment, written sometime between 1917 and 1922, in which this new musical space is most radically explored, as The Dying One gives up his soul. This final section is characterized by several features anticipated in *Herzgewächse* (the high, wordless coloratura soprano of The Soul, the *senza misura* writing, the static effect of repeated ostinato arpeggiations of celesta, harmonium, and harps, the "angelic" voice of the high solo violin), but also by a radically new element. Placed at a distance from the main orchestra are no less than four separate groups of instrumentalists and singers, two of them placed at different heights above the orchestra and two at different horizontal distances. This is far more than music theatre; it makes literal the spatialization of different orchestral sonorities that had, until then, been more conceptual, defined by distinct timbres and material rather than the actual direction of the sound source. Its debt to Mahler is twofold: first, it builds on Mahler's use of off-stage effects, and second, it seeks to realize the levels of ascent to heaven depicted by Goethe in Part II of *Faust* which forms the basis of Part II of Mahler's Eighth Symphony.

The threshold at the center of *Herzgewächse* connects to its massive expansion in *Die Jakobsleiter* a decade later, but it is also a transformation, both technically and expressively, of what takes place much earlier in the groundbreaking Second String Quartet, Op. 10 (1907–08), truly a threshold work itself. This points to a continuity of metaphysical concerns in Schoenberg's work that runs from at least 1907 to 1922 and the inseparable link between those metaphysical concerns and Schoenberg's search for a new musical language. Just as *Herzgewächse* evokes the world of Wagner's "Im Treibhaus," so the Second Quartet makes a similar elision of the erotic and spiritual, in its alliance of an attenuated tonal language and a post-Brahmsian motivic process. The result is music that is powerfully directed by an intense sense of searching or longing, but towards an unfulfilled goal (just as Schoenberg had explored in his *Verklärte Nacht* of 1899). Adding a soprano to the quartet for the final two movements, Schoenberg sets two texts by Stefan George expressing a spiritual, disembodied kind of longing, but the tone of both the poetry and the music once again look back to Wagner's *Tristan*. In the setting of "Litanei" that forms the third movement there is also more than an echo of Wagner's *Parsifal* – of the spiritual pain and longing of Amfortas, imprisoned by an erotically charged stasis. The variation structure creates a sense of being stuck in the same place, while the music nevertheless attempts to reach beyond itself. The overall character is one of lament, a prelude to the threshold moment constituted by the opening of the fourth movement.

What is the character of the world to which the threshold here gives access? It is new, strange, light, ungraspable, weightless, self-contained. All these qualities are underlined by George's text, which begins with the emblematic line "I feel the air of other planets." The musical world Schoenberg presents at this most famous of musical thresholds is one stripped of its hitherto subjective elements – the searching, lyrical lines of the forgoing music give way to the proposition of some supra-subjective state. At a parallel moment in *Die Jakobsleiter* (mm. 600–1), Gabriel delivers the line, "Then is your 'I' extinguished," as The Dying One expires and The Soul flies heavenwards. In this way, the Second Quartet makes an essentially metaphysical proposition – that subjective yearning breaks through to a radically new, more expansive state, and thus anticipates both *Herzgewächse* and *Die Jakobsleiter*. All three works contrast a disembodied, weightless music of arrival in a new, spatialized musical landscape, with the sense of longing evoked by the residual chromatic tensions of an enervated tonal harmony. In *Die Jakobsleiter* this is most audible in the *espressivo* counterpoint associated with the One who is Called, whose lyrical string accompaniment recalls not just Mahler but also Schoenberg's own earlier style in *Gurrelieder*. In other words, the Second Quartet anticipates the later oratorio fragment in aspects of character, plot, and structural narrative, of which *Herzgewächse* might be seen as a miniature version.

The Four Orchestral Songs, Op. 22 (1913–16) are similarly located in the gap between longing and fulfillment. The first sets a poem entitled "Seraphita," loosely inspired by Balzac's novel, by the English Decadent poet Ernest Dowson.[28] Its opposition of the storms of life and the anticipation of an otherworldly state read like a microcosmic version of Schoenberg's text for *Die Jakobsleiter*. Musically, it juxtaposes a chromatic, searching melodic line with moments of angelic vision (note the use of the solo violin in mm. 32 and 37ff.). The remaining three songs, all to texts by Rilke, draw out related topics – the ineffability of what is sought, the necessity of watching and waiting (the use of the cor anglais in the third song echoes the third act of *Tristan* in this respect), and the premonition of things to come.

The threshold divides two quite different spaces. It is less a mediation of opposites, which implies interaction and transformation, than a statement of mutual exclusivity. The threshold, by definition, implies leaving one space behind in order to enter into another. While the oppositions of these works are often between *Tristan*-esque longing and a fleeting vision of the longed-for completion, in Schoenberg, as in Mahler, spiritual thirst and malaise often turns to disgust at the distance between the two. Irony and negativity are often the outward signs of this. This Mahlerian triangulation is taken up prominently in some of Schoenberg's works.[29] In *Die glückliche Hand* the juxtaposition of longing, desire, and parodic irony is externalized in the mocking laughter of the chorus and the use of popular musical styles to undermine the claims of an autonomous "authentic" expression (as so often in the scherzos of Mahler symphonies or in Berg's *Wozzeck*). This explains the close proximity in Schoenberg's output of a luminous piece like *Herzgewächse* and the parodic grotesquerie of *Pierrot lunaire*.

Schoenberg wrote to Kandinsky, on August 19, 1912, to say that *Pierrot* was "a preparatory study for another work, which I now wish to begin: Balzac's Séraphita."[30] That might seem an odd connection to make, but *Pierrot* makes explicit that ironic negativity and grotesque parody are the direct result of a spiritual longing. This is clear not just from the text, which draws on similar topics of longing and waiting, but in the way that Schoenberg's skeletal ensemble and use of *Sprechstimme* produce a photographic negative of Wagnerian tone and delivery. Desire turns to poison as, for example, in the "Valse de Chopin." *Pierrot lunaire*, with its recurrent themes of sickness, despair, drunkenness, and madness, may be extreme in its unrelenting negativity and parody, but it is not alone in Schoenberg's works of this period. The Scherzo movement of the Second Quartet, parodic elements of the Serenade, Op. 24, and the sketch for a *moto perpetuo* scherzo (the "Totentanz der Prinzipien") from Schoenberg's unrealized Symphony, all express this negative "other" of metaphysical aspiration.[31]

While the significance of the threshold as both structural and expressive device comes to the fore in Schoenberg's atonal period, it is by no means lost with the move to twelve-tone composition. The central division of *Herzgewächse* anticipates what was to become the center of both horizontal and vertical symmetries in the later music of the Schoenberg school. That palindromes and mirror inversions were conceived of as more than merely technical devices is made explicit in Webern's settings of the poetry of Hildegard Jone, where the recurrent metaphysical relation of inner and outer worlds is explored through the structural inversions of Webern's music.

Modernism

Herzgewächse, I have argued, is emblematic of the technical and expressive concerns that define Schoenberg's work in the Expressionist years, *c*.1908–23. But what erupts in this music is not confined to Schoenberg, as is clearly evidenced by the commonality of interests he shared with Webern, Berg, Kandinsky, Steiner, Dehmel, George, Rilke – and many others. My broader suggestion is that the metaphysical and theosophical turn of the *fin-de-siècle* must be seen within a larger context and that, in its reactivation of central ideas in Western thought, it marks a moment of seismic change in the geology of Modernism. It mounted an aesthetic critique not only of the idea of representation, but of the philosophy and culture of materialism that, in the aesthetic sphere, was reinforced by representational art. The diminutive form of *Herzgewächse*, no more than a fissure when viewed in isolation, is the surface manifestation of forces that run down through the sedimented layers of social and cultural history, back through the poetry of the Symbolists to Wagner, Schopenhauer, and thus to German Romanticism and philosophical Idealism.

It is easy to be so engrossed by individual phenomena (Schoenberg's own biography, his religious beliefs or artistic credo) that one fails to see them as part of a wider and largely subterranean system. Of course, philosophical metaphysics is by no means the same thing as the theosophy to which Kandinsky and others responded and on which Schoenberg drew in various ways (as in the libretto to *Die Jakobsleiter*). Neither is it equivalent to what I have called the metaphysical proposition of Schoenberg's music, with its division of "earthly" and "unearthly" marked by threshold moments and distinctive oppositions of musical materials.[32] But all three have in common their critical stance towards a prevailing social materialism and philosophical positivism. In short, all three assert that the structures of rational knowledge, representation, and language are inadequate in the face of the totality of the world and our experience of it. Moreover, the music we have examined proposes such an idea by means of its own materials and forms, irrespective of any text-setting.

Perhaps the idea of geological movement might allow us to preserve both the obvious moment of disjunction marked by aesthetic Modernism while at the same time understanding it as the product of far larger forces. The familiar idea that modernist music represents a rejection of classical values (much to the detriment of the modern age) is superficial; classical music of the late eighteenth century is marked by the same kinds of tensions that later erupt more violently through the musical surface in Schoenberg.[33] Scratch the surface of late eighteenth-century art and disorder abounds (Sterne, Gozzi, Coleridge, Schlegel, Beethoven, Turner, Hoffmann); scratch the surface of Modernism and order is everywhere (Schoenberg, Webern, Stravinsky, Klee, Mondrian, Le Corbusier). What happens in the early twentieth century (and this is why the role of metaphysics has a valuable explicative power) is that some art and music moves away from the teleology of human desire (as encoded by tonal music) and reaches out for a more objective, all-encompassing order – the difference between the first three movements and the finale of Schoenberg's Second Quartet. As precursors to both are the paradisial elaborations of Mahler's landscape music, presented as the site of spiritual encounter and of liberation from subjective desire.

In the same year that Schoenberg completed his Second Quartet, the art historian Wilhelm Worringer published his seminal book *Abstraction and Empathy*.[34] Here he set out the two principal modes by which art constructs itself in relation to the world – empathy, an attempt to represent the external world through mimesis, and abstraction, an attempt to render principles of order in material form. Schoenberg's exploration of the threshold between the two, announced definitively in the Second Quartet but which shapes his entire output, thus wrestles with two attitudes toward the world whose mutual tension defines Western thought. Hegel announced a thoroughly modern conception of art in his Lectures on Aesthetics, first given in the 1820s, with the idea that art necessarily outgrew itself, that a modern art (he called it "romantic") was self-critical in respect to its own material and its inadequacy for the expression of a spiritual content.[35] His contemporary, Beethoven, in foregrounding that element of self-critique, thus stands at the beginning of a process of musical Modernism which Schoenberg may have intensified but by no means initiated.

But music is not philosophy, nor does it merely embody some philosophical zeitgeist; on the contrary, it stands in a critical relation to philosophy.[36] It does so first and foremost because, unlike philosophy, music has necessarily to mediate between its particular materials (the sensuous physicality of timbre, rhythm, intensity) and their abstract, intellectual ordering (as phrase, section, form). Whereas philosophy is thought in the abstract medium of language, music is thought through the concrete medium of its sonic materials. For Hegel and German Idealism, this was precisely what subordinated art to philosophy. Music, however, critiques this central idea of modernity (the primacy of rational abstraction) by engaging with its aspiration yet without quitting the realm of the sensuous. Schoenberg inherited this tension as both an artistic and metaphysical problem which shaped an essentially self-critical activity, the defining aim of which was to point beyond itself, to mediate between a human, lyrical, and subjective component, and the urge towards some trans-subjective order. Schoenberg's metaphysics may indeed have led him into the quite different domains of psychology, philosophy, and religion, but at its heart was a tension that not only shaped his own music, but which defines the musical modernism of which his music remains emblematic. Schoenberg's enthusiastic letter to Kandinsky (August 19, 1912) about his plans to set *Séraphita* is instructive in this regard:

> Balzac's "Seraphita." Do you know it? Perhaps the most glorious work in existence. I want to do it scenically. Not so much as theater, at least not in the old sense. In any case, not "dramatic." But rather: oratorio that becomes visible and audible. Philosophy, religion, that are perceived with the artistic senses.[37]

For that reason, not only is Schoenberg's music itself better understood as the outward eruption of much larger and older forces, but it in turn offers insight into the wider geology of musical Modernism.

9 *Pierrot lunaire*: persona, voice, and the fabric of allusion

RICHARD KURTH

Since its 1912 composition and premiere, Schoenberg's *Dreimal sieben Gedichte aus Albert Girauds Pierrot lunaire* (Three Times Seven Poems from Albert Giraud's Pierrot lunaire), Op. 21 has aroused strong responses and extensive commentary, especially regarding its enigmatic approach to *Sprechstimme* (speaking voice or recitation) and its "atonal" idiom. This chapter, in three parts, synthesizes and extends some themes in the recent critical reception of the work.[1] The first part sketches a history of the Pierrot character in comedy and pantomime, including a description of the genesis and overall shape of Schoenberg's *Pierrot lunaire*. The second section explores how traditional vocal representations of subjectivity and lyric expression are renatured by Schoenberg's striking approach to *Sprechstimme* in the work. The final part demonstrates, through selected examples, how the music invokes a rich network of musical allusions, in tandem with tonal latencies that permeate its kaleidoscopic surface.

Pierrots old and new – *en blanc et noir*

Over the centuries, the Pierrot character has been portrayed by countless actors, pantomimes, and puppets.[2] Originating among Italian *commedia dell'arte* troupes active in seventeenth-century France, Pierrot first appears in 1660s comedies as a rustic and dumbfounded bumpkin, but in the eighteenth century he became the paragon of pastoral innocence, a pure (and often silent) fool. The nineteenth century gradually transformed him, radically, into a decadent *fin-de-siècle* dandy, obsessed with the moon. A resemblance with the moon was already suggested by his eighteenth-century *commedia* costume: a powdered white face, soft white hat and large ruffled collar, and loose jacket and trousers of flowing white silk. By the nineteenth century he had become a darker figure, often completely mute, and the distant and intoxicating moon had become his emblem, muse, and mirror. This was his triumphant period on the stages of Paris, where he was reinvented in the 1830s by the pantomime Jean-Gaspard ("Baptiste") Deburau and his apostles. Pierrot's new lunatic persona aroused delirious enthusiasm among a diverse company of poets – Baudelaire, Banville, Gautier, Verlaine, Laforgue – because the mute Pierrot's miming gestures allegorized the sufferings and growing isolation of the modern poet.

Among other things, Deburau restyled Pierrot's make-up. The pantomime powdered his face to a perfect blankness to heighten its mute expressivity. He rouged his silent but elastic lips, added dark shading around his searing eyes, and topped his moon-like face with a black skullcap – to evoke the dark side of the moon, and an open cranium exposed to pernicious celestial influences. The contrast of this black void atop his white face signifies a deep split in Pierrot's psyche, manifested thereafter by the two main *fin-de-siècle* types of Pierrots: the moon-like white Pierrots of Aubrey Beardsley's etchings, who are pale, diaphanous, narcissistic, and androgynous; and the lunatic black Pierrots in tailcoats, seen in the cartoons of Jules Chéret and Adolphe Willette, who are evil geniuses inspired by seductive, grotesque, and sinister comic gaiety, or hallucinogenic and sacrilegious maniacs tormented by every fear and guilt.

Pierrots of both polarities waft and swerve through *Pierrot lunaire: Rondels bergamasques*, the 1884 collection of fifty French poems by the Belgian poet Albert Giraud (1860–1929). As Robert Vilain notes, Giraud uses Pierrot's inner and outer landscape to explore the artistic challenge of bringing Parnassian poetic restraint into contact with Symbolist poetic sensuousness, without falling into Decadent excesses.[3] Pierrot's white-or-black polarity here symbolizes a debate in Belgian poetic circles, with the Parnassian and Decadent creeds at the respective poles. In his 1893 German translation of Giraud's poems, Otto Erich Hartleben (1864–1905) preserved their basic Parnassian formal element – the rigid thirteen-line *rondel* form – but he refocused the poems as expressions of subjective crisis rather than aesthetic debate.[4] Hartleben intensified the imagery and sound of the poems, making them sizzle and blaze in a stunning display of sonic pirouettes and explosions, so that the poems render the mute pantomime's antic gestures and poses back into a spectacular verbal substance, perfectly suited to the novel mode of recitation Schoenberg would create in his 1912 *Pierrot lunaire*.

During the 1910–11 Berlin season, the actress Albertine Zehme gave three recitals featuring the Hartleben translations in melodramatic settings (with piano accompaniments) by Otto Vrieslander. Schoenberg moved to Berlin in October 1911, and Zehme approached him in January 1912 to commission more elaborate and adventurous settings of the poems. Schoenberg was fascinated by her proposal and ideas. On March 10, 1912 he signed a contract to compose at least twenty melodramas, with piano and two additional instruments, and he started composing immediately, writing "Gebet an Pierrot" (with piano and clarinet in A)

Table 9.1 *Titles, poetic character-shading (black/white), instrumentation, and instrumental character-shading in the three parts of* Pierrot lunaire. *(Instruments in parentheses enter midway through the respective melodrama.)*

1. Mondes**trunken**/Moon**drunk**	Piano		Flute	Violin	Cello
2. Colombine	Piano	(Clarinet in A)	(Flute)	Violin	
3. Der **Dandy**/The **Dandy**	Piano	Clarinet in A	**Piccolo**		
4. Eine blasse Wäscherin/A pale washerwoman		Clarinet in A	Flute	Violin	
5. **Valse de Chopin/Chopin Waltz**	Piano	Clarinet in A	Flute		
6. **Madonna**	(Piano)	**Bass Clarinet**	Flute	(Violin)	Cello
7. Der kranke Mond/The Sick Moon			Flute		
8. **Nacht/Night**	Piano	**Bass Clarinet**			Cello
9. Gebet an Pierrot/Prayer to Pierrot	Piano	Clarinet in A			
10. Raub/Robbery		Clarinet in A	Flute	Violin	Cello
11. **Rote Messe/Red Mass**	Piano	**Bass Clarinet**	**Piccolo**	**Viola**	Cello
12. **Galgenlied/Gallows Song**			**Piccolo**	**Viola**	Cello
13. **Enthauptung/Beheading**	Piano	**Bass Clarinet**		**Viola**	Cello
(wordless reprise of No. 7)		**Bass Clarinet**	Flute	**Viola**	Cello
14. **Die Kreuze/The Crosses**	Piano	Clarinet in A	(Flute)	(Violin)	(Cello)
15. Heimweh/Nostalgia	Piano	Clarinet in A		Violin	
16. **Gemeinheit!/Dirty Trick!**	Piano	Clarinet in A	**Piccolo**	Violin	Cello
17. **Parodie/Parody**	Piano	Clarinet in A	**Piccolo**	**Viola**	
18. **Der Mondfleck/The Moon Fleck**	Piano	**Clarinet in B♭**	**Piccolo**	Violin	Cello
19. **Serenade**	Piano	(Clarinet in A)	(Flute)	(Violin)	Cello
20. Heimfahrt/Homeward Journey	Piano	Clarinet in A	Flute	Violin	Cello
21. O alter Duft/O ethereal fragrance	Piano	in A/(**Bass**)	Fl./(**Picc.**)	Vln/(**Vla**)	Cello

on March 12. The instrumentation expanded rapidly as Schoenberg worked, eventually requiring five players and eight instruments; each melodrama uses a distinct combination of instruments, sometimes changing midway through. Schoenberg eventually chose twenty-one of the fifty poems, including twelve from Zehme's March 1911 recital, which had featured twenty-two poems arranged in three groups of six, seven, and nine poems, respectively. Schoenberg finished the individual settings in early July, and then completely revised his preliminary ordering so as to fashion an overall narrative in three groups of seven poems each – thus the "dreimal sieben" (three times seven) in the work's title.[5] Each group represents a contrasting facet of Pierrot's psychology in a multipart narrative of his exploits. After an open rehearsal on October 9 for invited guests and the press, the work was premiered on October 16, 1912. A five-week tour of thirteen cities followed immediately.[6]

Table 9.1 outlines the titles, grouping, and instrumentation of the melodramas. To show continuity and contrast, and observe affiliations with specific instruments, I associate the overall character of each movement with either a white or black Pierrot. (Bold type identifies the "black" Pierrot movements; some movements appear in mixed type, if they combine "white" imagery with "dark" character.) Bass clarinet, piccolo, and viola function like alter egos (to the clarinet, flute, and violin, respectively); they tend to appear in "black" numbers, and grotesquely distort the music's registral and timbral proportions. Overall, dark movements outnumber light ones, approximately two to one. Parts I and III are both fairly balanced, though differently paced, while Part II is almost entirely dark and diabolical. The lunar phases also structure Schoenberg's grouping. Part I begins with Pierrot enraptured by the full moon, but he slips progressively into illness as the moon wanes, and Part I ends with the dying moon as a mere sliver. Pierrot's depraved exploits in Part II mostly take place during the ensuing moonless phase, but a new crescent moon appears near the end (in No. 13). Pierrot becomes more comic as the moon waxes throughout Part III, until it is full again at "Heimfahrt" (No. 20). Morning sunlight dissolves the whole nocturnal world in "O alter Duft" (No. 21). Only this closing melodrama uses all eight instruments: the "white" instruments appear first; the "black" siblings enter near the end, but their dark connotations fade in the morning light.

Susan Youens interprets Schoenberg's selection and tripartite framing of twenty-one poems as an allegory on the condition of the modern artist.[7] Reinhold Brinkmann reinforces this interpretation when he notes that in comparison with other contemporaneous settings of the Giraud/ Hartleben poems, only Schoenberg's *Pierrot* cycle "elevates the puppet Pierrot to the level of an allegorical figure, to a model of identification for the late artist of modernity, for the problematic state of subjectivity, for the crisis of identity and cohesion of the I."[8] The eccentric sounds of the *Sprechstimme* certainly contribute to the expression of identity crisis and alienation, in rich and fascinating ways. But the sense of disorientation arises first from the discontinuous contrasts between the many black and white Pierrots that swerve through the poems, representing the obsessions of the modern psyche generally, not just the delusions of a single individual artist.

The electrifying diversity of the instrumental music also challenges the listener. Yet there are many factors, though often concealed, that do help to integrate it. Stephan Weytjens has shown the extensive use of varied motivic repetition in each melodrama, and Jonathan Dunsby believes that a "motivic essence" (and an unidentified *Grundgestalt*) unify Schoenberg's inventive music.[9] Many recent critics hear *Pierrot lunaire* as thoroughly parodic – like the eponymous pantomimes and puppets – and replete with satiric musical references and ironic allusions. As Brinkmann puts it, "There is not a single piece in *Pierrot lunaire* that is not based upon pre-existing material. The entire cycle indeed is music about music."[10] The musical references are concealed and distorted by Schoenberg's enigmatic harmony, which effaces their original tonal moorings, but the music is nonetheless replete with lambent fragments of tonal sensation. The hidden references also invoke a massive supplementary intertext of musical works with their own dramatis personae, much like the larger cast of *commedia* characters from which Pierrot emerged.

The mimetic voice: *Sprechmelodie* and alterity

The instrumental music in *Pierrot* is so remarkably inventive that some listeners, including Stravinsky, have wished the voice would fall mute – like a pantomime – to let the instruments sound alone.[11] But the unfamiliar mode of vocal production is surely the most important component in *Pierrot*, because it transmits and transfigures the word-sounds. The enigmatic quality of the *Sprechstimme* is the paramount aspect of *Pierrot*: it revolutionizes the musical use of the voice, and displaces the artifice of bel canto style that hitherto counted as the "natural" and authentic expression of subjectivity.[12] In fact, for her March 1911 recital, Albertine Zehme wrote a passionate program note on the aesthetics of recitation, questioning the naturalness of singing and calling for a wider expressive palette: "The singing voice, that supernatural, chastely controlled instrument, ideally beautiful precisely in its ascetic lack of freedom, is not suited to strong eruptions of feeling . . . For our poets and composers to communicate, we need both the tones of song as well as those of speech."[13] Undoubtedly, she showed this program note to Schoenberg, and her ideas probably influenced his approach to *Sprechstimme* in *Pierrot*.

Before *Pierrot lunaire*, Schoenberg experimented with different notations and approaches to modulating *Sprechstimme*, in *Gurrelieder* and *Die glückliche Hand*; and he would do so again in several later pieces.[14] Numerous factors have been proposed as influences on Schoenberg's unique approach to *Sprechstimme* in *Pierrot lunaire*: contemporaneous melodramatic works by other composers (especially Humperdinck's 1897 *Königskinder*); the Berlin cabaret world in which Schoenberg briefly participated in 1901; Karl Kraus's famous Viennese recitations; and perhaps even Jewish cantilation.[15] None of these possible influences is mentioned, confirmed, or denied in any of Schoenberg's recorded statements about *Pierrot lunaire*.

Schoenberg believed at this time that poetic language conveys meaning directly through its sensuous sounds (rather than through syntax, semantics, concepts), and he had proclaimed in a recent essay that he "had completely understood . . .the poems of Stefan George from their sound alone."[16] This statement resonates with Symbolist tenets valorizing poetic sound as the purified manifestation of meaning. Schoenberg must have been pleased to discover a similar conviction in Albertine Zehme's March 1911 program note: "The words that we speak should not solely lead to mental concepts, but instead their sound should allow us to partake of their inner experience."[17] The oracular *Sprechstimme* and brilliant instrumental gestures in *Pierrot lunaire* are vividly and inventively responsive to what Zehme calls the "inner experience" of the words. Schoenberg composed the *Pierrot* melodramas very rapidly, describing the experience as the "unmediated expression of sensual and mental gestures. Almost as though everything was directly transcribed."[18] The music is a transcription of vocal and instrumental gestures that Schoenberg imagined spontaneously in response to each poem's sonic material. In this period he had complete faith that word-sounds alone could transmit the full poetic content and shading, and he rendered afresh this "inner experience" of the words in new instrumental and vocal gestures, vividly perceived and notated in precise detail. The resulting music is definitely associative and representational, but Schoenberg's prefatory comments in the 1914 score have often been misunderstood to mean the opposite:

> Never do the performers have the duty here to shape the tone and character of the individual pieces out of the meaning of the words, but always only out of the music. So far as tone-painterly representation of events and emotions given in the text was important to the composer, it can in any event be found in the music.[19]

Schoenberg is in fact underlining his music's representational agency.[20] But he warns that because the music so precisely captures meanings and associations awakened during the creative moment, any attempt by performers to add expression could distort and destroy its intense specificity. He also wants the reciter (and instrumentalists) to avoid adding *pathos* that would make the performance, and the work, seem either affected or maudlin: "I have always stressed that this piece must be performed in a light manner, without pathos," he wrote of "Die Kreuze" in 1928, and in 1940 he referred to "the light, ironic-satiric tone . . . in which the work was originally conceived."[21] Like all the great nineteenth-century manifestations of the Pierrot persona, Schoenberg's *Pierrot* is a work of levity and wit, in which macabre images dissolve ironically into cathartic laughter.

Schoenberg actually used the word "*Sprechmelodie*" to describe his approach to *Sprechstimme* in *Pierrot*. Fidelity to the notated rhythms is crucial, but proper characterization of pitch and tone are the crucial properties. In the Foreword to the score, he outlined the concept carefully, first stating:

> The melody indicated by notes for the speaking voice [*Sprechstimme*] is not meant to be sung (apart from a few specifically marked exceptions). The performer has the task of transforming it, with due consideration for the prescribed pitches, into a speech-melody [*Sprechmelodie*].[22]

Sprechmelodie transforms the sonic material of language into a new musical resource. Schoenberg formulated specific directives for the desired concept of vocal modulation:

> [The performer must remain] fully aware of the contrast between singing tone and speaking tone: singing tone strictly maintains the pitch, while speaking tone gives it at first, but abandons it immediately either by falling or rising. But the performer must take great care not to fall into a sing-song form of speaking. That is absolutely not intended. And by no means should one strive for realistic-naturalistic speech. On the contrary, the difference between an ordinary speech and one that contributes to a musical form must be made clear. But it must also never be reminiscent of singing [*Gesang*].[23]

The last sentence makes it clear that "*Sprechgesang*" (speech-song) is definitely not what Schoenberg wants; Schoenberg avoided this term, but it has been widely used by others, creating unnecessary confusion even in otherwise perceptive and useful studies.[24] Schoenberg uses "*Sprechmelodie*," by which he means an expressive and artistically coordinated succession of *spoken* pitches, timbres, and rhythms, without the sustained vowels of song. *Sprechmelodie* is already inherent in the continuous frequency and timbre fluctuations of normal speech, and has long been shaped artistically in poetry and drama, by authors, readers, and actors. It is a natural vocal attribute, ready to become a new musical resource when shaped artistically by the composer in specific ways and contexts.[25]

Spoken pitch is inherently musical. It is in constant motion, across large intervals and microtonal ones; vowel timbres change continuously, and consonants are much more varied and incisive than in song. Schoenberg's *Sprechmelodie* replaces the bel canto emphasis on sustained pure vowels with a fantastic new mobility. It forces *continuous* change in both pitch and vowel timbre, and by magnifying the profile of the consonants, it also forces *discontinuous* change in vowel sounds. It produces a mercurial kaleidoscope of vocal tones and timbres, giving the voice new articulations and percussive effects, comparable to the extended bowing techniques used by the string instruments in the work. Ferruccio Busoni, after a private performance conducted by Schoenberg in 1913, described the declamation as "affected" but also "almost like a new instrument, charming and expressive."[26] Schoenberg's student Erwin Stein also compared the *Sprechmelodie* to an instrument in a seminal 1927 essay on the topic.[27]

This newly enriched vocal instrument can register the sonic material of language with utmost vividness, fulfilling Schoenberg's and Zehme's belief that the meaning and inner experience of words is conveyed purely through their sounds. But the heightened expressive capacities of this "instrumentalized" voice also alienate it from everyday vocalization, in which words function as semantic units, and only secondarily as inflected sound. *Sprechmelodie* still "speaks," but it also supersedes meaning through its extraordinary sonic palette. As Guy Michaud said of Verlaine's poetry, "the language is vaporized and is reabsorbed into the melody."[28] The *Sprechmelodie* in *Pierrot* transforms Hartleben's already heightened language into an acrobatic display of vocal gestures and timbres. It is also grotesque, in that the timbral capacities of the voice are distorted by immense increases in every dimension, to register more vividly the music of the poetic language.

The alterity of *Sprechmelodie* arises from this vertiginous liberty. It releases vocal sound and expression from the shackles of an outdated notion of beauty, but its free and rapid inflections also relinquish the ability of bel canto song to delineate subjective states through a more limited scale of positions relative to a tonic. The newly "instrumentalized" voice of *Sprechmelodie* denatures bel canto's most beautiful artifice – its constructed tonal representations of subjectivity and identity.

However, a growing number of analysts now acknowledge the fleeting tonal residues that arise everywhere in Schoenberg's music.[29] The beginnings of a methodological approach to this complex phenomenon have emerged recently in the theoretical literature.[30] Schoenberg's idiom in this period demonstrates his fine-tuned ability to create multiple *simultaneous* tonal implications that, in constant flux, are neutralized through superimposition or juxtaposition. (The basic elements are diminished-seventh, whole-tone, and fourth chords; they are fragmented and recombined to simultaneously intensify and neutralize their traditional implications.) Schoenberg was not out to destroy tonality, and in 1921 he derided the term "atonal," offering "polytonal" and "pantonal" as preferable alternatives.[31] It was the *structural obligations* of tonality that he wished to elide, and it is only from his concept of "suspended tonality" (*aufgehobene Tonalität*), all-too-briefly defined in his 1911 *Harmonielehre*, that we can find any historically relevant theoretical bearings for the music of *Pierrot*.[32] Schoenberg's published discussions of suspended tonality give very few examples, and his music in the period of *Pierrot* realizes the concept far more subtly and intensively, maintaining intricate webs of tonal latencies that collectively suspend tonality without completely negating it. Busoni may have been referring to these sorts of fleeting sensations in *Pierrot* when he remarked in a 1913 letter that it was "as if a large musical mechanism had been assembled from crumbled ingredients . . . put to uses other than those for which they were originally designed."[33]

In *Pierrot*, each instrument projects its own diaphanous shroud of fragmentary, shifting tonal latencies; contrapuntal superimposition of the different instrumental strata suspends these tonal residues in a neutral balance, something like a Calder mobile. *Sprechmelodie* plays an important role in keeping the suspension in motion, because – unlike sung pitches – it will generally not interfere with the sensitive pitch-specific balancing of tonal residues. Although Schoenberg's preface asks the reciter to give "due consideration" to the notated pitches, the main priority is the agility and timbral variety that characterize *Sprechmelodie*. In fact, recorded performances conducted by Schoenberg attest to his increasing lenience about pitch accuracy in the *Sprechmelodie*.[34] Nevertheless, the notated *Sprechstimme* pitches always participate in the musical structure, and not only in the obvious places where they double an instrument or collaborate in strict canonic imitation.[35] The optimal *Sprechmelodie* performance will convey the notated pitches as boundaries for the continuous pitch fluctuations in order to help project the specific manner in which tonalities are neutralized and suspended in each passage. After all, the notated *Sprechstimme* pitches are fundamental components of the spontaneous sonic/expressive content that Schoenberg imagined and heard in response to the poems, and of the harmonic/contrapuntal idiom that captured his experience.

The fabric of allusion: echoes of Schumann in the shadows of tonality

Pierrot lunaire, writes Reinhold Brinkmann, "offers a historical diagnosis" and "critical commentary on itself, on its own representational intent. In an extreme state of self-reflection, *Pierrot lunaire* is music about its own presence . . . music about music, music about a specific musical tradition."[36] For Brinkmann, fragments of specific musical works constitute what Busoni (quoted above) called "crumbled ingredients"; thus *Pierrot* weaves into its fabric parodic allusions to a panoply of works, genres, and composers – including Wagner's *Parsifal*, Strauss's *Ein Heldenleben*, and Schumann's *Carnaval* – in addition to numerous contrapuntal devices (passacaglia, retrograde and inversion canons, fugue) and traditional forms (trio sonata, barcarolle, waltz).[37] The *Parsifal* and *Ein Heldenleben* parodies appear in the first and second melodramas Schoenberg composed, so the idea of musical caricature – the analog of pantomime – must have been part of his "ironic-satiric" concept from the outset. There are also instances of self-parody: for instance, Jonathan Dunsby hears an echo of Op. 19, No. 4 in "Valse de Chopin," while Stephan Weytjens observes in "Colombine" a clear quotation from *Herzgewächse*, Op. 20.[38]

Example 9.1 (a) Schoenberg, "Mondestrunken" (No. 1), m. 1 (piano only). (b) Schoenberg, "Entrückung," String Quartet No. 2, Op. 10, IV, m. 1 (second violin only). (c) Schumann, "Mondnacht," *Eichendorff Liederkreis*, Op. 39, V, mm. 1–3. (d) Schumann, "Hör' ich das Liedchen klingen," *Dichterliebe*, Op. 48, X, mm. 1–2. (e) Schumann, "Am leuchtenden Sommermorgen," *Dichterliebe*, Op. 48, XII, m. 11

Brinkmann's idea that *Pierrot* is replete with ironic referentiality raises many fascinating questions. Are the allusions structural components of the work, or just witty moments of brilliance that emerge and then dissolve? How dense is the network of allusions, and what are its techniques of concealment? What criteria validate a "real" allusion? (Some putative references invoke striking musical or poetic intertextualities, while others may simply reflect a listener's personal associations.) To begin exploring such questions, the following discussion offers some new examples for consideration and debate, supported by several types of evidence. Passages that allude to tonal compositions will also help expose some of the tonal latencies in Schoenberg's music.

The "'Mondestrunken" motive (see Example 9.1a) is our starting point since it opens the cycle. It nicely exemplifies how Schoenberg concatenates familiar symmetrical harmonic configurations in order to superimpose multiple tonal implications: it contains an augmented triad, diminished-seventh chord, five-note whole-tone subset, and three tritones (the maximum possible in a seven-note set); these subsets are all tonally multivalent, in diverse ways. The motive's signature rhythm and contour are easily recognized, and it reappears in many guises throughout the cycle. It also evokes numerous musical allusions.

The "Mondestrunken" motive depicts the flooding moonlight that intoxicates the poet ("Den Wein, den man mit Augen trinkt"). It is surely a self-parody of the ascending eight-note motive from Schoenberg's "Entrückung" (third movement of the Second String Quartet, Op. 10), which depicts presentiments of celestial fragrance ("Ich fühle Luft von anderem Planeten").

The second violin entry (see Example 9.1b) best illustrates the close similarity, since it shares six pitch classes with the "Mondestrunken" motive (including the same augmented triad and diminished-seventh chord). Both poetic contexts involve celestial rapture, but the parody-allusion makes an "ironic-satiric" and grotesque comparison between the moon-drunk Pierrot and the soul's transcendental ecstasy in "Entrückung." The inverted contours of the two motives delineate that contrast.[39]

The "Mondestrunken" figure also echoes the beautiful descending figure from Schumann's "Mondnacht" (from the *Eichendorff Liederkreis*, Op. 39), probably the most beloved moonlit meditation in the entire Lied tradition (see Example 9.1c). This parody also invokes ironic contrasts, setting Eichendorff's affirmative celestial contemplation against *Pierrot's* decadent intoxication, and the Romantic isolation expressed elsewhere in the *Eichendorff Liederkreis* against the modern alienation allegorized in the Giraud/Hartleben poems.

As noted above, Brinkmann and Youens both interpret *Pierrot* as an allegory on the artist or poet of modernity. This identification emerges in "Mondestrunken" (No. 1), "Madonna" (No. 6), and "Die Kreuze" (No. 14), which are the only movements that specifically mention the poet or his verses. Indeed, the cello (Schoenberg's own instrument) enters in "Mondestrunken" precisely at the words "der Dichter." Schumann's *Dichterliebe*, Op. 48 is the obvious model for a song cycle about poetic subjectivity and psychological crisis. This discussion will henceforth focus entirely on numerous allusions to *Dichterliebe* that emerge in *Pierrot*.

The "Mondestrunken" figure, for instance, evokes a wistful memory of *Dichterliebe* X (see Example 9.1d), a song that in fact is about nostalgic recollection of song ("When I hear the song / that once my sweetheart sang"). The motive also parodies the enharmonically multivalent arpeggiations of *Dichterliebe* XII, in which Schumann's devastated poet, mournful and pale, falls mute and hears illusory voices – much like a sick and melancholy Pierrot. (Example 9.1e shows m. 11, precisely where the poet falls mute ("stumm"), and where a descending augmented triad D-B flat-G flat and diminished-seventh chord skeleton B flat-E-C sharp strikingly resemble similar components in the "Mondestrunken" motive.)

The preceding allusions all involve detailed intervallic similarities and poetic associations or contrasts. Brinkmann noted a different sort of allusion to *Dichterliebe*: the reprise of the flute monolog "Der kranke Mond" (No. 7) as an interlude – without *Sprechstimme* but with new instrumental parts – between "Enthauptung" and "Die Kreuze" (Nos. 13 and 14).[40] Brinkmann noted that *Dichterliebe* is the obvious model for this kind of structural recollection, because the postlude from *Dichterliebe* XII (a song just mentioned above) returns at the end of the entire cycle,

Example 9.2 (a) Schoenberg, "Madonna" (No. 6), mm. 1–3. (b) "Madonna", m. 24.
(c) Schumann, "Im Rhein," *Dichterliebe*, Op. 48, VI, mm. 57–8

transposed to D flat major. In both *Dichterliebe* and *Pierrot*, the reprise comments wordlessly upon a traumatic experience endured by the poet. In fact, the structural reprise in *Pierrot* also links the waning crescent moon of No. 7 to the waxing crescent moon of No. 13, and thereby also connects the adjacent movements "Madonna" (No. 6) and "Die Kreuze" (No. 14), which are both points of intense musical and narrative climax, share religious imagery, brood on the poet's suffering, and are the only melodramas that end with *fortissimo* outbursts.

In fact, "Madonna" (No. 6) makes striking structural allusions to *Dichterliebe* VI, and these can also help illustrate the tonal latencies of Schoenberg's remarkable idiom. In *Dichterliebe* VI, itself a parody of a chorale-prelude in E minor, the rejected and deluded poet ironically compares his faithless beloved to the beatific Madonna in the Cologne Cathedral altarpiece. Schoenberg's "Madonna" conceals ironic allusions to this song, perhaps initially stimulated by the shared religious iconography. In "Madonna" the poet hails the blood-red moon as the Mother of all sorrows; she rises over the "altar" of his verses, bleeding from unhealable wounds while holding her son's "corpse" – symbolizing a leaf of poetry – in her emaciated hands. Schoenberg's music doesn't parody Schumann's directly, although "Madonna" is also a mock baroque texture, which many critics interpret as an allusion to Bach's music.[41] "Madonna" does, however, project specters of Schumann's E minor that are suspended in its penumbral harmonic fabric.

In the opening passage (Example 9.2a), the cello ascends and descends in distorted scales that nonetheless create a liminal pitch-class focus on E/F flat. Above this, the flute melody projects a very strong sense of dominant harmony in E minor, highly embellished, but with durations and contours lending constant emphasis to dominant-function scale degrees. (The piano also repeats a B major triad five times near the end of the preceding melodrama.) Meanwhile, the opening *Sprechmelodie* pitches – sharing five pitch classes with the "Mondestrunken" figure! – project a strong sense of submediant harmony from parallel E major (C sharp minor), which morphs chromatically into subdominant harmony (A minor) at the word "Schmerzen." Multiple harmonic functions in E are thus diversely represented and superimposed contrapuntally, to suggest but suspend the tonality. (The bass clarinet drifts like a specter through fragmentary references to other centers.)

"Madonna" then orbits through numerous other fragmentary tonal references, but E minor reemerges at the final cadence (Example 9.2b), where the dominant chord B-D sharp-F-A-C (with diminished fifth F), is superimposed over E, with the root B prominently sustained in the cello. The tonal function of this sonority is obscured by the low register, loud dynamic, unusual spacing, and the manner of inverting the ninth chord. But it is nevertheless a compressed echo of the ending from *Dichterliebe* VI (Example 9.2c), where the same harmony (except with the perfect fifth F sharp) unfolds linearly, but in the same general register. The final crashing chord of "Madonna" hides this quotation, and all the other facets of allusion and parody between the two pieces, by smashing the whole edifice.

The ending of *Pierrot* on a nostalgic note and in full morning sun ("O alter Duft," No. 21) also evokes further parallels with *Dichterliebe*. The opening words "O alter Duft aus Märchenzeit" (O ethereal fragrance from fabled times) are matched by languid parallel thirds in mm. 1–2, and an E major triad at the phrase cadence in m. 3 (Example 9.3a). Other similar tonal cues arise throughout the song. Many critics hear the E major triad as a tonic here, and also at the end of song.[42] This tonal orientation is easy to hear, and it also forges an unmistakable – but so far unnoticed – allusion to the title, key, and final sonority of *Dichterliebe* XV ("Aus alten Märchen winkt es" [Out of the old fairy tales beckons]), which closes with the identical pitches in the piano right hand. The closing words of the Schumann song also describe how morning sun dissolves the idle dreams of the previous night. But like that fleeting dream-image, the sense of tonic function about the E major triad in Example 9.3a can also dissolve, and take on another identity: as a dominant substitute in C sharp/D flat major. The reader can test this idea at the piano, noting in particular the right hand D flat-F third and bass A flat that immediately precede the E triad, the clarinet's D-D sharp-C sharp sigh above it, the C-C sharp gesture that sets the left hand in motion at the outset, and other factors that emerge with clear tonal potency if a C sharp major triad is appended to the

Example 9.3 (a) Schoenberg, "O alter Duft" (No. 21), mm. 1–3. (b) "O alter Duft," mm. 26–30

excerpt. The fact that there is no literal resolution to C sharp here (except for the subtle clarinet figure) is absolutely typical of Schoenbergian suspended tonality, which necessarily entails suppression of the tonic sonority.[43]

The ability of the opening passage simultaneously to evoke both E major and C sharp major further strengthens the *Dichterliebe* allusion, because the E major of *Dichterliebe* XV gives way suddenly to C sharp minor in *Dichterliebe* XVI ("Die alten bösen lieder" [The old evil songs], a song with words and images ripe for ironic reference at this point in *Pierrot*). D flat major is attained later, precisely when the postlude from *Dichterliebe* XII (already mentioned earlier) is reprised. The multiple tonal latencies in the opening of "O alter Duft" thus simultaneously allude to both of the last two songs of *Dichterliebe*. Schoenberg's manner of suspending tonality gives his music this unprecedented allusiveness.

Like *Dichterliebe*, *Pierrot lunaire* also ends with nostalgic retrospection, very faint and subtly nuanced (see Example 9.3b). The strings wistfully remember the piano's opening thirds, and E major sensations are kept mysteriously aglow – by the piano triads (subdominant and two dominant substitutes) and by the closing low E octave – and then evaporate.

Meanwhile the *Sprechmelodie* is reprising a piano figure from m. 11, and uses C sharp three times, each one longer. As the voice also dissolves into inaudibility, it descends to a low F – intentionally beyond the singer's range – joining the C sharps to create a delicate echo of Schumann's closing D flat major. (This can be tested at the piano, again with great care for the fragility of the sensations in question.) In this intricate manner, quixotic tonal fragrances of E major and D flat major are superimposed once more, with the latter especially frail, but dissolving last – along with the entire atmosphere of allusion.

Some may also perceive another lingering diaphanous tonal sensation here: a delicate gravitation towards an F root. The suspension of tonality always produces multiple valences, arising from the counterbalanced instabilities that are needed to suspend tonality. These liminal sensations also heighten the sense of nostalgic yearning that ends Schoenberg's cycle. Like *Dichterliebe*, there is also a harmonic reference back to the tonal coordinates of the first song, and the analytically inclined reader will find residues of these same three tonalities in "Mondestrunken," especially at its lambent close. Such delicate and ephemeral harmonic traces, like the dreamy visions in "O alter Duft," are indices of the diaphanous world of suspended tonal sensibility that Schoenberg uniquely created. Like the imaginary gestures of the pantomime, these evanescent allusions to tonality emerge almost inaudibly and then evaporate into the fragrant air of memory and imagination.

PART III

Schoenberg between the World Wars

10 Schoenberg as teacher

JOY H. CALICO

Schoenberg's impact as a composer is rivaled by his remarkable legacy as a teacher. Among the hundreds of students he taught in Europe and the United States, many went on to distinguished careers as composers, performers, and teachers in their own right; many more were left with an indelible impression of the encounter.[1] The deep devotion Schoenberg inspired in his pupils is evident in their accounts which reveal a brilliant, generous, and indefatigable teacher who could also be an authoritarian, capable of sarcasm and even intimidation. Something of the intensity of his relationship with his students can be gleaned from Heinrich Jalowetz's comments in a testimonial volume from 1912:

> Schoenberg *educates* the pupils in the fullest sense of the word and involuntarily establishes such compelling personal contact with each one that his pupils gather around him like disciples about their master. And if we call ourselves "Schoenberg pupils," this has a completely different emphasis from what it does for those who are inseparably linked to their teacher by virtue of a fingering that will make him happy, or the creation of a new figured bass. We know, rather, that all of us who call ourselves Schoenberg pupils are touched by his essence in everything that we think and feel and that we thereby feel in a kind of spiritual contact with everything. For anyone who was his pupil, his name is more than a recollection of student days; it is an artistic and personal conscience.[2]

This chapter examines Schoenberg's teaching career from three perspectives, beginning with an overview of his teaching activities, including his private studios and various institutional affiliations. His didactic writings and recollections of his students then provide the basis for a discussion of his pedagogical methods. The chapter concludes with a consideration of his mentoring practices, as exemplified in his complex relationship with Hanns Eisler.

Teaching in Europe and the United States

Schoenberg's teaching career was one of near-constant private instruction punctuated by periods of institutional employment. From 1898, when he accepted Vilma Webenau as his first student in Vienna, to 1933, when he left Berlin under the shadow of the Nazis, Schoenberg shuttled back and forth between the two cities, accepting teaching posts at a variety of schools, all the while teaching privately at his frequently shifting residences. He moved to Berlin in December 1901; a year later, on the recommendation of Richard Strauss, he was offered his first formal teaching position at the Stern Conservatory, a private German–Jewish institution, where he taught music theory from December 1902 to July 1903.

After returning to Vienna in 1903, he began teaching at the progressive Schwarzwald School for girls founded by feminist Dr. Eugenie Schwarzwald, who would continue as a major supporter of Schoenberg for two decades.[3] The noted musicologist Guido Adler sent him several pupils from the University of Vienna, including Anton Webern who started private lessons in 1904, the same year Alban Berg began studying with Schoenberg after family members saw Schoenberg's newspaper announcement that he was seeking students. In 1910 Schoenberg petitioned for a part-time position as *Privatdozent* (roughly comparable to a present-day adjunct) at the Academy of Music and Fine Arts. Theory instruction at the Academy was in a state of crisis and his selection as the best candidate to set the program aright, despite his lack of formal education, attests to the reputation he had already established as a teacher.[4] At the end of the year his application for full membership at the Academy was blocked by an organized anti-Semitic faction. Stung by the rejection, he repaired to the Stern Conservatory in Berlin in 1911. When the Academy in Vienna reconsidered later that year, he declined the offer despite his dire financial straits. He remained in Berlin until 1915, cultivating his career as a conductor and teaching a handful of private students, including the pianist Eduard Steuermann.

Shortly after returning to Vienna, Schoenberg began the first of two periods of military service (1915–16 and 1917). After World War I he pieced together a living from classes at the Schwarzwald School and through private instruction. His classes attracted significant numbers of pupils: in 1918–19 fifty-five students enrolled in the composition seminar; the following year it had twenty-two. The founding in 1918 of the Society for Private Musical Performances, discussed further below, also had an impact on his teaching activities. From 1918–25 he taught private students at his home in Mödling (fifteen kilometers south of Vienna). Among his students in this period were Hanns Eisler, Rudolf Kolisch, Paul Pisk, Karl Rankl, Erwin Ratz, Rudolf Serkin, and Viktor Ullmann.[5]

In 1925 he was awarded the most prestigious academic post of his career: upon Ferruccio Busoni's death, Schoenberg was appointed his replacement at the Prussian Academy of the Arts in Berlin. The selection was not without controversy; conservatives feared him as an iconoclast, while young modernists found him too traditional. Students in his composition seminar came from the United States, Switzerland, Austria, Romania, Russia, Greece, Spain, and Yugoslavia.[6] They included the American Marc Blitzstein; Josef Rufer, who became a prominent musicologist and twelve-tone scholar; and the composer Winfried Zillig. Despite the tremendous promise of this generation, many aspirations were thwarted by the exigencies of Nazi politics and World War II. When the Academy notified Schoenberg that his contract would not be honored on May 23, 1933, he was already in exile in Paris.

Schoenberg escaped Europe by accepting a one-year post at the newly founded Malkin Conservatory in Boston. Assisted by Adolph Weiss, who had been the first American to study with him in Berlin, he taught one class in Boston and one in New York.[7] The brutal New England winter and weekly travel wreaked havoc on his health (although eventually the Boston students came to him in New York to spare him the commute), and in 1934 he moved to Los Angeles. Private students sought him out on the West Coast soon after his arrival. In 1935–36 he taught part-time at the University of Southern California in the Alkin Chair of Composition before accepting a full professorship at UCLA, where he taught until his retirement in 1944. Among his pupils in California were the composers Wayne Barlow, John Cage, Lou Harrison, Earl Kim, Leon Kirchner, Leroy Robertson, and several students who would become his assistants and important proponents of his work: Dika Newlin, Richard Hoffmann, Leonard Stein, Clara Silvers Steuermann, and Gerald Strang.[8] He was also popular as a composition teacher in Hollywood circles, numbering among his students many major figures from the film industry, including Oscar Levant, David Raksin, Edward Powell, Alfred Newman, Hugo Friedhofer, and Franz Waxman.[9] Schoenberg continued teaching after retirement out of financial necessity. He held a seminar for composition students at UCLA in 1949 and lectured at the University of Chicago and at the Music Academy of the West, but mostly he taught at home, where he conducted classes and received some private students.

This extraordinary work history foregrounds two features: Schoenberg taught private students almost continuously between 1898 and 1951; and he enjoyed only two prolonged periods of stability in an erratic academic career (1925–33 at the Academy in Berlin, and 1936–44 at UCLA). His controversial reputation, lack of formal education, and Jewish identity impeded his ascension in the ranks of the European professoriate, but this also meant that a master teacher was redirected to a wide array of educational institutions – Jewish, feminist, university, private, public – where many students, who never would have encountered him within the standard system, benefited from his tutelage.

Pedagogy

His early association with the composer Alexander Zemlinsky notwith-standing, Schoenberg was essentially an autodidact, and that experience was the bedrock of his pedagogy. Unencumbered by the indoctrination of any curricular paradigm, he taught theory and analysis to his students as he had taught it to himself: as the bases for acquiring the craft of composition, and less as independent disciplines.

General course of instruction

Student accounts of his teaching are remarkably consistent, regardless of when and where they worked with him.[10] Schoenberg taught pupils of all levels, individually, in groups, and in formal classes; sessions tended to be several hours long. The trajectory of a composition course progressed from composing a classically constructed theme to mastering sonata form. For beginners he prescribed a study of harmony followed by counterpoint, leading eventually to composition; more advanced pupils studied analysis, compositional technique, and orchestration. Models for solving specific compositional problems were drawn almost exclusively from the Austro-German masters (Bach, Mozart, Beethoven, Brahms, Wagner, Bruckner, and Mahler); he made occasional use of his own compositions as well, choosing examples mostly, but not exclusively, from his tonal works. Analysis was of vital importance, since Schoenberg believed that "comprehension and appreciation of an ideal represented by great achievements of the past went beyond training in composition to form part of a moral education that developed the whole personality."[11] This general course of study is detailed in *Theory of Harmony*, his magnum opus first published in 1911. It was one of his first works published by Universal Edition, a relationship that proved fruitful not only for Schoenberg but also for his students. It was to have been the first in a series of such teaching manuals that he envisaged as comprising a comprehensive "aesthetic of music."[12] Others that remained incomplete were a counterpoint book *Composition with Independent Voices* (1911), and the more wide-ranging *Coherence, Counterpoint, Instrumentation, Instruction in Form* (1917).[13]

The harmonic theory of Simon Sechter, filtered through his student and successor at the University of Vienna, Anton Bruckner, is apparent throughout *Theory of Harmony*. Sechter's work is typical of Austrian *Stufentheorie* (step theory), in which all chord progressions are grounded in the diatonic scale.[14] The unfinished instruction manuals cited above are indebted to nineteenth-century scholars, including, for example, the formal theories of A. B. Marx.[15] He also drew upon Heinrich Bellermann's

1862 treatise "in the Fuxian tradition of species counterpoint," which included a noteworthy history of contrapuntal theory.[16] Grounding the *Theory of Harmony* in this theoretical canon served the same purpose as linking his compositions to the German masterworks: it endowed his project with authority and legitimacy. Of course, Schoenberg did not transmit this legacy precisely as he received it. He took what was useful and adapted or rejected the rest. He was primarily concerned with divorcing this inheritance from what he regarded as its impotent pedagogy, which had been grounded in aesthetic and stylistic criteria. Instead, he called for a modern pedagogy, infinitely pragmatic in nature. The speculative, even heretical, aspects of *Theory of Harmony* are most apparent in the chapter entitled "Non-Harmonic Tones," in which he asserts that any simultaneity can be a "chord," describing the evolution of harmonic technique as an "apparently endless climb up the overtone series."[17] He also posits that "dissonant harmony had a structural significance in tonal composition which though independent of consonant harmony" is still related to it.[18] These claims substantiated the new direction he had taken recently in his own compositions.

The *Theory of Harmony* begins with the statement, "this book I have learned from my students." Indeed, the dated assignments found in Berg's student papers occur in precisely the same sequence in which those exercises and topics are presented in the textbook.[19] Berg's instruction may be taken as a template, since Schoenberg used some of the same exercises when he taught at UCLA. Berg studied formally from 1904 to 1911; for the first three years he worked on harmony, counterpoint, and music theory, with some composition; thereafter he focused on composition. He began with the C major scale, described the chord for each diatonic pitch, and then composed musical progressions with them. Schoenberg's pedagogical innovation is evident even in this simple exercise, the pragmatism of which is in stark contrast to the standard manner of teaching harmony in Europe at this time, which simply required the realization of figured bass provided for the pupil. From there Berg's vocabulary of chords was expanded: 6/4 chords, seventh chords and their inversions, and diminished sevenths in major keys. Once Berg demonstrated proficiency in using these in original harmonic progressions, the process began again with minor keys. Finally, he learned cadential patterns, which prepared him for modulation via chromatic harmony.

When Berg advanced to the study of counterpoint, he found that Schoenberg retained the traditional five species based on rhythmic value, thus adhering closely to Bellermann, although with far more interest in the resulting harmonic progressions. The assignments progressed from whole-note cantus firmus exercises to two-part imitation with entries at different intervals, and culminated in the combination of all the species simultaneously. Next came canon and fugue, for which the pupil generated original themes suitable for invertible counterpoint. He "graduated" from counterpoint studies with the fugue for piano and string quartet in 1907. Although Berg had been writing pieces while studying harmony and counterpoint, he now began a dedicated course of composition. A comparison of his lessons with the textbooks Schoenberg would write in the United States reveals that the method of teaching composition also remained essentially unchanged. Everything emanated from the musical motive as the smallest unit. The pupil learned the principle of developing variation by composing a theme and variations that exploited a particular thematic motive. Concurrently Berg wrote short pieces, such as minuets and scherzos, in which the contrasting middle passage was treated as a development. The ultimate goal was a well-crafted work in sonata form, which Berg produced in his single-movement Piano Sonata, Op. 1 (1907–08).

Schoenberg's other theoretical books were written in the United States, beginning with the unfinished *The Musical Idea and the Logic, Technique, and Art of Its Presentation*, much of it drafted in 1934–36, but drawing on material he had been developing for some time.[20] The final four manuals addressed the specific needs of his American students, whom he considered industrious, intelligent, and creative, but inadequately prepared. These are *Models for Beginners in Composition* (published in 1942, revised edition, 1943); and three other books published after Schoenberg's death: *Structural Functions of Harmony* (written 1948, published in 1954); *Preliminary Exercises in Counterpoint* (written 1936–50, published 1963); and *Fundamentals of Musical Composition* (written 1937–48, published in 1967). As Dorothy Crawford notes, they "gave him many years of trouble but were clearly important enough to the legacy he intended to leave that he was willing to sacrifice much time from his own composition."[21]

Organizations for training musicians

In addition to the work he did within established institutions, Schoenberg was keen to develop new organizations for training musicians. In 1927 he drafted plans for an "International School for the Formation of Style" to expose musicians to the styles of composition and performance from the leading musical nations; he later also considered a "Musical Conservatory in Keeping with the Times."[22] In Los Angeles he wrote a proposal for a "School for Soundmen" for the Academy of Motion Picture Arts and Sciences. It was to have trained not only composers, arrangers, and orchestrators, each according to his particular subfield, but also sound technicians, engineers, and mixers.[23]

The most significant plan to come to fruition was the Society for Private Musical Performances.[24] Founded in Vienna in 1918, it sponsored regular concerts until December 1921 and occasional concerts until December 1923. Initially closed to the public and to critics, it provided a forum in which contemporary music was presented in well-rehearsed performances. Its significance for the sustenance of modern music is widely acknowledged, but its pedagogical value should not be underestimated. The Society provided students with invaluable experience in arranging, conducting, performing, and coaching; recruiting musicians; scheduling and overseeing rehearsals; and operating an arts organization. Its pedagogical significance is evident in the arrangements prepared by his students. Schoenberg believed that this task provided "great familiarity with an important piece of music and basic experience with the elements of composition," and allowed the audience to hear music it might not otherwise hear.[25] The first two seasons featured arrangements of orchestral works by Mahler, Strauss, Reger, Debussy, Ravel, Stravinsky, Webern, Berg, Busoni, Bartók, Skryabin, Hauer, and Zemlinsky; the third season, overseen by Erwin Stein in Schoenberg's absence, included the master's own music for the first time.[26]

His instructions regarding principles of arranging were not recorded, but students followed the practices evident in Schoenberg's own arrangements. Doublings were eliminated throughout, and essential divisi parts reassigned; three wind instruments played the parts of "firsts"; a harmonium picked up remaining wind and horn parts and some inner voices; piano covered the harp and some brass; strings played their parts as is, after divisi were removed.[27] When Erwin Stein proposed a chamber setting of Schoenberg's Op. 8 for the 1920–21 season, the project was given to the youngest generation of students. The arrangers began by annotating a full orchestral score to indicate reduced instrumentation. They then produced an ink score of their chamber version, and this was professionally copied into parts.[28] Like so many arrangements for the Society these were never performed, but the pedagogical purpose was fulfilled nonetheless.

The twelve-tone method
Schoenberg is alternately blamed for and credited with what some perceive to be the tyranny of dodecaphony in the mid to late twentieth century, and it is often assumed that this was a primary agenda advanced in his teaching. It is noteworthy that none of the instructional manuals above broach the subject, and he rarely presented it in his classes. Early on, after he announced the method to his circle in the spring of 1923, he did not instruct them further in the details of its use.[29] Mostly the disciples

gleaned what they could from poring over his recent scores. Webern started sketching with twelve-tone rows in 1922; in 1924 Eisler wrote the twelve-tone *Palmström*, while Erwin Stein was the first to explain it in print; Berg used twelve-tone rows in 1925 in the song "Schliesse mir die Augen beide," and in the Chamber Concerto. In a letter to Schoenberg Eisler reported that Steuermann had shown him Opp. 23 and 25 and explained them thoroughly; he praised the works, but noted that "one must study them closely in order to understand."[30] Lore circulated informally among the faithful, who worked it out among themselves and developed their own approaches to it. Later, in the United States, Schoenberg was more forthcoming; he analyzed his dodecaphonic Third String Quartet in great detail for a class, and taught an entire seminar devoted to his works based on theme and variation form in 1948–49.[31] Occasionally an advanced student might bring a dodecaphonic work to him for advice, just as Lou Harrison did with his Suite for Piano (1943), but Schoenberg would not review serial compositions by students who had not demonstrated mastery of sonata form, as was the case with Cage.[32]

Schoenberg as mentor

Schoenberg's students were fiercely devoted to him, particularly those he taught in Europe. Berg and Webern neglected personal relationships and their own careers in order to attend to the needs of their master. Testimony to the allegiance he inspired and, some might say, demanded, is found in the volumes students published in his honor, such as *Arnold Schönberg* (1912), the first book about him in any language,[33] and a special issue of the journal *Musikblätter des Anbruch* to mark his fiftieth birthday (1924). That year he also received an album of student photographs and tributes.[34] Such loyalty is attributable to personality and pedagogy, but also to Schoenberg's enormous investment in mentoring. Though less well known than the relationships with Berg and Webern, Schoenberg's decades-long association with Hanns Eisler provides a particularly interesting case study.[35]

Eisler came to Schoenberg in 1919, penniless and in ill health.[36] Schoenberg accepted him as a student knowing that he could not pay for his lessons, subsidizing his participation in the master class with tuition paid by others who could afford it. He procured for Eisler a part-time job as proofreader at Universal Edition, thus providing him with a bit of income, access to new music, and contacts in the publishing industry. By 1920 Eisler was in a group that met twice weekly for four-hour lessons at Schoenberg's home in Mödling. In the winter of 1920–21, Eisler and Max

Deutsch accompanied Schoenberg to the Netherlands as his assistants.[37] When they returned to Vienna in March, they devoted themselves to the Society for Private Musical Performances. Eisler was a member of the board, and arranged works for performance (Schoenberg's Op. 8, No. 1 and Op. 16; Bruckner's Symphony No. 7). In August 1922 Schoenberg wrote to a patron who had asked him to pass on a small donation to worthy musicians, saying he would send it to Eisler and Rankl. He described them as follows: "both as poor as they are gifted, as ardent as they are sensitive, and as intelligent as they are imaginative."[38] Ever insolvent, Eisler expressed his gratitude in music. In 1920 he wrote the Scherzo for String Trio built on a motive derived from his teacher's initials, A–E flat (eS in German), and he dedicated *Three Little Songs on Poems by Klabund and Bethge* to Schoenberg in 1922.

Eisler continued to be plagued by respiratory troubles, and he convalesced at the Schoenberg home on more than one occasion. He was there under such circumstances in 1923 when Schoenberg announced his discovery of the twelve-tone method. On March 29 the master determined that Eisler had completed his studies; his graduation piece was the Piano Sonata, Op. 1. Schoenberg instructed Steuermann to perform it at a Society concert in Prague, and recommended it to Universal for publication. He also agreed to be the dedicatee. Eisler thanked him profusely in a letter dated April 13, 1923:

> For years you have worried and fretted over me. If anything useful comes of me, it will be all thanks to you! Right now I am just a passionate beginner and a fluff, but what would have become of me if you had not taken me as your student!!! And I am indebted to you not only musically, for your teaching, your works, and your example. I hope I have also improved myself as a person . . . You always worried about my material condition, and I will never forget how you created a job for me at UE in the terrible winter of 1919–20. Otherwise I would literally have starved to death. Also the sojourn to Holland saved me from medical catastrophe, as my doctor confirmed for me at that time. I owe you everything (perhaps even more than I owe my poor parents), and I can only give you my word that I will do my best to please you, and to be a tribute to the name "Schoenberg student." [. . .] In highest veneration and gratitude, your very faithful student Hanns Eisler.[39]

His formal studies had ended, but Schoenberg continued to attend to Eisler's well-being. A month later he attempted to recruit a patron for his perennially impoverished pupil: "[he] . . . suffers from a lung condition due to malnutrition and a difficult assignment during the war . . . he is very gifted and poor and as a result of his compositions he will receive high praise, but no money!!!"[40]

In 1924 Eisler was hailed as the third great composer in the circle, next to Berg and Webern. He held that lofty position but briefly. In a harbinger of his imminent commitment to leftist politics, he expressed frustration to Zemlinsky about the insularity of the new music scene in 1925. Zemlinsky reported the conversation to Schoenberg, who received Eisler's complaints about modern music as a personal betrayal. In 1926 they exchanged emotional letters in which the former student stood his ground while reaffirming his devotion to Schoenberg, but to no avail; the master would not abide such impudence. The prize student became *persona non grata*.

Eisler still idolized Schoenberg, despite the difficulty of reconciling his music with the workers' movement to which Eisler was now fully committed. The common experience of exile brought a rapprochement in California. He remained in Schoenberg's thrall, as Bertolt Brecht observed in 1942: "Schoenberg is an old tyrant and Eisler confesses with a smile that he trembles and worries about his tie being straight or arriving ten minutes too early."[41] He used Schoenberg's musical anagram A–eS–C–H (A, E flat, C, B natural) in the dodecaphonic quintet *Fourteen Ways to Describe Rain*, and presented it to his teacher on his seventieth birthday. His Third Piano Sonata (1943) also invoked the A–eS motive, just as his Scherzo had twenty years before. Thanks to the Rockefeller Foundation grant Eisler received to support his film music research, he was finally in a position to repay some of Schoenberg's generosity, giving his former teacher $300 toward surgery for his son. The older man was reluctant to take the money and "Eisler jokingly said he might take a few lessons in return, whereupon Schoenberg said hastily 'if you still haven't learnt it I can't teach it to you.'"[42]

Eisler's leftist politics drew the attention of the House Committee on Un-American Activities in 1947, and he returned to Europe. Even in East Germany he was a staunch proponent of Schoenberg, a decidedly unpopular position in the communist state at that time. When he learned of his teacher's passing in 1951, he mourned his death in an essay that began with a Chinese proverb: "he who does not honor his teacher is no better than a dog."[43] Such was the devotion Schoenberg the teacher elicited in his pupils, a legacy virtually unrivaled in twentieth-century art music.

11 Schoenberg, satire, and the *Zeitoper*

PETER TREGEAR

The end of World War I was an especially difficult time for Schoenberg, as indeed it was for most of his compatriots. It was not only the scarcity of basic necessities such as food and coal that made for uncomfortable living. The total defeat of Austria-Hungary, the collapse of the Habsburg monarchy, the rise of new political movements inspired by the Russian Revolution in November 1917, and the creation of an Austrian Republic in November 1918 were described by the composer as "the overturning of everything one had believed in"[1] and the beginning of a "war against all that is low and beastly."[2] While his introduction of radical atonality was itself commonly thought to be a violent break with tradition, Schoenberg nevertheless maintained that it was precisely a respect for tradition that ultimately justified his compositional advances.[3] Now, however, the very idea of deferring to the past seemed in question. The third edition of his *Theory of Harmony* (1921) warns the reader of the dangers of using the spirit of the postwar age as an excuse for an equally iconoclastic approach to composition. "The sad part," he wrote "is just that the idea, 'one may write anything today,' keeps so many young people from first learning something accepted and respectable, from first understanding the classics, from first acquiring *Kultur*." It was now necessary, he believed, to distinguish between a composer (such as himself) who was a "prophet of the future," preserving and extending an intrinsically valuable musical tradition, and the "modern" composer, who was merely concerned with being "up-to-date." "Masters," he continued, "are the only ones who may never write just anything, but must rather do what is necessary: fulfil their mission."[4]

It is not surprising then, that both Schoenberg and many of his subsequent defenders preferred to project an image of the composer that was aloof from the messy, contingent world that now surrounded him.[5] It fitted best with his *l'art pour l'art* philosophy, and has helped preserve a popular view of the composer as a misanthropic and misunderstood genius. However, Schoenberg was far more directly engaged with postwar cultural and political developments than we have come to recognize, and ample evidence is to be found not just in his polemical writings, radio broadcasts, and teaching, but also in his compositions. Indeed, Schoenberg was particularly conscious at this time of his growing status and fame as a composer, achieved principally through international performances of works such as the *Gurrelieder* and *Pierrot lunaire*.

Signs of his growing engagement with postwar culture are already evident in the series of works Schoenberg composed between 1920 and 1923, whose significance today is largely based on the fact that they chart the emergence of the twelve-tone technique. The fifth movement of the otherwise functionally entitled *Klavierstücke* (Pieces for Piano), Op. 23, is, for instance, a sardonic waltz reminiscent of the many piano dances by Wilhelm Grosz, Ernst Krenek, Karol Rathaus, Egon Wellesz, and others popular at that time.[6] The eclectic form and unusual scoring of the Serenade, Op. 24 (clarinet, bass clarinet, mandolin, guitar, violin, viola, cello, and baritone) evokes the sound world of contemporary salon orchestras, and the Suite for Piano, Op. 25 is a playful rendering of a baroque keyboard suite, a choice of genre which gives nod to contemporary aesthetic currents associated with the slogans Neoclassicism and *Neue Sachlichkeit* (New Objectivity).

In addition, Schoenberg's marriage in 1924 to Gertrud Kolisch, a woman some 26 years his junior, provided him with a worldly-wise, intelligent, and energetic creative partner. In other ways he was also becoming aware that he was being eclipsed by this "up-to-date" younger generation, some of whom, like Krenek with his *Zeitoper* (opera of the times) and *Jonny spielt auf* (Jonny Strikes Up), were to achieve extraordinary popular success in the later half of the 1920s. The fact that a genre like *Zeitoper* which, as the name suggests, deliberately set out to reflect the aesthetic conditions of contemporary life, had proved so successful irritated and troubled Schoenberg in equal measure. One observable result was that he composed works explicitly satirizing these contemporary composers and the contemporary milieu despite the fact that the equally inescapable worldliness of satire was ultimately in conflict with his emerging self-perception as a "lonely" defender of tradition after the war.[7] Nevertheless, this conflict of aims and means was nothing if not a creative one, eventually inspiring a curious commentary on the *Zeitoper* genre, the one-act opera *Von heute auf morgen* (From Today to Tomorrow), and thereafter helping to shape the dramatic and musical core of *Moses und Aron*.

Three Satires (*Drei Satieren*), Op. 28

The explicit motivation for Schoenberg's first expressly satirical work of the 1920s seems to have been twofold: his negative experiences at the

Festival of the International Society for New Music in Venice in September 1925 (in particular the success of Stravinsky's Sonata for Piano [1924]), together with the difficulties he experienced rehearsing the Serenade, Op. 24; and reports of a speech critical of Schoenberg given by Krenek at the Congress of Music Aesthetics in Karlsruhe in the following month.[8] As he later recalled: "I wrote [the Satires] when I was very much angered by attacks of some of my younger contemporaries at this time and I wanted to give them a little warning that it is not good to attack me."[9] The text is far from subtle; the foreword to the three choruses, for instance, refers to "wie der Mediokre neckisch bemerkt" (as the mediocre person cheekily remarks – the pun being in the sound "kre–neck" lying between "Mediokre" and "neckisch."[10] The second movement refers to Stravinsky as "der kleine Modernsky," and the third mocks Hugo Riemann, whose 1916 edition of the *Dictionary of Music* had been critical of Schoenberg's *Theory of Harmony*.

Effective satire depends upon an audience's ability to engage closely with the styles and idioms under critique. Here, however, Schoenberg conspicuously avoided extending his satirical impulse to the score. The music is instead composed rigorously in the twelve-tone technique, an analysis of which reveals complex contrapuntal musical patterns. Indeed much later Stravinsky said that while he was upset at Schoenberg's rudeness, he was nevertheless flattered that he would express it using a canon of such ingenuity.[11] While he would have easily been able to parody and pastiche particular composers' styles, Schoenberg found himself in an aesthetic bind. Composing this kind of novelty could only result in a score characterized by "*mannerism*, not originality" and as such would be constitutionally obsolete, not new, music, which was a principal criticism he had of the music of Stravinsky.[12] Indeed, Schoenberg had been particularly annoyed to read a report of a comment that Stravinsky had made in New York early in 1925 that he was quite happy not composing "music of the future," rather he would write "for today."[13] Stravinsky's attitude was reflected more widely in the appearance of so-called *Gebrauchsmusik* (music for use), and music inspired by jazz or film music, or music which tried to reflect in its internal workings the stylistic heterogeneousness of contemporary urban life. Schoenberg's ideal of the authentic musical utterance was, however, constitutionally opposed to such aesthetic pragmatism or concession to popular taste. Music could never be a mere object for enjoyment or a means to some extrinsic end; rather it was a mode of cognition, which required submission to its own internal logic. Any composition which debased this logic in favor of easy gratification was, he thought, functionally obsolete as soon as it was composed, because it was not, in this sense, "new."[14]

Schoenberg's attitude owed much to the example of Karl Kraus, who similarly believed that the artist's duty was to maintain a steadfast loyalty to values immanent to the creative medium.[15] And like Kraus, Schoenberg's insistence upon it took on not only ethical, but also religious – and specifically Jewish-theological – resonances. The first two of the Four Pieces for Mixed Chorus, Op. 27, which were composed around the same time as the Satires, set texts which made the connection quite explicit: "Unentrinnbar," for instance, praises those who have "the strength to conceive of their mission, and the character that will not let them refuse it." The evocation of Jewish theology, and by implication, his Jewish heritage, was in part a response to increasing anti-Semitic attacks. As he wrote to Kandinsky on April 19, 1923, "I have at last learnt the lesson that has been forced upon me during this year, and I shall never forget it. It is that I am not a German, not a European, indeed perhaps scarcely even a human being (at least, the Europeans prefer the worst of their race to me), but I am a Jew."[16] In a letter to Berg in 1933, Schoenberg reflected upon his then recent reconversion to Judaism by noting that the text of the second movement of Op. 27, "Du sollst nicht, du mußt," was evidence that his return to the Jewish faith had in fact taken place "long ago."[17]

Schoenberg in Berlin

This increasing feeling of alienation helped to confirm Schoenberg's sense of himself as one who was destined "to become lonely," that he had the melancholy duty "of developing my ideas for the sake of progress in music, whether I liked it or not; but I also had to realize that the great majority of the public did not like it."[18] Nevertheless, his growing success as a composer also brought with it greater material independence which allowed him to cultivate a more open and comfortable lifestyle. Following the death of Ferruccio Busoni in 1924, Schoenberg, newly married, was wooed to Berlin to teach composition at the Prussian Academy of the Arts (Akademie der Künste) which enabled him to leave, as Stuckenschmidt observed, "many things behind in Vienna which had hitherto inhibited his character."[19] In contrast to the Austrian capital, Berlin had recovered from the shock of revolution and the subsequent ravages of hyperinflation with astonishing speed, and had by the middle of the 1920s, as Carl Zuckmayer put it, "a taste of the future about it."[20] It quickly became a center for artists, journalists, painters, and musicians from around the world, keen to discuss the nature of that future and how their art might respond. Their creations in turn filled the galleries, theaters, cinemas, nightclubs, and concert halls helping to create an atmosphere of now-legendary permissiveness and excitement.

The new, heterogeneous, dramatic forms being presented on the Berlin stage by figures such as Erwin Piscator and, later, Bertolt Brecht must, however, have appeared especially antithetical to Schoenberg. Berlin might well have become the center of gravity of German music, but for Schoenberg, what was lacking was precisely a "center of *gravity*," that is a collective will to take seriously the kind of technical and ethical concerns that now drove his own compositional style.[21] His commitment to the twelve-tone technique thus took on implicit political implications, not least in its superficial similarities to calls on the far right of politics for a renewal of German cultural and civil life, and in the context of his reputed comment five years earlier that in twelve-tone music he had "made a discovery which will ensure the supremacy of German music for the next hundred years." Indeed for Schoenberg, the proper register for German music was an art form which would steadfastly maintain the highest ambition, which would "always reach for the heavens." The rest, he declares, "only boasts with artifice."[22] The Suite, Op. 29, for piano, E flat clarinet, clarinet, bass clarinet, violin, viola and cello, and the Third String Quartet, Op. 30, both completed in 1926, not only served as demonstrations of the ability of his new compositional technique to support large-scale musical statements through atonal similes to sonata form or to replicate complex contrapuntal structures, but also showed his continuing commitment to the traditional forms of chamber music, and by extension, to the German ideal of absolute music. These compositional explorations culminated in the two Pieces for Piano, Op. 33a (1929) and 33b (1931) and his first composition for large orchestra since the Orchestral Songs, Op. 22 (1914–16), the Variations for Orchestra, Op. 31, which, in its incorporation of the B-A-C-H motive, registers its affiliation to the heart of the German musical pantheon.

Von heute auf morgen

And yet, soon after his arrival in Berlin, Schoenberg also made a decisive return to explicitly dramatic forms of music, something that he had avoided since the abandonment of the composition of *Die Jakobsleiter* (Jacob's Ladder) in 1922. In June 1926 he began work on his play *Der biblische Weg* (The Biblical Way) and by October 1928 he had drafted the first version of the text of *Moses und Aron*, then in the form of an oratorio. The composition of the music of *Moses und Aron*, however, was not to commence for some years. Instead, in October 1928 Schoenberg began work on *Von heute auf morgen*. The libretto, penned by Gertrud Schoenberg, writing under the pseudonym of Max Blonda, was apparently inspired in part by the manner of some of Schoenberg's circle of friends.[23] Gertrud had at this time also been working closely with her husband on several other libretti on contemporary subjects, including, it seems, one set in Monte Carlo, and another, with echoes of Debussy's *Jeux*, revolving around an international tennis competition.[24]

Von heute auf morgen became Schoenberg's most overt confrontation with the culture of the Weimar Republic. Like the Three Satires it was prompted in part by his annoyance at the extraordinary successes of a younger generation of composers, which at the time of its composition included not just Krenek's *Jonny spielt auf,* but also Kurt Weill's *Der Zar läßt sich photographieren* (The Tsar Has His Photograph Taken) and Hindemith's *Hin und zurück* (There and Back). These archetypal *Zeitopern* were for Schoenberg, as they have often been for many a critic since, representative of a shamelessly ephemeral genre, and thus constitutionally antithetical, it seemed, to the idea of authentic art. *Von heute auf morgen* thus satirizes both modern life *and* modern art. As he noted in his own introduction to a radio broadcast of the work that he conducted in Berlin on February 27, 1930, "the matter becomes serious when fashionable slogans shake the foundations of private life, the relationship between the sexes and the institution of marriage. . . . [W]hen the foundations are destroyed, rebuilding can only be superficial."[25] The consumer of the *Zeitoper* is by implication like the husband in the opera with the wandering eye, who is told by his wife that "behind the glittering mask you imagine a marvellous creation. You are dazzled by every new apparition that is fashionably dressed. But once the charm of novelty has worn off, you gaze disappointed into nothing."[26]

Once again, however, Schoenberg was also confronted with the problem of satire itself, which, given the inherently worldly, satirical, nature of the *Zeitoper* genre, was here especially acute. In both, an ideal norm of form or content is often conspicuous by its absence; rather the composer of a *Zeitoper* seems to share with the satirist a hope that an intended audience "will go through the strengthening exercise of finding it themselves."[27] Thus, a *Zeitoper* will make a virtue of the absence of an apparently consistent compositional voice, instead foregrounding devices such as parody, pastiche, and displays of the grotesque, forcing us to reflect on what might constitute an authentic aesthetic utterance in the modern world.[28] Schoenberg's opera, however, conspicuously avoids such a strategy. While there are signs of an attempt at musical satire through the use of instruments associated with the cabaret and nightclub (such as the soprano and alto saxophone, flexatone, piano, mandolin, and guitar), fleeting references to a tango, and even a brief quotation from Act I of Wagner's *Die Walküre*, typically such references are fully integrated into the overall timbre and dodecaphonic structure of the work, and thus softened in effect if not placed beyond our immediate grasp. "Better colourless than crude – better no humour than this disgusting slapstick which is rampant in Berlin," he wrote.[29] Even an easy opportunity to mimic *Zeitoper* stage effects, such as the "entrance" of one character by means of the telephone, is consciously avoided. Schoenberg notes in the score that the effect of a telephone call is to be achieved naturally, and "under no account via loudspeakers or megaphones," as if he wanted consciously to negate the craving for novelty that had followed in the wake of the appearance of such technology in *Jonny spielt auf.*[30]

The music is instead concerned principally with internal consistency, though we might note that the treatment of the twelve-tone row is here more supple than hitherto apparent in Schoenberg's dodecaphonic music, moving from a strict ordering of notes within a row toward free permutations of notes within hexachords. Nevertheless, both Rognoni and Rufer, apparently taking a lead from Schoenberg himself, saw this as a development once again supported by tradition, as it could be thought of as being analogous to Rameau's principle that the harmonic identity of a triad remained essentially the same, whatever the inversion in which it was found. It was justified ultimately by the "unity of the soundspace, where horizontal and vertical elements are considered as aspects substantially identical."[31] The force of musical tradition seems also to have influenced the overall form of the work, which can be considered as a kind of secret numbers opera within which passages of recitative are punctuated by short sections of arioso, arias, and ensembles. It is even possible to detect the outline of a classical four-movement symphony form;[32] though in so doing we would do well to remember Derrick Puffett's observation that these are usually not so much objective truth claims as "a representation of a certain way of seeing things, a way which we know from all kinds of evidence to have been characteristic of Schoenberg and his circle."[33]

Schoenberg suggested elsewhere that it was the libretto which held the key to the work's overall character, that "behind the straightforward plot something else is hidden: [namely] that everyday figures and events are being used to show how above and beyond the simple marital story the so-called modern, the fashionable exist only 'from one day to the next' (*Von heute auf morgen*), from an unsteady hand to a greedy mouth, in marriage no less than in art, in politics and in life philosophies."[34] The form and dramatic function of the music of *Von heute auf morgen* is then perhaps most concisely expressed by Adorno, who in his review of the work in 1930 wrote that "the music consumed the libretto."[35] Or, as Rognoni more expansively put it, "alienation does not invest in the artist's language, but is simply 'described' as an external fact which may be objectively dismantled and reconstructed by the composer like a sort of shifting *collage.*"[36] We observe the story unfold, all the while the music stares us down, like one of Schoenberg's famous self-portraits, demanding us to maintain an unwaveringly distant and critical standpoint towards it.

All the same, it could be argued that the stylistic montage evident in contemporary *Zeitoper* is ultimately a more effective artistic gesture for transporting a social context into a critical aesthetic sanctuary. At the very least, it makes for more effective, but also more approachable, satire. It is therefore hard to believe that at the same time, Schoenberg thought that this work would have the same kind of commercial success as was greeting other new works in the 1929–30 season, such as Max Brand's *Maschinist Hopkins*, Brecht and Weill's *Aufstieg und Fall der Stadt Mahagonny* (Rise and Fall of the City of Mahagonny), or Hindemith's *Neues von Tage* (News of the Day), the last of which superficially deals with some of the same subject matter. And yet so confident was he of its success that he rejected an offer of 30,000 marks from Bote und Bock for the publication rights, a decision that later proved financially disastrous.[37] Perhaps, as Adorno notes, "[e]ven if Schoenberg with his comedy *Von heute auf morgen*, was searching for success, it was – to his honour – refused him, by the complexity and the dark ferocity of its music ... The antinomy of opera and public came out to be a victory for the composition upon the opera."[38] Certainly compared to Schoenberg's other major works, *Von heute auf morgen* has had few performances – though it is a fate that it, of course, now shares with the vast majority of the *Zeitoper* genre.

Accompaniment to a film-scene (*Begleitungsmusik zu einer Lichtspielszene*)

Schoenberg's preoccupation with contemporary culture at this time is also reflected in his interest in cinema. He considered introducing a film sequence into *Moses und Aron* for the "Dance Around the Golden Calf," and had also discussed the use of film with Alban Berg who was later to recommend its use in the staging of his opera *Lulu*. The *Begleitungsmusik zu einer Lichtspielszene*, Op. 34 (1930) was composed in response to a commission by the publisher Heinrichshofen, and stands as Schoenberg's most overt artistic response to the burgeoning genre of film music, one then on the cusp of moving decisively from the live theater pit to the sound track. While not conceived with an actual visual narrative in mind, Schoenberg did offer the following synopsis for the work: Fear – Threatening Danger – Catastrophe. In so doing he may have been alluding to the books of themed musical excerpts that were the stock-in-trade of the silent movie accompanist. Both the quasi-expressionist synopsis and the fact that the music proved a success with contemporary audiences, though, also bring to mind the popular complaint made of later twelve-tone music that it rather lends itself to being used as the accompaniment to horror films. Certainly, as Dahlhaus wrote, in articulating the implied expressive content, the programmatic titles "transform [the work] into an illustrative one ... The listener feels he has been placed in the role of a spectator instead of being himself directly affected; and since it is film music (albeit only fictitious) he accepts the dissonances he would otherwise not tolerate."[39] Perhaps Schoenberg sensed this potential corruption of the relationship between the listener and the score when he tellingly remarked, "[The public] seem to like the piece – should I draw conclusions as to its quality?"[40] Later, in America, Schoenberg dabbled with the possibilities of film music once again, this time to accompany Metro-Goldwyn-Mayer's *The Good Earth*, but he could not accept the necessary level of compromise and subordination to the needs of the studio that the task would have required.

Another work from this time, the Six Pieces for Male Chorus, Op. 35 (1930) is also concerned with the relationship between an artist and society, not least because it was written for, and performed by, workers' choruses, but the work also demonstrates an attempt by the composer to mediate between tonal and twelve-tone systems. The texts set are again by Schoenberg, yet this time his concerns are not satirical but rather deliberately serious. In this respect they seem an apt precursor to *Moses und Aron*, the work to which Schoenberg was now returning with renewed vigor. And yet, that work too should be seen as but another elaboration, albeit now on an abstracted and monumental scale, of his struggle to articulate a musical response to the art and politics of the Weimar Republic without thereby becoming tainted by it. As Joseph Auner suggests, the metaphor of Moses and Aaron was only meaningful to him precisely because of the "tension and ambivalence" that had come to characterize his relationship to his public during the Weimar years.[41]

Conclusion

Given how decisively *Moses und Aron* seems to conceal the satiric impulse that is apparent in many of the works that it precedes, it has been easy to downplay or forget this broader historical context. Arguably, Schoenberg's reputation has suffered for it. Certainly in the hands of his critics both then and subsequently, his professed belief in *l'art pour l'art* became a statement that suggested both an unpleasant arrogance and an apparent lack of concern for social engagement through art.[42] Today the notion that a direct engagement with popular culture must always be destructive of the idea of authentic art arouses at the very least our suspicion, at worst, our derision. For all this, however, Schoenberg deserves not so much to be blamed as understood. Recognizing that he, like a character in *Der biblische Weg*, was "cursed by wishing to be Moses and Aaron wrapped up in one," allows us to resolve the apparent contradiction in his music of the 1920s between a profound commitment to the twelve-tone technique, and a genuine desire to engage with forms of popular culture. Although, in the end, Schoenberg did feel compelled towards a definitively antagonistic position towards mainstream culture, it is also worth remembering that he was far from alone in choosing such a path. It is more than merely ironic that both Krenek and, eventually, Stravinsky were themselves to adopt the twelve-tone technique in terms not altogether removed from those Schoenberg had come to represent in dramatic form at this time. While today we can take a considerably more nuanced view of the oppositions between high and low culture that buttressed much of his creative self-image, for many who followed more immediately in his footsteps, the effects of the stock market crash in America in October 1929 and the subsequent rise to power of the National Socialists in Germany seemed only to confirm the righteousness of the ethical stance that his music had come to represent. Such is the weight of history that has come to haunt our reception of Schoenberg, man and musician, from the Weimar era.

12 Schoenberg's row tables: temporality and the idea

JOSEPH AUNER

Schoenberg's interest in chords and melodies using all twelve tones emerged as early as 1910 during the composition of his opera *Die glückliche Hand*, Op. 18 (1910–13) and as he was writing the final chapters of his *Theory of Harmony* (1910–11). The sketches for his unfinished choral symphony, which he started in 1914, include a twelve-tone row and its transformations. During the years of World War I, and then more systematically in 1920–23, he experimented with ordered and unordered collections of various lengths, using a technique he described as "working with tones of the motif," in works and fragments including *Die Jakobsleiter*, the Five Pieces for Piano, Op. 23, and the *Serenade*, Op. 24. The Suite for Piano, Op. 25 (completed in 1923 and published in 1925) is the first piece to use twelve-tone techniques throughout, while the Wind Quintet, Op. 26 (1924) was the first to use a single row for all the movements.[1] And though he never stopped writing tonal music, the project of exploring the manifold ramifications and possibilities of the "method of composing with twelve tones related only to one another" remained at the center of his creative life for the next twenty-seven years.

In contrast to his extensive writings on tonal theory, however, Schoenberg wrote very little concerning the details of twelve-tone composition. The essay "Composition with Twelve Tones," published a year before his death in the first edition of *Style and Idea* (1950), was his most substantial public statement.[2] As a result, we primarily owe our understanding of Schoenberg's twelve-tone method to the work of three generations of composers, historians, and theorists who have produced an extraordinary body of scholarship and new compositions formalizing and extending Schoenberg's ideas.[3] These developments have necessarily brought with them considerable standardization in the pedagogy of twelve-tone theory and analysis. While some differences still persist, the adoption of a shared terminology, conceptual framework, and conventions of representation, have led to an ease of communication between scholars and composers and thus to the flourishing of what has become an important discipline in the field.

Yet it is just this sense of "discipline" that sits uncomfortably with Schoenberg's repeated warnings against orthodoxy, his resistance to establishing a "school" of twelve-tone composition, and his characterization of the essence of the method as "a real faith in what is uncertain, untested, problematic, dangerous."[4] There was always a tension in Schoenberg's mind between thinking of the method as the product of inevitable historical forces and thus, in some sense, as common property, or as something that he had created and that was individual to him.[5] With the extensive development of twelve-tone theory comes the potential for the creation of blind spots in our understanding of the differences between Schoenberg's conceptions and later formulations by composer-theorists with their own compositional agendas.[6]

It is important to remember that almost half a century separates us from the brief period after World War II when it appeared that the method and its serial offshoots would become established as a new common language to replace tonality. One must go back three decades further to the summer of 1921 when Schoenberg made his famous proclamation to his pupils about twelve-tone composition: "I have made a discovery thanks to which the supremacy of German music is ensured for the next hundred years."[7] Along with this temporal distance, we can only approach Schoenberg's conception of the method across the gulf created by the huge social, political, and cultural transformations of the twentieth century. Indeed, he started off the Preface to his unfinished treatise on *The Musical Idea and the Logic, Technique, and Art of its Presentation* from early in his American exile in 1934 with the simple statement: "German music will not take the path I have pointed out for it."[8] But of course, except in isolated instances, music in America, Great Britain, or anywhere else could hardly be regarded as having followed the path he indicated; on the contrary, our present day conceptions of twelve-tone composition are also shaped by three generations of composers, scholars, and critics who have worked hard to repudiate it.

The principles of the twelve-tone method in Schoenberg's formulation include:

1. "the constant and exclusive use of a set of twelve different tones";
2. a concern for avoiding "false expectations" of tonality that could be evoked by alluding to tonal harmony or by octave doubling that might suggest a root or tonic;
3. the use of the row to generate melodic and harmonic material, thus conceiving of "the two or more dimensional space as a unity";
4. the use of the basic set, along with its inversion, retrograde, and retrograde inversion in any transposition, resulting in the forty-eight possible row forms.[9]

And yet even from the perspective of Schoenberg's music, and even more so for Berg, Webern, or the many other composers who have adopted and adapted the method, recent scholarship has shown that each of these

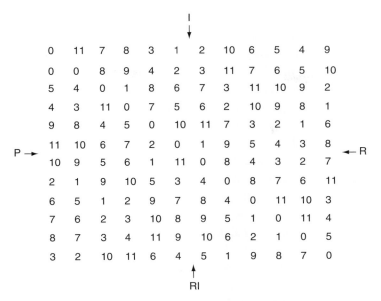

Figure 12.1 Matrix for Schoenberg's String Quartet No. 4, as given as Figure 5–9 in Joseph Straus, *Introduction to Post-Tonal Theory*, 2nd edn. (Upper Saddle River: Prentice Hall, 2000), 149

principles turns out to have a complex and inconsistent relationship to actual compositional practice. Determining precisely what constitutes a row – ordering, intervals, or the specific pitch class content – is not a trivial task. Tonal allusions and analogies occur frequently, sometimes playing a primary role in creating form. Reconciling the horizontal and vertical dimensions of a work poses enormous challenges. Many of the rows that composers have found the most interesting compositionally do not allow forty-eight independent transformations, but rather inversions will duplicate retrogrades, and so forth.

The complexity of coming to terms with Schoenberg's conception of the twelve-tone method can be illustrated by a consideration of what is seemingly the least problematic aspect of twelve-tone theory: how we represent the forty-eight row forms. Indeed the formalization and standardization of the method is nowhere more apparent than with the near-codification of the representation of the forty-eight row forms in the familiar twelve-by-twelve matrix or "magic square" (Figure 12.1).

The connotations of a "magic square" are not incidental here – as Stefan Kostka says in his book, *The Materials and Techniques of Twentieth Century Music*, "The matrix or magic square allows you to see all 48 versions after writing out only 12 of them."[10] And as with magic tricks, it can seem as though one is not supposed to inquire too closely into how it is done. Indeed there are various programs available that will generate and label the matrix automatically. With the "Matrix Maker" software, for example, one simply enters the row form, specifies a few preferences, and the Magic Square appears.[11] Not only will the program create a magic square from any row you enter, but it also provides a basic analysis of the row identifying the set type, its combinatorial properties, and other features. The implication from this and similar pieces of software is that the beginning stages of a twelve-tone analysis have become routine and applicable to any composer or piece.

Yet a study of Schoenberg's sketches – not to mention those of Berg and Webern – makes clear that the representation of the forty-eight row forms is anything but uniform. While, as we shall see, Schoenberg did at times use row tables comparable to the familiar matrix, he prepared many different kinds of graphic representations for most of his twelve-tone works. These include various ways of listing all forty-eight row forms systematically in tables, to a vast range of charts and sketches that use two or more of the available forms, along with numerous mechanical devices in the form of slide rules, card catalogs, and volvelles (information wheels).

In this chapter I will argue that Schoenberg's row tables were by no means a simple expedient or a preliminary phase of the pre-compositional activity, but were a dynamic and evolving medium in the creation of individual works and the development of the method of composing with twelve tones. The number and variety of the row tables and sketches suggests that their importance extended well beyond their practical use, but they seem to have served many purposes. Schoenberg's row tables can be understood on the one hand as an attempt to represent the unrepresentable "idea" at its most metaphysical, and on the other as a manifestation of the materiality and even tangibility of the row, whereby features such as layout and labeling are closely bound up with the musical relationships that make up the piece. Every way of representing row forms has its own characteristics and implications; just as there are significant connotations to how we label the rows in relation to the prime form, or even what we call the row, whether it be "series," "prime form," or "basic set." In her discussion of Webern's row tables, Kathryn Bailey has made a similar point about Webern's deep immersion in his very diverse row tables while composing:

> An acquaintance with the row tables suggests that Webern's inspiration was at least as much visual (and, one supposes, aural) as it was intellectual, and that the amazing symmetries for which he has been celebrated were as often unexpected discoveries as inventions. Here, as in the mountains, the "physical reality contains all the miracles."[12]

My point is not to claim that the row tables and sketches offer the only way or even the best way to understand, analyze, or perform Schoenberg's works; on the contrary, a significant body of research is emerging that advocates approaches to twelve-tone and serial music independent of the compositional methods used to create them.[13] But if we are going to think about the rows, it is important for us to be aware of the conventions we are adopting and the tools we are using. The history of tonal theory includes many different ways of representing the relationships between keys, and new ways of imagining tonal space are still emerging. In contrast, the lack of explicit discussion in much twelve-tone theory about the assumptions and implications of the making of row tables has closed off a potentially fruitful path of inquiry for musicologists, theorists, and composers. A study of the row tables can help us better understand Schoenberg's achievement in creating the method and the role that it played for him, not as a system or a simple solution to a compositional roadblock, but as a tool to stimulate new ways of thinking about potential musical relationships.

Origins of the matrix

Before looking in more detail at Schoenberg's row tables, it is useful to step back and briefly consider the origins of the current status of the "magic square" as a kind of default setting in our mental apparatus. Martha Hyde's groundbreaking 1983 article, "The Format and Function of Schoenberg's Twelve-Tone Sketches," remains the most extensive study, and I will be retaining her terminology here: the term "row tables" will refer to charts that present all forty-eight row forms, while "row sketches" present two or more forms of the row.[14] The relative neglect of Schoenberg's row tables is striking in contrast to the amount that has been written about his twelve-tone music, but also in comparison to the scholarship on Berg, Webern, and even Stravinsky in which the literature on the actual mechanics of making row tables is much more extensive. It is noteworthy that the Matrix Maker program even has a special option for generating "Stravinsky Verticals"; needless to say there is no option for Schoenberg slide rules or card catalogs.

There is, in fact, a rather remarkable silence concerning how one might go about making a row table in many theoretical and musicological sources. To my knowledge, neither Schoenberg, Berg, nor Webern published complete row tables in their lifetimes. Most of the earliest writings on twelve-tone composition also did not present row tables, including Erwin Stein's "Neue Formprinzipien" from 1924, Richard Hill's "Schoenberg's Tone-Rows and the Tonal System of the Future" from 1936, or Josef Rufer's book *Composition with Twelve Notes* from 1952.[15] But it is surprising that the substantial *New Grove* article on twelve-tone composition by George Perle and Paul Lansky similarly provides no indication of what row tables look like – with the exception of the passage on Stravinsky's music, which does include one of his row tables.[16] Many general surveys of twentieth-century music, such as those by Morgan, Salzman, and Taruskin, describe the basic features of twelve-tone composition and how one generates the forty-eight row forms, but do not provide complete tables. Even many theoretically focused studies, such as those by Smith Brindle, Perle, and Haimo, also lack complete row tables. The likely implication of this silence, particularly for beginning students, is either that it does not matter how you make a row table, or that it is assumed you already know.

The actual mechanics of making row tables have largely been left to the music theory textbooks, such as the Kostka book or Joseph Straus's *Introduction to Post-Tonal Theory*. Straus does acknowledge that there are different ways of writing the forty-eight forms, but only illustrates the twelve-by-twelve matrix. He writes:

> In studying a twelve-tone piece, it is convenient to have at hand a list of all forty-eight forms of the series. We could just write out all forty-eight either on staff paper or using the pitch class integers. More simply, we could write out the twelve primes and the twelve inversions (using the music staff, letter names, or pitch class integers) and simply find the retrogrades and retrograde inversions by reading backwards. The simplest way of all, however, is to construct what is known as a "12 x 12 matrix."[17]

But while it may be the most efficient way, it is hard to argue that the matrix is the simplest, since it only reveals its utility upon completion of a set of instructions that can seem arbitrary on first acquaintance. The simplest approach is what appeared in the earliest writings that did provide row tables, namely a list of all forty-eight forms showing the row, the inversions, the retrogrades, and retrograde inversions at every level of transposition. This is the technique used in Krenek's *Studies in Counterpoint* from 1940, one of the first tables published, and in Hanns Jelinek's *Instruction in Twelve-Tone Composition* from 1952.[18]

Schoenberg, Berg, and Webern similarly often constructed row tables by writing down all forty-eight forms, or as in a row table for Schoenberg's Piano Concerto, Op. 42 shown in Figure 12.2, that provides the twenty-four prime forms and inversions while leaving the retrogrades and retrograde inversions implicit. The table for the Piano Concerto is laid out with the prime form adjacent to its combinatorial inversion (that is, a version of the row, the first half of which shares no common tones with the first half of the prime form, thus allowing them to be used at the same time without duplicating any pitch class).[19] He then writes out all the transpositions

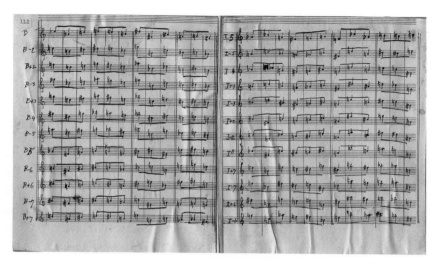

Figure 12.2 Row Table for the Piano Concerto, Op. 42. Arnold Schönberg Center

ascending chromatically and labeled according to the diatonic interval that separates them from the prime form or the inversion. Thus, in the table in Figure 12.2, "B-2" indicates the "basic shape," a term he often used for the row in English, transposed up a minor second. Schoenberg developed many different formats and ways of ordering the rows in such tables, each with their own implications for what sorts of relationships between rows are significant. His interest in what one can learn about how row forms relate by placing them in different contexts is especially evident in one of the tables for the Variations for Orchestra, Op. 31, which uses individual cardboard slips for each row, thus allowing them to be placed in any order.[20]

Yet despite the apparent utility of such tables for Schoenberg and other composers, one can now get the sense that they are somehow less legitimate than the matrix. Milton Babbitt, for example, writes:

> Schoenberg laid these things out by just writing down every single one of the twenty-four forms of the series (he was willing to read the retrogrades from right to left). And he wrote it all out in pitch-class notation, not in numerical notation. After writing down all set forms, he would write down what the distance was between the transpositions – plus one, minus one, plus two, minus two, and so on. The unity of all this evaded him completely.[21]

The disapproving tone echoes the much sharper criticisms of Schoenberg's conception of the method by Boulez and other serialists in the early 1950s. Ralph Lorenz suggests that the first published example of a magic square was in Babbitt's liner notes to the 1957 Columbia recording of *Moses und Aron*, followed in the early 1960s in foundational writings on

S	A	T	O	R
A	R	E	P	O
T	E	N	E	T
O	P	E	R	A
R	O	T	A	S

Figure 12.3 SATOR Palindrome

twelve-tone theory by Perle and others.[22] In Europe Boulez, Stockhausen, and Ligeti used matrices in ever more elaborate ways to determine pitch, rhythm, and other parameters together with the development of integral serialism and electronic music.[23] A seminal source was Webern's reference to the ancient Latin SATOR palindrome at the conclusion of his lectures on "The Path to Twelve-tone Composition" from the early 1930s.[24]

Schoenberg and the matrix

Because the magic square has become so familiar, it provides a useful starting point for a reconsideration of Schoenberg's row tables. As Figure 12.4 from one of the many row tables Schoenberg prepared for the Suite, Op. 29 shows, he was aware of the possibility of constructing a twelve-by-twelve matrix. But for Schoenberg the significance of the magic square was more complex and far-reaching than its present-day status as a simple tool would suggest. Indeed, I would argue that it was the almost metaphysical quality of such tables for Schoenberg that ultimately made them less useful in actual composition than the other formats he preferred. As in the textbook version, the table presents all the prime forms ordered according to the inversion of the row, though with the axes apparently reversed so that the prime form extends down the left side while the inversion runs along the top. I say "apparently" here because Schoenberg has ingeniously constructed the matrix with staves running in two directions. Thus it is possible to rotate the table so that the prime form actually runs along the bottom edge using the red staves, with the inversion moving up the left-hand side.

This is, of course, more than just a casual experiment. Through the remarkable alignment of pitches on both horizontal and vertical staves, as well as the elaborate intertwining of trichordal and tetrachordal segments for all the forms of the row, the table serves as a vivid physical representation of the foundational notion expressed in the essay "Composition with Twelve Tones": "THE TWO-OR-MORE-DIMENSIONAL SPACE IN WHICH MUSICAL IDEAS ARE PRESENTED IS A UNIT."[25] In the essay Schoenberg makes the well-known comparison between the unity of musical space, which demands "*an absolute and unitary perception*," and the mystical

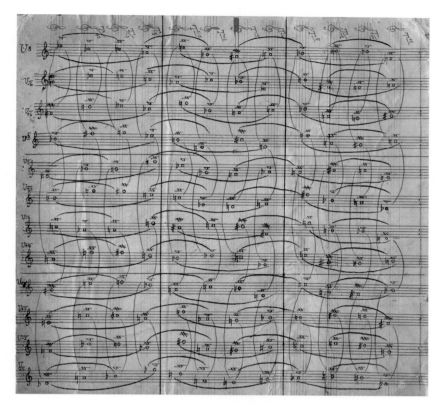

Figure 12.4 Row Table for the Suite, Op. 29. Arnold Schönberg Center

Swedenborgian image of heaven in Balzac's novel *Séraphita*, where "there is no absolute down, no right or left, forward or backward."[26]

I would argue that we now approach Schoenberg's conception of multidimensional space from quite a different intellectual perspective, one shaped primarily by writings of the serialist composers after World War II, such as Stockhausen's "... how time passes ...," that extend the concept into an equivalence of all musical parameters, so that pitch, dynamics, rhythm, timbre can be thought of as all manifestations of the same phenomenon.[27] Ligeti's analysis of Boulez's *Structures* from *Die Reihe*, for example, shows how one could interpret the numerical values in the tables in terms of pitches, rhythms, or dynamics.[28] Accordingly, such tables lead us to think of the equivalence of musical space in very abstract and metaphorical terms, in order to imagine, for example, the inversion of a series of rhythms or dynamics.

But for Schoenberg, the row tables were at the same time more literal and concrete as well as more metaphysical and even mystical. As noted above, his row table for Op. 29 presents the unity of musical space very literally with the staves moving in two directions and with the pitches on the staves retaining their relative positions so that the trichords and tetrachords in both the prime forms and the inversions preserve their identities as musical gestures. Because of the highly symmetrical nature of the row, these segmentations are saturated with the same groups of pitch classes (or invariant subsets) everywhere you look. This tangible quality brings to mind Schoenberg's explanation of the unity of musical space through an analogy to the capacity of our minds to recognize physical objects from any perspective. He writes:

> To the imaginative and creative faculty, relations in the material sphere are as independent from directions or planes as material objects are, in their sphere to our perceptive faculties. Just as our mind always recognizes, for instance, a knife, a bottle or watch, regardless of its position, and can reproduce it in the imagination in every possible position, even so a creator's mind can operate subconsciously with a row of tones, regardless of their direction, regardless of the way in which a mirror might show the mutual relations, which remain a given quality.[29]

On the other hand, another row table for the Suite, Op. 29 shows how far-reaching Schoenberg's notion of multidimensionality and "showing the idea from all sides" could become (Figure 12.5). Here Schoenberg super-imposes two 12-by-12 matrices; the lower one presents a set of inversions ordered not by the prime as would be usual, but by the inversion itself running down the left side. Thus it provides two sets of twelve inversions running in each direction. Attached to this matrix another one extends upward, here with the prime form moving up the left-hand side. This in turn determines the transpositions of another set of prime forms moving horizontally, which thus necessarily results in a set of prime forms in both dimensions. That such a table does not serve any practical purpose suggests that it had some other function.

The various row matrices for Op. 29, with their interlocked primes and inversions teeming with a profusion of trichords and tetrachords, point us to the fundamental nature of the musical Idea as something eternal, timeless, and unchanging, but something which, for that reason, can only be indirectly grasped. The challenge of representing the unrepresentable Idea is, of course, the central theme of Schoenberg's unfinished opera *Moses und Aron* (1930–32). Schoenberg's libretto is based on the opposition between the two title characters, with Moses given the charge to transmit God's message but lacking the ability to communicate, while Aron has the gift of persuasion but lacks a vision of the infinite. When Aron says "can you love what you *dare* not even imagine?" Moses replies: "Dare not? Unimaginable because invisible, because everlasting, eternal, because ever present, because almighty." In his unfinished treatise *The

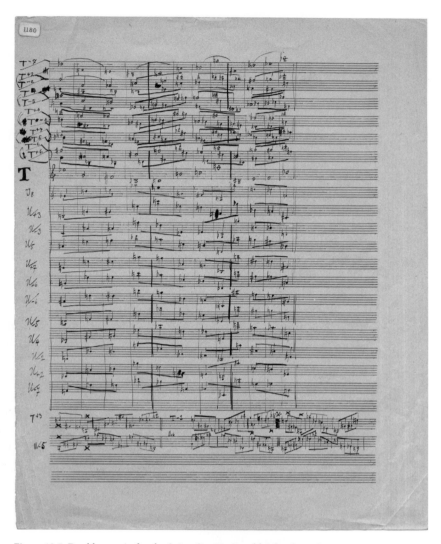

Figure 12.5 Double matrix for the Suite, Op. 29. Arnold Schönberg Center

Musical Idea, and the Logic, Technique, and Art of its Presentation, Schoenberg writes that melodic and harmonic progressions are components of the Idea, but only the visual and audible components that can be directly perceived by the senses, applying only "by analogy to that which makes up the actual content of a musical idea."[30] Just as in a contrapuntal composition where Schoenberg identifies the Idea as "all the possibilities for combination that obtain among the given voices,"[31] the matrices discussed above might be understood to suggest that the Idea of a twelve-tone work is not the row but the sum of all the relationships between all the manifestations of the row. Like the Idea, the twelve-tone row is imperceptible as a whole, but pervades all that one hears; as God says to Moses, "so will you perceive my message in everything." That Schoenberg thought of the row tables as a way to approach this metaphysical sphere can perhaps explain in part why he prepared so many different row tables for a single work, with Op. 29 being an extreme case.

Row sketches, temporality, and the art of presentation

This points us in turn to a fundamental aspect of Schoenberg's thought and music: while the Idea itself is eternal and unchanging, we can only attempt to grasp the Idea through its representation in time. Carl Dahlhaus explained the Idea as something that can only be approached indirectly through its unfolding in time, with an analogy to Torah exegesis: "Revelation is not in itself a comprehensible message, but becomes one only in the reflections which it experiences in human consciousness. And there is no limit to their number."[32] As Schoenberg wrote in "New Music, Outmoded Music, Style and Idea," "In a manifold sense, music uses time. It uses my time, it uses your time, it uses its own time. It would be most annoying if it did not aim to say the most important things in the most concentrated manner in every fraction of this time."[33] Many of Schoenberg's writings on the Idea focus on this crucial temporal dimension and the associated issues of recognition, memory, association, and understanding; this is the whole reason for the extended title for his book *The Musical Idea and the Logic, Technique, and Art of its Presentation*. In "Criteria for the Evaluation of Music," he similarly foregrounds temporal issues, writing that the critic must determine, "Is the time-space adequate for the importance or the unimportance of the ideas? Are main ideas distinctly differentiated from subordinate ideas in space by adequate proportions as well as in emphasis, so always to secure the predominance of the object? Is the breadth of the presentation justified?"[34]

There is similarly an implicit temporal dimension in Schoenberg's comparison of the unity of musical space, noted above, to our capacity to recognize physical objects in different positions. As a corollary to the objects moving in space, they must also move in time (and it is noteworthy that one of the objects he mentions is a watch, which would presumably be ticking off the seconds as it was rotated in space). It is not coincidental, I believe, that the sketch materials for one of Schoenberg's earliest twelve-tone pieces, the "Sonett" movement of the *Serenade*, demonstrate how important the temporal dimension was in representing the Idea (Figure 12.6). As many have discussed, the piece is based on a Petrarch Sonnet with eleven syllable lines. Schoenberg sets this text with a vocal melody based on repeated statements of a twelve-tone row. As a result the vocal line rotates through

Figure 12.6 Row device for the Serenade, Op. 24, Sonett. Arnold Schönberg Center

the row, starting each line at a different point. To generate the vocal melody, Schoenberg created a slide rule that made it possible to rotate the row to see each possible combination of the order numbers and the pitch series. We can thus think of the slide rule at rest as potentially embodying the various rotations of the row that appear in the vocal line, and which he worked out in a series of sketches. But only by actually manipulating the device in time and space are the individual rotations revealed.

He used similar slide rules for several pieces, including Op. 29, and there are a number of row tables that integrate moving components that reveal various features of the row forms as they change positions in time and space. Figure 12.7 shows one of Schoenberg's row sketches for *Moses und Aron*, along with a device for partitioning the row forms. Such mechanical row devices underscore the central role of the concept of "comprehensibility" or "Faßlichleit" for Schoenberg. As in the root word *Fassen*, meaning to grasp or seize, for Schoenberg to truly understand something meant to hold it in his hand. Throughout his life Schoenberg devoted enormous energies to various arts and crafts, with painting and drawing being the most significant, but also including binding his books, building furniture, making sets of playing cards, chess sets, and many other tools and devices. Of course the impossibility of trying to seize an Idea, of holding in your hand "thoughts that roam the cosmos," is the central theme of his libretto for the opera *Die glückliche Hand*. This pessimism is captured in the ironic title of the work (translated variously as "The Happy Hand," "The Fortunate Hand," "The Fateful Hand"), which he described as signifying the act of trying to grasp "that which can only slip away from you, if you hold it."[35]

While Schoenberg did use magic squares in composition, I would argue that it is precisely their mystical and atemporal aspects that limited their usefulness; we might think of the magic squares as existing in the realm of the pure Idea, of Moses. Moreover, the beautiful symmetries, completeness, and uniformity of the matrix for Op. 29 should also be regarded from the perspective of Schoenberg's ambivalence throughout his life to perfect symmetry and regularity. In *The Musical Idea* Schoenberg links symmetry to the primitive forms of music, claiming even that "perfect regularity (symmetry and the like) is not suited to music" or rather only to "petrified music."[36] Much more common and more closely integrated to the

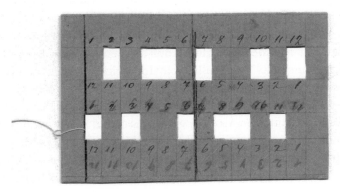

Figure 12.7 Row device for *Moses und Aron*. Arnold Schönberg Center

compositional process are the partial row sketches, such as those that appear on the bottom of the double matrix for Op. 29 in Figure 12.5, where he tries out contrapuntal combinations of row forms at different levels of transposition.[37] Unlike the magic square, which for Schoenberg points to a sphere beyond human imagining, such sketches exist in the realm of Aron and the temporality of the presentation of the timeless idea. And though it is common to regard Schoenberg as identifying most strongly with Moses, there is considerable evidence that characteristics associated with Aron also played a central role in his creative and intellectual life.[38]

The draft manuscript of the Piano Piece, Op. 33a, dated December 1928, can illustrate several important features of Schoenberg's row sketches (Figure 12.8). The first four systems contain a draft of the opening measures that is very close to the finished work in terms of the basic gestures and row structure. These measures use only the prime form and

Figure 12.8 Draft and row sketch for Op. 33a. Arnold Schönberg Center

its combinatorial inversion (notated at the bottom left of the page) along with their retrogrades. Halfway through the fourth system, however, the draft differs from the finished version with an awkward ostinato-like section that sounds as if a record got stuck. Only at this point does Schoenberg pause and make a small row sketch in which he writes out the two other combinatorial pairs he would go on to use in the developmental middle section (P^2/I^7 and P^7/I^0, or in Schoenberg's terminology T^2/U_4 and T^5/U_8); of the new forms sketched he used all but the transposition starting on E flat (P^5 or T^4).

Several things are significant about this sole surviving row sketch for the piece in the present context. The manuscript demonstrates, as others have pointed out, that row tables and sketches were not necessarily created prior to the composition of the piece, but were often produced during the composition. That Schoenberg apparently started the work with the intention of only using the original combinatorial pair underscores the limited role transpositions played in some of his shorter pieces. Accordingly, he did not necessarily start a work from an imagined constellation of forty-eight row forms swirling in the matrix from which he chose one, but rather he began with a row or a combinatorial pair and then generated other forms as needed. As in most of Schoenberg's row tables, the sketch also indicates something of how Schoenberg thought of the register and contour as well as the segmentation of the row. In contrast to the matrix, the layout and labeling of the row sketch demonstrates that

Schoenberg conceived of the pitch space much more literally in terms of the relationship to the prime form of the row, with transpositions above and inversions below, and with the combinatorial pairs arching out from the center.

In comparison to a matrix, Schoenberg's row sketch also makes it much easier to see significant features of the piece, such as his use of row forms starting on the first three pitches of the row: B flat, F, and C. This literal pitch space is reflected as well in Schoenberg's manner of labeling the transpositions and inversions in terms of diatonic intervals above or below the basic set. Thus T^5 is the theme a perfect fifth above, while U_4 is the inversion a perfect fourth below. The older practice in twelve-tone theory of identifying the initial form of the row as P0 retains this primacy to some degree. But the fixed-*do* system of labeling row forms where C always equals 0, which has emerged as the dominant approach, obscures the sense of distance in musical space of the transpositions from the prime form, and undercuts the primacy of the basic set so central to Schoenberg's conception of the method. Moreover, there is also an implicit connection between the use of the fixed-*do* system and the reliance on the twelve-by-twelve matrix as the imagined background of a twelve-tone work. In other words, to label the prime form of Op. 33a as P^{10} (that is, as the row form starting on B flat, where C always equals 0) places the row from the outset within the context of the other forty-seven row forms, with a possible implication that choice of transpositional level is to some degree arbitrary.

The final example shows the row sketch for the fifth movement of the Six Pieces for Male Chorus, Op. 35, "Landsknechte" (mercenaries), published and premiered in 1930 (Figure 12.9; the text and translation, with an indication of the row usage, is given in Figure 12.10).[39] There are several points of similarity between this sketch and that for Op. 33a. As with Op. 33a, this is the only row chart he used for the piece. Also similar to the Op. 33a row sketch, the "Landsknechte" sketch shows the prime and inversion at the center with the combinatorial pairs unfolding in an irregular arch form out from the central pair. The changing handwriting and paper indicate that the row sketch did not precede the composition of the piece, but was produced over the course of the compositional process. It appears that he started out with just the prime form, inversion, and the combinatorial inversion at the perfect fifth below, as evidenced by the title of the movement ("Landsknechte") written directly above the prime form. As the piece progressed he added other transpositions above and inversions below, which even necessitated attaching the sketch to another page when he ran out of staves (thus U_{-7} and the title at the top are written on a different piece of paper). It is also noteworthy that he made some mistakes writing down the transposition of T^{+6}, not because

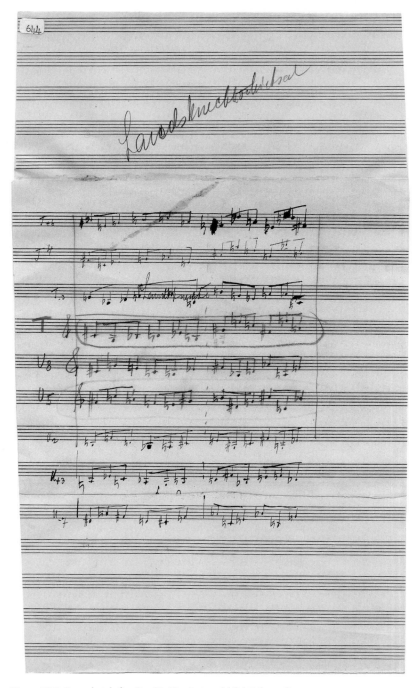

Figure 12.9 Row sketch for Op. 35, No. 5. Arnold Schönberg Center

German	English			Tempo
	Tu-tu-ru, tu-rum-pu-ru	P0	T	Langsames Marschtempo
Einmal muß man sterben,	We all have to die sometime,	P0/I5	T/U5	
Aber wer denkt daran!	but who thinks about it?			
Und wie ist das: Sterben?	And what's that: to die?			
Ach was!	So what!			
Leben weiß man in jedem Augenblick.	We know how to live in each moment.			Rit
Ebensolang: aber es geht weiter.	Just for that very moment, but things go on.	I0	U8	Langsamer
	Tu-tu-ru, tu-rum-pu-ru			Tempo 1
Tapp, tapp, hopp, hopp!	Tapp, tapp, hopp, hopp!	I5	U5	
Auf die Weide!	To the pasture!			
Oh, heute regnets; wenig Gras – kein gutes--.	Oh, it's raining today; little grass – none good –.			
Herrlich: hier bin ich allein!	Marvelous: I am alone here!			
Der beste Platz! Kein andrer findet her.	The best spot! No one else will find it.			Rit
Eine fette Weide für alle.	A luxuriant pasture for us all.	P5	T4	Langsamer
Vertragt euch: es ist genug für jeden!	Make peace: there's enough for everyone!	P5/I10	T4/U2	molto calando
	Tu-tu-ru, tu-rum-pu-ru			accel Pesante
Weg! Die Weiber sind mein!	Go away! The women are mine!			Viel rascher
Lauf! oder ich spieße dich auf!	Run, or I'll run you through!			
Stirb! So, hier bin ich Herr!	Die! Now I'm the master here!			Langsamer
Für die Jungen ist gesorgt.	The young are provided for.	P0/I5	T/U5	
Ach was, Junge!	The young, so what!	P3/I8	T-3/U+3	
Man lebt jetzt eben!	Live for the moment!	P9/I2	T+6/U-7	Sehr breit
Oho, es reicht nach Blut?	Oh, there's a smell of blood?	P0	T	allmählich rascher
Nach unserem Blut und Fleisch.	Of our flesh and blood.	I5	U5	
Also dorthin gehts?	So, that's the way it goes?	I0	U8	
Werden wir jetzt schon geschlachtet?	Will we be slaughtered already?	P3 I2	T-3 U-7	accel
	Tu-tu-ru, tu-rum-pu-ru	P0/I5	T/U5	Etwas langsamer als I.
Man sollte fliehen:	One ought to flee:			
Man ist gelähmt!	One is paralyzed!			langsamer rit
Was könnte es nützen?	What's the use of that?			
	Tu-tu-ru, tu-rum-pu-ru			a tempo
Landsknechtsschicksal!	Mercenaries' fate!			

Figure 12.10 Text and row usage, Op. 35, No. 5

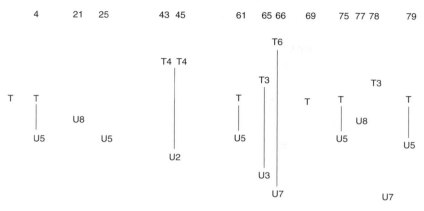

Figure 12.11 Row forms in Op. 35, No. 5

we expect Schoenberg to be perfect, but rather as it shows that the generation of such row forms was far from automatic.

As a result of the close correlation between the row sketch and the compositional process of the work, the sketch also embodies the succession of rows over the course of the piece. Figure 12.11 plots the sequence in which the row forms appear, starting out with the basic set, then expanding outward to the more distant transpositions before returning to the original combinatorial pair. In most cases the move to different row forms is connected to the text and is marked on the musical surface by tempo, textural, and dynamic changes (as shown in Figure 12.10). The sketch thus makes it possible to see much more clearly than a matrix allows the various characteristic ways Schoenberg created analogies to tonal motion, moving away from and returning to the initial hexachordal level. Schoenberg works to make this more than metaphorical by designing the row so that all of the dyads in the prime form are held invariant, though obviously reordered, in its combinatorial companion I5. All of these dyads are made extremely explicit in the music, often presented as ostinato figures in the individual parts. As the piece moves from the center of the chart outwards, each level of transposition is marked by a different number and type of returning dyads, just as every degree of transposition of a diatonic scale preserves a unique set of common tones.

The row sketch thus can be understood as representing the temporality of the compositional process as well as the temporal progression of the row forms in the work, and by implication all the relationships between the row forms of ordered and unordered invariant subsets that shape the piece. That all of this is derived from the basic set at the center provides a concrete example of Schoenberg's claim: "The theme is so created that it already holds within itself all these many Gestalten through which this will be made possible."[40] In comparison to the generic twelve-by-twelve matrix, this partial row sketch so bound up with the making of this piece can also illuminate a distinction between science and art that Schoenberg makes in one of his earliest writings, "On the Presentation of the Idea," from August 19, 1923. He writes: "Science aims to present its ideas exhaustively so that no question remains unanswered. Art, on the other hand, is content with a many-sided presentation from which the idea will emerge unambiguously, but without having to be stated directly. Consequently, in contrast, a window remains open through which, from the standpoint of knowledge, presentiment demands entry."[41]

Conclusion

The richness and complexity of the examples I have presented here, which are only a small percentage of what is available through the Arnold Schönberg Center, should make clear why I will not attempt to make any sort of general statement about Schoenberg's row tables and sketches in these concluding remarks. While there was some standardization in his working methods later in his life, his continual development of new ways to imagine the twelve-tone method in works like the *Ode to Napoleon* or the String Trio, suggests that he did not regard twelve-tone composition as something that could be ultimately defined or reduced to a system.

At the very least, I hope that these images suggest that it would be worthwhile in our approach, even to such basic analytical tasks as preparing a row table, to maintain the attitude that row tables were for the composers – and can be for us – powerful heuristic devices for understanding the characteristics and capacities of the musical material, and not something we should leave to a computer program. Now that so many of these sketches and row tables are available through the Arnold Schönberg Center, students and scholars in history, theory, analysis, composition, and performance would be well-served by wrestling with the metaphysics and materiality of Schoenberg's creative process.

13 Immanence and transcendence in *Moses und Aron*

RICHARD KURTH

Schoenberg's opera *Moses und Aron* dramatizes – along philosophical, theological, and psychological lines – the predicament of the prophet, who grasps the essential unrepresentability (*Unvorstellbarkeit*) of the Divine, but cannot communicate an understanding that supersedes language and concepts. Although Schoenberg may resemble his protagonist Moses in some respects, the opera cannot be reduced to an allegory on the modern artist's intractable position. Rather, it examines the human condition from multiple perspectives, by exploring the distinct spiritual and psychological experiences of Moses, Aron, and the Jewish *Volk*, through their diverse capacities for awareness, insight, expression, and belief. The opera is fundamentally concerned with the limits of perception and knowledge, and with the potential for human spirit and intellect (*Geist*) to supersede those limits. The music's fabric of sound, more than the events portrayed or the ideas articulated by the words, conveys the experience and import of those epistemological limits.

In his book *Metaphysical Song*, Gary Tomlinson elucidates how opera has always echoed contemporaneous systems of epistemology and metaphysics, using the sonorous presence of the human voice to point toward the super-sensible realm – as each philosophical (and operatic) age conceived it.[1] The philosophical ground for modern opera is given by Kantian epistemology, in which human intuition and thought are fundamentally limited to immanent and sensible phenomena, and cannot access the transcendental realm of noumena. In modern opera, Tomlinson writes, "The noumenon becomes the modern cipher of the supersensible world."[2] No opera articulates the quest for the noumenal more explicitly than Schoenberg's *Moses und Aron*.

In an influential commentary on *Moses und Aron*, Theodor Adorno claimed that its music is representational, and that the totalizing capacities of the twelve-tone method invoke a fatal tension in the work. Tomlinson encapsulates the crucial inferences in Adorno's critique, laying bare their vertiginous circularity, when he writes: "In the process of representing metaphysics through an integrated musical totality . . . Schoenberg loses *the possibility of representing the impossibility of representing metaphysics* – the most basic premise on which the whole endeavor of *Moses und Aron* was predicated."[3]

This chapter offers a counterpoise to the Adornian polemic, by questioning some of its fundamental assumptions, and by contextualizing and reinterpreting others. Attending to the music's most elemental components, and to Schoenberg's own statements, I will argue that the music's function is not to represent metaphysical or theological conundrums (as Adorno thinks), but to enact epistemological ones: the music indicates and performs the limits of sensible phenomena and immanence, to reach the boundary that is superseded by noumena and transcended by the pure Divine idea.

The chapter begins with a critique of Adorno's commentary on the opera, then sketches Schoenberg's own notions of higher meaning in artworks, and concludes with short analyses that show how the music in *Moses und Aron* exemplifies his artistic beliefs.

Opera as sacred art? *Moses und Aron*, Schoenberg and Adorno

Theodor Adorno's 1963 lecture on *Moses und Aron*, published under the title "Sakrales Fragment" (Sacred Fragment), is a cornerstone in the opera's reception history.[4] Adorno's influential critique has resonated throughout subsequent discussions of the opera, especially in the more recent commentaries by Philippe Lacoue-Labarthe and Gary Tomlinson.[5] As a pupil of Alban Berg and member of the Schoenberg circle, Adorno was generally an insightful champion of Schoenberg's work. But some tensions developed between the two men in the later years, partly in connection with Thomas Mann's *Doktor Faustus*.[6] And Schoenberg's resolute personality and confident directness sometimes grated on Adorno, whose virtuosic philosophical prolixity could in turn irritate the composer. In striking ways, their personalities and relationship ironically replicate the tension between Moses and Aron in the opera, and this analogy may have had a subliminal effect on Adorno's response to the opera. Although the final paragraphs of "Sakrales Fragment" praise aspects of the opera, the essay conducts an extended *agon* against Schoenberg. Despite some powerful insights, Adorno's polemic misrepresents some fundamental aspects of the opera. Contradictions lie beneath its polished discourse, and it distorts Schoenberg's aesthetic intentions and attitudes.

Adorno's critique hinges on two main accusations, the first being that Schoenberg aimed to write a belated "sacred" work, unaware that (in Adorno's opinion) such products of bourgeois ideology and nostalgic theology are untenable after Kant and Hegel; as Adorno writes: "The impossibility is historical, that of sacred art today."[7] Adorno accuses

Schoenberg of "a residue of naiveté" and assumes that *Moses und Aron* was innocently intended as a sacred work, a sort of Old Testament riposte to Wagner's *Parsifal*.[8] Adorno argued that "the fact that *Moses und Aron* was written as an opera does not disqualify it" from being a "sacred work of art."[9] But in fact Schoenberg had rejected and abandoned treatments of the material using two traditionally sacred genres: a cantata *Moses am brennenden Dornbusch*, of March 1926; and an oratorio prose text *Moses und Aron: ein Oratorium*, of October 1928. Between these, Schoenberg wrote the agitprop stage play *Der biblische Weg* (The Biblical Way, completed July 12, 1927), in which the protagonist Max Aruns tries – but fails – to establish a modern Jewish state in Africa. Aruns passionately expresses some distinctive religious positions, but he is principally a man of action and a political prophet, not a religious one. Despite its title, the play focuses on psychological, political, and social dynamics, and Schoenberg continued in that vein by ultimately deciding to cast *Moses und Aron* as music drama. By April 1930, he was describing the *Moses und Aron* project as an opera, and on the "Kompositionsvorlage" (the working copy of the libretto) dated July 17, 1930 he crossed out the word "Oratorium" and definitively wrote "Oper" in its place.[10] Even if he first considered a sacred work, Schoenberg eventually shaped the material as tragic *opera seria*.

Der biblische Weg and *Moses und Aron* differ in many ways, but they share underlying content and themes.[11] The play's contemporary setting points to timely and urgent issues for the present and future, but the focus is also on human psychology and behavior. Although Schoenberg based his opera on biblical sources, his libretto adapts and alters the biblical narrative significantly, to portray also the forces of human psychology and behavior that pose ineluctable obstacles to spiritual evolution.[12] Opera requires dramatic situations, actions, and pacing that permit sung expression in solos and ensembles and that allow instrumental music to be a fundamental agency for the projection of meaning; contrasts between Moses and Aron propel the opera's tragic narrative, and are musically supported by the opposition of speech (Moses) and melos (Aron), and by concomitant differences in the instrumental and choral parts. In the play, Max Aruns combines aspects of both Moses and Aron in one persona, but in both works prophets and political leaders meet with tragic failure: humanity is unready for their higher vision, and is too divided even to form a viable polity.

Adorno's prejudice about sacred art leads him to misunderstand not only the dramatic emphasis on human psychology and behavior, but also the basic character of the many choral textures in the opera: "the pathos of the music . . . at every moment embodies a communal 'we,' a single impulse of a predetermined collective consciousness, something like the unanimity of a congregation. Otherwise, the predominance of choral writing would be unthinkable."[13] But the *Volk* in the opera are disorderly and factionalized; they rarely show collective agreement or communal worship – except, ironically, in the Dionysian orgy around the Golden Calf. *Der biblische Weg* likewise portrays, as Bluma Goldstein notes, a "diverse and contentious population of socialists, capitalists, intellectuals, Zionists, assimilationists, and orthodox Jews."[14] The opera's choral textures are densely polyphonic, displaying the *disunity* of the *Volk*. We repeatedly witness an isolated Moses, and an uncomprehending, quarrelsome, and unsympathetic *Volk*. The audience has no sense of a congregational "we," only of a divided "them" and an isolated "him." Moses stands alone at the beginning, and at the end. In fact, Adorno also misrepresents the concept of individual genius, as it applies to both Schoenberg and the Moses of the opera: "The belief in genius, that metaphysical transfiguration of bourgeois individualism, allows no doubt that everything is open to the great ones at any moment, and that they can constantly achieve the greatest things."[15] But Adorno forgets that Schoenberg had portrayed the genius as doomed to a cycle of rejection and failure in *Die glückliche Hand* (1910–13), which Michael Mäckelmann calls a "*conceptual* precursor" of *Moses und Aron*.[16] The opera likewise narrates the opposite of what Adorno claims: the great Moses fails. The opera is not a sacred work; it is a tragedy – for Moses, and for Aron and the *Volk*. Schoenberg also failed, since he was unable to complete Act III, although many agree that Acts I and II together constitute a compelling artistic whole.

To be sure, in the ensuing years Schoenberg did write compositions that are unquestionably intended as "sacred" works, either devotional or congregational: *Kol Nidre*, Op. 39 (1938), *Dreimal Tausend Jahre*, Op. 50a (1949), *Psalm 130* (De Profundis), Op. 50b (1950), and his incomplete last work, the *Moderner Psalm*, Op. 50c (1950). The latter bears obvious similarities with the opening scene of *Moses und Aron*, but these also underscore how different is the rest of the opera. The question is not whether Schoenberg held religious beliefs or wrote "sacred" works, but whether *Moses und Aron* is such a work. Moses does articulate Schoenberg's most fundamental religious belief, that the sacred is inexpressible and beyond imagination. But contra Adorno, the opera is a sacred work only in being an extended demonstration of the *impossibility* of conveying the sacred. By thinking Schoenberg to be naive, Adorno himself failed to perceive that Schoenberg made this impossibility the opera's fundamental axiom. To counter Adorno's claim that *Moses und Aron* is sacred art, one need only observe that few audience members will leave a performance with any sense of renewed religious devotion.

The second axis of Adorno's attack on the opera is his claim that its twelve-tone idiom is totalizing and authoritarian in character. But Adorno often ascribes his own grandiose claims to Schoenberg's music, then censures the composer for not heeding them; for example, "Every music that aims at totality, as a simile of the absolute, has its theological dimension, even if it is unaware of it."[17] The idea that the opera's music "aims at totality, as a simile of the absolute" is Adorno's, and does not comport with the composer's perspective (as will be shown later). Adorno prized Schoenberg's earlier Expressionist "atonal" works as authentic artistic reflections of post-Enlightenment modernity, especially for their departure from the obsolete values of tonality. The Expressionist works reflect a late phase of individualistic society: "the spiritual content available at such a stage of consciousness cannot be anything else but that of the individual expressing himself. Hence the definition of Schoenberg's music as extreme expression, which accompanied it to the threshold of the twelve-tone technique."[18]

Schoenberg's own conception of the twelve-tone technique notwithstanding, Adorno viewed it as a regressive ideology of totalization and domination over the compositional material. He claims that because of "the sovereignty that Schoenberg commands over his music" in *Moses und Aron*, "the eruptive, expressive passages become images, metaphors of expression in a double sense. The overall plan . . . domesticates them and renders them inauthentic."[19] But Adorno's own concepts would more cogently argue that the expressive and "eruptive" moments must be authentic precisely by virtue of wrenching themselves from the putative oppressive grip of the system. By typecasting Schoenberg's twelve-tone practice as authoritarian, and as a shift in expressive attitude, Adorno overlooks how the opera narrates a crisis of expression, exemplified in the tragic positions of both Moses and Aron, whose problem is not to represent God, but to communicate the idea of an unrepresentable God.[20] Contra Adorno, the drama – and the music, as we will see later – continually remind us that unrepresentable totalities cannot be illustrated.

Adorno dwells at length on the Second Commandment, which is clearly one of the opera's underlying concerns, but he slights Schoenberg's understanding of it: "The prohibition on graven images [*Bilderverbot*], which Schoenberg heeded as few others, nevertheless extends further than even he imagined."[21] Because the *Bilderverbot* dominates his focus, Adorno cleaves to the idea that the music must be pictorial. He fixates on the visual, repeatedly insisting that the music tries to illustrate the Absolute, and that it naively contravenes the *Bilderverbot*, and "verges on heresy."[22] Preoccupied with images, Adorno asserts what he calls "the pictorial essence [*Bilderwesen*] of the music"[23] and claims that it is "the intractable duty of the music[,] to be an image of the imageless [*Bild des Bilderlosen*]."[24] So preoccupied is Adorno with the pictorial, rather than the sonorous, that he grandly credits Schoenberg with having "actually rendered visible one of the antinomies of art itself."[25] But Adorno's fixation on image rather than sound goes against an aesthetic imperative that Schoenberg had already expressed in 1912: "The assumption that a piece of music must summon up images of one sort or another . . . is as widespread as only the false and banal can be."[26] Aside from the Divine voice emanating from the Burning Bush in the first scene, and again briefly in the fourth scene, there is no place in the opera where the Divine is represented.[27] Jewish law prohibits pronunciation of the Divine Name, but to imagine the holy voice is no heresy. As Bluma Goldstein notes, Jewish tradition grants special immediacy to the auditory, and Deuteronomy 4: 12–15 prohibits visual but not aural representations: "The Lord spoke to you out of the fire; you heard the sound of words but perceived no shape – nothing but a voice . . . therefore, be most careful . . . not to act wickedly and make for yourself a sculptured image in any likeness whatever."[28] The breathtaking vocal/instrumental sonority that Schoenberg conceived and created in the Burning Bush scene is extraordinary precisely because it is so purely – and blindingly – aural and oracular.

The aesthetics of incomprehensibility

The opera's music is not a naive attempt to depict and manifest the ineffable or the Divine. Instead, it exemplifies the Kantian sublime.[29] Its aim is to sound the limits of immanence, of the phenomenal, and of human comprehension. That perspective on the music will now be anchored in some of Schoenberg's own statements.

Schoenberg's religious and aesthetic convictions converge on the notion that inspired insight can sometimes exceed the limits of human perception and understanding, and burst through to the noumenal. Artworks must explore the margins of comprehensibility, in order to stimulate intuition and spirit to higher awareness.

It was noted above that Schoenberg's libretto alters the Old Testament narrative. Already in the 1912 essay "The Relationship to the Text," Schoenberg had noted that "no one doubts that a poet who works with historical material may move with the greatest freedom."[30] Earlier in that essay, Schoenberg describes how opera librettos relate to music – at least for composers who write their own librettos:

> in the case of Wagner it is as follows: the impression of the "essence of the world" *received through music* becomes productive in him and stimulates

him to a poetic rendering [*Nachdichtung*] in the material of another art. But
the events and feelings which appear in this rendering were not contained in
the music, but are merely the material which the poet uses only because
so direct, unpolluted and pure a mode of expression is denied to poetry, an
art still bound to subject-matter.[31]

If this tells us anything about Schoenberg's own approach, then we must
invert Adorno's claim that the music provides "an image of the imageless":
just the opposite, the dramatic action provides a secondary transmutation
of the music, which is the primary creative impulse and the imageless art
par excellence. The characters and events in Schoenberg's opera must be
understood as a visible and comprehensible supplement to the non-verbal
experience and understanding that the music transmits directly in its own
way. But what exactly does Schoenberg's music signify?

Schoenberg begins "The Relationship to the Text" by refuting the
notion – nonetheless belabored by Adorno – that music must conjure
images. He then formulates an axiom, fundamental to his aesthetic canon,
on the relation between music and reason (*Vernunft*):

> There are relatively few people who are capable of understanding, purely in
> terms of music, what music has to say. The assumption that a piece of music
> must summon up images of one sort or another . . . is as widespread as only
> the false and banal can be . . . Even Schopenhauer, who at first says
> something really exhaustive about the essence of music – in his wonderful
> thought, "The composer reveals the inmost essence of the world and utters
> the most profound wisdom in a language which his reason does not
> understand" – even he loses himself later when he tries to translate details of
> this language which reason [*Vernunft*] does not understand into our terms.
> It must, however, be clear to him that in this translation into the terms of
> human language – which is abstraction, reduction to the recognizable – the
> essential [*Wesentlich*], the language of the world, *which ought to remain
> incomprehensible and only perceptible* [*nur fühlbar*], is lost.[32]

Here Schoenberg adopts Schopenhauerian thought, at least to the extent that
"the essential" (*das Wesentlich*) is inaccessible to reason (*Vernunft*). It is at
best *"only perceptible,"* and music is therefore its most direct artistic medium.
It should also remain incomprehensible – at least to human cognition – and
this is a fundamental feature of artworks that must be embraced. Already in
1909 Schoenberg had pronounced: "the artwork is a labyrinth."[33]

In an important letter to Kandinsky from August 19, 1912, Schoenberg
characterizes artworks as puzzles or enigmas that bring us in contact with
the "incomprehensible":

> We must become conscious that there are puzzles [*Rätseln*] around us. And
> we must find the courage to look these puzzles in the eye without timidly

asking about "the solution" [*Lösung*]. It is important that our power to create such puzzles [that is, artworks] mirrors [*nachbildet*] the puzzles with which we are surrounded, so that our soul may endeavor – not to solve them – but to decipher [*dechiffrieren*] them. What we gain thereby should not be the solution, but a new method of coding or decoding [*Chiffrier- oder Dechiffrier-Methode*]. The material, worthless in itself, serves in the creation of new puzzles. For the puzzles are an image [*Abbild*] of the incomprehensible [*Unfaßbaren*]. And imperfect, that is, a human image [*Abbild*]. But if we can only learn from them to consider the incomprehensible [*das Unfaßbare*] as possible, we get nearer to God, because we no longer demand to understand him. Because then we no longer measure him with our intelligence [*Verstand*], criticize him, deny him, because we cannot reduce [*auflösen*] him to that human inadequacy [*Unzulänglichkeit*] which is our clarity.[34]

For Schoenberg, the artwork-*Rätsel* provides an "imperfect, that is, human image" of *das Unfaßbare* (the incomprehensible); it shows *Unfaßbarkeit* (incomprehensibility), and indicates the human inability to grasp the ineffable. Understood in this way, the music in *Moses und Aron* does not contravene the *Bilderverbot*: it does not represent God, but only the associated qualities of *Unfaßbarkeit* and *Unvorstellbarkeit*, and it does so with a *Rätsel*, not a *Bild*. Such an artwork nevertheless brings us "nearer to God" because it shows us the membrane between phenomena and noumena, between immanence and transcendence – a boundary where we can recognize the limits of human reason, realize that what we call "clarity" is merely "inadequacy," and conclude that we must accept a fundamental *Unlösbarkeit* (insolubility, irreducibility) in the artwork and also the higher *geistliche* (spiritual) essence that it signifies. Adorno's assumption that Schoenberg tried to represent the unrepresentable clashes badly with Schoenberg's declared aesthetic position, which aimed instead to enact the human limits of incomprehensibility (*Unfaßbarkeit*) and unrepresentability (*Unvorstellbarkeit*). For Schoenberg, the artwork is the modern, quasi-secular medium for contemplating the *Unfaßbare*, and it supersedes traditional concepts and approaches to the "sacred." Later we will see how Schoenberg adheres to this approach in his twelve-tone idiom, which helps him produce artistic puzzles that enact *Unfaßbarkeit*.

Schoenberg's artistic credo alters radically the relation of the artwork to its public. In a March 1930 essay Schoenberg wrote: "Called upon to say something about my public, I have to confess: I do not believe I have one."[35] Already in February 1928 Schoenberg had noted: "Surely I have said it often enough. I do not believe that the artist creates for others."[36] These remarks totally undermine Adorno's notion of a communal "we" in the opera. The greatest tension in the work is not some contravention of the *Bilderverbot*, but the bold gesture of writing an opera – the most public of musical genres – that puts *Unfaßbarkeit* and *Unvorstellbarkeit* at its very center, and whose narrative and compositional means perform the rupture between the visionary artist and a puzzled, uncomprehending public.

As an "anti-*Parsifal*," Schoenberg's opera destroys the Wagnerian fantasy of redemption – individual or collective. By returning to an earlier stage in religious history, the biblical setting undercuts Wagner's medieval Grail fantasy and the illusions of the bourgeois age to assert a fundamental *Unerlösbarkeit* in the human spiritual condition. In *Moses und Aron* there is no *reine Tor* to reclaim the spear, heal the wound, and give the audience the illusion and catharsis it craves. Instead there is Moses's exhortation to purify thinking ("reinige dein Denken!"), although a *reine Gedanke* (pure idea) will always remain *unvorstellbar, unfaßbar*, inexpressible. The opera is not directed to a public, but at the epistemological limit, at *reine Geist* (pure spirit). Schoenberg gives us no catharsis, makes no concession to the public. He offers *Unlösbarkeit* in place of Wagnerian *Erlösung* (redemption).

The limits of musical immanence

How does Schoenberg's music signify *Unfaßbarkeit*?

In an unpublished manuscript dated July 23, 1927, just eleven days after completing *Der biblische Weg*, Schoenberg describes the ineffable quality of certain ideas:

> For there are thoughts (as I well know) that one can think hundredfold with perfect clarity, but that dissipate [*zerflattern*], often as soon as one wants to articulate them, and always when one wants to write them down. The presentation of a thought is in most cases a reduction to the comprehensible [*Faßliche*]; fewer can be presented than can be thought: even among the comprehensible ones.
>
> But it appears there are ideas that may indeed be thought, but not articulated, not further extended. There appears to be a knowledge [*Wissen*] which remains reserved only for those minds which are chosen for it; a secret knowledge [*Geheimwissenschaft*] that cannot be disseminated; for which our language has no words; that one can think, but cannot – and may not – reproduce [*wiedergeben*]!!³⁷

Schoenberg articulates here a new form of the *Bilderverbot*: what cannot and may not be expressed is not necessarily the traditional notion of the Divine, but is nonetheless a window toward the *Unfaßbare* or *Unvorstellbare*, a glimpse of a hidden knowledge of the noumenal. The secret knowledge described here seems closer to esoteric *gnosis* than to *scientia*; it is experienced by a select few, not acquired through the application of logic and reason. These are also the kind of inexpressible thoughts that motivate Moses's expressions of verbal inadequacy: "Ich kann denken, aber nicht Reden" (I can think, but not express) and "O Wort, du Wort, das mir fehlt" (O word, you word, that fails me). But the capacity Moses lacks is one he could never possess, because transcendental ideas are not commensurable with language. Despite their clarity, they are cognitively unstable and are evaporated by the impulses and mechanisms of expression. They are suspended at the boundary between immanence and transcendence. In other words, they have the quality of musical tones and musical ideas – which decay and dissipate once sounded, can be produced in the musical imagination and retained by force of concentration, even notated, but their meaning cannot be fully captured by language or reason.

The music of *Moses und Aron* enacts in aural experience these limits of non-verbal thinking and perception. The twelve-tone idiom is ideally suited for this task, *pace* Adorno's claims about its totalizing tendencies, because it creates tone-configurations that probe the limits of musical cognition and memory. Schoenberg's music does not *communicate the content* of the kinds of thoughts described above; but as a labyrinth or puzzle, the musical artwork does *enact the experience* of such a thought, as a blend of clarity, irreducibility, and incomprehensibility. Two short excerpts from the opera will indicate how the music does this.

Moses's first words in the opera (mm. 8–11) address the Divine presence emanating from the Burning Bush by listing God's essential properties: "Einziger, ewiger, allgegenwärtiger, unsichtbarer, und unvorstellbarer Gott!" (Unique, eternal, omnipresent, invisible, and unrepresentable God!). These words are accompanied by instrumental music that seems to suspend the flow of time (see Example 13.1a). The music preceding and following this critical passage uses the row forms labeled **P** and **I9(P)** on Example 13.1b, subdivided into the segments enclosed in boxes. These row forms are hexachordally combinatorial, as is Schoenberg's normal twelve-tone practice.[38] But for the list of Divine attributes, Schoenberg deploys row forms that are *not* hexachordally combinatorial, **I10(P)** and **T10(P)**, shown on Example 13.1c. In mm. 8–10, the sonic frame for Moses's declamation is given by four solo instruments playing six tetrachords, interrupted by fermatas. Boxes and circled numbers on Example 13.1c indicate how the tetrachords are derived from the two row forms. Bold type highlights the pitch classes (one per tetrachord) played by the English horn, as the highest voice in each chord. These declaim the six-note motive D–E flat–D flat–G–F–F sharp, which is partly concealed in the dark and mysterious chords, but which is a prominent leitmotiv in the

Example 13.1a Schoenberg, *Moses und Aron*, mm. 8–11

Example 13.1b Combinatorial row forms **P** and **I9(P)**, as segmented in mm. 1–7 and 11–15
cf. English Horn, mm. 8–10

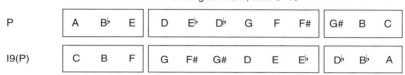

Example 13.1c Row forms **I10(P)** and **T10(P)** as segmented in mm. 8–10

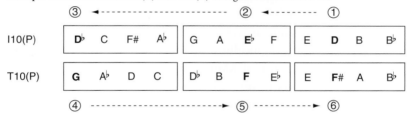

surrounding measures and throughout the opera; its original derivation from row form **P** is indicated on Example 13.1b.[39]

These features have been widely recognized, but the unusual row pairing in mm. 8–10 has puzzled analysts.[40] This passage constitutes a compact musical labyrinth in several ways. Horizontal brackets beneath Example 13.1a link inversionally related chords, indicating a palindrome under the relevant inversion operation, to show that the music is its own mirror image in both its temporal and its harmonic-intervallic dimensions (in tandem). The English horn motive signals this mirroring by projecting an interval palindrome, <+1,−2,+6,−2,+1>, but the other instrumental lines are not palindromic individually. The enigmatic, labyrinthine quality of this music arises from its double inward-folding, which figuratively reverses-and-suspends the flow of time and the extension of (musical) space. Michael Cherlin has discussed other inversional palindromes in Act

I, and his two principal examples each "portray a central mystery of the drama"; he notes that palindromes of this type are "esoteric" and difficult to perceive, in part due to "wonderfully Hegelian" aspects of their coming-into-unity.[41] The double reflexivity of the palindromic scheme in mm. 8–10 is almost self-negating, for it neutralizes both temporal immanence and spatial immanence. This musical *Rätsel* makes the listener experience *Unfaßbarkeit*, precisely while Moses is acknowledging the *Unvorstellbarkeit* of the Divine. The palindromic design can be partially perceived, but not completely comprehended. The English horn motive gives the listener an inkling, but the timbre and dissonance of the chords otherwise obscure the full extent of the palindrome. Adorno viewed the twelve-tone technique as *ideology*; but for Schoenberg its task was to stimulate aural *ideation*, and to probe the limits of perception and comprehension.

The doctrine in "The Relationship to the Text" suggests that Moses's words here are a "*Nachdichtung*" of this enigmatic music: while the music performs its own *Unfaßbarkeit*, Moses refers in parallel to invisibility and *Unvorstellbarkeit*. But Moses is also naming God, and the musical construction observes a traditional Jewish precaution in this regard. I suspect that Schoenberg's use of tetrachords refers to the *Tetragrammaton*: the manner of writing the holy Name as YHWH, omitting the vowels so that the sacred sonic aspect of the Name – the Divine vowel sound – is not represented graphically and the *Bilderverbot* is not transgressed. The music's tetrachordal *Klangfarbenmelodie* also has a sublime and supernatural vowel quality – created by the unique combination of wind, string, and low brass instruments – and it thereby breathes life into its own manner of manifesting the Divine Name. Moses himself does not pronounce the Name, but Michael Cherlin has noted that the vowel sounds in Moses's list of Divine attributes form a powerful progression, becoming successively longer, darker, and more open; they culminate on the "o" of "Gott," to echo the pure, infinite "O" that emerges from the Burning Bush in mm. 1–3 and 5–7.[42] Even though the instrumental *tetragrammata* intone vowel-like sounds, the music respects the *Bilderverbot* and the traditions that govern writing the Name. Perhaps Adorno sensed all this when he remarked (about Schoenberg's music in general) that "Schoenberg's expressive urge . . . has as its secret model the revelation of the Name,"[43] echoing an earlier essay in which he had written that "what [music] says is as appearance simultaneously determined and concealed. Its idea is the form of the Divine Name. It is demythologized prayer, freed from magical effects; the ever-futile human attempt to name the Name, not to communicate meanings."[44] Schoenberg was apparently aware that he had found the *only* row forms from which he could construct the passage by extracting the six-note motive from the *tetragrammata* of two inversionally palindromic row forms.[45] This explains why he departed from his normal combinatorial procedures for this passage. The passage is both a *Rätsel*, and also a brilliant solution to the problems invoked by the *Bilderverbot*. Evidently, Schoenberg's ability to observe the *Bilderverbot* extended much further than Adorno imagined.[46]

Many passages in the opera are like this – miniature musical puzzle-labyrinths, complete in themselves and yet nothing but hermetic fragments. In mm. 57–8, for instance, Schoenberg creates another short enigmatic musical unit that is effectively described by the words emerging from the Burning Bush, "so vernimmst du meine Stimme aus jedem Ding" (so shall you perceive my voice in all things). (See Example 13.2a.) This passage is derived from a single row form (Example 13.2b), and again

Example 13.2a Schoenberg, *Moses und Aron*, mm. 57–8

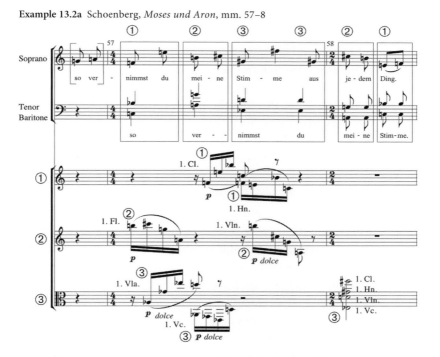

Example 13.2b Row form I2(P) as segmented in mm. 57–8

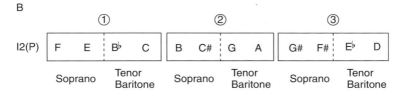

tetrachords are associated with the Divine voice. Example 13.2a uses a short-score format to show how each tetrachord (again labeled by a circled number) appears in the orchestra as an independent instrumental gesture, and is soon echoed with a new contour and instrumental timbre. These instrumental echoes can be heard piecemeal with careful attention, but the total effect is purposefully fleeting and difficult to grasp. Meanwhile, three solo singers project two simple palindromes: each tetrachord is subdivided into dyads, assigned in alternation to the soprano or to the tenor-baritone duet; the soprano (excluding the anacrusis) presents a melodic palindrome (with register slightly varied at the end), while the male voices present a palindrome of simultaneous dyads (with simple rhythmic elaboration). The vocal palindromes are quite easy to notice individually, but harder to perceive in combination, and become nearly inscrutable when surrounded by the fleeting orchestral accompaniment. Moreover, the listener's attention here is actually commanded by the otherworldly *Sprechchor*, which is not shown on the example. The musical construction again signifies the hermetic density of phenomenal immanence in space and time, and takes the listener to the limits of comprehension; the words ironically reinforce the point, for the Divine voice may be omnipresent, but our human capacity to perceive it is limited. It is not expected that the listener will cut through the music's immanent *Unfaßbarkeit*, and apprehend its structures. Such things, as Schoenberg said in "The Relationship to the Text," should remain "incomprehensible and only perceptible."[47] They will nonetheless subconsciously work their mystery on the receptive listener.

The opera's music is effectively a succession of enigmatic and paradoxical shards of musical *Unfaßbarkeit*.[48] The characters, words, and events on stage are a poetic-dramatic rendering of Schoenberg's belief that the margins of comprehensibility are the essential realm of both art and spirit. The fragmentary, enigmatic, and hermetic shards of sounding creation emerge and then dissipate, so concentrated in their layered combination, so replete with immanent tone-relations and self-reflective musical phenomenality, that they immediately reach the limits of aural comprehensibility. The sounds are experienced on the membrane of our eardrums, but their realm is also the tympanum between the phenomenal and the noumenal, between immanence and transcendence. The artwork cannot cross that boundary, but it can sustain the limits of *Unfaßbarkeit* in order to point beyond. *Moses und Aron* transcends Adorno's category of sacred art, and it achieves – in a necessarily fragmentary and immanent way – the sublime.

14 Schoenberg, the Viennese-Jewish experience and its aftermath

STEVEN J. CAHN

This chapter considers what made Arnold Schoenberg's participation in the culture of the Austro-German world possible, from the perspectives of a German-Jewish historical context and a theory of Viennese-Jewish identity. Taking a broad perspective requires a focus on matters larger than the individual. A simple reduction of Schoenberg's hyphenated Jewish identity to matters of personal belief, individual choice, or a facet of artistic expression would forgo too many questions that encompass the concerns of a people: a family history, a sacred text and law, a drive to be granted rights and recognized as fully human, an attempt to thrive in the majority culture, a desperation not to suffer annihilation, an opportunity to raise a family in a new country, a hope to help build a new nation. By virtue of their magnitude and urgency, these questions, vital to Schoenberg, help to place his work in a fitting context.

In a recent history of the German people, there is no mention of Schoenberg's name.[1] The names that do appear, Bach, Handel, Haydn, Mozart, Beethoven, and Wagner, embody the narrative of a people who from a foundation resting on 200 years of German tradition (J. S. Bach), turned toward Enlightenment (Haydn and Mozart), a circumspect embrace of Utopianism (Beethoven), and an uneasy pairing of iconoclasm and German purity (Wagner). Though Schoenberg could have occupied a loosely defined space within the world of culture, as do Freud and Einstein, the fictional Adrian Leverkühn, the tragic protagonist of Thomas Mann's *Doktor Faustus*, displaces Schoenberg in this narrative. Leverkühn's pact with the devil not only brought him the secrets of Schoenberg's intellectual property – the method of composition with twelve tones related one to another – but the death of a beloved nephew and a fatal case of neurosyphilis. If one wishes to reflect the history of the German people through its composers, Leverkühn represents the catastrophic descent into Nazism. Schoenberg as a composer who did not belong to this people cannot assume an apt historical function.

By contrast, in a four-volume history of German Jewry in modern times, Schoenberg's name occurs in three of the four volumes.[2] He occupies an important cultural space among German-Jewish artists and intellectuals. In the context of that history, the basic preconditions for his participation in German culture are set forth, and these begin with laws that permitted Jews to live in cities, and encouraged their subsequent migration to Central Europe's capitals.

Steps toward emancipation (1852–72): a tale of two fourteen-year-olds

In 1852, embarking early in a wave of Jewish migration in the aftermath of the Revolution of 1848 – an event that incited anti-Jewish rioting while it advanced the cause of Jewish emancipation – the fourteen-year-old Samuel Schönberg left home to become "an apprentice in a business."[3] He headed westward through the culturally Slovak region of the Hungarian Kingdom, from his native Szécsény to Bratislava, Hungary's former seat of government, and made his way by steamboat along the Danube to the imperial city – Vienna.[4] His journey is reminiscent of that of another fourteen-year-old who left home in 1743, decades before the 1812 edict that emancipated the Jews of Prussia, and made his way northward from Dessau to Berlin – over 100 kilometers – on foot.

Moses Mendelssohn left Dessau to continue rabbinical studies in Berlin, where he would become both a leading philosopher of the Enlightenment and a successful businessman. His example of self-formation through education (*Bildung*) made him an influential figure upon subsequent generations of German Jews; the intellectual aspirations in philosophy, science, literature, and music of the young Arnold's Jewish cohort evince the transmission of Mendelssohn's example. Berlin, a city of Slavs and Germans, was highly restrictive to Jews. In 1750, when Mendelssohn, a Jew of limited means, turned twenty-one, he became subject to the stringent terms of the new Revised General Code enacted that year.[5] Harsh regulations and punishing taxes diminished his opportunities in business and marriage while augmenting his financial woes with punishing taxes. This byzantine Code of Frederick II's bureaucrats placed those like Mendelssohn in the precarious Class Five, the category of *unprotected* Jews, a measure that intensified the degree of repression and exploitation inflicted upon those least secure.

One hundred years later, Samuel Schönberg's prospects in Vienna appeared more promising. After the Revolution of 1848, which pressed for equal rights, emancipation, and freedom of religion, residency restrictions for Jews in Vienna had been relaxed. Compared to Mendelssohn's risk of expulsion, Samuel Schönberg's chances were decidedly less and his choice of occupation somewhat greater. From an economic standstill, Vienna, by then a railway hub, lurched into commercial activity and seethed with newly arrived small businesses. But few prospered amid the fierce competition; moreover, equality and rights for Vienna's Jews were still not settled issues. In governmental acts of 1851 and 1853, rights granted to Jews in 1848–49 were revoked, and restrictions concerning property ownership and professional opportunities were reinstated.[6] Further liberalization would await a new constitution in 1867.

If the matter of cementing Vienna's liberal aspirations was still over a decade off, in the intervening century Jewish religious practice in some communities had undergone significant liberalization. While Moses Mendelssohn was learned in Jewish law and adhered to Jewish observance, Samuel Schönberg, by all accounts a "freethinker," sympathized with the attitudes of Jewish reform; he no longer felt obligated to many of the practices of traditional Jewish observance.[7] By 1871 a majority of German Jews shared this attitude.[8]

Ten years younger than Samuel Schönberg, Arnold's mother Pauline Nachod arrived in Vienna from Prague as a child with her parents and five siblings. In 1852 Prague, in both number and percentage, had a larger Jewish population than Vienna, though in the coming decades Vienna's Jewish population would exceed Prague's. Distantly descended from an illustrious ancestry, Rabbi Judah Löw (the Maharal of Prague, 1525–1609) and a line of synagogue cantors, Pauline Nachod's family tree was musical and traditional. Her family had long been associated with the *Altneushul*, a synagogue that has stood in Prague since the thirteenth century. Why Josef Gabriel and Karoline (née Jontof-Hutter) Nachod, after the birth in 1853 of their youngest child, Anna, uprooted their family to move to Vienna is a matter for speculation. One motivation may have been to escape anti-Jewish violence that broke out before Easter 1848 and led to attacks against Jewish shops, while another may have been the apparent upswing in Vienna's economy. As Jews migrated from the country to the city, Prague's Jewish population grew, but not as fast as Vienna's.

In 1852, serving a community scarcely 6,000 strong, less than one percent of the Viennese population, the Israelitische Kultusgemeinde (IKG) of Vienna was founded after imperial recognition of Vienna's Jewish community in 1849 and ratification of the Provisional Community Decree in 1852.[9] With oversight of Jewish schools and the power to tax community members directly, the IKG managed the community's life-cycle needs as a religious communal welfare organization, not a political one. Newly operational when Samuel Schönberg arrived and the Nachod family settled, the IKG served this mid-century ripple of immigration, which in the coming decades would flow in waves from the eastern backwaters of the empire into Vienna. By 1900 the Jewish population would surpass 146,000, representing 8.7 percent of the Viennese population.

Table 14.1 *Conversions in Schoenberg's family*

Name/birth date/relation to AS/godfather	Marries	Apostasy	Age	Conversion
Schönberg, Arnold, 09/13/1874, "Franz Walter" (added), Walter Pieau (?)	Mathilde 10/18/1901	03/02/1898	24	3/25/1898
Kramer, Emil Wilhelm, 01/06/1872, brother-in-law, A. F. W. Schönberg	Ottilie 1899	11/02/1900	29	1/06/1901
Schönberg, Ottilie, 06/09/1876, sister, A. F. W. Schönberg	Emil Kramer 1899	11/23/1900	25	1/06/1901
Zemlinsky, Mathilde, 09/07/1877 Schoenberg's wife, H. Kleinfeld, *Küster*	Arnold 10/18/1901	10/11/1901	24	10/18/1901
Zemlinsky, Alexander, 10/24/1871, brother-in-law, A. F. W. Schönberg	Ida Guttmann 1907	3/29/1899	36	6/11/1907
Guttmann, Ida, 06/26/1880, sister-in-law, A. F. W. Schönberg	Alexander 1907	5/10/1907	27	6/11/1907

In September 1874 the birth of "Arnold Schönberg" would be entered in the IKG's register with the infant's Hebrew name written אברהם (*Avraham*). Likewise, twenty-three years later Schoenberg's separation from the community and release from its financial obligations were recorded by the IKG on March 2, 1898. His apostasy was followed by his conversion to Protestantism, March 25, 1898, when he received a third name, "Arnold Walter Franz Schönberg." Years later in Paris on July 24, 1933, a new spelling, "Arnold Schoenberg," would be introduced in the improvised document for his reentry into the Jewish community. This document would serve as a proxy in effect restoring his name to the IKG roster and reestablishing his Jewish identity on a communal basis while distancing him from the German-speaking world and nullifying the "Walter Franz." Arnold Schoenberg amounted to a fourth name, the one he would soon take to America, his next yet unknown destination. The gravestone in Vienna's *Zentralfriedhof* reverts to the German "Arnold Schönberg."

For Schoenberg and his family, apostasy and Protestant conversion appear to have been tied to family, marriage, and assimilation.[10] Indeed, the date of Mathilde's conversion is the date of her wedding to Schoenberg. The only conversions in which Schoenberg played a role involved his sister's and his wife's families (see Table 14.1). Though the total number of Jews in Schoenberg's age group who converted was small, the percentage of Jews converting reached its peak around 1898.[11] Among the well-known apostates of this period are the composer and conductor Gustav Mahler, the journalist and critic Karl Kraus, and the artist Richard Gerstl; each had ties to Schoenberg, but none had a comparable situation: Mahler was older and conversion was required to direct the Vienna State Opera; Kraus, Schoenberg's contemporary, was wealthier and antithetical to the Zionist movement led by Theodor Herzl; Gerstl was from an intermarried family. There is no generalizing about the individual motivations for renouncing Judaism and decision about conversion.[12] But in light of the heightened anti-Semitism of the time, the Schoenberg family and this limited group from his generation became what had been rare in the Vienna of their parent's day: they became *baptized Jews*. This is a term used advisedly to indicate that despite conversion they were still seen as Jews, and would be vulnerable to a new ideological and racist upsurge in anti-Semitism.[13]

When Samuel Schönberg and Pauline Nachod married on March 17, 1872, it was still "a hopeful moment."[14] Since 1867, when the Jews of Vienna achieved equality and fundamental goals of emancipation were realized, a period of stability seemed at hand, especially since Vienna had not yielded to its penchant for granting rights to Jews and then rescinding them. But the underpinnings of Jewish practice, identity, and communal life in Vienna had also been shifting in profound ways for over two decades. Various kinds of change would continue to affect all aspects of Jewish identity as Schoenberg and his cohort reached adulthood.

First, Jews in modern Europe had come to be defined narrowly in terms of personal religious belief rather than collectively (for example, as a nation without a land).[15] On this narrow criterion, derived from Christianity, adherence to a romantic theology attained preeminence as a dimension of personal identity. It was a criterion for *belonging* imposed upon Judaism and alien to it.

Second, by the close of the nineteenth century, after decades invested in assimilating German culture, Jews would come to identify as imperial subjects with respect to national allegiance, Germans with respect to culture, and Jews with respect to ethnic identity and religion.[16] This was different from their past status as members of Jewish communities residing in German-speaking lands. To manage the transition from communal identity vis-à-vis the state to personal identity, many of Samuel and Pauline's generation had embraced assimilation as the proper direction for their children. In 1934 Schoenberg would regard their certitude in assimilation as "a replacement for messianic belief."[17] Assimilation created a vacuum in Jewish education and affected the connection of Jewish youth to Jewish community. Between 1917 and 1934 Schoenberg would grow critical of its effects.

Third, as Michael Meyer observes, the ethical message of the Hebrew prophets had largely displaced Jewish ritual law for a majority of German Jews as their religious focal point: "ethical monotheism had become the foundation of their Jewishness."[18] Nuria Schoenberg-Nono recalls that the Schoenbergs taught their children that a good person holds to ethical conduct and belief in one God. This foundation in *ethical monotheism* was a pillar of faith for his three families: the Jewish family in which he was raised, the Protestant family with Mathilde (née Zemlinsky) of Jewish ancestry, and the Catholic family with Gertrud (née Kolisch), a Catholic of Jewish ancestry (the three children of this marriage were raised Catholic as a precondition of the marriage).

Fourth, in 1879 a corrosive racial anti-Semitism gained a foothold in the German-speaking world marked by the publication of a malicious book by Wilhelm Marr, *The Victory of Judaism Over Germanicism*. Racial anti-Semitism derived from French works by Count de Gobineau and Joseph-Ernest Renan would be infused into the culture, undermining the recognition of long-awaited and hard-won rights.[19]

Fifth, in 1896 Theodor Herzl, whose life would make a strong impression on Schoenberg, published *Die Judenstaat*; Zionism, the Jewish national cause, would take hold in Vienna.

Ultimately, the "gravest challenge" to "the German-speaking Jews of Austria" would follow in the wake of World War I when the monarchy would collapse.[20] But this was in the offing. At a moment when the promise of the 1852–72 period seemed to assure a brighter future for a young Jewish family, Samuel and Pauline Schönberg set up their home in the Leopoldstadt, Vienna's Second District, the site of seventeenth-century Vienna's Jewish ghetto. Situated in the mainstream of Jewish life, in what was and is again today Jewish Vienna, Arnold Schoenberg was born, the second day of Rosh Hashanah, September 13, 1874.

On this Viennese-Jewish background, Schoenberg not only becomes an indispensable figure for modern German-Jewish history, but the contexts and concepts of modern German-Jewish history become indispensable for Schoenberg. The view taken here is that the research program of modern German-Jewish history – identity, emancipation, anti-Semitism, Judaism, Jewish apostasy, and Jewish philosophy – helps to delineate these factors in Schoenberg's Jewish identity and clarifies their impact upon Schoenberg's artistic enterprise. Moreover, as a theory of specifically Viennese-Jewish identity, the concept of tripartite identity treats the cultural, political, and ethnic-religious as autonomous spheres; their shifting entanglements define the case of Arnold Schoenberg.[21]

Bildung and "tripartite" identity

In Vienna, where emancipation arrived decades after its launch in Berlin, Jews aspired to reenact what had occurred following the Emancipation Edict of 1812. Amos Elon describes the second generation in Berlin as one that attained its status through success in commerce and its pursuit of

Kultur. Since their father's hard-won *exceptional* status, which superseded his *unprotected* status, did not extend to them, the young Mendelssohns were on their own making a place in society:

> In the eyes of the young, the key to integration was through the cult of
> *Bildung,* as defined in Goethe's novel *Wilhelm Meister*: the refinement of the
> individual self and character in keeping with the ideals of the
> Enlightenment. Even as they remained Jews, *Bildung* and *Kultur* would
> make them 100 percent German.[22]

Wilhelm von Humboldt, Prussian Minister of Education (1809), founder of the University of Berlin (1810), and frequent visitor to the Jewish salons of Berlin, understood *Bildung* as the path to emancipation and full citizenship leading from Judaism through Protestantism, ultimately to secular humanism.[23] Jews would not be emancipated as Jews per se, but as individuals who would shed their Judaism over time. This would occur not through the embrace of Christian dogma, but by "accepting Christianity as the historical and cultural agency that had molded their intellectual and moral life."[24] Thus *Bildung* required inhabiting and learning one's way around a secular world of culture premised in emphatically Christian terms. *Bildung* was a single yet vital mode of assimilation.

Schoenberg's pursuit of *Bildung* occurred through his youthful, amateur participation in the Polyhymnia Society and his friendships within a better-educated, almost exclusively Jewish cohort. *Bildung* led them through the avenues of music as well as art, literature, philosophy, science, politics, and religion. The spread and persistence of this "cult" (or secular religion) reached Schoenberg and his cohort through its narrow transmission via musical channels. Earlier Jewish-born Berlin musicians such as Giacomo Meyerbeer and Felix Mendelssohn were its representatives par excellence. Adolph Bernhard Marx made *Bildung* and its assumption of the unique potential of each individual fundamental to his theory of musical form.[25] *Bildung* achieved wide transmission from Berlin's precariously positioned parvenus to Vienna's aspiring bourgeoisie.

However, in the 1890s becoming "100 percent German" was not the categorical imperative in multinational, multiethnic Austria that it was in Germany. On Rozenblit's theory of Jewish identity in Habsburg Austria, Jews avowed a "tripartite identity," retaining their attachment to Jewish ethnicity while declaring loyalty to the Emperor and adopting the prevailing German culture.[26] This model is apt for the Schoenberg family. On account of his father's place of birth in a Slovak region of Hungary, Schoenberg was a Hungarian subject – he was called up for military service as such – and culturally Slovak.[27] In his relationship to the state, he was not recognized as a German, but would be culturally assimilated as Viennese. Schoenberg's ethnic-religious Jewish identity, even free of the gravitational pull of the IKG, would have a life of its own without conflict imposed by national allegiance, official state religion, or culture. It would continue in Berlin, where *Der biblische Weg* would be completed, and in America, where the Fourth Quartet, Op. 37 (1936) would be composed swiftly during the long gestation of "A Four-Point Program for Jewry" (1933–38), a singularly prescient document foreseeing the Holocaust.

Given the independence of the three tracks of tripartite identity – national, cultural, ethnic – two questions vis-à-vis tripartite identity persist: first, did Schoenberg's push toward cultural assimilation necessarily entail a pull away from ethnic-religious identity? While there is fierce tension, Jewish sources inform Schoenberg's critique of Vienna. Second, were the creative interactions between Schoenberg's autonomous affiliations with German culture and Jewish ethnicity continuous or sporadic? The quality of these interactions could be harmonious, as in the visionary settings of Rilke in the Orchestral Songs, Op. 22 (1916), or in tension.[28]

Biblical sources as cultural and political critique

In Schoenberg's writings, cultural and ethnic affiliations were mutually refracted in ongoing critical dialogue that reached a point of crisis in 1933–34. As early as 1909, when Schoenberg condemned the Viennese cultural milieu, he did so using language not inherent to German high culture. The young Schoenberg's pursuit of *Bildung* occurred in an environment less than classically German. By attending *Realschule*, a junior high school designed for the majority of students, and not the *Gymnasium*, which admitted children who were elite academically, from wealthy families and occasionally from poor Jewish families, Schoenberg's education in German high culture missed a key component. As William Kangas notes, Schoenberg's *Realschule* curriculum lacked the foundations in Greek and Roman "mythos" indispensable to German high culture.[29] In lieu of studies in Greek and Roman civilizations, the Hebrew Bible became Schoenberg's touchstone. Jewish civilization, not Greek or Roman, is Schoenberg's historical frame of reference. Allusion to the Hebrew Bible occurs throughout Schoenberg's writings; discussion of two instances must suffice.[30]

Writing in 1909, Schoenberg compares Vienna to Sodom and Gomorrah. Schoenberg, unlike his namesake Abraham, however, laments the few righteous individuals for whose sake Vienna is spared:

> So it would almost be better were there not the few "decent men." Were there not these few righteous men in Sodom and Gomorrah, perhaps God would

repent of his ways, become angry and make it possible for a new culture to arise out of the desert salt. This is a feeble hope.[31]

This is not a homily, but an ironic commentary on Genesis 18: 17–33, a scene of bargaining, itself ironic. It not only demonstrates Schoenberg's conversance with the Hebrew Bible, but something more. The allusion reveals his affinity for Abraham's sense of morality epitomized by Abraham's questions to God: "Will you really sweep away the innocent along with the guilty? . . . The judge of all the earth – will he not do what is just?"[32] The self-centered individual would not pose such questions, but the ethical monotheist would. Contending with this biblical passage, Schoenberg engages the ethical monotheistic outlook of prophetic Judaism and maps the Viennese world around him into the biblical context of Sodom and Gomorrah. Schoenberg lays irony and ethics edge to edge, a juxtaposition that ignites *the torch* whose incendiary and illuminating effects could "make it possible for a new culture to arise." To lament the righteous ten on whose account a corrupt Vienna is not only sustained, but goes unpunished as it grows ever more depraved, is a way to rebuke a city that causes Schoenberg to lament God's compassion.

Schoenberg's rhetoric of rebuke, born of this volatile mixture of the ethical and the ironical, is akin to that of Karl Kraus, whose journal *Die Fackel* (The Torch) Schoenberg read devotedly and contributed to occasionally.[33] For Schoenberg, the ironic rhetoric of rebuke, an attitude adapted from the tone of prophetic Judaism, would be integral to several works that do not allude to or quote biblical text. A passage from the text of *Die Jakobsleiter* (1915) illustrates the point. The One Who Is Called proclaims:

> I sought beauty. To it I sacrificed everything: no aim was sacrosanct, no means clear-cut . . . I looked into brightness everywhere . . . I saw only my sun, was aware only of the rhythm of beauty.

The Angel Gabriel supplies the rebuke:

> Nevertheless you are self-satisfied: your idol grants you fulfillment before you, like those who seek, have tasted the torments of longing. Self-sufficiency keeps you warm. Heathen, you have beheld nothing.[34]

One work that does use biblical text to express both critique and faith, in much the spirit as the passage alluded to from Genesis, is *A Survivor from Warsaw*. It epitomizes the "entanglement" between Jew and German that finds expression in an "oratorical moment" of extreme concision.[35] In the text of the *Sh'ma Yisroel*,[36] instructions to hear, to affirm (the Oneness of God), to love, to teach, and to rise repudiate each dehumanizing action taken by the Nazi soldiers against the Jews recounted in the Narrator's text: to roust them (mm. 25–42), beat them (mm. 43–61), count them (mm. 62–79), and deliver them to the gas chamber (mm. 69–79, 97–9).[37] Here the critique of fascism is presented in juxtaposition to a biblical text whose significance is not merely symbolic, but whose meaning is vital given its context in the work: the *Sh'ma* is recited for its own sake as a Jewish response to this reality, not because it promises a reward for suffering. The *Sh'ma*, a startling interruption in the narrative, is itself interrupted on the word *uvekumecho* (and when you rise). Schoenberg's pattern of row transformations leads inexorably from the choral *Sh'ma* to the return of the martial fanfare of the Nazi soldiers at its original transposition level. The ending's orchestral bombast, epitomized by the return of the trumpets, belongs not to the power of the *Sh'ma*, but to the military power on the verge of annihilating the defenseless contingent. Hardly a triumphant conclusion, it indicates, with irony on their attempt to rise, the imminent moment of the Jews' annihilation on which the survivor's memory shuts down and the extermination goes undepicted. *A Survivor from Warsaw* is a culminating work during a lifetime of Schoenberg's contending with anti-Semitism.

Bildung and anti-semitism

There is deep-seated anger in Schoenberg's 1909 rebuke of Vienna, the city in which his artistic personality was formed. Fueled by issues of cultural politics, sexual mores, and anti-Semitism, his anger is not counterbalanced with nostalgic writing about the Vienna of his youth. And if there is one city about which people wax nostalgic, it is Vienna. Schoenberg also refrains from writing with candor about his personal experience of Vienna's anti-Semitism. Moshe Lazar notes that during 1910–11 there is an absence of remarks from Schoenberg that address anti-Semitic attacks leveled against him and against Jews in general, including the 1911 Beilis blood-libel case.[38] Schoenberg does not write an essay about the humiliating experience of his family's 1921 vacation on the Mattsee[39] from which they were expelled as non-Aryans; he makes little more than ironic use of it in a note to Alban Berg:

> it got very ugly in Mattsee. The people there seemed to despise me as much as if they knew my music. Nothing happened to us beyond that.[40]

There may have been early negative impressions and humiliating experiences from his upbringing in Vienna that went unreported, but not unremembered.

This dearth of early anecdote forces H. H. Stuckenschmidt in his biography of Schoenberg to improvise cautiously about the early years.

Schoenberg completed no autobiography comparable to Bruno Walter's or Artur Schnabel's. Both authors recount their adventures in *Bildung* and place themselves squarely in the German-Jewish milieu. Gershom Scholem would assign those like Schoenberg, Walter, and Schnabel to the "broad Jewish liberal middle class" who "adhered to the monotheistic belief and to a puritanical prophetic ethic that still observed High Holidays, Sabbath eve, Seder, and memorial anniversaries."[41]

Schoenberg's sketch for the third movement of his Jewish Program Symphony dated February 9, 1937 and entitled "The Sacred Feasts and Costumes," contains references to Bar Mitzvah and reading from the Torah, the Passover Seder, Purim, Yom Kippur, and Chanukah. These references and the musical content may hint at Jewishly familiar touchstones from Schoenberg's growing up. The confrontational titles of the other three movements – 1. "Predominance provokes envy"; 2. a) "What they think about us," b) "What we think about them," c) "conclusion"; 4. "The day will come" – suggest the experience of a harsher reality and a desire to make a clean break from assimilationism and political ties to the German world.

Karl Popper, the philosopher, came from the kind of Viennese-Jewish family that in Scholem's words attempted to make "a clean break" and convert to Protestantism. From his perspective in the well-to-do First District, Popper offers this assessment:

> I believe that Austria before the First World War, and even Germany, were treating the Jews well. They were given almost all rights, although there were some barriers established by tradition, especially in the army ... although Jews, and people of Jewish origin, were equal before the law, they were not treated as equals in every respect. Yet I believe that the Jews were treated as well as one could reasonably expect.[42]

Artur Schnabel, the pianist and composer, was raised in Vienna under harder material circumstances – closer to Schoenberg's than to Popper's. Concerning Vienna's anti-Semitic mayor, Dr. Karl Lueger, about whom Schoenberg is virtually silent, Schnabel has an unfortunate episode to recount. Schoenberg's experience with the Lueger regime was mixed. In 1903 Lueger helped Schoenberg by authorizing an annual pension for him. But in 1911 the Christian Socialists, the political heirs of Lueger, interfered with Schoenberg's chances of gaining a professorship. Schnabel, without animus, recalls the effects of Lueger's anti-Semitism:

> Encouraged by Lueger, it was a favorite sport of patriotic male adolescents to bully and beat, with a jolly brutality, children whom they thought to be Jewish. I was molested only once, and I am not sure whether the motive for the attack was Austrianism or mere drunkenness on the part of a few lads. Though a very happy child in general those days, I learned the meaning of fear.[43]

This incident probably occurred after 1895 when Lueger first became mayor; Schnabel would have been about fourteen. Schnabel does not make too much of this episode which darkens an otherwise optimistic account of self-formation and growing mastery of German culture. In all likelihood, Schoenberg suffered similarly to Schnabel. When Schoenberg writes that anti-Semites made their argument "*durch die Faust*" (by beating it into us), it is hard not to take Schoenberg at his word.[44]

Bildung and anti-Semitism relate tortuously. *Bildung* anathematized anti-Semitism and fostered a German-Jewish symbiosis, thus serving as a valid basis for German-Jewish identity, yet *Bildung* also contained a latent anti-Judaism that sought to emancipate Jews not only from degradation and persecution, but from Judaism itself. The emergence of racial anti-Semitism adds an additional dimension to the formation of identity.

Contending with racism: relations with Richard Dehmel and Richard Gerstl

Insight into the question of anti-Semitic racism can be gained from a brief look at the artistic relationships Schoenberg maintained with the poet Richard Dehmel and the painter Richard Gerstl. Both influenced Schoenberg. Dehmel's influence is evident in Schoenberg's song settings as well as the string sextet setting of *Verklärte Nacht*. Gerstl's influence, evident from 1908, exerts itself when Schoenberg devoted himself to painting with the hope of a supplemental career as a portraitist. These relationships, which should be understandable within the aims of *Bildung*, take Schoenberg outside *Bildung's* proper domain. "Jewishness," as opposed to "Judaism," becomes the pressing issue of anti-Semitic racism that lurks in the question: can Jewishness be overcome?

In 1908 Richard Dehmel, famous as the *poet of the young*, published the essay "Culture and Race," a fictitious dialogue between a German poet, "free of any *Rassedogma*," and a Jewish artist from Berlin. The poet, in his conclusion, argues that:

> talent is not the product of any one race. As for culture, its highest achievements would be impossible without the mixing of different races, since complicated temperaments which feel the need to express the contrasts and conflicts deriving from their personal identities can only evolve out of mixed blood origins . . . environment rather than race [is] the determinant of cultural forms.[45]

Liberal attitudes toward race like Dehmel's could excite Schoenberg's enthusiasm. Dehmel's liberality would only have encouraged Schoenberg to propose collaboration in 1912 on a wide-ranging work in which modern man regains religion:

> for a long time I have been wanting to write an oratorio on the following subject: modern man, having passed through materialism, socialism and anarchy and, despite having been an atheist, still having in him some residue of ancient faith (in the form of superstition), wrestles with God and finally succeeds in finding God and becoming religious. Learning to pray! . . . But I could never shake off the thought of "Modern Man's Prayer," and I often thought: If only Dehmel . . .[46]

However, after World War I, Schoenberg's engagement with the poet seems to end for good just as Dehmel's attitude toward Jews changes. In 1919 Dehmel composed the manuscript "Einfluss des jüdischen Volkstums auf das Deutsche" (Influence of Jewish Customs on the German). According to this postwar manuscript, Dehmel perceives *mixed culture* as a "danger" and regards Jews as having "too much influence."[47] This was a line that in Schoenberg's view "nationalistic Germans," paragons of *Bildung*, such as Richard Strauss, Hans Pfitzner, and Wilhelm Fürtwangler, did not cross. Without subscribing to racist anti-Semitism, they could "consider everything German as superior" and have "a small anti-Semitic tarnish," but Schoenberg did not identify them with racial anti-Semitism and Nazism.[48]

Richard Gerstl, called the Austrian Van Gogh, came from a Jewish family in flux: his father was born Jewish, his mother converted to Judaism from Roman Catholicism. By 1898 Gerstl converted to Roman Catholicism. His mother would eventually be accepted back to the church and his father would convert to Roman Catholicism in 1904. According to Gemma Blackshaw, from 1905 to 1910, when the Christ image was iconic for young male artists, Gerstl and Schoenberg explored the use of this icon for the expression of conflicted Jewish identity.[49] For them the Christ image, without explicit consideration of any question of Jewish race, symbolized both "socio-cultural exclusion and belonging." Blackshaw understands Schoenberg's series of painted gazes as following Gerstl's emulation of the sudarium, the cloth used by St. Veronica to wipe the sweat from the face of Jesus that then became imprinted with the image of Jesus; Schoenberg invests these images with an intensely focused and colored gaze. Gerstl, on Blackshaw's view, was engaged in testing the possibility of identifying with Christ as the "ideal of overcoming Judaism," and in following this path suggested by Otto Weininger, of overcoming *Jewishness* as well. Blackshaw reads the final laughing self-portrait as Gerstl's last word on the folly of his Jewish-Christ enterprise. Schoenberg painted two very different "Visions of Christ." In general, he concerned himself more with grotesquerie and satire. According to

Schoenberg's Viennese-American pupil Richard Hoffmann, Schoenberg's many self-portraits were largely to hone his skill at portraiture. Blackshaw's point is that the interpretation of Gerstl's images requires consideration of Jewish identity, which applies to the interpretation of Schoenberg's art as well.

Theories of Schoenberg: accounting for the Jewish work of the American years

The majority of Schoenberg's Jewish-themed compositions and writings originate after 1933 in America (see Table 14.2).[50] Few are performed. And while they are not the works on which Schoenberg's reputation rests, they are provocative. Commentators have tried to integrate these final works into the sweep of religious interest that permeates Schoenberg's work. Peter Gradenwitz proposes a thesis characteristic of German histor-iography: "Schoenberg's inner religious development seems to have been dictated almost independently of his formal confession."[51] "Inner reli-gious development" does not insist upon synchrony between formal religious confession and belief while it suggests aims and purposes (telos) that will ultimately converge with Schoenberg's formal confession. This is pleasing in a novelistic sense. In this narrative Schoenberg achieves unity with himself, if not with God. André Neher connects "inner religious development" with the penitential act of *teshuva* (return) and understands Schoenberg's biography to represent in Jewish terms a drama of *teshuva*.[52]

Alexander Ringer theorizes a continuous connection between Schoenberg's music and Jewish symbolism.[53] Thus for him the task of interpreting each work means thinking about underlying Jewish mystical concepts and Jewish musical practice. Steven Schwarzschild places the emphasis on the proximity of Schoenberg's compositional methods, espe-cially twelve-tone serialism, to the Marpurg neo-Kantian philosophy of Hermann Cohen, which amounted to a highly idealistic German-Jewish synthesis and symbiosis.[54] Schwarzschild points to a passage from one of Schoenberg's letters to Kandinsky to show that the creative imagination is just that – creative:

> when the artist reaches the point at which he desires only the expression of inner events and inner scenes in his rhythms and tones, then "the object in painting" has ceased to belong to the reproducing eye.[55]

Consonant with Schwarzschild's view, William Kangas understands Schoenberg to be motivated by a "quest to think through the meaning of music in ethical terms ... music, ethics and Jewish identity existed in a

Table 14.2 *Selected Jewish-themed writings and works by Schoenberg,*
1923–50

Year	Composition/text	Description	Subject	Source/author
1923–26	*Der biblische Weg* (The Biblical Way)	Theatrical play	Political. To possess the land, return to the biblical path.	A. Schoenberg
1930–32	*Moses und Aron*	Opera in 2 acts, complete and Act 3 text	A theological debate unfolds through a series of biblical scenes	Selections from Exodus, from Burning Bush through wanderings and death of Aaron (Act 3).
1933–38	A Four-Point Program for Jewry	Political essay	Fate of European Jewry. "Is there room in the world for almost 7,000,000 people? Are they condemned to doom?"	A. Schoenberg
1934	*Jeder junge Jude* (Every Young Jew)	Political essay	Assimilation as a false messianic hope	A. Schoenberg
1936	Violin Concerto, Op. 36	Finale: Allegro	"Triumphal March for Palestine"	A. Schoenberg
1938	*Kol Nidre*, Op. 39	Jewish liturgical, choral	Jewish mysticism (special light hidden at creation). Repentance. Annulment of vows	Yom Kippur traditional liturgy, modified and enhanced by Rabbi Jacob Sonderling and A. Schoenberg
1945	"Genesis" Prelude, Op. 44	Chorus and orchestra	The Creation evinced through wordless chorus and large orchestra	First verses of Genesis
1947	*A Survivor from Warsaw*, Op. 46	Oratorio. Narrator, men's chorus and orchestra	A Narrator recalls: Nazi soldiers round up Jewish men, who recite part of the *Sh'ma Yisrael* before their deaths	English text by A. Schoenberg, based on various reports, with a portion of the *Sh'ma Yisrael* up to the word *uvekumecho* [and when you rise]
1949	*Israel Exists Again* (fragment)	Chorus and orchestra	"Israel exists again, though invisibly"	A. Schoenberg
1949	*Dreimal tausend Jahre*, Op. 50a	Chorus a cappella	Rebuilding the Temple in Jerusalem	Dagobert Runes
1950	*De Profundis* (Out of the depths) *Mima'amakim* Op. 50b	Psalm for mixed chorus, a cappella	Redemption of Israel from all its iniquities	Book of Psalms, Psalm 130 Composed for the Chemjo Vinaver *Anthology of Jewish Music* (1953)
1950	*Moderner Psalm*, Op. 50c	Speaker, chorus, orchestra	On the necessity of prayer, "and yet I pray . . ."	A. Schoenberg

self-reinforcing structure."[56] Ethics took Schoenberg to Jewish identity, not vice versa.

A theory based on the history presented in this chapter would suggest that the experience of the period from the relative security of the 1870s to the Holocaust had the trajectory spiritually, culturally, and politically of an avalanche. The listener is never safe from this. Schoenberg places before his listeners a precarious scene, where a beleaguered, bewildered, or uncomprehending subject (as soloist or chorus) responds spontaneously to circumstances that resist resolution. The situation, one of life and death without theodicy as a presupposition, speaks to a modern condition, while the context, which may partake of irony and/or tragedy offset by some deep hope, may have an explicit or implicit religious dimension. The expressly religious works are noteworthy for their ability to present a subject's attempt to address the supernal world as a spontaneous response in a moment of crisis. *A Survivor from Warsaw* has already been addressed along these lines. The setting of Psalm 130 (*De Profundis* or *Mima'amakim*), Op. 50b offers a striking example, especially when compared to the setting by Franz Liszt that occurs in *St. Stanislaus* (1886). Liszt erects a cathedral; his setting is pictorial and theatrical, representing the "depths" and depicting the text; it is in every sense a Western setting. Schoenberg's setting is about the people who are using this psalm for prayer: their emotional and mental states, and their desire that Israel be redeemed without knowing when or how. Schoenberg does not try to imitate traditional Jewish prayer, but comes to a similar effect through his own musical language.

Musically, the Psalm and the other religious works shun traditional or ritualistic formulas, and it is from this, in part, that the sense of the spontaneous arises. But it is also this novelty and incongruity in the avoidance of conventional Western musical-religious codes that keep the composer's expression of religious belief and identity in flux.

PART IV

Schoenberg's American years

15 Cadence after thirty-three years: Schoenberg's Second Chamber Symphony, Op. 38

SEVERINE NEFF

In 1939 Arnold Schoenberg resumed work on his Second Chamber Symphony, a composition he had first started thirty-three years earlier. Thus Schoenberg, that quintessential Modernist, was confronted directly with a prototypical issue of contemporary composition: what is the underlying sense of writing tonal music after the atonal and twelve-tone revolutions that he himself initiated and brought to fulfillment? Was the Second Chamber Symphony, far from being a retrogressive exercise in nostalgia as suggested by many Modernist scholars and composers, a step forward for him instead?[1] In what follows, I will discuss ways in which Schoenberg indeed employed hitherto unexplored tonal structures and even alluded to serial procedures. These features are evident in particular in the codas and cadences of each movement, which he composed in 1939, notably the same passages he failed to complete in 1906–08 when he first worked on the piece, or when he returned to it in 1911 and 1916.

Yet, paradoxically, the work's final triad is presented in a virtually identical fashion to that of "Litanei" (Litany), the third movement of the Second String Quartet, Op. 10, composed in 1908.[2] Both works end with an extremely low E flat minor triad swelling in crescendo, only to break off into abrupt silence. Stefan George's poem "Litanei" is a prayer for an end to earthly misery. In 1908 Schoenberg followed his setting of "Litanei" with his first major atonal work – the renowned interpretation of George's "Entrückung" (Transport), which describes the transport of the soul from earthly suffering to transcendent ecstasy.[3] In December 1939, at the onset of World War II, Schoenberg considered ending the Symphony with a third movement set to his own philosophical-religious text, *Wendepunkt* (Turning Point). Ultimately he rejected the idea, leaving only silence after the Symphony's final cadence. Thus its dark, E flat minor triad ushers in the last decade of Schoenberg's creative life – one in which works of a religious as well as political nature continued to preoccupy his psyche, including the Prelude for Orchestra and Mixed Chorus, Op. 44; *A Survivor from Warsaw*, Op. 46; *Dreimal tausend Jahre*, Op. 50a; *De Profundis*, Op. 50b; *Moderner Psalm, Nr. 1*, Op. 50c. As Reinhold Brinkmann writes: "For my understanding of Schoenberg's life and output, it is in these works of a religious-political engagement that his path reaches its goal and fulfillment."[4]

My chapter begins with a brief summary of Schoenberg's thoughts on returning to tonality after writing non-tonal music. These comments set the stage for a discussion of the Second Chamber Symphony as a Janus-faced work – combining materials conceived intermittently between 1906 and 1939, including a final triad plainly recalling that of the third movement of the Second String Quartet written in July of 1908. Schoenberg would further refer to the quartet's large-scale schema by introducing the human voice into the Symphony's proposed third movement. He intended to set its philosophical-spiritual text, *Wendepunkt*, as a melodrama. Although Schoenberg ultimately rejected that plan for a third movement, I contend that *Wendepunkt* continued to be central to his thinking about the work as a private, *post festum* program – thus further underscoring my thesis that the Symphony approaches the ethos of Schoenberg's late religious-political works.

"Tonal oder atonal?"

Unlike many modernist composers of the postwar era, Schoenberg was never obsessed by a compositional dichotomy between tonal and non-tonal music; but rather held the belief that such matters were merely a stylistic concern. In a letter to composer Roger Sessions, he writes: "A Chinese poet speaks Chinese, but what is it he *says*?"[5] And, more specifically, in his essay "On Revient Toujours" (1948) he writes: "the older style was always vigorous in me; and from time to time I had to yield to that urge. This is how and why I sometimes write tonal music. To me *stylistic* differences of this nature are not of special importance."[6] To understand Schoenberg's statement fully, it is necessary to realize that he always uses the word *Styl* (style) in opposition to his philosophical notion of "musical idea," which, as a metaphysical concept basic to all of Schoenberg's thought, necessarily eludes definition.[7]

In practice, Schoenberg addressed only what he termed the material presentation (*Darstellung*) of the musical idea.[8] He saw style as an aspect of presentation, common to craftsmen and artists alike: "Every man has a fingerprint of his own, and every craftsman's hand has its personality . . . Style is the quality of a work and is based on natural conditions, expressing him who produced it."[9] For Schoenberg, a consummate Idealist, the purpose of style differed radically depending on whether craftsmen or artists were concerned. It was his view that while craftsmen often see a change in style opportunistically, as a sure method of acquiring critical attention, artists must not be concerned with such expedient matters. For them, style is a means of truthfully presenting a musical idea that

First Movement:
A Section (mm. 1–52)   E minor, "roving"
B Section (mm. 53–94)   A minor, "roving"
A' Section (mm. 95–140)   E minor, "roving"
Coda (141–65)   E minor, "roving"

Second Movement:
Exposition:
First Group (mm. 166–218)   G major "roving"
Second Group (mm. 219–63)   "roving"

Development: (mm. 263–82)   D major, "roving"
Recapitulation:
Theme from First Group (mm. 282–337)   G major "roving"
Theme from Section B, Movement (mm. 338–90) "roving"
Second Group (mm. 391–439)   "roving"

Coda (mm. 440–89)   E♭ minor, "roving"

Figure 15.1 The Symphony's form and tonality

transcends time and space: "[An artist] will never start from a preconceived image of a style; he will be ceaselessly occupied with doing justice to the idea (*Gedanke*). He is sure that, everything done which the idea demands, the external appearance will be adequate."[10] Hence the composer's task is to choose the appropriate method to present a musical idea, so that it can escape the boundaries of a given society or era and speak spiritually and philosophically to humanity as a whole:

> My personal feeling is that music conveys a prophetic message revealing a higher form of life towards which humanity evolves. And it is because of this message that music appeals to people of all races and cultures.[11]

Schoenberg maintained that if listeners are to comprehend a piece of music, its presentation must include a varied repetition of the materials, in order to ensure that they remain in the listener's memory to help foster understanding.[12] He writes: "Music is only understood when one goes away singing it and only loved when one falls asleep with it in one's head, and finds it still there on waking up the next morning."[13] And indeed, the layout of the Symphony is in particular dependent on the key and themes of the first movement returning in the coda of the second (Figure 15.1).[14] The slow pace and mournful character of Schoenberg's first movement, however, is highly unusual for a symphony – in mood, only the initial funeral march in Gustav Mahler's Fifth Symphony seems a possible precursor. Unlike Mahler, however, Schoenberg presents his movement not in a traditional sonata-allegro form, but in a subtle ternary design instead.[15] In the nineteenth century the ternary or *lied* forms were typical of the slow middle movements of symphonies or chamber works and character pieces for solo keyboard – or works that prefigured them such as the first movement of Beethoven's "Moonlight"

Sonata. Thus in his first movement, Schoenberg paradoxically used a design associated with intimate performance in the most public of genres, the symphony.

The form of the Symphony's second movement, too, is refractory to a traditional schema, although a modified sonata-allegro model seems presumable. The opening follows a fairly traditional sonata structure; but from the middle of the movement onward, the formal complexity increases markedly. The movement begins in an unambiguous G major, the second group is mostly "roving" in tonality, although there are references to E flat minor, the tonic of the first movement. As a result, at the beginning of the development section, it is difficult to hear the D major emphasis as a dominant relating to a tonic. Further on, in the recapitulatory passages, Schoenberg avoids asserting the material in any of its original keys. All of this combines to lend a developmental character to this section, weakening the tonal weight of the thematic recapitulation and transferring any sense of balance to the extended coda, while it reiterates the materials of the first movement.[16]

Composing the Symphony, 1906–16

Schoenberg made his initial sketches for the Symphony on August 1 and 14, 1906 (Figure 15.2). He worked extensively on the piece during the summer of 1907; and by August 1908 he had completed a draft of the first movement up to the beginning of its coda (m. 143), and one of the second up to the end of the second group (m. 252).[17] At this point he abandoned the piece and turned to composing the Second String Quartet, Op. 10 and *The Book of the Hanging Gardens*, Op. 15, claiming in a later essay that his response to the poems of Stefan George led to an all-consuming, exclusive preoccupation with atonal works.[18]

He continued to write atonal works until 1910 when he returned to the tonal *Gurrelieder*, abandoned nine years earlier. Days after completing its orchestration on November 7, 1911, he became preoccupied with *Das Lied von der Erde*, the symphony composed by his supporter and benefactor Gustav Mahler. The premiere of Mahler's work took place posthumously, in Munich on November 20, 1911, seven months after the composer's death. Schoenberg's students Alban Berg, Anton Webern, and Paul Königer attended the performance; but, for financial reasons, Schoenberg could not accompany them. Two days after the premiere, in Schoenberg's presence, Webern played through Mahler's score at the piano. Both of them were deeply moved. In his diary Schoenberg wrote, "We couldn't speak."[19]

SKETCHBOOK III [MS 77, CASG86-C290]

Pages	Movement sketched/ drafted	Dates included
32–5 [Sk210–3]	I, 20 sketches	August 1, 14, 1906
38–9 [Sk216–7]	I, 5 sketches, draft of mm. 1–57	
46 [Sk224]	I, 1 sketch	
76–81 [Sk254–9]	I, 5 sketches, draft of mm. 57–143;	July 8, 1907
	II, 1 sketch, drafts of mm. 3–10, 43–85	
84–5 [Sk 262–3]	II, 4 sketches, drafts for mm. 43–55,	[July/August 1907]
	86–105	
87–88 [Sk 265–6]	II, 2 sketches	[July/August 1907]

FAIR COPY 1907/8 [MS 42, 86CO]

[1241–1269]	I, mm. 1–14	January 14, 1907
	II, mm. 166–252	August 29, 1908

SKETCHBOOK III (CONTINUED FROM ABOVE)

116 [Sk 300–2]	II, 1 sketch	November 23, 1911;
	II, drafts for mm. 251–92	[corrections from 1939]
117 [Sk 303]	II, 1 sketch, draft for mm.	
	293–308	
118 [Sk 304]	II, 1 sketch containing inventory of 22	[1911], December 6, 1916
	themes	
118a–b [Sk 305–6]	Text of *Wendepunkt* glued into sketchbook	[1911? 1916?]
118c [Sk 307]	1 sketch	[1911]
118d–e [Sk 308–9]	I & II, 21 sketches	
118f [Sk 310]	1 sketch	
119 [Sk 311]	II, 2 sketches	[1911, 1916]
120–7 [Sk 312–9]	II, 30 sketches	[1916]
130 [Sk 322]	II, 1 sketch	

LOOSE PAGES CUT OUT OF SKETCHBOOK III [MS 42, 86C5]   [1939]

1 [recto 1279]	I, 1 sketch	
2 [recto/verso 1280]	II, 4 sketches	
3–5 [recto 1282/3; recto U343/1298a; verso U344/1298b; recto U345, 1298c]	I, 19 sketches	

12 PAGES (RECTO/VERSO) IN HANDMADE SHEAF [MS 42, 86C6]   October 12, 1939

1 [1270]	2 sketches, draft (mm. 309–15)	
2 [1271]	2 sketches, draft (mm. 316–27)	
3–6 [1272–78]	draft (mm. 316–489)	

LOOSE SHEETS CONTAINING DRAFTS AND SKETCHES FOR A REJECTED THIRD   November 5, 1939/
    MOVEMENT [MS 42, 86-C4, -C5, -C6]   January 27, 1940

[1284–97]	13 sketches; fair copy of mm. 490–508; draft of mm. 490–618	
[U346–51/1298d–i]	30 sketches	
[U505–6]	4 sketches	
[U556–58]	10 sketches	

ABORTED FAIR COPY (MM. 1–25) [MS 42, 1281, 86C3]

FAIR COPY OF THE   October 21, 1939
PARTICELL (now lost)

SCHOENBERG'S PERSONAL COPY OF THE *PARTICELL*   October 21, 1939
[MS 42, 1207–40, 85C935, 85C937]
(extant)

PARTS HAND-COPIED BY SCHOENBERG   [1939]
[NO NUMBER ASSIGNED]

Figure 15.2 Chronology of sketches and drafts (1906–40)
(This chart summarizes information in Arnold Schönberg, *Sämtliche Werke*, Section IV: *Orchesterwerke*, Series B, Vol. 11, Part 2, *Kammersymphonien*, ed. C. M. Schmidt (Mainz and Vienna, 1979), 104–202; and W. Frisch, *The Early Works of Arnold Schoenberg, 1893–1908* (Berkeley: University of California Press, 1993), 250; Arnold Schönberg Center website, www.Schoenberg.at/archive/music/work/op/compositions op. 38 sources e.htm. Archive nos. and possible dates appear in brackets.)

The very next day Schoenberg returned to his own Symphony, undoubtedly motivated and inspired by Mahler's work, though there is no direct structural influence. To refresh his memory of the Symphony's material, Schoenberg wrote out a list of all its major themes and their variants.[20] He also attempted several separate drafts of the second movement extending through the development and into the first group of the recapitulation – only to stop work on the piece once again, to turn to composing the atonal *Herzgewächse*, Op. 20 (started December 19, 1911) and *Pierrot lunaire*, Op. 21 (begun March 12, 1912).

Thoughts of the Symphony arose again in 1915, during World War I, when Schoenberg was anticipating his conscription into the Austrian army. He then drew up a new last will and testament and made a commitment to finish lingering projects. After being discharged from the military for medical reasons in 1916, he made numerous sketches for the second movement's recapitulation and the transition to its coda, significantly altering the instrumentation. In a letter dated December 12, 1916 to his friend, teacher, and brother-in-law, the composer Alexander von Zemlinsky, he explained:

> I've decided to finish my 2nd Chamber Symphony – the one I started in 1907 (!) and haven't touched since then.[21] Two movements have been written – one of them finished except for the final bars and the other completed up to the halfway point. I'm going to fuse them into *one* movement; that will be the first part. That's to say that I'm planning a 2nd part (my intention back then), but maybe I won't after all. But I'm *not* going to write the piece for solo instruments; I'm going to write a new score at once for (a mid-sized) *orchestra*. I think, after all, that it is a mistake to score for solo strings opposed to so many winds, because then one option is lacking; no single instrument, no single group could dominate in a loud *tutti* over all the rest – but the music needs it, the way it is conceived.[22]

Sometime between 1911 and 1916 Schoenberg had added a text for Part II called *Wendepunkt* (Turning Point) which, as noted above, was to be set as a melodrama.[23] *Wendepunkt* describes a soul's journey toward spiritual awareness: a general feeling of mourning, a turn toward happiness, a reversion to mourning, and a dismissal of it through the soul's acknowledgement of spiritual salvation (see Figure 15.3).[24] *Wendepunkt*'s subject matter distinctly recalls the libretto of the oratorio *Die Jakobsleiter* – both address earthly misery and salvation through prayer.[25] It is tantalizing to speculate what musical language Schoenberg might have intended for a setting of *Wendepunkt*. But, be that as it may, in the end, Schoenberg never sketched any music for the text, though he wrote on January 30, 1917 to the pianist and composer Ferruccio Busoni that he did wish to finish the Symphony.[26] By April 1917, however, Schoenberg had

Auf diesem Weg weiterzugehen war nicht möglich.
It was impossible to continue along that path.
Ein Lichtstrahl hatte eine Trauer sowohl allgemeiner, als
A beam of light had shed its illumination on a grief of both a general
auch besonderer Natur erhellt. Abhängend [von der Laune] nicht
and special kind. Depending not only
nur von ihrer [seinen inneren] Konstitution, sondern auch von den
on its makeup, but also on
Launen äußerer Zu[Glücks]fälle, kann eine Seele gegen den
the moods of outward happenstance; a soul can no more
Glücksfall sich sowenig unempfindlich verhalten, vie vorher
react insensitively to the whim of fortunate happenstance
gegen das Unglück [und antwortet in/mit/einem zunächst]
than it could to prior misfortune.
In plötzlichem Umschlag antwortet sie mit [einer] fröhlichem [Beschwingtheit]
In a sudden sea change, it responds with cheerful contentment,
Behagen, erhebt sich dann mit mächtigen Aufschwung
arises then with a mighty
träumt von seligen Erfüllungen, sieht sich als Sieger,
about-face, dreams of blissful fulfillment, calling itself a victor,
stürmt weiter, fühlt ihre [seine] Kraft immer mehr wachsen, und sammelt,
storming further, feeling its power ever growing and growing, collecting together
im Wahn eine Welt besitzen [erobern] zu können, die sie schon
everything it can in its mad delusion that it could possess a world which it already
für die ihre hält, alles was in ihrer Fähigkeit liegt, um
thinks is its own,
in einem mächtigen Anlauf eine überirdische Höhe zu erreichen.
in order to attain an extraterrestrial height in a mighty surge.
Was notwendigerweise geschehen müßte, besorgt der Zufall:
Happenstance ensures that that which needs must happen does indeed occur;
wie die angesammelte Kraft ausbrechen soll, versagt sie;
just as the amassed power is to break out, it falters
ein kleines aber hinterlistiges Ereignis – ein Stäubchen im Uhrwerk – ist imstande, sie
*   an ihrer*
– something tiny yet insidious – a speck of dust in the clockwork – is able to prevent the
   soul from
Entfaltung zu hindern.
blossoming as it might.
Dem Zusammenbruch folgt Verweiflung, danach die Trauer. Sie ist erst
[allgemeiner]
After the collapse comes despair, and then mourning. The grief is at first
[wieder allgemeiner und besondrer Natur. Dann auch besond]
besondrer, dann auch allgemeiner Natur. Vom äußeren
of a special, then of a general kind. Proceeding from the outward
Ereignis ausgehend glaubt die Seele [ihren Ab] den Grund zuerst
occurrence, the soul first believes it has found the reason therein,
in diesem zu finden, sucht ihn dann in ihrer Konstitution.
but then searches further within its makeup.
Das ist die eigentliche Vollendung dieses [des] Zusammenbruchs. Aber das be-
Thus is the actual completion of that collapse. But that
deutet kein Ende; ist im Gegenteil ein Anfang; ein neuer
does not signify an end; on the contrary it is a beginning;
Weg zum Heil zeigt sich, der einzige, der ewige. Ihn
a new path toward salvation is revealed, the only and eternal one
zu finden war der Zweck alles vorherigen Erlebens.
and the purpose of all foregoing experience was to find that path.

Figure 15.3 The text of *Wendepunkt* [Turning Point]
(Transcription by Christian Martin Schmidt. Passages crossed out in the original appear in brackets. Translation by Grant Chorley. Mr. Chorley and Severine Neff gratefully acknowledge the astute comments of Nuria Schoenberg Nono on the English text.)

turned to writing a pedagogical/theoretical text titled *Coherence, Counterpoint, Instrumentation, Instruction in Form*,[27] and by June he had begun composing the score of *Die Jakobsleiter*.

Twenty-two years passed before the Symphony came to Schoenberg's mind again. In the summer of 1939 his friend, the conductor Fritz Stiedry, asked for an orchestral work for his ensemble called the New Friends of Music Orchestra, motivating the composer to return to the unfinished project he had begun thirty-three years earlier.[28] That occurred on the eve of an historical cataclysm: Hitler invaded Poland on September 1, 1939; France and England declared war on September 3, and World War II began. It is striking that Schoenberg's other attempts to finish the Symphony coincided with grave turning points in his own life – Mahler's departure from Vienna for New York in 1907 and his death in 1911, and Schoenberg's military service in 1916–17, for example. Yet another turning point came to Schoenberg's life in the autumn of 1939: on November 5 Schoenberg filed the papers that would lead to his becoming an American citizen.[29] Once again, it was at just such a decisive moment that he returned to the Symphony.

Cadence after thirty-three years

> For the past month I have been working on the Second Chamber Symphony. I spend most of my time trying to find out: "What did the author mean here?"
>
> After all, in the meantime my style has become much more profound, and I have difficulty in making the ideas which I wrote down years ago without too much thought (rightly trusting my feeling for design) conform to my present demand for a high degree of "visible" logic. This is one of my greatest difficulties, for it affects the material of the piece.
>
> However, this material is very good; expressive, rich and interesting. But it is meant to be carried out in the manner that I was capable of at the time of the Second Quartet.[30]

That is Schoenberg's description of his work on the Symphony when he returned to it in 1939. He discovered "what the author meant" by copying out parts of the symphony and analyzing their contents.[31] Once he had become familiar with it again, he began altering earlier drafts and composing the codas of both movements. Interestingly, the movements' final cadences, though written in the language of extended tonality, are unlike any found in his early major tonal works, the Suite for String Orchestra (1934) or *Kol Nidre*, Op. 39 (1938), all of which end with variants of V-I. The movements of the Symphony conclude with #IV-I progressions, a cadence modified in the first movement by the use of

Example 15.1 #IV at the cadence to both movements (in the two-piano reduction by Schoenberg)
(a) First movement (b) Second movement

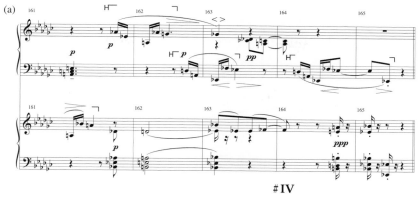

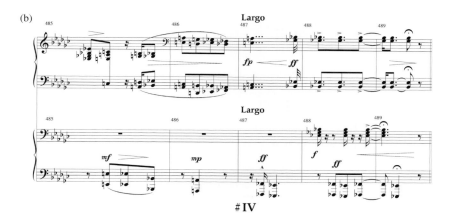

fourth chords (see Example 15.1). Two years later, he used #IV–I to close the *Variations on a Recitative for Organ*, Op. 40, a work whose harmony, in his words, "fills out the gap between my *Kammersymphonien* and the 'dissonant music.'"[32] Thus Schoenberg understood such a unique cadence as a logical consequence of his earlier explorations of extended tonality.

#IV and I are built on scale degrees that have a very remote tonal relation. But for Schoenberg, any connection is possible, even if it lies at the boundaries of a given tonality.[33] Schoenberg chose #IV to I for a cadence by deducing the Symphony's contextual logic. #IV is highlighted as the second chord of the entire work after the tonic (spelled enharmonically [cf. m. 1]); meanwhile, the scale degree #4 consistently appears at major articulative junctures and in the oft-repeated main theme (see, for example, the appearance of #IV at mm. 48–51 and 439–47). By reiterating

Example 15.2 Two sketches for the first movement's coda (a) Stopping on the dominant (b) The sketch beginning at m. 144

the scale degrees #4 and 1 at places where traditionally a dominant/tonic relation would appear, Schoenberg was able both to undermine the Symphony's sense of tonality and integrate its highly individualized thematic and harmonic materials.

Schoenberg's sketches from 1939 also document his notion of limiting the power of several traditional V^7-I cadences that he composed into the work in 1906.[34] In a sketch made in 1939 for the onset of the coda, he stops at the V^7 chord in m. 140 as if not knowing what to do with it (compare Example 15.2a). In the final version, the dominant-tonic resolution is immediately followed by an abridged version of the main theme and an abrupt shift of register. The ensuing viola-cello line in Example 15.2b highlights perfect fourths a tritone away from each other (first on a flat' and e flat' [mm. 144–5], and the d' and a' doubled in octaves [m. 145]). Such events severely weaken the effect of a traditional cadence.

Example 15.3 Surface permutations of trichord X (a) Permuted forms of trichord X
(b) Permutations of trichord X in the main theme, mm. 141–6, movement one

The only other surviving sketch for this same passage (compare
Example 15.2b) shows that the viola-cello theme in mm. 144–9 was indeed
central to Schoenberg's compositional thought. Its material centers on a
trichord (that I call X) in the main theme, which he presents in transposition, inversion, retrograde, and retrograde inversion (compare
Examples 15.3a and 15.3b). Thus this theme exhibits a surface logic
associated with the twelve-tone method. Compare, for example, similar
passagework in the Fourth String Quartet, Op. 37, the twelve-tone work
composed prior to the Symphony: for example, mm. 602–9 in the second
movement. This method of variation appears solely in portions of the
first movement composed in 1939.

Such surface permutations return only in the coda to the second
movement, also written in 1939. Here, however, we must also take seriously Schoenberg's admission to Stiedry that the Symphony was "meant
to be carried out in the manner which I was capable of at the time of the
Second Quartet." In voicing and register, the Symphony's final tonic triad
recalls the last sonority of "Litanei" from the Second Quartet's third
movement (compare Example 15.4). Both E flat minor triads are dark in
timbre, growing ever louder, only to be cut off abruptly into utter silence.
Both chords act as resolutions, yet they beg for continuation. The end of
"Litanei" reflects George's text in which a despondent individual, weary of
life's emotional battles, prays for release from misery: "Take from me love,
Give me thy peace." Schoenberg's setting of these lines is astounding – in
singing *Liebe* (love), the soprano covers an expanse of more than two
octaves in a single beat (see Example 15.4a, mm. 65–6). Analogously, at the
last climactic point of the Symphony, a tritone on 1–#4 instantaneously
descends over two octaves from the first violin's e flat''' on the downbeat of
m. 483 to the basses's a, on the second beat (see asterisk, Example 15.4b,
m. 483). This stunning descent makes the depth of the subsequent cadence
even more breathtaking, as if a dark abyss had suddenly opened up
beneath our feet, giving release into a void.

Example 15.4 The Symphony and "Litanei" (a) The final cadence of "Litanei" from the Second String Quartet, Op. 10 (b) The end of the coda and final cadence of the Symphony

Example 15.4 (cont.)

The rejected third movement

In November 1939 Schoenberg was not clear at first on how he wanted the Symphony to end. He drafted 127 measures of another movement, which he described to Stiedry:

> Whether I shall write a third movement (or even a fourth or fifth, which is also not out of the question) is not yet certain. I have not been able to find my old sketches – it is too hot to look for them. So I have no idea whether or not I

Exampe 15.4b (cont.)

can resume with one of the *many plans, which exist* [emphasis added] for the
completion. My preliminary idea is to have a slow third (final) movement, a
heroic Maestoso.[35]

This quotation is telling – in the surviving manuscripts, at least, there are
in fact no extended "plans" for the completion of the Symphony – only the
text of *Wendepunkt*. Here I would like to speculate for a moment on the
relation of that text to the final score, for it may suggest that an additional
movement was in order. I contend that *Wendepunkt* turned from a text to
be set as a melodrama to a *post festum* program for the work, outlining the
soul's progress through mourning, jubilation, a reversion to mourning,
and finally heavenly salvation through prayer. The emotional tone of the
Symphony parallels this sequence of feelings (see Figure 15.4). The

Auf diesem Weg weiterzugehen war nicht möglich.
It was impossible to continue along that path.
*Ein Lichtstrahl hatte eine Trauer sowohl
    allgemeiner, als*
A beam of light had shed its illumination on a grief of
    both a general
*auch besonderer Natur erhellt. Abhängend [von der
    Laune] nicht*
and special kind.

{Opening of first movement
    mm. 1–165}

*In plötzlichem Umschlag antwortet sie mit [einer]
    fröhlichem [Beschwingtheit]*
In a sudden sea change, it responds with cheerful
*Behagen, erhebt sich dann mit mächtigen
    Aufschwung*
contentment, arises then with a mighty
träumt von seligen Erfüllungen, sieht sich als Sieger,
about-face, dreams of blissful fulfillment, calling itself a
    victor,

{Opening of second
    movement mm. 166–438}

*Dem Zusammenbruch folgt Verweiflung, danach die
    Trauer. Sie ist erst [allgemeiner]*
After the collapse comes despair, and then mourning.
    The grief is at first
*[wieder allgemeiner und besondrer Natur. Dann
    auch besond]
besondrer, dann auch allgemeiner Natur.*
of a special, then of a general kind.

{Beginning of final coda,
    mm. 439–78}

Weg zum Heil zeigt sich, der einzige, der ewige. Ihn
A new path toward salvation is revealed, the only and
    eternal one
zu finden war der Zweck alles vorherigen Erlebens.
and the purpose of all foregoing experience was to find
    that path.

{Rejected third movement}

Figure 15.4: *Wendepunkt* as a private program

opening movement establishes the mood of mourning, while the G major beginning of the second movement is quite clearly jubilant. The beginning of the second movement's coda signals the return to mourning and the E flat minor of the opening movement.[36] But what has become of the soul's new beginning, its turn down a new path towards heavenly salvation through prayer? This could hardly be represented by the final cadence, for the dark E flat-minor triad brings the Symphony to one of the most solemn and tragic endings in all of Schoenberg's works.

More likely, the "new" beginning was to be the unrealized third movement. Unsurprisingly, its first draft begins with the triads in an adagio chorale style resembling the coda of the second movement (see Example 15.5a).[37] After this, the general contour begins to progress upward toward a heavenly realm. At a dramatic shift toward high registers, Schoenberg literally writes the word "ascending" into his draft (see Example 15.5b). Ultimately, high violin lines soar into space (see Example 15.5c) like those representing the Soul in the oratorio *Die Jakobsleiter* (see Example 15.5d). The parallels between the works' texts are obvious. *Wendepunkt* describes the soul's acknowledgement of salvation through prayer, while the libretto

Example 15.5 Parallels With *Die Jakobsleiter* (a) The opening of the third movement (b) Sketch of movement three with the word "ascending" (c) The high violin in the Symphony (d) The soul in *Die Jakobsleiter*

of *Die Jakobsleiter* expounds on it, tracing the spirit's journey from an earthly condition to its heavenly meeting with God.

Schoenberg only set half the text of the oratorio, stopping at the soul's transformation through prayer and death. The Second Chamber Symphony stops at an analogous place – if my reading of the program is correct. It is well known that in many works Schoenberg sought to communicate the rise to a transcendental state, and that he repeatedly was unable to portray it musically.[38] *Die Jakobsleiter, Moses und Aron,* and the *Moderner Psalm Nr. 1,* Schoenberg's last work, all break off at that same point, "unfinished." I contend that the Second Chamber Symphony is part of this group of works to which Schoenberg constantly returned, and which embodied his most important philosophical and religious concerns and his greatest intellectual and spiritual preoccupations.

The Second Chamber Symphony is the only one of the four that Schoenberg ever considered "finished."[39] Writing to Stiedry in the spring of 1940, he said that the abandoned third movement was not "unconditionally necessary," and that it had merely appended certain "observations" on the "musical and psychic problems" already exhaustively presented in the two completed movements.[40] Could it be that only under the consecration of tonality, renewed and enriched by thirty-three years of unparalleled expansion of his musical vocabulary, Schoenberg could face the tragic reality that for him, as the darkness of World War II gathered, the prayerful return to mourning rather than the soul's transcendence was the ultimate cadence?

16 Schoenberg's collaborations

JENNIFER SHAW

Collaboration, according to current English-language dictionaries, can mean to work in conjunction with others on literary, artistic, or scientific works: in 1940, however, it also became the label for a treacherous collusion with an enemy and, in particular, with the Nazis. Over the next sixty years the boundaries between these dual meanings – at once laudable and reprehensible; creative and destructive – became tangled and fused. For instance, our governments collaborate in bringing international criminals to justice as well as in occupying other nations' sovereign territory: in other words, "collaboration" is not a pure term. Yet even before 1940 the reality of artistic collaborations had become tainted and untenable for many, especially in Germany and Austria. Within a year of coming to power in January 1933, the National Socialists passed civil service laws that banned membership of the Reich Chamber of Culture to those who "did not possess the necessary reliability (*Zuverlässigkeit*) and aptitude (*Eignung*) for the practice of [their] activity."[1] When racial laws were passed soon after, and it became clear that at least 75 percent Aryan ancestry was an essential criterion for "reliability," many artists – Aryans and Jews alike – attempted to distance themselves from their artistic collaborators who were now, by law, considered racially and artistically "alien," and who therefore were also deemed to be unreliable and inept. The effect, as Schoenberg explained in a speech that he gave in 1935, little more than a year after leaving Berlin via Paris for a new life in America, was that Jews, "deprived of their racial self-confidence, doubted a Jew's creative capacity more than the Aryans did."[2] To the many émigré composers who, like Schoenberg, had fled from Germany to North America, it therefore seemed imperative to assimilate – to become like, to "fit in," as Schoenberg explained – and yet also to stand out as capable, reliable, and original creators.

And so, at the same time as influential musicologist Herbert Gerigk and other Nazi propagandists were busy rewriting Germany's official artistic history in order to marginalize and denigrate Jewish musicians as plagiarists and deviants, so, too, did émigré composers revise their own histories. Shaped by the politics of crisis, in these migrant success stories, artistic collaborations – especially those that might call a composer's sole creative abilities and rights into question – were given, at best, a minor role. It is a narrative that continues to exert much power today, especially in accounts of Schoenberg's compositional development; and it is a narrative that Schoenberg also seems to have found compelling. In several published documents he depicts himself as the stereotypical genius composer, alienated from his peers and unmoved by popular trends. This attitude is reflected in his famous *Self Portrait, Walking* of 1911 in which, with his back to the viewer, he walks away, denying us that intimate or (as in his "Vision" paintings) confronting relationship with the gaze. Likewise, in an aphorism that he wrote in 1928, Schoenberg cynically discredits the brief period of popularity that he experienced in the years after World War I:

> It was a period of deepest depression as I saw myself suddenly surrounded, hemmed in, besieged, by a circle of admirers I had not earned.
> I overcame them, starved them out, remained deadly serious, moralized to the point of suicide – they fell off like rotten fruit – I am rid of them.
> What good that does me!
> Finally alone again![3]

Certainly there are well-known episodes that support this narrative of genius and alienation, among them the "scandal concerts" of 1908 and 1913 that ended in riots and, perhaps most notoriously, Schoenberg's attempts to dictate terms in exchange for his collaboration on the Metro-Goldwyn-Mayer film of Pearl Buck's *The Good Earth*. According to Salka Viertel, another successful émigré who attended the single (and singular!) meeting in 1935 between Schoenberg and MGM director Irving Thalberg, Schoenberg declared that, for a fee of $50,000, he would need to have "complete control" not just over the music but also over the dialogue, and that the actors "would have to speak in the same pitch and key as I compose ... it would be similar to *Pierrot lunaire* but, of course, less difficult."[4] Viertel then, at Schoenberg's request, sang some of *Pierrot* for Thalberg, who, according to Viertel, seemed stunned. Not surprisingly, Thalberg chose the easier option of purchasing the rights to some Chinese folk songs, which the head of MGM's sound department then used as the basis for the movie's soundtrack.

Yet such statements that seem to reflect extremes of alienation and control need to be read in the context of Schoenberg's actions. For instance, in 1928, a few months after Schoenberg wrote the remark about "starving out" his rotten-fruit admirers, he began to court new listeners in Berlin by bringing his music into line with new trends. Moreover, Schoenberg did in fact consider and suggest major collaborations, and several of these resulted in completed, successful projects. A selected list of some of these collaborations is given in Table 16.1. This list

Table 16.1 *Arnold Schoenberg's Collaborations: A Selected List*

Year	Collaborator/s	Title/Project	Comments
1904–05	Alexander von Zemlinsky	Society of Creative Musicians	Concerts for one season in Vienna with Gustav Mahler as inaugural president
1909	Marie Pappenheim	*Erwartung* (Expectation), Op. 17	Collaborated on libretto. Opera completed; staged June 1924
1911–12	Wassily Kandinsky	*Blaue Reiter* Exhibition and Almanac	Paintings by Schoenberg displayed at the *Blaue Reiter* Exhibition in Munich 1911; Schoenberg's essay "The Relationship to the Text" published in the *Blaue Reiter Almanac* 1912
1912	Richard Dehmel	"Modern Man" oratorio	Dehmel supplied already written oratorio text; used by Schoenberg in Symphony (begun 1914, not completed)
1913	Alexander von Zemlinsky	*Merlins Geburt* opera	Discussed adaptation of Eduard Stucken's play
1913–14	Marie Pappenheim	*Séraphita* oratorio	Text adaptation of Balzac's *Séraphita*; text not completed
1918–21	Alban Berg, Erwin Stein, Anton Webern, Eduard Steuermann, and other former students of Schoenberg	Society for Private Musical Performances	Society operated in Vienna with Schoenberg as president; branch in Prague (with Zemlinsky as president); lasted until 1923
1923	Wassily Kandinsky	Bauhaus collaboration	Schoenberg declined Kandinsky's invitation to direct the Weimar music school
1923–24	Josef Matthias Hauer	Composition school and twelve-tone textbook	Projects discussed only
1928	Gertrud Schoenberg	*Tennis-Spiel* (Tennis Match)	Libretto and some musical ideas sketched; not completed
1928–29	Max Blonda [Gertrud Schoenberg]	*Von heute auf morgen* (From Today to Tomorrow)	Opera completed; staged February 1930
1930	Lázló Moholy-Nagy	*Begleitungsmusik zu einer Lichtspielszene*, Op. 34 (Accompaniment to a Film Scene)	'film music for no film' conducted by Otto Klemperer at the Krolloper, November 1930, but without proposed "film" set by Moholy-Nagy
1930	Franz Werfel	*Der biblische Weg* (The Biblical Way)	Schoenberg's request for assistance to revise Schoenberg's script refused by Werfel
1933–	Various (including Franz Werfel, Ernst Toch)	Efforts to establish a Jewish State	Plans begun in Paris; Schoenberg continued to support efforts in the United States
1934	Hanns Eisler	Proposed Music Institute in Russia	Outline discussed only
1935	MGM (Irving Thalberg)	*The Good Earth* film music	Met with Thalberg; script marked and some musical sketches begun
1938	Rabbi Jacob Sonderling	*Kol Nidre*, Op. 39	Collaborated on text for the "Kol Nidre" service; performed October 1938
1944–45	Nathaniel Shilkret, Aleksander Tansman, Darius Milhaud, Mario Castelnuovo-Tedesco, Igor Stravinsky, Ernst Toch	Prelude, Op. 44	Commissioned by Shilkret. First seven movements of the *Genesis* Suite performed November 1945, Los Angeles; recorded by RCA 1946

1949–50	Dika Newlin	Style and Idea	Revised essays for publication in volume edited by Newlin
1950–51	Karl Rankl, Hermann Scherchen	*Die Jakobsleiter* (Jacob's Ladder)	Schoenberg asked Rankl and Scherchen to complete the orchestration of the first part of his oratorio; after Schoenberg's death Gertrud asked Winfried Zillig to complete the work (1961 concert performance)
1954	Hermann Scherchen	*Moses und Aron*	*Dance of the Golden Calf*, performance version (fragment), premiered by Scherchen in 1954

is intended as a representative sample only: there are many more works, including *Pierrot* and *Die glückliche Hand* for instance, that could be argued in some respects to be products of collaborative ventures and others where the boundaries between collaboration and influence are unclear. Yet, for the purposes of this chapter, I have chosen to define the parameters of Schoenberg's collaborations quite narrowly as instances where we know that Schoenberg worked with another on a project, or specifically asked someone to collaborate with him, or was approached by others with a view to collaboration. So, for example, I have excluded the more slippery categories of his transcriptions and arrangements of other composers' works and his students' transcriptions of his works, as well as projects in which the influence of others – but not explicit collaboration – may have played a significant role in a work's genesis. Take, for instance, Schoenberg's interactions with the Russian painter Wassily Kandinsky which resulted in two unambiguous collaborations: the display of four of Schoenberg's paintings (including *Self-Portrait, Walking* and two of the 1910 "Visions") as part of the *Blue Rider* Exhibition held in Munich in December 1911 and the publication of his essay "The Relationship to the Text" in the *Blue Rider Almanac* of 1912.[5] At the same time, there are other important aspects and outcomes of their relationship that cannot be regarded as collaborations: the January 1911 concert in Munich at which the performance of Schoenberg's Op. 11 piano pieces served as direct inspiration for Kandinsky's painting *Impression III (Concert)*; Schoenberg's dedication of a copy of his 1911 *Theory of Harmony* to Kandinsky; Kandinsky's praise for Schoenberg's music in his 1912 treatise *On the Spiritual in Art*, and his active promotion of Schoenberg's music, painting, and ideas. Also difficult to categorize in this context are Kandinsky's assistance in arranging for Schoenberg to conduct his *Pelleas und Melisande* in St. Petersburg in December 1912, and the possible mutual influence of each other's ideas about form, theory, light, and color as documented by their correspondence in 1912–13 while Kandinsky was completing his opera *Der gelbe Klang* (The Yellow Sound) and Schoenberg was working on his opera *Die glückliche Hand*. In these instances – and many others – the evidence for and nature of the collaborative relationship are difficult to reconstruct.

Nevertheless, the list of documented collaborations is surprisingly extensive. I have chosen to outline several of Schoenberg's collaborations that occurred in 1913, 1923, 1928, and 1944 – that is, in selected years over a thirty-year period – in order to convey an idea of their scope and success. My interest in them centers on the construction of an alternative narrative that focuses on the nature and extent of cooperative creativity and invention in these projects. While there is no overarching explanation of why Schoenberg chose to collaborate or why some projects succeeded while others failed, we can relate Schoenberg's shifting views about collaboration to his sense of how he was perceived by his public, his peers and, most importantly, by his sense of how he believed his creative abilities would be judged in historical accounts.

The 1913 collaborations

In 1913 Schoenberg considered two major collaborations. The February 1913 premiere of his *Gurrelieder* in Vienna was to remain Schoenberg's greatest critical and popular success, and it was a success that Schoenberg sought to replicate when, later in 1913, he consulted his brother-in-law Alexander von Zemlinsky about dramatic subjects suitable for collaboration. The subject that initially appealed most to Schoenberg was *Merlin's Birth*, the first in a sequence of eight plays by Eduard Stucken concerning the quest of the Arthurian knights for the Holy Grail. Schoenberg's choice of Stucken's text, and of Zemlinsky as his collaborator, was designed to have wide popular appeal. Schoenberg deeply admired Zemlinsky both as a conductor and as a successful opera composer, so he must have had some hopes that Zemlinsky would be involved in the text adaptation and production – and perhaps even that he would compose some of the music. Perhaps, too, Schoenberg saw the possibilities of creating a series of Grail operas. Yet Schoenberg never made clear the proposed nature of his collaboration on this project with Zemlinsky and, within a month of receiving Stucken's text, Schoenberg, in a November 1913 letter to his brother-in-law, suggested that it might be a topic that Zemlinsky would be better suited to tackle alone. He confessed to Zemlinsky that his interest had shifted to more ambitious collaborative projects, as he now intended to compose a dramatized musical setting that Dr. Marie Pappenheim had begun to adapt for him of Balzac's *Séraphita*.[6]

Postcards and letters sent between November 1913 and May 1914 indicate that Schoenberg told Pappenheim of his desire to set *Séraphita*, and Pappenheim then proposed that she would provide the libretto for Schoenberg, much along the lines of their successful collaboration that, in 1909, had resulted in the monodrama *Erwartung*.[7] Although Schoenberg accepted this proposal, mailing brief comments about the libretto drafts to Pappenheim, they never completed their *Séraphita* adaptation. Initial work was promising, with Pappenheim mentioning that – in just one afternoon – she had completed the entire first scene.[8] But in none of Pappenheim's brief communications is the form that the libretto was to take or her progress with the adaptation made clear. Indeed, one suspects that these may have been critical issues that were never resolved, given Pappenheim's deep reservations about the work's form, and the conflict she perceived in making the work either too much of a human drama or, on the contrary, something that amounted to "no more" than a mystery play.[9]

From these remarks we can probably also assume that Pappenheim's adaptation of Balzac's tale did not match Schoenberg's vision. As Schoenberg noted in a November 1913 letter to Alma Mahler, what began as a mystical oratorio setting of "one of the most glorious books in existence" had, in his mind, become a massive theatrical project, demanding its own purpose-built theater and at least 2,000 singers.[10] Of course Schoenberg must have meant to impress Alma with the parallels he was drawing between his ambitious new project, Wagner's opera dramas, and Gustav Mahler's symphonies and, relying on funds from the Mahler Foundation to support his work, Schoenberg probably also calculated that it may not have been in his interest to include a reference to a proposed collaboration with Pappenheim. More surprising, however, is that in a letter sent to his publisher at Universal Edition at the beginning of 1914, in which Schoenberg outlined possible publication projects, the composer remained silent about both the *Séraphita* theater project and about any collaboration with Pappenheim.[11]

By May 1914 Schoenberg was, instead, engrossed in the composition of a multi-movement choral symphony. As his first task for this new project, Schoenberg chose the texts for his symphony's movements. Although not designed with a tight narrative structure, as in Stucken's Grail drama, nor with the dramatic intensity that Pappenheim envisioned in her *Séraphita* adaption, the movements were to be connected by a number of poetic texts that explored the themes of creation, love, and death. They, too, were designed on a massive scale requiring the kinds of vocal and instrumental forces that, once war broke out just weeks later, were clearly impossible to assemble. Despite his grand plans for the symphony, Schoenberg only sketched about twenty pages of music. In 1917 some of that music and one of his own texts for the symphony became the first part of his *Die Jakobsleiter* (Jacob's Ladder) oratorio, but that, too, remained unfinished.[12] So, his plans for a collaborative work, with aspects of text-setting, production, and maybe even some of the music allocated to others, ended up as an oratorio for which Schoenberg alone wrote both the music and text: in the oratorio text there are obvious allusions to other sources – Balzac's *Séraphita* and biblical verses among them – but by no stretch of the imagination is this a collaborative work.

Collaborations of 1923 and 1928

Many of Schoenberg's other ambitious collaborations met a similar fate. For instance, in November 1923 the composer Josef Hauer, who (to Schoenberg's consternation) had also been experimenting with twelve-tone composition in the form of his "tropes," wrote to Schoenberg to suggest that they establish, jointly, a composition school. Schoenberg supported this idea and, in turn, suggested that they author, jointly, a textbook on "the possibilities of achieving logical form by the use of twelve tones."[13] Despite their theoretical and aesthetic differences, Schoenberg suggested that they would alternate chapters in the hope that "we may incidentally arrive at a basis for smooth collaboration." Not surprisingly, neither the school nor the textbook materialized. Likewise, Kandinsky's April 1923 invitation to Schoenberg to direct the Bauhaus music school in Weimar – a project on a similarly ambitious scale – was declined by the composer, as he had heard reports of anti-Semitic comments made by Kandinsky and other artists on the Bauhaus faculty. Yet the intention to collaborate is clear, at least on Kandinsky's part, and, despite Schoenberg's serious – and well-founded – reservations about Bauhaus attitudes and beliefs, the collaborative possibilities must have held great appeal.

More successfully, Schoenberg's collaborations in 1928 with his second wife, Gertrud, in fact resulted in draft ideas for a number of dramatic works and one completed opera. Among Gertrud's papers are drafts of several comic librettos that originate from this time. One, entitled *Rien ne va plus*, is set in a casino in Monte Carlo. Another, *Tennis-Spiel*, revolves around an international tennis competition and comedy of errors of identity.[14] The one project that the Schoenbergs did complete was a moderately successful twelve-tone *Zeitoper* (opera of the times) that they entitled *Von heute auf morgen* (From Today to Tomorrow), in which, in the domestic setting of their living room, a modern husband and wife flirt with contemporary fashions in dress, music, and relationships before reaffirming the status quo. The music of this one-act opera, as Schoenberg explained to many of the opera house directors whom he approached to stage the work, was "entirely" his; the libretto, however, he claimed was "entirely" that of his (male) collaborator (*Mitarbeiter*) Max Blonda, a pseudonym designed to disguise Gertrud's identity and gender. Schoenberg confessed that he had suggested some lines here and there, but in fact the libretto drafts and notes indicate that Schoenberg had a major hand in the construction of the libretto and, conversely, that Gertrud's stage directions – and her explicit textual references to *Rheingold*, *Siegfried*, and *Die Walküre* as well as to popular dance music heard on the radio – guided Schoenberg's musical allusions to these works and genres.

Although both Arnold and Gertrud were convinced that their opera would be a great success, the production closed after just four performances at the Frankfurt Opera House and, apart from a Berlin Radio broadcast in February 1930, the opera was not performed again until after Schoenberg's death. Although Gertrud remained intimately concerned with her husband's creative efforts and business affairs, there were no further collaborative attempts between them that resulted in completed musical works. *Von heute auf morgen* has, however, achieved modest commercial success in more recent recordings and performances, among them the 1997 film version *Du jour au lendemain* by Danièle Huillet and Jean-Marie Straub, featuring the Frankfurt Radio Symphony Orchestra, conducted by Michael Gielen, with vocal soloists Richard Salter (Husband), Christine Whittlesey (Wife), Claudia Barainsky (Female Friend), Ryszard Karczykowski (Tenor), and Annabelle Hahn (Child): the film's soundtrack, which consists entirely of Schoenberg's music for *Von heute auf morgen*, was also commercially released in 1997. At the very least these performances and recordings have resulted in an acknowledgement of Gertrud's role during this period of her husband's life as one more central, and practical, than that of muse.

Collaborations in the 1930s and 1940s

With the exception of his partnership with Marie Pappenheim on *Erwartung* in 1909, *Von heute auf morgen* was perhaps Schoenberg's most successful and satisfying collaboration; yet it was to be his last completed collaboration of any kind for almost ten years. At this time, that is around 1930, Schoenberg stopped proposing any further musical collaborations. At the same time he began to record his thoughts about originality and creativity. This seems to have been in direct response to increasing attacks from writers in Germany and Austria on his ability to create new and "authentic" works.

In Germany Schoenberg was singled out as a locus of hostility. So, for instance, Herbert Gerigk (whose views are documented in the many publications he edited, including the journal *Die Musik* and the Nazi-commissioned *Lexicon of Jews in Music*) argued that Schoenberg's chromaticism merely imitated the innovations of Brahms and Wagner, and that his "rootless" twelve-tone method was part of an international, Jewish, Bolshevist plot to subvert the "well-rooted" musical heritage of the true German *Volk*. Put most crudely, in the Nazi's *Entartete Musik* or "Degenerate Music" exhibition of 1938 visitors could listen to a gramophone recording of Schoenberg's Serenade, Op. 24 as "an attempt to undermine the essence of the German musical expression, the triad."[15] Ironically, the one "collaboration" that was singled out in the Degenerate Music and Art exhibitions, a photograph of Oskar Schlemmer's set for the 1930 Berlin production of Schoenberg's opera *Die glückliche Hand* (included as an illustration of how Schoenberg's "madhouse fantasy" was reflected in both music and stage design), was one that Schoenberg would have disowned, as he, too, hated Schlemmer's set.[16]

The hostilities, however, had begun much earlier. In 1925 Alfred Heuss accused Schoenberg of deliberately cultivating a "principle" of "rootlessness" and non-assimilation as a means to destroy the German musical tradition.[17] Such charges Schoenberg regarded as unfounded: as he wrote in a 1931 essay, he deserved credit for having written "truly new music which, being based on tradition, is destined to become tradition."[18] Schoenberg also hit back at those who accused him in the late 1920s of copying the latest trends for dance-forms and for one-act operas by replying that he had obviously plagiarized the one-act form of his own, prewar opera *Erwartung* and had stolen "old style" counterpoint and dance forms from *Pierrot lunaire*.[19] Such charges of plagiarism and lack of originality, were, however, harder to deal with, and Schoenberg genuinely feared that "the small bit of fame for originality" that he felt due to him would be attributed, through the Nazi's revisionist projects, to others, and, in particular to his former student Anton Webern and to Josef Hauer.[20] Such fears lingered: even after World War II, when Schoenberg fell out with Thomas Mann over Mann's attribution in his novel *Dr. Faustus* of twelve-tone composition to the fictitious character of Adrian Leverkühn, Schoenberg sent Mann a mock encyclopedia entry that Schoenberg himself had written that attributes twelve-tone composition to Mann and dismisses "spurious" claims that the minor composer Schoenberg could have been the originator of it, since "Only a real inventor is in a position to give such an illuminating presentation. Schoenberg would never have had the capacity for work of this kind."[21] As Schoenberg's response suggests, even after the war, the wording and effect of the civil service law that banned membership of the Nazi Chamber of Culture to artists who "did not possess the necessary reliability and aptitude for the practice of activity" continued to resonate. In Schoenberg's 1948 response to Mann, Schoenberg puts on display his fear that he would be viewed by history as unreliable, unoriginal, and lacking in creative capacity.

So the fact that Schoenberg, in 1944, readily agreed to a major film music collaboration is all the more surprising. Nat Shilkret – best known as Director of Light Music in the 1920s and 1930s at RCA Victor and for his many Hollywood compositions of the 1930s and 1940s – commissioned Schoenberg and a number of other émigré composers living in Los Angeles each to write a piece for choir, narrator, and orchestra for the MGM pilot for a film setting of the Book of Genesis. Schoenberg was asked to write the "Prelude" to the *Genesis* Suite: other movements completed included the "Creation" by Shilkret, "Adam and Eve" by Aleksander Tansman, "Cain and Abel" by Darius Milhaud, "Noah's Ark" by Mario Castelnuovo-Tedesco, "The Covenant" by Ernst Toch, and "Babel" by Igor Stravinsky. This takes us to chapter 11 in the Book of Genesis, and indicates that Shilkret may have planned another eighteen or so pieces: other composers, including Bartók, Hindemith, and Prokofiev had agreed to write music for later chapters. Schoenberg completed his piece in just seven days in September 1945. The Suite was premiered by the Janssen Symphony Orchestra in Los Angeles in November 1945 and recorded by RCA in 1946. The *Genesis* movie, however, was never made.

Very little was known about this work until the early twenty-first century, as it had been assumed that a fire at Shilkret's home in the 1960s had destroyed all the scores apart from the pieces by Schoenberg and Stravinsky; however, while researching his doctoral dissertation on Castelnuovo-Tedesco's film music, James Westby located full scores of Castelnuovo-Tedesco's "The Flood" and Milhaud's "Cain and Abel." Westby then tracked down the basic "short scores" of each movement that Shilkret had registered in 1945 with the United States Copyright Office in order to obtain copyright protection. The Milken Archive of American Jewish Music then commissioned Hollywood film composer Patrick Russ to reconstruct the movements by Shilkret, Tansman, and Toch from the copyright scores and the 1946 recording.[22] The music was recorded in 2000 and the narration added in 2003 (this was done by actor Edward Arnold in the 1945 concert premiere, by Pastor Osborne in the 1946 recording and, in the Naxos recording, released in 2004, by six narrators: Sigurd Brauns, Barbara Feldon, Tovah Feldshuh, David Margulies, Isaiah Sheffer, and Fritz Weaver). The full score of Tansman's "Adam and Eve" movement surfaced after 2000 and has yet to be (newly) recorded.

Schoenberg was on friendly terms with Milhaud, Tansman, and, at times, with Toch. Yet, despite the real possibilities for actual co-composition, all the composers involved seemed to have viewed the "collaboration" purely as a business arrangement: according to the contract that each signed, each was to write his short movement and, on completion and delivery, was to be paid a very modest fee by Shilkret, who retained sole rights to each piece. The fee varied: Tansman, Milhaud, Castelnuovo-Tedesco, and Toch were each paid just $300 for pieces of between five and eleven minutes' duration. Stravinsky, for his five-minute "Babel" fugue, was quoted a fee of $1,000, while Schoenberg – who, in contrast to his previous encounter with MGM, readily accepted the contract terms – was paid $1,500 for his five-minute Prelude.[23]

But perhaps that pragmatic attitude in itself was a statement about collaboration: that is, that in the closing stages of World War II, these seven composers – six of them recent émigrés, six of them Jewish – agreed to combine their extremely diverse musical styles – twelve-tone, tonal, and polytonal, contrapuntal and homophonic, serious and "light" – into one, potentially immense work intended to reach the widest possible audience. For example, in the final minutes of Schoenberg's *Genesis* Prelude (which is, in fact, a prelude and fugue), a vocalise chorus enters with a final statement of the fugue subject, with the twelve-tone row partitioned between the vocal and instrumental parts, before the Prelude ends on C octaves. It is followed immediately by Shilkret's setting of the "Creation" which is tonal, homophonic, and predictably, its first cadence strongly establishes the key of C major. Schoenberg's and Shilkret's pieces are also linked loosely by their use of a vocalise chorus and, in fact, several of the pieces use the chorus as a "texture" in this way – only Stravinsky's "Babel" piece calls for the chorus to sing texted parts. Yet, despite the use of vocalise and "C-ness" at the end of Schoenberg's piece and in the opening of Shilkret's, there is no attempt in the Suite to assimilate or to compromise individual voices, or even to speak the same musical language.

Mirroring collaboration

In a chapter on diatonic triads in his *Theory of Harmony*, Schoenberg observed that "the work of art is capable of mirroring what we project into it. The conditions our conceptual power imposes, a mirror image of our own nature, may be observed in the work. This mirror image does not, however, reveal the plan upon which the work itself is oriented, but rather the way we orient ourselves to the work."[24] So, as Schoenberg then explains, if we position ourselves differently to the work, we will see new mirror images. In an essay published in California in 1948, Schoenberg demonstrated this with reference to twelve-tone composition: while the Nazis had labeled his twelve-tone compositions "Bolshevik" since it could be argued that all notes in the row are equal (not that this was Schoenberg's view), they had tolerated the twelve-tone music of Danish composer Paul von Klenau, perhaps, as Schoenberg suggests, because they could also choose to interpret the row in a "fascist" way, in which (in Schoenberg's words) the prime row is seen as the Führer, the source of all power and function, and originator of all other events in a work.[25] So, here we have the same technique, but two different orientations – and two radically different interpretations.

Viewing these collaborative works from different perspectives may also provide us with new interpretations of them. Take the historical position of Schoenberg's Prelude and its context in the *Genesis* Suite, written just after Schoenberg's seventy-first birthday – a decade after he had been in the United States, and at the very end of the war in Europe when Schoenberg himself was being asked to pass opinion on the possible political collaborations of Richard Strauss and Wilhelm Furtwängler. Take its content and meaning: on the recording released in 1946 and remastered in 2001 Schoenberg's *Genesis* Prelude bears MGM's title (but not Schoenberg's) of "The earth was without form," but this is clearly not a formless or ahistorical piece: its strictly controlled, expressive content and defined, fugal structure are strongly grounded in the German traditions of Bach and Haydn. At the same time, Schoenberg's use of his twelve-tone idiom and vocalise, rather than texted song, deliberately render the Prelude linguistically and musically "rootless," but we can also hear that this is not a music that is derivative, nor is it "homeless and speechless" – terms Schoenberg had used on his sixtieth birthday to describe his first years of exile in North America. On the contrary, the music depicts the intensely creative but, crucially, not chaotic, state before Genesis; that is, before ideas become tangible, before the creative vision is realized. Perhaps, most significantly, the symbolic importance of Schoenberg's *Genesis* Prelude and the *Genesis* Suite as a whole lies in their ability to demonstrate that, if we share vocabulary and the means to communicate, even if common verbal and musical language are absent, we can reclaim collaboration as a meaningful and creative act.

17 Listening to Schoenberg's Piano Concerto

WALTER B. BAILEY

Behind the words of Schoenberg's 1946 essay "Heart and Brain in Music," one can hear the aging composer railing against those who had branded him as a heartless intellectual.[1] This particular criticism stung him acutely, even though he believed that it reflected more on the naivety of his critics than on a realistic interpretation of his works. For Schoenberg, "heart" and "brain" could not be separated in the compositional process, nor did he believe that the great composers of the past had considered them separately. While purporting to address the relative importance of inspiration and conscious construction in all manner of music, Schoenberg obviously sought to demonstrate in this essay that the perceived complexity of his own music – and especially that of his twelve-tone works – was congruent with long-standing musical traditions that valued the cerebral and the emotive equally.

To illustrate his thesis, Schoenberg cited musical examples in which passages produced via inspiration were difficult to differentiate from those resulting from extensive conscious effort. For example, as an illustration of a melody that listeners would most likely identify as emotive and "inspired," Schoenberg provocatively cited the beginning of his Concerto for Piano and Orchestra, Op. 42, written four years earlier (1942). The irony, as Schoenberg undoubtedly intended, was that this conventionally lyrical theme occurred in a twelve-tone work (Example 17.1). The existence of such a theme, he implied, proved that the twelve-tone method, which had earned him "the title of constructionist, engineer, mathematician, etc., meaning that these compositions are produced exclusively by the brain without the slightest participation of something like a human heart," was far from "heartless."[2]

For the purposes of his essay, Schoenberg was content to leave the Piano Concerto after simply noting the existence of this lyrical melody, but there is more to be said about the Concerto in light of Schoenberg's essay, the sketches for the work, and – above all – the sound of the Concerto. Like most composers, Schoenberg wrote the kind of music that he wanted to hear, and during the 1940s his musical taste was remarkably varied. The String Trio, Op. 45 (1946), for example, is a complex, dissonant, twelve-tone work that makes few concessions to the

Example 17.1 Schoenberg, Concerto for Piano and Orchestra, Op. 42, mm. 1–8

uninitiated listener, despite its reliance on a sophisticated web of references to earlier musical styles.[3] In contrast, *A Survivor from Warsaw*,
Op. 46 (1947), a twelve-tone work for narrator, men's chorus, and orchestra, employs accessible, illustrative musical ideas to intensify its emotional
subject. The *Ode to Napoleon Buonaparte*, Op. 41 (1942), also dodecaphonic, is similarly accessible, and it even includes references to tonal idioms
as accompaniment to the recitation of a dramatic poem by Lord Byron.
Falling somewhere between the String Trio and the *Ode to Napoleon* in
regard to accessibility, the dodecaphonic *Phantasy for Violin with Piano
Accompaniment*, Op. 47 (1949) has many of the attributes of conventional
virtuoso display pieces. The *Variations on a Recitative* for organ, Op. 40
(1941), by way of contrast with these twelve-tone works, is a tonal composition that offers a new take on the key of D minor that Schoenberg had
explored in earlier works such as *Verklärte Nacht*, Op. 4 (1899), *Pelleas und
Melisande*, Op. 5 (1903), and the String Quartet No. 1, Op. 7 (1905).
Another tonal work, the Theme and Variations in G Minor for band,
Op. 43 (1943) is didactic, intended to prepare young musicians for the
rigors of contemporary music. The varied sounds of these works suggest
that during the 1940s Schoenberg was still in the process of exploring the
ramifications of the twelve-tone method and reconciling it with his earlier
musical experiences. Points that Schoenberg made in "Heart and Brain in
Music," taken together with the compositional evolution of the Piano
Concerto and the score of that work, illuminate one particular facet of
that exploration.

Although Schoenberg rejected the notion that specific aspects of music
originate exclusively in "heart" or "brain," calling such an idea an "outmoded misconception," he recognized that listeners had in the past
assigned certain musical qualities to emotional or intellectual origins. He
observed that musical features perceived to stem from emotional sources
traditionally included "the beautiful melody or phrase, the beautiful – or,
at least, sweet – sound, [and] the beautiful harmony." Although he did not
define "beauty" in this context, he implied it was associated with conventional, tonal harmony and emotive, rhythmically regular themes that were
easy for listeners to follow. He "ascribed to the co-operation of the heart
and brain" qualities such as "dynamic contrasts, changes of tempo,

accentuation, features of rhythm and accompaniment," and a work's larger organization; he noted that such features engaged "the interest of a listener without considerable appeal to his feelings." Counterpoint, in his assessment of its conventional value, appealed to the brain, and was "tolerated only if it [did] not destroy the warmth of the dreams into which the charm of the beautiful has led the listener." In admitting the existence of such conventions, Schoenberg also recognized the possibility of tailoring compositions to appeal to a large audience, but he claimed that such pandering was never his goal.

> I believe that a real composer writes music for no other reason than that it pleases him. Those who compose because they want to please others, and have audiences in mind, are not real artists. They are not the kind of men who are driven to say something whether or not there exists one person who likes it, even if they themselves dislike it. They are not creators who must open the valves in order to relieve the interior pressure of a creation ready to be born. They are merely more or less skillful entertainers who would renounce composing if they could not find listeners."[4]

In practice, however, Schoenberg often took into account his intended audience when composing, and it is likely that the varied sounds of his works from the 1940s resulted from his recognition of how their audiences might differ.[5] In this light, it seems natural that his Piano Concerto, presumably intended for a public performance in a large hall before an audience of symphony subscribers, should be more accessible in sound than the String Trio, which was intended to be played at a conference of music critics sponsored by an elite university.[6] Another aspect of "audience" also might have affected the sound of the Concerto: the pianist who commissioned it. Oscar Levant, a Broadway and Hollywood celebrity, had studied briefly with Schoenberg and completed some compositions under Schoenberg's direction, but he was known chiefly for his works in popular style; thus, it has sometimes been assumed that the Concerto's style reflects Levant's tastes.[7] But even if Schoenberg were catering to Levant's preferred style, it was presumably not his intention to descend to the level of "entertainer" with the Concerto's accessible first theme, but merely to acknowledge the nature of the genre and its likely audience – and maybe even the taste of its intended performer. Even these acknowledgements do not fully explain Schoenberg's motivation in casting the theme as he does; his deeper motivation is revealed only in some of his first sketches for the work.

The Concerto is a single-movement work cast in four contrasting sections that mimic the movement-types and order of an eighteenth-century symphony: first movement, scherzo, slow movement, and dance-like finale. Early sketches for the Concerto include a brief extramusical program that

Example 17.2 Schoenberg, sketches for Concerto for Piano and Orchestra, mm. 1–8 of the first version of the theme (from sketches 113 and 120)

represents Schoenberg's first "idea" for the work and informs its formal outline: "1. Life was so easy; 2. Suddenly, hatred broke out; 3. A grave situation was created; 4. But life goes on."[8] Such a program suggests an emotive, inspired beginning for the work at odds with Schoenberg's perceived intellectualism; although Schoenberg did not mention extra-musical programs in his brief discussion of commonplace perceptions of emotive versus intellectual aspects of music, one assumes that he would have identified them with the "heart" aspect of this dichotomy. Although this program affects the larger formal scheme of the work, it is not an exclusively abstract, musical consideration. Indeed, the obviously auto-biographical nature of this program – Schoenberg's successful life in Berlin, the disruptions caused by the rise of the Nazis, his flight from Europe and the advent of World War II, and the eventual resumption of his life in Los Angeles – places the program firmly in the realm of the heart. Thus the opening of the Concerto – the lyrical twelve-tone theme – represents the "good old days" before political events turned the world upside down. The percussive scherzo, by way of contrast, captures the outbreak of hatred. The "grave situation" of exile and war is presented in the intense slow movement, and the resumption of Schoenberg's life becomes a gentle finale. Clearly, his very first thoughts on the Concerto engaged not only his emotions, in the form of the program, but also his intellect, as illustrated by the historically grounded formal scheme. Thus, the initial conception of the Concerto captures the balance of heart and brain of which Schoenberg wrote in his essay.

With his large-scale conception of the Concerto in mind, Schoenberg invented a musical idea that communicated the idea of "ease" and reso-nated with his own past: a lilting melody that suggests a Viennese waltz. For Schoenberg, this theme was a gift, born of inspiration. As he explained in his essay "Composition With Twelve Tones," he sometimes fortuitously discovered a twelve-tone row fully realized in the shape of a theme, rather than constructing a row and then extracting a theme from it; this was one of those situations.[9] Schoenberg's sketches show that the theme occurred to him replete with many of the rhythmic and textural qualities that he associated with accessible tonal music (Example 17.2). But as he began to work with the twelve-tone theme, he came to understand that its pitches did not fulfill the quality that he required of the row in all his mature twelve-tone works, namely, that it be combinatorial. Retaining the theme's rhythmic shape and general melodic contour, Schoenberg changed specific pitches until the row met his requirements, and he then reapplied it to the portions of the work he had outlined so far.[10] This particular step in the compositional process, which he did not mention in his essay "Heart and Brain in Music" when he quoted the theme, intensified the irony of his citation of the theme as an emotive/inspired-type melody: his sketches demonstrate that he reworked his first take on this heartfelt melody into something that fulfilled his technical expectations for twelve-tone compositions, yet retained the surface qualities of his original theme. So the irony is not only that a twelve-tone theme could be emotive and lyrical, but that a musical inspiration could be subjected to abstract musical processes and still emerge as an emotive entity. The first theme of the Concerto is therefore an even better example of the interdependency of the emotive and the intellectual than Schoenberg had implied in his essay.

As he continued to work on the first section of the Concerto with the revised theme, Schoenberg sustained the theme's lyrical, accessible quality in a manner not typical of most of his twelve-tone works. As he would eventually observe, his mature works did "not promote easy understanding" because they required "intense attention to grasp and a good memory to keep in mind what is going on."[11] In the first section of the Concerto, he focused on the musical characteristics of what he often termed "popular and dance music," such as periodic phrasing, which served as aids to memory. As he later wrote in the essay "Brahms the Progressive," "Construction by phrases of the same length, especially if their number of measures is two, four or eight times two, and if subdivision into two equally long segments adds a certain kind of symmetry, contributes much to memorability; knowing the first half, it is almost possible to conjecture the second half."[12] In the spirit of this technique, the theme of the first section of the Piano Concerto is constructed largely of pairs of four-measure phrases, often in antecedent-consequent relationships, with significant repetition on several levels. The theme itself, of more than forty measures, is stated twice completely – first in the piano and then in the orchestra as the piano adds a counter melody – before giving way to passages where it is developed jointly by piano and orchestra; it is subsequently sounded yet again in shortened form at the end of this third, developmental portion of the first section of the Concerto.

Congruent with this very regular melodic construction and large-scale repetition, the triple meter expressed in the first measures remains constant throughout, providing a rhythmic background of remarkable consistency; in addition, a dotted rhythmic figure repeats frequently to unify the rhythmic surface of the section. As a further aid to accessibility and memorability, the texture is quite simple – even sparse – at the beginning of the Concerto, and this quality brings the melody to the fore; only gradually is the texture complicated with additional lines. In light of Schoenberg's assessment of the perceived role of counterpoint, the counterpoint that exists here – melody and counter melody superimposed or brief echoes of melodic motives – does not "destroy the warmth." The light texture also reveals the relative consonance of the theme and its accompaniment: consonant intervals and widely spaced chords do not challenge the conservatively tuned ear. All of the musical ingredients also unfold at a relatively slow pace; simplicity, periodicity, repetition, and this slow unfolding of the material make it possible for listeners to fully grasp it before it becomes more complicated – a rarity in Schoenberg's works, which, as noted by Schoenberg above, tend not to "promote easy understanding." As a result, the opening section of the Concerto fulfills the requirement of "the beautiful melody or phrase, the beautiful – or, at least, sweet – sound, [and] the beautiful harmony," and it thus appears emotive and inspired rather than cerebral; it also matches the affect of the "good old days" expressed in the extramusical program.

By way of contrast, the second section of the Concerto relies less on "beauty" and more on rhythmic energy, in a manner which, according to Schoenberg's assessment of the conventional perception of these elements, suggests more of a cooperation between heart and brain. This new section is remarkably different from the first, which is in keeping not only with a "new" movement but with the outbreak of "hatred" indicated in the program, yet it retains certain musical characteristics that guarantee it a similar accessibility. The driving rhythm, duple meter, percussive orchestration, and faster tempo provide an immediate contrast with the first section, but an emphasis on regular phrasing, here largely in two-measure groups, relates the two sections. Similarly, the austere harmonic formations of the second section, featuring the perfect intervals of fourths, fifths, and octaves, contrast with those of the first, but they are not significantly more dissonant in sound. New, syncopated rhythmic figures produce a strong visceral interest that is intensified by a recurring dialogue between orchestra and piano, and these features contrast strongly with the lyricism of the first section. But these obvious surface contrasts are counterbalanced by a sub-surface regularity and relative consonance that matches the first section of the Concerto. Thus, the Concerto remains fairly easy to listen to and understand through the end of its second section, suggesting more "heart" than "brain."

With the third section of the Concerto, Schoenberg introduces additional contrasting elements that produce a greater complexity than had been evident in the previous sections. This "slow movement" carries the weight of the Concerto, as indicated by the "grave situation" called forth in the program: its serious nature is conveyed not only by the slow tempo, but also by the darker color of the orchestration, a generally lower range, richer rhythmic palette, denser counterpoint, and more dissonant harmony. Even though the phrasing is still based largely on two-measure units, these new qualities – especially the slow tempo, rhythmic variety, and complex counterpoint – tend to obscure any immediate appreciation of periodicity. Frequently, at least three melodic strands are superimposed, and florid subdivisions of the beat are common. Whereas an octave filled in by a fourth or fifth was a typical piano chord in the second section, here typical figurations include major or minor ninths, or major sevenths, enclosing smaller intervals. As a result of these more complex phenomena, this section of the Concerto sounds difficult: although the general sweep of the music is emotive in the Expressionist manner that Schoenberg evolved in his freely atonal works, its sound outpaces his descriptions of conventionally "inspired" or beautiful music, cited earlier. Indeed, the "situation" of the program is so "grave" that it cannot be expressed in the rather conventional musical language of the first two sections of the Concerto. Ironically, the musical effects used to depict this gravity seem to defeat the perception of this section as conventionally emotive.

The fourth section of the Concerto heralds a return to some of the surface qualities of the earlier portions of the work, but the affect of the third section still lingers. Schoenberg reintroduces a simpler, homophonic texture at the beginning of the fourth section and joins it with a regular duple meter, a repeating and memorable rhythmic pattern suggestive of a gavotte, and catchy themes constructed so as to suggest triads without relying on them exclusively. Constructed from a fairly clear alternation of new themes and their developments, the section culminates in a restatement of the theme from the first movement. Although these qualities almost recapture the "life was so easy" accessibility of the first section of the Concerto, the level of dissonance – reminiscent of that of the third section – is now much higher. For example, the melodic pitch "G," which occurs on the first downbeat in the primary melody of this section (m. 330), is accompanied by an F sharp and a G sharp to create a chord that sounds bitingly dissonant, even though these pitches are spread out over two octaves. This dissonance, which is sustained and repeated, is strangely at odds with the simple, lyrical theme, and the effect of their combination is disconcerting. In similar fashion, the development of themes in this section proceeds at a much faster pace than in the first section of the Concerto: exact repetition is rare here and the listener needs more of an "intense attention to grasp and a good memory to keep in mind what is going on." If interpreted from the perspective of the program, these particular qualities suggest that Schoenberg wished to depict his recent life without recourse to the rose-colored glasses that he had trained on his "easy" earlier life. Clearly, "life goes on" did not imply a resumption of the "easy" life represented at the beginning of the Concerto; instead, life as resumed was colored by the gravity of the recent past and retained some of its darkness. Thus, if the final section of the Concerto is not as accessible as the first and thus seems less emotive, its complexity is well merited in light of the autobiographical program.

Regarding the work as a whole, the relative engagement of heart and brain can be described and explained in a number of ways. From the perspective of the conventional, yet outmoded, understanding of the emotive and intellectual components of music that Schoenberg described, the Concerto encompasses an arc from heart to brain, as the "beauty" of the beginning of the work gives way to more complex features. In this view, the greater complexity of the final section of the Concerto results from a self-conscious decision on Schoenberg's part, presumably at the behest of his brain rather than his heart. Schoenberg would have been able to predict this rather conventional assessment of the work, but his own reading of it would have been far different. Although Schoenberg did not specifically address the role that intellect played in the creation of the Concerto, he did explain how intellect contributed to the evolution of another work. Regarding successive reworkings of a theme in one of his earlier tonal works, the First Chamber Symphony (1906), Schoenberg noted that the intellectual component at work in this process had nothing to do with contrapuntal complications or harmonic progressions. Instead, he stated that before he even considered harmony and counterpoint, he had to shape the theme itself from the motivic ideas that first occurred to him:

> The task . . . was to retard the progress of development in order to enable the average good listener to keep in mind what preceded so as to understand the consequences. To keep within bounds and to balance a theme whose character, tempo, expression, harmonic progression, and motival contents displayed a centrifugal tendency: this was here the task . . . it was not complexity which stood in the way of perfection, nor was it the heart which erred nor the brain which corrected.[13]

Apparently for Schoenberg, the essence of this particular theme needed taming, and he labored to build from it a theme that would not outpace the tracking abilities of most listeners. In the process, he had to temper his initial idea – to slow down the development of the material that came to him naturally – to allow listeners to keep up. It seems that in the case of the Piano Concerto, Schoenberg's inspiration handed him the beginning of a lyrical theme without those "centrifugal" tendencies, yet he still needed to adapt it to his own needs, first to bring it into line with his expectations for twelve-tone materials, and then to control its development to match his aesthetic idea for the work, as expressed in the first element of his extra-musical program. To those ends, Schoenberg strengthened the theme by making it combinatorial, then he created from it an expansive first section for the Concerto with uncharacteristic large-scale repetition rather than fast-paced development. In considering the relationship between the four sections of the Piano Concerto, it therefore seems obvious that Schoenberg exercised as much intellectual power to retard the development of the first and second parts as he did to construct the complexities of the third and fourth. Yet all of this self-conscious construction was motivated by the emotional program that dictated its larger form. In this work, there is no question that heart and brain were inextricably connected. As Schoenberg observed in general:

> It is not the heart alone which creates all that is beautiful, emotional, pathetic, affectionate, and charming; nor is it the brain alone which is able to produce the well-constructed, the soundly organized, the logical, and the complicated. First, everything of supreme value in art must show heart as well as brain. Second, the real creative genius has no difficulty in controlling his feelings mentally; nor must the brain produce only the dry and unappealing while concentrating on correctness and logic.[14]

Inspired by an autobiographical program, Schoenberg created a Piano Concerto that begins with an exceptionally lyrical and accessible musical idea that is then expanded in an unusually obvious manner. From this distinctive starting point, Schoenberg created a decidedly conservative work: out of respect for his original musical idea and for the overriding program, Schoenberg employed a restrained mode of expression, avoiding aggressive contrasts and challenging developments that would have been too jarring with the original conception of the work. Thus the distinctive sound of the Concerto can be traced back to the program itself. Regarding other works from the 1940s, none of them stems from exactly the same aesthetic origins, and their diverse sounds match their own unique situations. The existence of such a varied body of works from this decade counters those critics who dismissed Schoenberg as a heartless intellectual: Schoenberg addressed the needs of each work in turn rather than subjecting them to an overriding system. The intellectual component is certainly apparent in these works, but it is always modulated by Schoenberg's very human heart.

18 Schoenberg reception in America, 1933–51

SABINE FEISST

Like countless refugees from Nazi Europe, Arnold Schoenberg spent an important part of his creative life in America (1933–51). Here he not only produced significant works, but also contributed greatly to America's musical culture. Yet, little research has been done on Schoenberg's American years and the reception of his work. Moreover, scholarly impressions of his American career tend to convey a variety of predominantly negative interpretations. Numerous Schoenberg commentators claim that he was an isolated figure, that his music was rarely performed and "could not fall on fertile ground," and that his work was either misunderstood or ignored.[1] In this chapter, I will challenge some of these perceptions and examine the question of American Schoenberg performances, along with aspects of the theoretical and compositional reception of his work in America.

Schoenberg performances and press reactions

The common view that Schoenberg's music was "practically not performed" in America is a myth inviting scrutiny.[2] It partly grew out of Schoenberg's own worries about the dissemination of his music. He was troubled by the lean years of the Great Depression and World War II, when the arts saw major cutbacks, and was concerned about the conservatism predominating musical life in America. Yet his anxiety might have been prompted also by the feeling of what his fellow émigré Ernst Krenek called the "'echolessness' of the vast American expanses" – a notion implying that artists, for lack of feedback, were unaware of the full scope of their work's reception.[3]

When Schoenberg arrived in America in 1933, he was no stranger to Americans and his music was not entirely unknown. In fact almost all of his works composed before his emigration had received hearings and many of the more than two hundred documented performances had obtained press coverage.[4] Thanks to his and his supporters' intense networking, Schoenberg's music continued to receive hundreds of performances across the country throughout the 1930s and 1940s. Although

[247]

Schoenberg often stressed his indifference toward the music market, he strove for a wide dissemination of his music, along with audience appreciation and monetary benefit from his art.

In the 1930s conductors such as Otto Klemperer, Sergei Koussevitzky, Eugene Ormandy and Frederick Stock performed his orchestral music. Their programming, however, complied with the populist leanings at that time. In these depression years, orchestras lost private funding, struggled against declining concert attendance, and could not risk disaffecting audiences with peculiar-seeming music.[5] Thus almost all of the *circa* one hundred documented orchestral performances of the 1930s featured Schoenberg's tonal music, *Verklärte Nacht*, *Pelleas und Melisande*, the First Chamber Symphony, excerpts from *Gurrelieder*, and his Bach, Handel, Monn, and Brahms arrangements. Even Schoenberg himself preferred to conduct his old and new tonal compositions.

The focus on tonal works conformed to his own "pedagogical" strategy to first familiarize Americans with his most accessible music in order to prepare them for his atonal works. While audiences seemed generally pleasantly surprised by what they heard, East Coast critics were puzzled by the incompatibility of these works with Schoenberg's iconoclastic reputation. Upon hearing Schoenberg conduct his *Pelleas und Melisande* in Boston in 1934, a critic wondered, "Why a work this unrepresentative should have been selected by Schönberg (he himself and no other made the selection) remains a riddle as unsolvable as that of the sphinx itself."[6] Schoenberg's new tonal Suite in G (1934) even provoked mockery in the press. "Has the much advertised Californian sunshine thawed out the gloomy apostle of the twelve-tone Grundgestalt and left him singing roundelays among the poppies?" wrote a New York reviewer.[7] The West Coast critics, in contrast, reported mostly favorably, but seldom thoroughly and meaningfully, on his music.[8]

Schoenberg's chamber music could also be heard regularly in major American cities throughout the 1930s. Among the more than ninety performances, however, renditions of his atonal works prevailed. Infrastructures for the dissemination of modern chamber music had been developed since the 1920s thanks to the endeavors of Edgard Varèse, Henry Cowell, and others. The Abas, Manhattan, Pro Arte, and Kolisch String Quartets played his last three Quartets. The Kolisch Quartet not only premiered the Fourth Quartet in 1937 in Los Angeles, but also recorded and performed all four Quartets as a cycle in several American cities.[9] Richard Buhlig, Jésus Sanromá, and Eduard Steuermann among other pianists repeatedly played works from Opp. 11 through 33b.[10] Schoenberg's *Book of the Hanging Gardens*, *Pierrot lunaire*, and Woodwind Quintet, however, received altogether only about a dozen performances. These events, often presented at small venues and attended by people from the literary, art, and dance scenes, were generally announced in the press, but seldom reviewed. The premiere of the Fourth Quartet, however, was an exception. It even received a sympathetic review in the *New York Times*, which pointed out the work's Romantic qualities, the sizeable concert attendance, and positive audience response.[11]

Despite Schoenberg's perception in 1949 "that the number of performances sank to an extremely low point," concerts featuring his orchestral works in the 1940s had doubled, not least thanks to his seventieth and seventy-fifth birthdays in 1944 and 1949, and Antony Tudor's popular ballet *The Pillar of Fire* based on *Verklärte Nacht*.[12] American orchestras gave more than 200 performances including premieres of the dodecaphonic Violin and Piano Concertos, *Ode to Napoleon*, Prelude to the *Genesis* Suite, and *A Survivor from Warsaw* conducted by Leopold Stokowski, Artur Rodzinski, Werner Janssen, and Kurt Frederick. Moreover, Dimitri Mitropoulos performed and recorded the Violin Concerto and Serenade, reviving the Five Orchestral Pieces in 1948 and Variations for Orchestra, Op. 16 in 1950. Yet again, performances of tonal works prevailed, with only about ten percent featuring his Modernist output. Schoenberg's initial push for his tonal music had turned into a situation comparable to that of Goethe's *Sorcerer's Apprentice*: "Spirits that I've cited my commands ignore." Schoenberg's hopes that his atonal and dodecaphonic music would become a staple of American orchestra concerts were shattered by the late 1940s.

But conversely, in the realm of chamber music, hearings of his atonal works outweighed performances of his tonal compositions. The over one hundred renditions (out of *circa* 190 performances) of such pieces as *Pierrot lunaire*, *Book of the Hanging Gardens*, and his progressive string and piano works document an increasing interest in modernism against a still conservative musical background marked by a focus on Neoclassicism and Americana. Schoenberg benefited from the emergence of contemporary music groups and the presence of open-minded émigré musicians such as the Galimir, Kolisch, and Pro Arte Quartets, and the pianist-composers Erich Kahn and Eduard Steuermann. But an increasing number of American-born artists including the Fine Arts, Juilliard, and Walden Quartets, the singer Rose Bampton, the pianists Buhlig, William Masselos, Frances Mullen, Leonard Stein, and David Tudor also performed his music. Institutions such as the New School for Social Research and the New Friends of Music in New York, Black Mountain College in North Carolina, and Evenings on the Roof in Los Angeles played a vital role in promoting European (and American) modernism. From 1939 to 1953

numerous performances and lectures on this subject were given at Black
Mountain College. Here Heinrich Jalowetz, Schoenberg's student, and a
college professor from 1939 to 1946, mounted an influential festival on the
occasion of Schoenberg's seventieth birthday in 1944. The creative exchange
of such Schoenbergians as Rudolf Kolisch, Steuermann, Marcel Dick, Ernst
Krenek, and Mark Brunswick gave Schoenberg reception in America a
boost. Significantly Roger Sessions, who also attended the festival, consequently became an active Schoenberg supporter after having been skeptical
of Schoenberg's ideas. Initiated in 1939 by writer Peter Yates and his wife,
pianist Frances Mullen, the Evenings on the Roof were an important
chamber concert series, specializing in modernist repertoire and featuring
between 1939 and 1954 nine all-Schoenberg programs and West Coast
premieres of *Herzgewächse*, Op. 20, the Serenade, Op. 24, Four Pieces for
Mixed Chorus, Op. 27, the String Trio, Op. 45, and *Dreimal tausend Jahre*,
Op. 50a.

Most press and audience responses to Schoenberg performances in the
1940s were sympathetic. This was due to the fact that performances of
Schoenberg's tonal orchestral works dominated the programming and
that performances of his chamber music by and large did not receive
detailed press coverage, if it received any at all. Among the non-tonal
orchestral works, the Five Orchestral Pieces and *Ode to Napoleon* generally prompted a favorable feedback, the Piano Concerto and *A Survivor
from Warsaw* elicited mixed reactions, while the Violin Concerto and
Variations for Orchestra initiated antagonism from critics and
audiences.[13] Interestingly, the verdicts of *New York Times* critic Olin
Downes, commonly perceived as a Schoenberg detractor, varied greatly.
He reviewed positively *Verklärte Nacht*, the First Chamber Symphony,
Second String Quartet, Five Orchestral Pieces, and *Pierrot lunaire*.[14] Yet,
he dismissed *Pelleas und Melisande*, the Orchestral Variations, Second
Chamber Symphony, Piano Concerto, and *A Survivor from Warsaw*.[15]

The performances and emergence of recordings of Schoenberg's
modernist music and his provocative contributions to newspapers
inspired lively debates on atonality and dodecaphony in widely circulated
journals (*New Yorker*, *Newsweek*, *Partisan Review*, *Time*, and so on),
especially from the mid 1940s on.[16] Schoenberg critics including
Downes, Daniel Gregory Mason, and Tibor Serly questioned the validity
and success of his techniques.[17] Schoenberg supporters such as Dika
Newlin, René Leibowitz, and Roger Sessions defended his progressive
stance insisting on its integrity, relevance, and inevitability.[18] These
debates were paralleled by discussions about avant-garde versus mass
culture in intellectual circles, which intensified after the massive cultural
changes in the Soviet Union in the 1930s. Additionally, in the late 1940s

several of Schoenberg's public protests – his infamous complaint about American conductors neglecting his works, his denigration of Aaron Copland, and disapproval of Thomas Mann's best-selling novel *Doctor Faustus* (1948) – strongly reverberated in the press and drew attention to him and his music. But they left the impression that he was a neglected and bitter artist.[19]

Commentaries on Schoenberg's compositional techniques

Much ink has been spilled to explain, criticize, and defend Schoenberg's innovations ever since the notorious early performances of *Verklärte Nacht*. In America his work has generated commentary since *circa* 1907. By the time he settled there, Americans had been confronted with numerous discourses on his *Harmonielehre* and atonal music. His students, including Egon Wellesz, Erwin Stein, and Adolph Weiss, had informed Americans about the rudiments of dodecaphony starting in the mid 1920s.[20]

In America, as he had done in Europe, Schoenberg left speculation about the twelve-tone technique to his adherents. He limited public discussion of it to the basic talk "Composing with Twelve-Tones," which he presented to non-specialist audiences between 1934 and 1946 and included in his book *Style and Idea* (Philosophical Library, 1950). Thus Schoenberg's relative silence on dodecaphony left much room for idiosyncratic interpretations of this subject. In 1936 American musicologist Richard Hill published an influential in-depth study on Schoenberg's dodecaphony. Herein he identified the ways in which Schoenberg treated the set horizontally and vertically and combined different row forms. He also recognized for the first time in print the phenomenon that Babbitt later termed "inversional combinatoriality." Despite this insight, however, Hill criticized Schoenberg for using the row in complex and non-linear ways, claiming that the row's "motival significance has been completely destroyed."[21] Hill called for a more thematic treatment of the row and adherence to its temporal pitch order. Soon thereafter Krenek, seemingly building on Hill, published two introductions to dodecaphony, *Here and Now* (Norton, 1939) and *Studies in Counterpoint Based on the Twelve-Tone Technique* (Schirmer, 1940), promoting a thematic and polyphonic use of tone rows.[22]

Among other publications of the 1930s, Marion Bauer's textbook *Twentieth-Century Music* (Putnam's Sons, 1933) deserves mention for its inclusion of a chapter on Schoenberg's atonal works, which despite its sketchy analyses had a special meaning for many musicians, including Milton Babbitt. Merle Armitage published the anthology *Schoenberg* (Schirmer, 1937) with contributions by Schoenberg and many of his champions. And Schoenberg himself emerged with a variety of essays in such venues as *Modern Music*, *American Mercury* and Armitage's *George Gershwin* (Schirmer, 1938).[23]

The 1940s saw many more printed tributes to Schoenberg due to his seventieth and seventy-fifth birthdays, issued by such friends as Brunswick, Jalowetz, and Sessions, but also by some of his American students, including Lou Harrison and Dika Newlin.[24] Jalowetz wrote in 1944 a comprehensive essay on Schoenberg's music featuring a detailed analysis of his Piano Concerto.[25] Author of numerous Schoenberg articles, Newlin published the musico-cultural study, *Bruckner, Mahler, Schoenberg* (New York, King's Crown Press, 1947). While many surveys of modern music included sizeable Schoenberg chapters, Schoenberg himself published articles, the treatises *Models for Beginners in Composition* (1942) and *Theory of Harmony* (1949), and the essay collection *Style and Idea* (1950).

In the 1940s knowledge about atonality and dodecaphony was further advanced. In his 1943 essay "New Developments of the Twelve-tone Technique," Krenek discussed the "trend towards exploring the extramotival function of the series," analyzing Schoenberg's non-thematic use of the row in the Violin Concerto and works by himself and his student George Perle.[26] Concurrently Perle published his first essays on his twelve-tone modal system and twelve-tone tonality combining dodecaphonic ideas with hierarchic relations among pitch classes and chords comparable to those existing in tonal practice.[27] These systems, which Perle substituted for the (in his opinion) "fortuitous" harmonic relationships in dodecaphonic music, imply a critique of Schoenberg's handling of the harmonic dimension in dodecaphonic composition. In 1946 Babbitt completed his Ph.D. dissertation at Princeton University, "The Function of the Set Structure in the Twelve-Tone System," which was, due to a lack of competent readers, not officially accepted until 1992, but became nevertheless a widely read and authoritative manuscript on dodecaphony in America. Drawing on set theory, Babbitt rationalized and extended the theoretical foundation of Schoenberg's, Webern's, and Berg's twelve-tone ideas. Moreover, he created a soon widely used mathematicized terminology including "pitch class," "set," "aggregate," and "combinatoriality" to describe manifold serial concepts.

Yet René Leibowitz, a Polish-born French composer and passionate Schoenberg promoter, arguably made an even greater impact on the music scene at the time with his enthusiastic landmark study *Schoenberg et son école* (1947), which appeared in 1949 in an English translation by Newlin, presenting for the first time broad coverage of Schoenberg's, Berg's, and Webern's music. While this book was welcomed and widely read, it was criticized by Aaron Copland for its "dogmatic" and "fanatical tone," and by Babbitt and Perle for its superficial musical discussions and use of "misleading" analogies between tonal and twelve-tone music.[28] With his scathing 1950 review of Leibowitz's book, Babbitt officially published for the first time his sophisticated insights into dodecaphony and set the stage for many detailed studies of twelve-tone music in the years to come.[29]

Both Babbitt and Perle also criticized Schoenberg's essay "Composing with Twelve Tones," published in 1950, questioning his evocation of serialism's historical lineage and his analogies to tonal music to validate its use.[30] And as if Schoenberg had foreseen this essay's critiques, he claimed in 1950 that he wrote "a superficial explanation" of the twelve-tone method against his "'free' will."[31] His apologetic position, however, reflects his apprehension of the looming ideologies of serialism. The generalization of Schoenberg's methods resulted, according to Sessions, in "attention on the *means*, rather than on the music itself," which was something Schoenberg tried to avoid.[32]

The preoccupation with Schoenberg's techniques after World War II was furthered by the growth of college education prompted by such measures as the 1944 GI bill, a tendency toward teaching specialized rather than general knowledge, and a focus on science and technology. Lending itself to theorization and science-inspired thinking, Schoenberg's work was soon institutionalized, researched, and taught at major American universities. Its study propelled the rise of American music theory and denoted a sea change in musical thought and practice in America.

Schoenberg's impact on composition in America

During the 1930s and 1940s Schoenberg inspired gradually more composers to explore his ideas and above all serialism – perhaps the most easily traceable Schoenberg influence in American music. During Schoenberg's American sojourn, serialism developed into an important compositional trend marking American music for several decades.

Adolph Weiss, who studied with Schoenberg from 1925 to 1927, was one of the first Americans who composed twelve-tone works and whose dodecaphonic Piano Preludes (1927) and Sonata da Camera (1929), each accompanied by a brief analysis, were the first twelve-tone works published in America (1929 and 1930). These pieces inspired composers such as Wallingford Riegger, who soon thereafter extensively experimented with this method. In *Dichotomy* for chamber orchestra (1932) Riegger used an eleven-note and a thirteen-note row in their prime, retrograde, and inversion forms as themes with variations in a freely chromatic context. Weiss's and Riegger's focus on the linear-thematic and contra-puntal possibilities of dodecaphony, however, differed from Schoenberg's mature twelve-tone techniques in which the twelve-tone set is often treated as referential background. Despite a widespread unawareness of these procedures, Schoenberg, on the occasion of the publication of his Klavierstück, Op. 33b in Cowell's *New Musical Quarterly* in 1932, abstained from "musical explanations concerning his work, since his musical viewpoint [is] well known."

Interest in the use of dodecaphony in America grew thanks to Schoenberg's popularity as a teacher and the presence of other European refugee composers including Paul Dessau, Hanns Eisler, Kahn, Krenek, Steuermann, and Stefan Wolpe who employed and/or helped disseminate it in various ways. Wolpe and Krenek, who both emigrated to America in 1938, had adopted the twelve-tone technique shortly before Hitler's rise to power and kept using it in idiosyncratic ways. Wolpe, a left-wing activist composer, shifted his focus from Neoclassical approaches to serial tech-niques in the late 1920s, believing that serial music symbolized not merely resistance to fascism, but rather the new social liberation. In America he generally held on to a personalized serial technique, surely for political reasons gaining in urgency during the Cold War when Soviets suppressed artistic freedom and Senator Joseph McCarthy persecuted leftist artists. Wolpe often alternated between diatonicism, octatonicism, and twelve-tone techniques, employed pitch cells within completely chromatic set-tings, and combined serial ideas with traditional harmonic devices. Later Wolpe refrained from the constant exhaustion of the chromatic palette, giving fewer notes greater weight and exploring pitch sets with fewer or more than twelve pitches.[33]

For Krenek, his adherence to serialism was partly a political gesture, withstanding its ban by the Nazis and mediating it to another culture. Krenek was perhaps most instrumental in using and promoting thematic, modal, and unorthodox approaches to dodecaphony. In his *Lamentatio Jeremiae Prophetae* (1942) he used modal counterpoint and applied the principle of rotation to the row, dividing it into two hexachords and systematically alternating the pitches within these hexachords. Thematic and modal treatments of the row became popular in the 1940s and early 1950s with composers such as Ben Weber, Walter Piston, Ross Lee Finney, Copland, and Sessions.

From the 1930s through the 1950s American Schoenberg students, including John Cage and Harrison, also used serialism in their works. Yet since they heavily engaged in experimentalism, they tend to be overlooked as heirs of the Schoenberg legacy despite the fact that to them Schoenberg had remained a lifelong inspiration. Cage, a student of Schoenberg from 1935 to 1936, explored various unorthodox forms of serialism between 1933 and 1938. He used a twelve-tone row and its transformations in his Sonata for Clarinet (1933), unordered rows of twenty-five pitches based on the principle of non-repetition in Sonata for Two Voices (1933), and rows as collections of small motives subjected to various serial transformations in *Metamorphosis* (1938). In comparison, Harrison, who studied with Schoenberg in 1943, alternated between serial composition and multitudinous other techniques for much of his career. Modeled after Schoenberg's Suite, Op. 25, his Piano Suite (1943) is based on a thematically treated quasi-all-interval set. This lyrical work, which Harrison wrote during his studies with Schoenberg, is one of the rare student twelve-tone compositions that he actually supervised and endorsed. Later Harrison used various serial approaches, involving very lyrical tone rows with tonal implications or with fewer than twelve notes, as well as permutation principles in such compositions as *Schoenbergiana* (1945), Symphony on G (1948–65), and *Rapunzel* (1954).

Babbitt and Perle, Schoenberg scholars since the 1930s, emerged in the 1940s as perhaps the most dedicated and influential "serial" composers, taking dodecaphony to new levels of sophistication. Babbitt developed dodecaphony into an intricate system of structurally interrelated sonic textures articulated by pitch, rhythm, timbre, dynamics, and register. In his *Three Compositions for Piano* of 1947 he pioneered new types of combinatoriality and invariance and developed, earlier than his European colleagues, integral serialism by serializing duration and dynamics. Further, Babbitt expanded Schoenberg's approach to what he called "partitioning" by constructing trichordal rows whose four forms could be superimposed to unfold horizontally and vertically at the same time. These so-called arrays would then lead to more complex types of textures such as all-partition arrays and superarrays. While Schoenberg and Babbitt both believe in musical progress, in contrast to Schoenberg's emphasis on emotion and intuition, Babbitt stresses quasi-scientific and technical qualities in his music. As Babbitt greatly illuminated Schoenberg's work, his penchant for logical positivism and academicism, however, reinforced the cliché of Schoenberg's music being "cerebral."

As mentioned above, Perle developed his own twelve-tone modal system in the late 1930s. In such works as his *Two Rilke Songs* of 1941, he conceived twelve-tone sets with ascending and descending circles of fifths, which determined the vertical dimension of the work. Next Perle refined this tone-centered approach, now termed "twelve-tone tonality," through the use of cyclic sets – twelve-tone sets consisting of symmetrical cells that can be combined in pairs to form symmetrically interrelated arrays of chords. Only marginally related to Schoenberg, twelve-tone tonality became the focus of many of Perle's compositions since the 1940s. As Perle found fault with certain aspects in Schoenberg's twelve-tone works, including the Violin Concerto, he also rejected Babbitt's approach to serialism due to its musical and perceptual complexity.

In 1949 Kurt List, former student of Berg and Webern, wrote to Schoenberg that as the editor of the music publishing firm Boelke-Bomart he had seen many dodecaphonic works, reporting that "twelve-tone music is now very 'fashionable'" and that most young American composers now write music based on rows.[34] Indeed, young composers, including Newlin, George Rochberg, and Gunther Schuller, but also established figures such as Piston, Copland, Sessions, and Finney, began to explore serialism. Having been controversial and greeted with a mixed reception, Schoenberg's ideas gained momentum thanks to a myriad of favorable circumstances. Highly esteemed performers and spokesmen suggested the relevance and prestige of his music. Moreover at the beginning of the Cold War era, serialism became a symbol of creative freedom in Europe and America in that it epitomized resistance against the stifling cultural politics of both the Nazi and Communist regimes. In America McCarthyism arguably motivated left-wing composers (among them Copland) to balance their formerly politically oriented and audience-friendly music with abstract serial works.[35] Furthermore, music conveying socialist or patriotic messages was less in demand after the war. Neoclassicism, the most popular style in the 1930s and 1940s, seemed outmoded too, as many composers, among them its most prominent representative Stravinsky, abandoned it in favor of serialism shortly after Schoenberg's death. With the renewed faith in progress, science, and technology, there was an increased interest in intellectually based, abstract, and avant-garde music. In 1948 and 1949 such works as Riegger's dodecaphonic Third Symphony and Babbitt's serial Composition for Four Instruments began to receive prestigious awards.

Conclusion

Schoenberg's presence in America led to manifold responses to his music reflected in performance, scholarship, and composition. He obtained support from three groups: fellow émigrés, his American students, and Americans outside his circle. Despite his worries about being neglected, he received numerous performances nationwide, though the renditions of his tonal music outweighed those of his atonal works. The number of performances of Schoenberg's modernist music, however, needs to be gauged against the background of a general musical conservatism conditioned by economically strained times, and also compared with the still smaller number of performances of progressive works by such fellow émigrés as Bartók, Krenek, and Wolpe, or indigenous composers including Ives, Riegger, and Sessions. Aside from performances, Schoenberg also received attention in many journalistic and scholarly publications, reflecting a growing interest in musical Modernism and music theory. The diverse theoretical and practical interpretations of dodecaphony filled the gap Schoenberg created with his silence on this subject, but also generated consequences he might not have anticipated. During a time when dodecaphonic music was largely banned in Nazi Europe, ever more American composers began developing their own take on serialism and conveying their fascination with Schoenberg to younger generations. Finally, Schoenberg's ideas benefited from political and societal changes in the postwar era, attaining new political and cultural values. Schoenberg's ideas undoubtedly fell on fertile ground, growing into one of the strongest influences on American music for a quarter century.

19 Schoenberg: dead or alive? His reception among the postwar European avant-garde

RICHARD TOOP

Immediate postwar responses

From the early 1950s onwards, the response of "radical" young European composers to the Schoenberg legacy was highly diverse. On the one hand, in 1951, Pierre Boulez wrote a notorious polemical article announcing that "Schoenberg is Dead"; on the other, one of Luigi Nono's first works was the *Variazioni canoniche sulla serie di l'opus 41 di Schoenberg* (1950), and in 1955 he established direct family ties by marrying Schoenberg's daughter Nuria (they had met the previous year at Hans Rosbaud's premiere performance of *Moses und Aron* in Hamburg). For elder spokesmen of the postwar period such as Theodor W. Adorno, Schoenberg was the exemplary apostle of progress, as opposed to the "reactionary" Stravinsky. But precisely this kind of patriarchal espousal aroused suspicion and resistance among the young, to both the dodecaphonic and Neoclassical camps. Of the Second Viennese School, it was often the equally "patriarchal" Schoenberg who was rejected in favor of an emergent Webern mythology on the one hand (initially, the young "Darmstadt generation" was often characterized as post-Webernian), and a fascination with Berg's esoteric late-Romanticism on the other.

Significantly, none of these young Europeans had ever encountered Schoenberg in person. In principle, both Nono and Stockhausen should have done so: one of the main reasons for Stockhausen's going to the 1951 Darmstadt Summer Courses (at the instigation of Herbert Eimert) was that Schoenberg was scheduled to give the composition class, and Nono was there too. But Schoenberg was too ill to travel, and was replaced by Adorno: the latter's hostile encounter with Stockhausen following a performance of the two middle movements of Karel Goeyvaerts's Sonata for 2 Pianos (in which Stockhausen had been the second pianist) has often been recounted.[1] Now, just suppose that Schoenberg had been well enough to travel to Darmstadt: could that have changed the course of European new music? One must assume that his response to Goeyvaerts's work would have been at least as antagonistic as Adorno's. But can we believe that Stockhausen would have been as confident in defending this innovative but not particularly distinguished piece against one of the giants of contemporary music as he was against Adorno? Assuming that Schoenberg's objections would have been much the same as Adorno's, though probably much more emphatically expressed, can we imagine that the twenty-two-year-old Stockhausen would have accused him too of "looking for a chicken in an abstract painting?" Or that Schoenberg would even have allowed discussion on the matter? This could have been a real crisis for Stockhausen: how sure can we be that, in the months following Darmstadt, he would still have gone on to compose *Kreuzspiel*, and all the works that followed from it?

It's a similar story with Luigi Nono. The preceding year (1950), in Darmstadt, Hermann Scherchen had conducted the premiere of Nono's *Variazioni canoniche*, and since Nono had been following Scherchen around Europe as an assistant from 1948 onwards, it's possible that the latter had mentioned him to Schoenberg, with whom he had enjoyed a friendship dating back forty years. At the 1951 Darmstadt courses, Scherchen gave the premiere of the young composer's *Polifonica – Monodia – Ritmica*, and again, one wonders how Schoenberg might have reacted: probably less negatively than he would have done to Goeyvaerts's sonata, but negatively nonetheless. I imagine he would have been irritated by the rather anodyne Webernisms of the first three minutes, somewhat more engaged by the sharper, more "Schoenbergian" figure at the end of the first part, reluctantly tolerant of the "Mediterranean" *Monodia* section, and, finally, dismissive of the constructivist final section, whose obsession with unpitched percussion sounds might well have reminded him of his former American student John Cage ("not a composer, but an inventor – of genius"). If so, and if he had expressed his views with his usual intransigence, how would Nono have responded?

At one level, this is all futile speculation, and yet ... is it too much to suggest that, in many respects, Schoenberg's demise was a "fortunate death" for the emerging young serialist European avant-garde, as indeed was Webern's? One has a sense of Schoenberg, and with him the whole Second Viennese School, conveniently dying (to cite the subtitle Boulez once had in mind for his *Structures*) "At the Borders of the Fertile Land," that is, as a musical Moses who reaches the borders of the Promised Land, but never enters it. This is a concept that Boulez emphatically dismisses at the end of "Schoenberg is Dead,"[2] but twenty-three years later, in "Schoenberg, the Unloved?," he takes a more equivocal view of it.[3]

Not surprisingly, "Schoenberg is Dead" unleashed enormous resentment, especially in the United States. But this would scarcely have bothered the young Boulez, who in matters of polemics was an unashamed street fighter. To a degree, one might surmise, Schoenberg's status became caught up in the crossfire between Boulez and his former teacher René Leibowitz, or rather, the former's unremitting attacks on the latter, who was a fervent but somewhat academic advocate of Schoenberg. It's hard to underestimate the savagery of these attacks. Writing to Cage late in 1951, shortly after the article's publication, Boulez claims "I believe that this putting things clearly was indispensable in order to be able to separate me from the dodecaphonic academicians."[4] Though this may be partly true, it is scarcely the whole story. It seems to me that at this stage, the young Boulez was engaged in all-out Oedipal rebellion, and that in this enterprise, "small" but physically present father figures in Paris such as Leibowitz and Jacques-Louis Monod probably paled into insignificance next to the "legendary" Schoenberg. In this context, however, Leibowitz's apparent Schoenberg idolatry could scarcely have helped (recently, Boulez described him as "an epigone of the very worst kind. He swore only by Schoenberg. Schoenberg was the truth, the Bible."[5]).

In any case, Boulez's attacks on Schoenberg had not waited for his death. Already in *Trajectories* (1949) he had expressed sharp reservations. The essay begins by comparing *Pierrot lunaire* with two works that responded to it – Stravinsky's *Three Japanese Lyrics* and Ravel's *Trois Poèmes de Stéphane Mallarmé* – and while ultimately finding much more significance in *Pierrot*, Boulez endorses Stravinsky's initial impression of *Pierrot*, as expressed in his *Autobiography*, as representing "a retrogression to the out-of-date Beardsley cult." Yet at the same time Boulez suggests that this correct aesthetic judgement blinded Stravinsky to the technical solutions that the work offered – albeit transitorily – to the "problem of language," by which he primarily means pitch structure. Here too, though, he sees a contradiction between form and content: "the most serious charge one could level at *Pierrot lunaire* [is] the lack of a profound coherence and a 'uterine' relationship between its language and its architecture."[6] But this, he feels, is only reinforced when Schoenberg, having subsequently evolved a twelve-tone technique, uses it to write "a march, a minuet, a waltz . . . the novelty of the language has altered nothing in the way of thought which preceded that language; a malaise simply accentuated by what followed."[7] As a concrete instance of this, he cites Schoenberg's reluctance to renounce the convention of melody and accompaniment: for the young Boulez, "accompaniment" has no place in current musical thinking.

The point at issue here is not whether Boulez's accusations are reasonable: in many respects they clearly are not. But *Trajectories* partly documents the historical upbeat, in Europe, to the musical *tabula rasa* of 1951, and Boulez, one may surmise, is looking for pretexts to sweep as much as possible off the table. As it happens, he could have used Schoenberg's own words in his defense. In a letter of December 21, 1948 (so, ironically, at almost exactly the moment when Boulez was writing *Trajectories*)

Schoenberg wrote to the critic Olin Downes: "Now finally as to your question whether I believe composers are as a rule fair or unbiased critics of other composers: I think they are in the first instance fighters for their own musical ideas. The ideas of other composers are their enemies. You cannot restrict a fighter. His blows are correct when they hit hard, and only then is he fair."[8]

Perhaps one should point out that this early polemic precedes any notion of a "Darmstadt avant-garde": in 1948/9 the twenty-four-year-old Boulez is an isolated "voice crying in the wilderness." Maybe, by the time of "Schoenberg is Dead," the situation has changed a little, but not much: Goeyvaerts, Nono, and Stockhausen have met up at Darmstadt in 1951, but Boulez isn't there, and personally, I would be inclined to suggest that this "Darmstadt avant-garde" doesn't really exist as a palpable force until 1954 (and even then, only as a marginal one: it's not until 1957 that one of them [Stockhausen] gives a composition course there.)[9] Be that as it may, "Schoenberg is Dead" doesn't just resume the critiques of *Trajectories*: it takes them a great deal further, with the aim of total dismissal: "pour en finir avec le pouvoir de Schoenberg," so to speak. Let's recall the abrasive opening lines:

> Taking a position on Schoenberg?
> Certainly, it's one of the most pressing necessities; nevertheless, it's a fleeting problem, defying wisdom: perhaps an investigation with no satisfactory outcome.
> No point in denying it: the Schoenberg "case" is, above all, irritating, because it involves such blatant inconsistencies.[10]

Pierrot is now hailed as a "resounding triumph,"[11] and the "initial phase" of atonality is at least cautiously praised, in so far as "aesthetics, poetic, and technique are all in phase ... whatever flaws one may be able to find in these areas individually."[12] But that's as far as the good news goes. Schoenberg's alliance of dodecaphony with traditional forms and syntactic details is denounced as "a direction as wrong as any in the history of music."[13] It's not just his strategy that is lampooned, but even its technical execution: "From Schoenberg's pen flows a stream of infuriating clichés and formidable stereotypes redolent of the most wearily ostentatious romanticism ... those fake appoggiaturas, those arpeggios, tremolandos and note repetitions, which sound so terribly empty ... finally, the depressing poverty, even ugliness of the rhythms."[14]

But this kind of rabid Schoenberg-antipathy is, frankly, unique among the young European avant-garde of the period around 1950. It may seem ironic, coming from the composer who – among this group – arguably learned most from Schoenberg, but it raises a broader question: how much specific influence did Schoenberg's music exert on young Europeans in the early 1950s? At a technical level, rather little: neither the motivic processes of Schoenberg's twelve-tone practice nor the linked theoretical perspectives that fascinated Milton Babbitt and many North-American composers after him made much apparent impact on them. In the early 1950s Nono analyzed Schoenberg's Variations for Orchestra in his classes, along with those of Webern (Op. 30), but in this respect he was something of a lone voice among the younger avant-garde, for whom Webern was the natural point of reference, if any was needed. One aspect of Schoenberg's practice that did make a limited impact was *Sprechstimme*, not so much in its solo form, as in *Pierrot*, the *Ode to Napoleon*, and *A Survivor from Warsaw*, as in its choral one, which would initially have become familiar from *Moses und Aron* rather than *Die glückliche Hand*. Early examples include two Boulez cantatas – *Le soleil des eaux* and *Le visage nuptial* – as well as Nono's *España nel Corazón* (the second part of his *Epitaffio per Frederico García Lorca*) and *La victoire de Guernica*. On the other hand, while the range of novel vocal techniques in late-fifties works as diverse as Cage's *Aria* and Stockhausen's *Carré* include *Sprechstimme*-like elements, one would hesitate to ascribe these to Schoenberg's influence.

This, perhaps, is the point at which to recall that, in Italy, the most significant link between the young composers and the older Malipiero/ Dallapiccola generation was provided not by Nono, but by Bruno Maderna (1920–73). Maderna has said that he was already studying *Pierrot lunaire* at the age of eighteen, just before the outbreak of World War II. It's a reminder that the Nazi proscription of the Second Viennese School initially had only limited impact in Italy (another key figure of the future European avant-garde, Mauricio Kagel, living on the other side of the planet in Buenos Aires, claimed that he already encountered works by Schoenberg and Webern in his mid teens, that is, around 1945.)[15] Maderna's later description of his rationale for studying Schoenberg is particularly instructive: "certain problems, and certain solutions, were of interest to me; but, like others of my generation, I thought that a work like *Pierrot lunaire*, however important it might be, was something different from our own things: it was 'German,' just as we were 'Italian.'"[16] Similar thinking may have underlain Luciano Berio's decidedly negative response to Schoenberg's twelve-tone works. But there are other factors: "One of the reasons for the objective difficulties involved in coming to grips with the neo-classical Schoenberg of, say, the Wind Quintet is – quite apart from the general incompatibility and indifference between rhythm and pitch – the frankly repulsive character of the dodecaphonic 'themes' which disfigure the discourse, and whose useless recurrence I find utterly depressing."[17]

So why was Luigi Nono's attitude so different? One can't reduce it to the anti-fascist aspects exemplified in the *Ode to Napoleon* and *A Survivor from Warsaw*, even though Nono described the latter work, in 1961(!), as "the aesthetic, musical manifesto of our era." Rather, it seems that his sustained exposure to Austro-German music as a result of his association with Scherchen had a decisive impact: he writes that he "got to love the German tradition" in a way that Berio, for example, did not. Specifically, one can't overemphasize the importance that Nono attached to one of Schoenberg's lesser-known (though utterly fascinating) works: the one-act opera *Die glückliche Hand*, which the young Boulez also cited with approval. However, their approbatory motivations are different. Boulez sees the work primarily as a first deployment of *Sprechstimme*, whereas for Nono (again, in 1961) it has a much greater significance: for him, it is "the starting point for a modern conception of music theatre."[18] Accordingly, when – as noted above – Nono heads the score of his first opera, *Intolleranza* (1960), with the inscription "For Arnold Schoenberg," it seems fair to assume that he has, not least, the composer of *Die glückliche Hand* in mind.

The Nono case is, of course, exceptional, because it is the only one to address directly the humanitarian aspects of some of Schoenberg's late work, albeit from a perspective, a Euro-Communist one, that would have been alien to the politically conservative Schoenberg. As noted above, Nono's first acknowledged work was the *Variazioni canoniche sulla serie di l'opus 41 di Schoenberg*, Schoenberg's Op. 41 being the *Ode to Napoleon*. The choice of this series as basic material is clearly ideological rather than compositional: it has as much, and indeed more, to do with Schoenberg's choice of Byron's anti-Napoleon text, as a thinly veiled allusion to Hitler's "final solution," than it has with this particular dodecaphonic series.

As for the third member of a – partly mythologized – Darmstadt triumvirate, Karlheinz Stockhausen cites a recital of Schoenberg's piano music, given by Else Lasker-Schüler at the Cologne Musikhochschule during his student days, as a primary motivation for his engaging with the world of New Music after an essentially conservative training. But technically, his initial knowledge of twelve-note methods came from Frank Martin and Hermann Heiss, and a little later from reading a small textbook by Herbert Eimert.[19] On the whole, it seems that for Stockhausen, Schoenberg was an ethical model, rather than a musical one. He has remarked (to the present author, among others) that as a young composer, he often felt that he had Schoenberg peering over one shoulder and Stravinsky over the other: not as stylistic influences, but as a radical form of "quality control." But whatever he may have thought of Schoenberg's music (and in the early 1950s he probably knew far less of it than Boulez did), he did view him, unlike Stravinsky, as a model of exemplary artistic intransigence.

This emerges clearly from part of a conversation with Theodor Adorno, broadcast on Hessischer Rundfunk in April 1960. Here the name Schoenberg often crops up, though (predictably) almost always on Adorno's lips rather than Stockhausen's. Yet there is one significant exception. Stockhausen refers to a tape of Schoenberg (in conversation with a music publicist), which he had heard at Gertrud Schoenberg's house, presumably during his 1958 US tour. When the topic of "accessibility" was raised, he says, Schoenberg suddenly became angry, and said (in Stockhausen's paraphrase):

> Do you think that when Nansen was going to the North Pole, he first sent round a questionnaire to see if one should actually do that now, and whether this was the right time? Can't you see that the mental activity that is expressed in music through artistic activity is closely allied to the activity undertaken by someone who is discovering new things in the field of science, in the field of philosophy, or, let's say, the whole field of mental endeavor? Music is a matter of the mind: one has to accept that.[20]

In the late 1950s some collateral damage to the Schoenberg image was inflicted by Igor Stravinsky, who had become an ardent Webernist, but was now also showing considerable interest in Boulez and Stockhausen, and was in the process of composing brief, radically "fragmented" post-Webernesque works such as the *Movements* for piano and orchestra, and the *Epitaphium*. The first volume of "conversations" with Robert Craft, published in 1959, includes certain comments strikingly similar to those of Boulez almost a decade earlier, including outright rejection of the sensibility of late works such as the Fourth String Quartet and the *Ode to Napoleon* (which Stravinsky compares to César Franck!). Yet there are also some limited affirmations: "We – and I mean the generation who are now saying 'Webern and me' – must remember only the perfect works, the Five Orchestral Pieces, Op. 16 (except for which I could bear the loss of the first nineteen opus numbers), *Herzgewächse*, *Pierrot*, the *Serenade*, the *Variations for Orchestra* and, for its orchestra, the *Seraphita* song from Op. 22. By these works Schoenberg is among the great composers."[21]

Responses from the 1960s onwards

All these are responses from a first, structuralist phase of European "new music," predating the major impact of Cage's work, though some composers were already engaging with limited forms of indeterminacy. During the 1960s, one might reasonably claim, Schoenberg became a non-issue for those young composers who felt themselves to be part of an avant-garde. Indeterminacy and variable forms apart, principal preoccupations included a new fascination with timbre and texture – in this context, exceptionally, Ligeti and others have acknowledged the significance of the *Farben* movement of Schoenberg's Op. 16 – and a stylistic pluralism that already anticipates the Postmodernism of a decade later. But by this stage, (some of) Schoenberg's work is "classic" repertoire, and the same is true of Webern's: it no longer has "exemplary" status. So when a fragment of the "Peripetie" movement of Op. 16 opens the celebrated third (collage) movement of Berio's *Sinfonia* (1968), I don't believe one can take this as espousing a view of Schoenberg's historical or current significance: it's simply an expedient appropriation of a very spectacular gesture at the "peripeteia" of the movement. Nevertheless, a certain Oedipal residue remains, exemplified in Paolo Castaldi's orchestral piece *Schoenberg A-B-C* (1969), where the latent tonality of passages from Schoenberg's Variations for Orchestra is emphasized (and rendered rather banal) by *added* notes! A comparable but more restrained attitude is apparent in Dieter Schnebel's "tonal" analysis of the opening bars of Schoenberg's Violin Concerto.[22]

But from the mid 1970s Schoenberg comes back into the spotlight, and here we can usefully focus on three composers: Helmut Lachenmann (b.1939), Brian Ferneyhough (b.1943), and Wolfgang Rihm (b.1952), all of whom established significant reputations during the 1970s. Prima facie, they seem to represent quite different trends: Lachenmann obsessed with a social interpretation of the energy latent in sound, Ferneyhough with late-Modernist structuralism, and Rihm with spontaneous expression. These are, of course, glib formulations: as one unravels what lies behind them, more and more points of similarity, if not exactly agreement, start to emerge. At a surface level, one can say that all three composers share more or less the same level of historical distance from Schoenberg. By the time their careers started to gain some momentum, Schoenberg had been dead for about twenty years, and there had been a whole generation's worth of avant-garde debate about his significance. More generally, one can say that, however radical these composers may be in their particular ways, they have no involvement in the *tabula rasa* strategy of (parts of) the preceding generation. These are all composers who have engaged, both personally and through their work, with notions of "tradition" in which Schoenberg represented, perhaps, the last stage, the last post. That their personal styles all seem to coalesce at the chronological upbeat to European Postmodernism is probably no coincidence, but there is no uniformity of outcome.

Here, perhaps, we need to consider lines of historical continuity. Lachenmann's is the most direct, and also the most complex one: his early experience of Schoenberg, it seems to me, was essentially threefold. On the one hand, there were direct encounters with the music: by the 1960s there was no difficulty in hearing Schoenberg's work, or getting to know the scores (surprisingly, these even figured in his studies with the conservative Johann Nepomuk David).[23] On the other, there were ideological/philosophical views of Schoenberg, as mediated respectively by Nono and Adorno. Lachenmann not only studied with Luigi Nono, but became his virtual amanuensis in terms of debates with other members of the European avant-garde. His autonomous comments on Schoenberg begin about a decade later, as his own compositional career is beginning to achieve serious momentum.

For Lachenmann, it appears, Schoenberg's principal significance lies not so much in individual compositions (which are only rarely referred to in Lachenmann's writings) as in two partly related socio-aesthetic aspects: his insistence on the moral obligations of the artist, and his seemingly fearless initial response to a crucial historical moment. In the former respect Lachenmann may seem close to Nono, but on the whole, I think, it's Adorno who casts the more visible shadow. Schoenberg's moral achievement is, according to Lachenmann, essentially twofold: an insistence on art's obligation to be "truthful," and his "demand that the uncomfortable has a right to exist, given the domination of the comfortable,"[24] which in turn involves a "redefinition of the concept of beauty."[25]

Naturally, this directly reflects Lachenmann's view of his own aims and responsibilities as a composer. Historically, he praises Schoenberg for having pushed an inherent dialectical conflict between the consistent extension of development-based sonata style and prevailing bourgeois aesthetics to a point not just of crisis but of unconcealable and irreparable fracture. But this is also where his Schoenberg-critique comes into play: "what he opened up in terms of method and material, he immediately closed down: it remained tied to his idiom, both stylistically and expressively."[26] In this sense Schoenberg fails, but Lachenmann doesn't judge this entirely negatively: "so with Schoenberg there's still a sort of barb that riles us: a criterion for failure that we sympathize with, or envy."[27] Yet on the other hand, he confidently asserts "The morality of Schoenberg's thinking, and the obligation, compositionally, to be consistent and persistent, is something that serial music has understood and adopted."[28] (Clearly, "serial music" here means that of the postwar avant-garde.)

Of these three case histories, the Rihm one is, perhaps, the simplest. Looking through his extensive writings, one finds the phrase "Schönberg um 1910" (Schoenberg around 1910) time after time. Just how wide a net the word "around" is meant to cast is never quite clear, but I suspect it's a rather narrow one: perhaps 1909–11. It would surely include The Three Pieces, Op. 11 (the last of which Rihm quotes in his own *Klavierstück 5*), the Five Orchestral Pieces, and *Erwartung*, Op. 17. But is the Second String Quartet, Op. 10 there at the start, and *Pierrot lunaire*, Op. 21 at the end? That's not so certain. In any case, it may be that for the young Rihm, at least, "around 1910" was at least as important in this recurrent formulation as "Schoenberg." While early pieces of his show a certain stylistic engagement with this era, it's not nostalgic, but highly equivocal. I would surmise that it is the inspired groping for new certainties at the moment of transition, coupled with the often flamboyant gestures of the first three pieces mentioned above, that particularly appealed to him.

Perhaps the most unexpectedly obsessive engagement with Schoenberg at the turn of the twenty-first century has been that of the English-born Brian Ferneyhough. In the first place, to state the obvious, he is English, not Austro-German, and there is nothing in his early upbringing that would have predisposed him towards a Schoenbergian orientation (in fact, his epiphanic moment vis-à-vis "new music" came from hearing a recording of Varèse's *Octandre*).[29] Nevertheless, his student years in London coincided with a period at the BBC where William Glock was advocating the latest "new music," especially that of the European avant-garde, and Hans Keller was an eloquent and persistent advocate of Schoenberg's work. And by the time he wrote his first spectacular large-scale works, such as *Firecycle Beta* and *Transit*, Ferneyhough had long since left England, and was living in Freiburg.

For him, the engagement with Schoenberg goes back a long way, and operates at many, partly contradictory levels. Initially, during the student period, there was simple absorption: "I came to be very impressed by the works of Schoenberg heard little by little during this period, particularly the Wind Quintet (I was much occupied with wind instruments at the time myself), *Pierrot*, the Violin Concerto, and the [First] Chamber Symphony. Probably the importance of these works for me lay in the still personally unresolved conflicts of received musical norms of one sort or another and the gradual desire to move into areas which I had not at that stage succeeded in 'legitimizing' to myself."[30] Note that in this account, tonal, free atonal, and twelve-tone works sit side by side, at a far remove from the outlook of the young Boulez, who dismissed everything prior to the Op. 11 *Klavierstücke* as having largely "documentary" status. This is particularly intriguing since the most obvious stylistic influence on Ferneyhough's early music is precisely those early works of Boulez composed around the time of *Trajectories*. One might think that this simply reflects an early stage in Ferneyhough's thinking, but that's not so. For example, the opening of the First Chamber Symphony still hovers, albeit with slightly ironic intent, in the background composition processes of Scene 6 of his opera *Shadowtime* (2003).

Ferneyhough has often talked about Schoenberg's Second String Quartet as a "threshold work," by which he means "a category of compositions typified by what I understand to be a *surplus* of meaning, caused by their straddling the divide or fault line between one way of perceiving and another in a way somehow embodied in the actual texture."[31] This doesn't mean that the work in question is necessarily judged to be a triumphant success: its importance may lie in the fact that it addresses dichotomies in a way that, in terms of criteria of period and genre, can only lead to "failure," albeit a failure that is somehow more artistically significant than any "success" could have been (which in part relates to Lachenmann's "criterion of failure" cited above).

In more concrete terms, Ferneyhough's Fourth String Quartet (1990) was commissioned as a potential companion piece to Schoenberg's Second Quartet, and likewise has a solo soprano part in two movements. But far from being a complementary act of homage, Ferneyhough's Quartet offers him an opportunity to reflect on everything that has changed since 1908 in the relationship between vocal and instrumental utterance, and even the (im)possibility – already investigated in his *Etudes transcendantales* (1985) – of continuing to "set" texts in a way that implies that musical and verbal meaning can be at least contiguous.

Yet perhaps the most curious (but also significant) manifestation of Ferneyhough's Schoenberg-preoccupation lies in his idiosyncratic use of the series of *Moses und Aron* in his own *Carceri d'Invenzione* cycle (1981–86). It represents the opposite pole to the "omaggio a Schoenberg" evident in Nono's *Variazione Canoniche*; far from providing the source material for the *Carceri* cycle, let alone being quoted in some overt form, it operates as a sort of "ghost in the machine," secretly filtering and reordering the basic materials in a way that only the composer and the most assiduous analysts could be aware of: Schoenberg as hidden cipher, perhaps in an arcanely Talmudic role.

With this trio of composers (Ferneyhough, Lachenmann, Rihm) it may well be that one aspect of the Schoenberg legacy comes to an end. These are, in all probability, the last significant European composers whose approach to composing will have been decisively shaped by their engagement with the "Schoenberg" phenomenon. If so, they mark the end of a profound musico-intellectual history whose surface has only been scratched here, and which invites much further reflection.

Notes

Chapter 1 Introduction

1. A. Schoenberg, *Theory of Harmony*, trans. R. E. Carter (Berkeley and Los Angeles: University of California Press, 1983), 2.
2. J. Auner, *A Schoenberg Reader: Documents of a Life* (New Haven and London: Yale University Press, 2003), 105.
3. H. H. Stuckenschmidt, *Schoenberg: His Life, World and Work*, trans. H. Searle (New York: Schirmer, 1978), 73.
4. T. W. Adorno, "On the Social Situation of Music," in *Essays on Music*, ed. R. Leppert, trans. S. Gillespie (Berkeley and Los Angeles: University of California Press, 2002), 397.
5. T. W. Adorno, *Philosophy of Modern Music*, trans. A. Mitchell and W. Blomster (New York: The Seabury Press, 1980), 105; A. Huyssen, *After the Great Divide: Modernism, Mass Culture, Postmodernism* (Bloomington and Indianapolis: Indiana University Press, 1986), 53–4.
6. A. Schoenberg, "Attempt at a Diary," trans. A. Luginbühl, *Journal of the Arnold Schoenberg Institute* 9/1 (1986), 9.
7. Auner, *A Schoenberg Reader*, 7.
8. Many of these can be viewed on the Arnold Schönberg Center webpage, and see *Arnold Schönberg Catalogue raisonné*, eds. C. Meyer and T. Muxeneder (Vienna: Arnold Schönberg Center, 2005).
9. Cited by I. Pfeiffer, "Introduction," *Schoenberg, Kandinsky, Blaue Reiter und die Russische Avantgarde: Journal of the Arnold Schönberg Center* 1 (2000), 33.
10. Cited in *Arnold Schoenberg/Wassily Kandinsky: Letters, Pictures and Documents*, ed. J. Hahl-Koch (London: Faber, 1984), 136.
11. Hahl-Koch, *Arnold Schoenberg/Wassily Kandinsky*, 21.
12. See R. Specht, "Schoenberg Among the Workers: Choral Conducting in Pre-1900 Vienna," *Journal of the Arnold Schoenberg Institute* 10/1 (1987), 28–37, and J. Auner, "Schoenberg and His Public in 1930: The Six Pieces for Male Chorus, Op. 35," *Schoenberg and His World*, ed. W. Frisch (Princeton: Princeton University Press, 1999), 85–125.
13. *Berliner Börsen-Courier*, January 26, 1916.
14. J. A. Smith, *Schoenberg and His Circle: A Viennese Portrait* (New York: Schirmer Books, 1986), 81–102.
15. Auner, *A Schoenberg Reader*, 123–4.
16. J. Shaw, "Schoenberg's Choral Symphony, *Die Jakobsleiter*, and Other Wartime Fragments" (Ph.D. Dissertation, State University of New York at Stony Brook, 2002).
17. A. Schoenberg, *Coherence, Counterpoint, Instrumentation, Instruction in Form*, ed. S. Neff, trans. C. Cross and S. Neff (Lincoln: University of Nebraska Press, 1994), 19.
18. See J. Straus, *Remaking the Past: Musical Modernism and the Influence of the Tonal Tradition* (Cambridge, MA, and London: Harvard University Press, 1990), 45–8, and R. Stephan, "Schoenberg and Bach," trans. W. Frisch in *Schoenberg and His World*, ed. Frisch (Princeton University Press, 1999), 133.
19. Excerpts from Schoenberg's published essay, which arose from a 1918 symposium organized by architect Adolf Loos on the postwar direction of the arts, are reprinted in *Style and Idea: Selected Writings of Arnold Schoenberg*, ed. L. Stein, trans. L. Black (Berkeley: University of California Press, 1975), 369–73.
20. Schoenberg, "Speech on the Jewish Situation," *Style and Idea*, ed. L. Stein, 502.
21. Schoenberg, "How I came to Compose the Ode to Napoleon," in Auner, *A Schoenberg Reader*, 291.

Chapter 2 Schoenberg's lieder

1. A. Schoenberg, "The Relationship to the Text," in *Style and Idea: Selected Writings of Arnold Schoenberg*, ed. L. Stein, trans. L. Black (Berkeley: University of California Press, 1984), 141–5.
2. See *Ernst Challiers Grosser Lieder Katalog* (Berlin: Challier, 1885). Supplements or *Nachträge* were published every two years well into the twentieth century.
3. E. Kravitt, *The Lied: Mirror of Late Romanticism* (New Haven and London: Yale University Press, 1996), 20.
4. The "Valse de Chopin" by Joseph Marx on the lieder program of February 4, 1912 is a setting, composed in 1909, of the same poem from the Giraud-Hartleben *Pierrot lunaire* that Schoenberg would set in May 1912. Just over a month after the February concert, Schoenberg signed his contract for *Pierrot* and began composing the first melodramas.

5. J. Auner, *A Schoenberg Reader: Documents of a Life* (New Haven and London: Yale University Press, 2003), 119.
6. Schoenberg, "How One Becomes Lonely," in *Style and Idea*, 49.
7. Auner, *A Schoenberg Reader*, 78.
8. This specific sonority is labeled triadic tetrachord 9B by Simms, who observes that it appears frequently in Schoenberg's compositions and even in his theoretical writings. See B. Simms, *The Atonal Music of Arnold Schoenberg, 1908–1923* (New York and Oxford: Oxford University Press, 2000), 17.
9. W. Ruf, "*Herzgewächse, Op. 20*" in *Arnold Schönberg: Interpretationen seiner Werke*, ed. G. Gruber (Laaber: Laaber Verlag, 2002), vol. I, 293.
10. W. Ruf, "Vier Lieder," *Arnold Schönberg: Interpretationen seiner Werke*, vol. I, 324.
11. See A. Schoenberg, "Analysis of the Four Orchestral Songs, Op. 22," trans. C. Spies, *Perspectives of New Music* 3/2 (1965), 1–21.
12. T. W. Adorno, "Haringer und Schönberg," in *Gesammelte Schriften*, ed. R. Tiedemann (Frankfurt: Suhrkamp, 1984), vol. 18, 427.
13. See the detailed analysis by Jacques-Louis Monod in Arnold Schoenberg, *Three Songs for Low Voice and Piano*, Op. 48, rev. edn (Hillsdale, NY: Boelke-Bomart, 1979); and also T. Ahrend, "Drei Lieder für Gesang und Klavier Op. 48," in G. Gruber (ed.), *Arnold Schönberg: Interpretationen seiner Werke*, vol. II (Laaber: Laaber Verlag, 2002), 162–71.

Chapter 3 Schoenberg and the tradition of chamber music for strings
1. See W. Frisch, *The Early Works of Arnold Schoenberg: 1893–1908* (Berkeley: University of California Press, 1993), 32–47.
2. *Ibid.*, 33. See also Oliver W. Neighbour, *Foreword* to the *String Quartet in D Major, 1897* (London: Faber Music Limited, 1966).
3. See W. Bailey, "Changing Views of Schoenberg," in *The Arnold Schoenberg Companion* (Westport: Greenwood Press, 1998), 3.
4. For an alternative analysis see Frisch, *The Early Works of Arnold Schoenberg*, 31–47.
5. Rhythmic cross-currents within the Third Quartet are studied by Jeff Nichols, "Metric Conflict as an Agent of Formal Design in the First Movement of Schoenberg's Quartet Opus 30," *Music of My Future: The Schoenberg Quartets and Trio*, eds. R. Brinkmann and C. Wolff (Cambridge, MA: Harvard University Department of Music, 2000), 95–116. Cross-currents within the Fourth Quartet are studied by R. Kurth, "The Art of Cadence in

Schoenberg's Fourth Quartet: Metric Discourse or Metric Dialectic?," *Journal of the Arnold Schönberg Center* 4 (2002), 245–70.
6. See M. Cherlin, "Dialectical Opposition in Schoenberg's Music and Thought," *Music Theory Spectrum* 22/2 (2000), 157–76.
7. I discuss such retrospective and prospective hearings within the First String Quartet, Op. 7, in Chapter Four of *Schoenberg's Musical Imagination* (Cambridge University Press, 2007).
8. See Frisch, *The Early Works of Arnold Schoenberg*, 33.
9. See Neighbour's notes to the appendix to the score cited in note 2 above.
10. For related discussions of the string quartets and the Trio, see D. Lewin, "Inversional Balance as an Organizing Force in Schoenberg's Music and Thought," *Perspectives of New Music* 6/2 (1967–8), 1–21.
11. Frisch discusses the dating of *Verklärte Nacht* in *The Early Works of Arnold Schoenberg*, 110.
12. A. Schoenberg, *Style and Idea: Selected Writings of Arnold Schoenberg*, ed. L Stein, trans. L. Black (Berkeley: University of California Press, 1975), 80.
13. Frisch, *The Early Works of Arnold Schoenberg*, 109–39, summarizes earlier analyses of the form and provides his own analysis.
14. R. Swift, "1/XII/99: Tonal Relations in Schoenberg's *Verklärte Nacht*," *19th-Century Music* I/1 (1997), 3–14. Swift provides a formal overview on page 7. The most significant discrepancies between our readings occur in Part One, Swift's "Sonata 1." Swift understands mm. 1–28 as an introduction, whereas I consider the passage as part of the principal theme group (1a in my figure). More significantly, Swift hears mm. 50–2 as part two of the first group, whereas I interpret the passage as the second theme. For Swift mm. 63–104 form a bridge to the second group; I hear most of this as continuing the second theme (already begun at 50), with m. 100 and following as comprising the closing section of the exposition. Finally, Swift considers mm. 181–7 to be a shortened recapitulation of the first group; I hear this as part of the development. Frisch criticizes Swift's reading (*The Early Works of Arnold Schoenberg*, 114–66), making several observations that are congruent with my own hearing; however, Frisch essentially dismisses the idea of understanding the work through the lens of sonata form: "At issue here is the necessity of invoking sonata form at all, when so many distortions are required to make it fit" (*ibid.*,

115). For me, the dialectic with sonata form is pervasive and essential to the work.

15. The collected program notes are found in *Arnold Schoenberg: Self-Portrait*, edited by Nuria Schoenberg Nono (Palisades, CA: Belmont Music Publishers, 1988), 119–23.

16. Wagner introduces the motive in m. 37 of the third scene of *Das Rheingold*. See Cherlin, *Schoenberg's Musical Imagination*, Chapter Five, "Uncanny Expressions of Time in the Music of Arnold Schoenberg."

17. See, M. Cherlin, "Schoenberg and *das Unheimliche*: Spectres of Tonality," *The Journal of Musicology*. Vol. 11/3 (1993), 357–73, and M. Cherlin, "Memory and Rhetorical Trope in Schoenberg's String Trio," *Journal of the American Musicological Society* 51/3 (Fall 1998), 559–602.

18. See Kurth, "The Art of Cadence in Schoenberg's Fourth String Quartet."

19. See W. Bailey, *Programmatic Elements in the Works of Schoenberg*, Studies in Musicology 74 (Ann Arbor: UMI Research Press, 1984), 151–7.

Chapter 4 Two early Schoenberg songs

1. W. Kinderman and H. Krebs (eds.), *The Second Practice of Nineteenth-Century Music* (Lincoln: University of Nebraska Press, 1996). Curiously, Bailey, though frequently cited, is not himself represented by an essay. See also my article/review of this book, which both praises its virtues and criticizes its weaknesses: R. P. Morgan, "Are There Two Tonal Practices in Nineteenth Century Music?" *Journal of Music Theory* 43/2 (Fall, 1999), 135–63.

2. G. Vogler, *Handbuch der Harmonielehre* (Prague: K. Barth, 1802); G. Weber, *Versuch einer geordneten Theorie der Tonsetzkunst*, 3 Vols. (Mainz: B. Schott, 1817–21); F. J. Fétis, *Traité complet de la théorie et de la pratique de l'harmonie* (Paris: Schlesinger, 1844); C. F. Weitzmann, *Die neue Harmonielehre im Streit mit der alten* (Leipzig: C. F. Kahnt, 1861); K. Mayrberger, *Die Harmonik Richard Wagner's an den Leitmotiven aus "Tristan und Isolde" erläutert* (Bayreuth: Bayreuther Patronaterverein 1881); G. Capellen, "Harmonik und Melodik bei Richard Wagner," *Bayreuther Blätter* 25 (1902), 3–23.

3. A. Schoenberg, *Harmonielehre* (Vienna: Universal Edition, 3rd edn, 1922), 459–60. Schoenberg's remarks appear in a brief section entitled *"Über schwebende und aufgehobene Tonalität"* (Concerning Fluctuating and Suspended Tonality), most of which is devoted to *schwebende Tonalität. Aufgehobene*

Tonalität, discussed only in the final paragraph, is quite different: its "purely harmonic aspect . . . involve[s] almost exclusive use of explicitly vagrant chords. Every major or minor triad could be interpreted as a key, even if only in passing." All quotations are taken from the English translation: A. Schoenberg, *Theory of Harmony*, trans. R. E. Carter (Berkeley: University of California Press, 1978). Page citations are given first for the English translation, then for the German edition.

4. *Ibid.*, 384; 459–60

5. A. Schoenberg, *Structural Functions of Harmony*, ed. L. Stein (New York: W. W. Norton, 1969), 111–13. All page citations are for this volume. Schoenberg also discusses tonal expansion in several of his articles but without analytical commentary. See especially "Problems of Harmony," the fourth numbered section of "Brahms the Progressive," and portions of "My Evolution" and "Opinion or Insight?," *Style and Idea: Selected Writings of Arnold Schoenberg*, ed. L. Stein, trans. L. Black (Berkeley: University of California Press, 1975), 267–86, 402–5, 81–4 and 259–60.

6. Schoenberg, *Structural Functions of Harmony*, 111.

7. For more on this, see my article/review of *The Second Practice of Nineteenth-Century Music*, cited in Footnote 1.

8. R. Bailey, "An Analytical Study of the Sketches and Drafts" in the Norton Critical Score, *Richard Wagner: Prelude and Transfiguration from Tristan und Isolde*, ed. R. Bailey (New York: W. W. Norton, 1985), 113–46.

9. *Ibid.*, 120. The preceding summary of Bailey's theory draws on his 116–20. Although Bailey does not stress a connection to Schoenberg, he does begin his comments by quoting *Harmonielehre* on the "transition from twelve major and twelve minor keys to twelve chromatic keys" (Schoenberg, *Harmonielehre*, 389, 466).

10. C. Lewis, "Mirrors and Metaphors: Reflections on Schoenberg and Nineteenth-Century Tonality," 19th*-Century Music* 11/1 (1987), 29–30.

11. For a more detailed analysis, see my "Circular Form in the *Tristan* Prelude," *Journal of the American Musicological Society* 53/1 (2000), 69–103.

12. Lewis, "Mirrors and Metaphors," 26 and 38.

13. Given "Lockung"'s complexity, a few additional comments on the graph are in order.

The non-Schenkerian top voice remains fixed on g" throughout. In both sections A¹ and A², however, g" moves to an "interrupted" f" (more weakly the second time), and it acquires double neighbors in the B section: f sharp" (prolonged mm. 32–40) and g sharp"(= A flat) (m. 42), the latter continuing into section A³ as part of the final V7 prolongation (m. 48). Though g" appears at m. 50, it is still subordinate to a flat", which resolves back to g" only at m. 60 as the song ends. Though most prolongations in the top voice (consisting largely of prominent high notes in the voice) support the form, overlaps result frequently from more surface features. The last measure of section A², for example, has a full-measure melodic upbeat to section B; and the G sharp ending section B becomes (enharmonically) part of the prolonged dominant seventh spanning most of section A³. Note that this V7 prolongation, which initiates A³ (in contrast to the C minor beginnings of A¹ and A²), subsumes the (later) C minor prolongation of mm. 51–3, and thereby strengthens E flat in the final section.

14. Another late-tonal feature of "Lockung" (also discussed in *Harmonielehre*) is that its background consists largely of dominant, rather than tonic, prolongations.

15. Each of the four main sections has one pivot (the one at m. 32 being the one not redirected immediately to E flat). It is tempting to consider the chord at m. 57 in section A³ as an important structural pivot as well, since it appears after the music has veered yet again toward C minor (mm. 51–4), which could be interpreted as an altered vi7 of C, becoming iv7 of E flat. But as mentioned in note 13, I prefer to see this last, rather weak reference to C as part of the final dominant prolongation in E flat, and thus a more surface phenomenon. The chord at m. 57 is nevertheless heavily articulated; and it contains a B minor triad, the key (but not mode) of the B section, with its fourth note – G sharp – the root of the chord with which that section ends.

16. Lewis, "Mirrors and Metaphors," 33. Lewis appears to hedge his bets here, though not sufficiently to take back his essential point. As he writes: "I suggest that F functions as more than a coloration, and as more than an extended neighbor; it is rather the other half of a perhaps rudimentary tonic complex." *Ibid.*

17. While the tonic-saturated tonality of "Traumleben" needs no additional explication, a word about the graph may again be useful. The top voice, which is also non-Schenkerian, prolongs g sharp' throughout, always heard in conjunction with the tonic triad (mm. 4, 7, 9,

12, 25, 31) and usually at points of important formal division. Though there are two relatively weak linear motions outlining a third span, B to G sharp (mm. 1–5 and 19–25), the overriding quality is static, supplying a tonally frozen yet sensuous and floating quality appropriate to Julius Hart's somewhat smarmy poem. The song's paradoxical fluidity stems partly from the numerous overlaps: for example, each of the four principal E cadences, notated with half notes (unlike the two E chords with top-voice B), simultaneously supply cadential goals and points of departure, the elision underscored by the piano's ongoing rhythm.

18. The only apparent exception occurs in the final cadence before the Postlude (m. 31), where the top voice descends by step through a lowered second degree (F again) to a conclusive E, creating a strong sense of vocal-textual closure. This is obviously a critical event in the song; but since the piano maintains G sharp a third above the voice's E, I prefer to view this span ultimately as a middleground rather than background phenomenon. Like "Lockung," "Traumleben" thus reveals that increasingly common late-chromatic characteristic: an immobile top voice at the background level.

19. See E. T. Cone, "Sound and Syntax: An Introduction to Schoenberg's Harmony," *Perspectives of New Music* 13/1 (1974), 21–40.

20. Lewis, "Mirrors and Metaphors," 37.

21. Schoenberg, *Harmonielehre*, 153; 185.

Chapter 5 Arnold Schoenberg and Richard Strauss

1. For a discussion of the poetic idea acting as a structural basis of Strauss's work, see the author's article, "Hans von Bülow and Richard Strauss: the Master and his Ardent Follower," *Musicology Australia* XVI (1993), 28–38.

2. R. P. Morgan, *Twentieth-Century Music: A History of Musical Style in Modern Europe and America* (New York: W. W. Norton, 1991), 29.

3. H. H. Stuckenschmidt, *Schoenberg: His Life, World and Work* (London: John Calder, 1978), 61.

4. From the Arnold Schönberg Center website at http://www.schoenberg.at.

5. *Ibid.*

6. *Ibid.*

7. *Pelleas und Melisande* is scored for seventeen woodwinds, eighteen brass, two harps, and a string orchestra totalling sixty-four parts.

8. As quoted in Stuckenschmidt, *Schoenberg*, 63.

9. For a discussion of the enigmatic contradictions associated with the composer, see M. Kennedy, *Richard Strauss: Man, Music,*

Enigma (Cambridge University Press, 1999), 3–5. Note in particular Kennedy's comment regarding how Strauss could have been mistaken "for a prosperous bank manager."

10. Stuckenschmidt, *Schoenberg*, 63.

11. *Ibid.*

12. Universal Edition was founded in Vienna in June 1901, just over two years prior to the date of this letter.

13. Stuckenschmidt, *Schoenberg*, 66.

14. *Ibid.*, 68.

15. The fourth piece was completed four days later, on July 18.

16. Schoenberg is referring to his performance of *Pelleas und Melisande*, directing the Orchester des Wiener Konzertvereines in Vienna on January 25, 1905.

17. Stuckenschmidt, *Schoenberg*, 71.

18. *Ibid.*, 70.

19. *Ibid.*, 220.

20. Daniel M. Raessler, "Schoenberg and Busoni: Aspects of their Relationship," *Journal of the Arnold Schoenberg Institute* 7/1 (1983), 7–27.

21. *Ibid.*, 7.

22. As quoted in Stuckenschmidt, *Schoenberg*, 221.

23. As quoted in Raessler, "Schoenberg and Busoni," 12.

24. Stuckenschmidt, *Schoenberg*, 72

25. Along with music, the other six chambers included cinema, fine art, literature, the press, radio, and theater.

26. Kennedy, *Richard Strauss*, 271.

27. Stuckenschmidt, *Schoenberg*, 73.

Chapter 6 Interpreting *Erwartung*

1. Theodor W. Adorno, *Philosophy of Modern Music*, trans. A. G. Mitchell and W. V. Blomster (New York: Continuum, 1973; first published 1949); Willi Reich, *Schoenberg: A Critical Biography*, trans. L. Black (New York: Praeger, 1971); Carl Schorske, *Fin-de-siècle Vienna* (New York: Vintage Books, 1981); Susan McClary, *Feminine Endings: Music, Gender, and Sexuality* (Minneapolis: University of Minnesota Press, 1991); Daniel Albright, *Untwisting the Serpent: Modernism in Music, Literature, and the Other Arts* (Chicago and London: University of Chicago Press, 2000).

2. J. Breuer, "Fräulein Anna O.," in J. Breuer and S. Freud, *Stüdien über Hysterie* (1895), reprinted in *The Standard Edition of the Complete Psychological Works of Sigmund Freud*, trans. and ed. by J. Strachey with A. Freud, Vol. II (1893–95), (London: Hogarth Press and the Institute of Psycho-Analysis, 1953–74).

3. A. Schoenberg, "New Music: My Music" (1930) in *Style and Idea*, ed. L. Stein, trans. L. Black (Berkeley: University of California Press, 1984), 105.

4. P. Bekker, "*Erwartung*," in *Arnold Schönberg zum fünfzigsten Geburtstage*, special issue of *Musikblätter des Anbruch* VI/7–8 (1924), 277. Copy with Schoenberg's marginal annotation in Arnold Schönberg Center (ASC) archive, Vienna.

5. Dr. M. Unger, "Ein neuer Schönberg," *Dresdener Nachricht*, June 10, 1924; *Deutsche allgemeine Zeitung*, June 13, 1924; and *Fränkischer Kurier* (Nuremberg), June 29, 1924. ASC clippings file: opus 17, 19240606. Thanks to Rosemarie Greenman for translation assistance. Translations of archival material are by Greenman or myself unless otherwise noted.

6. [No author named], "Das deutsche Theater zum Musikfest," *Montagsblatt Prag* [no date]. ASC 19240606.

7. [A. Aber], [no title], [*Leipziger Neuste Nachrichten*], [no date]. ASC 19240606.

8. Dr. E. H. Müller, [no title], *Dresdener Anzeiger*, November 6, 1924.

9. F. A., "Buhne und [word illegible]: Arnold Schönberg: *Erwartung*; Ravel: *Die spanische Stunde*," [no periodical title], [no date]. ASC 19240606.

10. [No author], [no review title], [*Arbeiter Zeitung*], [no date]. ASC 19240606.

11. [No author], reviews in, respectively, *Kreutz-Zeitung*, June 11, 1930; *Vossische Zeitung*, June 10, 1930; *Der Tag*, June 8, 1930; and *Zeitschrift für Musik*, July 1930, transcribed and translated in M. S. Namenwirth, "Twenty Years of Schoenberg Criticism: Changes in the Evaluation of Once Unfamiliar Music," Ph.D. Dissertation, University of Minnesota, 1965.

12. [No author], *Der Reichsbote*, June 14, 1930, in Namenwirth, "Twenty Years of Schoenberg Criticism."

13. [No authors], reviews appearing, respectively, in the *Vossische Zeitung*, June 10, 1930; *Der Tag*, June 8, 1930; and the *Berliner Boerson Zeitung*, June 10, 1930.

14. [No author], *Der kleine Journal*, June 13–17, 1930, in Namenwirth, "Twenty Years of Schoenberg Criticism."

15. N. Pisling-Boas, "Schönberg Er[wartung] . . . Staatsoper am Platz der Republik," [No periodical title], ASC 19300706.

16. H. H. Stuckenschmidt, "'*Erwartung*' und '*Die glückliche Hand*': Schönberg-Abend in der

Krolloper," [no periodical title, no date], ASC 19300706.

17. [No author], review in *Deutsche Allgemeine Zeitung*, June 10, 1930, in Namenwirth, "Twenty Years of Schoenberg Criticism."

18. [No author], review in *Der Reichsbote*, June 14, 1930, in Namenwirth, "Twenty Years of Schoenberg Criticism."

19. *Zeitschrift für Musik*, July, 1930, in Namenwirth, "Twenty Years of Schoenberg Criticism."

20. T. W. Adorno, *Philosophy of Modern Music* (New York: Continuum, 1973), 42.

21. O. Fries, "Expressionistische Musikdramatik in Zurich," *Düsseldorfer Stadtanzeiger* 22 (Nov 1949). ASC 19491031.

22. W. Reich, "[?] and in Switzerland – Inter[national . . .]: Zurich Sees Experimental Presentation," *Christian Science Monitor*, December 10, 1949. ASC 19491031.

23. W. Reich, *Schoenberg, A Critical Biography* (New York: Praeger, 1971).

24. H. T., "Schoenberg's 'Erwartung' Heard with Dorothy Dow as Soloist," *New York Times*, November 16, 1951. ASC 19511115.

25. See "Second-wave" feminist critiques, including: P. Chesler, *Women and Madness* (Garden City: Doubleday, 1972); K. Millett, *Sexual Politics* (New York: Doubleday, 1970); and especially B. Friedan, *The Feminine Mystique* (New York: Dell Publishing, 1963).

26. S. Freud, *Three Essays on the Theory of Sexuality* (1905), reprinted and abridged in *Freud on Women: A Reader*, E. Young-Bruehl, ed. (New York: W. W. Norton, 1990), 137.

27. Pappenheim to Schoenberg (c.1915) regarding *Seraphita*, Schoenberg Correspondence, Music Collection, Library of Congress (LOC).

28. Breuer and Freud, "On the Psychical Mechanism of Hysterical Phenomena: Preliminary Communication" (1893), rpt. with *Stüdien über Hysterie* in *The Standard Edition*, 8.

29. The following sources are held at the Arnold Schönberg Center and may be viewed online: Manuscript draft libretto in Marie Pappenheim's hand, Archive numbers 2401–26; Typescript libretto, carbon copies, Archive numbers 2427–31; Draft reduced score, in Schoenberg's hand, 2367–86. The autograph fair copy is held at Pierpont Morgan Library, New York.

30. Schoenberg to Fräulein Rothe, September 12, 1910, Universal Edition Collection, Musiksammlung, Wiener Stadt- und Landesbibliothek.

31. See E. Keathley, "Revisioning Musical Modernism: Arnold Schoenberg, Marie Pappenheim, and *Erwartung*'s New Woman," Ph.D. Dissertation, State University of New York at Stony Brook, 1999, Chapter 3.

32. D. Newlin, *Schoenberg Remembered: Diaries and Recollections, 1938–1976* (New York: Pendragon Press, 1980), 211.

33. Pappenheim to Schoenberg, [September 9, 1909], LOC.

34. Keathley, "Revisioning Musical Modernism," Chapter 3.

35. *Ibid.*, Chapter 2; Karl Fallend, "über Marie Frischauf-Pappenheim," *Literature & Kritik* (July 1996); Police and Austrian Communist Party documents, Pappenheim-Frischauf, Marie. "Lebenslauf" and "Fragebogen," copies in Pappenheim file, ASC.

36. See H. Anderson, *Utopian Feminism: Women's Movements in fin-de-siècle Vienna* (New Haven: Yale University Press, 1992).

37. Included in the Pappenheim file at the ASC are copies of Bundes-Polizeidirektion in Wien, Zentrals[. . .] gegen Pornographie, "An das Landesgericht für Strafsachen, Münster-Verlag, Wien," March 25, 1934; and twenty newspaper clippings by or about Marie Pappenheim-Frischauf, dating from 1927 to 1998.

38. See Keathley, "Revisioning Musical Modernism," Chapter 2; Anderson, *Utopian Feminism*.

39. Anderson, *Utopian Feminism*, 167. Rosa Mayreder, *Zur Kritik der Weiblichkeit* (Jena: Diederichs, 1905), English edition, *A Survey of the Woman Problem*, trans. H. G. Scheffauer (New York: G. H. Doran Company, 1913).

40. Anderson, *Utopian Feminism*, 168.

41. R. Felski, *Beyond Feminist Aesthetics: Feminist Literature and Social Change* (Cambridge, MA: Harvard University Press, 1989), 135.

Chapter 7 The rise and fall of radical athematicism

1. A. Beaumont (trans. and ed.), *Ferruccio Busoni: Selected Letters* (New York: Columbia University Press, 1987), 388–9.

2. A. Schoenberg, *Zusammenhang, Kontrapunkt, Instrumentation, Formenlehre [Coherence, Counterpoint, Instrumentation, Instruction in Form]*, ed. S. Neff, trans. C. M. Cross and S. Neff (Lincoln: University of Nebraska Press, 1994), 8, 9.

3. A. Schoenberg, "My Evolution," in *Style and Idea: Selected Writings of Arnold Schoenberg*, ed. L. Stein, trans. L. Black (Berkeley: University of California Press, 1984), 88.

4. The March 12, 1912 entry in Schoenberg's diary reveals Schoenberg's feelings of competition with his students and its consequences. Schoenberg, *Attempt at a Diary*, trans. A. Luginbühl, *Journal of the Arnold Schoenberg Institute* 9/1 (1986), 39.

5. Schoenberg, "The Young and I," in *Style and Idea*, 94.

6. See J. Auner, *A Schoenberg Reader: Documents of a Life* (New Haven and London: Yale University Press, 2003), 236.

7. Schoenberg, "Anton Webern: Klangfarbenmelodie," in *Style and Idea*, 484.

8. *Ibid.*, 484–5.

9. Copy of the letter in the Arnold Schönberg Center, Vienna.

10. It cannot have helped matters that Webern's Op. 5, No. 3 is clearly based on the motives and themes from the Scherzo of Schoenberg's String Quartet, Op. 10, No. 2. See H.-K. Metzger, "Webern und Schönberg," in *Die Reihe. Information über serielle Musik*, vol. II: *Anton Webern* (Vienna: Universal Edition, 1955), 48.

11. J. Auner, "Schoenberg's Aesthetic Transformations and the Evolution of Form in *Die glückliche Hand*," *Journal of the Arnold Schoenberg Institute* 12/2 (1989), 104.

Chapter 8 Schoenberg, modernism, and metaphysics

1. See A. P. Lessem, *Music and Text in the Works of Arnold Schoenberg. The Critical Years, 1908–22* (Ann Arbor: University of Michigan Research Press, 1979), 171.

2. *Ibid.*, 16; and W. Ruf, "Herzgewächse, Op. 20" in *Arnold Schönberg – Interpretationen seiner Werke*, ed. G. Gruber (Laaber: Laaber Verlag, 2002), 284.

3. Ruf, "Herzgewächse, Op. 20," 285.

4. A similar change of tone and texture can be seen in the later serial songs of Webern to metaphysical texts by Hildegard Jone, e.g., "Herr Jesus mein," Op. 23, No. 3.

5. Ruf, "Herzgewächse, Op. 20," 290.

6. *Ibid.*, 293. Heinz-Klaus Metzger sees Op. 22 not as the end of a phase (of free atonality) but as the possible beginning of a new development that, in the end, failed to materialize. "Zu Schönbergs Orchesterliedern Op. 22" in *Musik-Konzepte Sonderband: Arnold Schönberg*, eds. H.-K. Metzger and R. Riehn (Munich: Edition Text + Kritik, 1980), 52.

7. M. Cherlin, *Schoenberg's Musical Imagination* (Cambridge University Press, 2007); J. M. Christensen, "Arnold Schoenberg's Oratorio *Die Jakobsleiter*," (Ph.D. Dissertation, UCLA, 1979); C. M. Cross and R. A. Berman, (eds.), *Political and Religious Ideas in the Works*

of Arnold Schoenberg (New York: Garland, 2000); B. K. Etter, *From Classicism to Modernism. Western Musical Culture and the Metaphysics of Order* (Aldershot: Ashgate, 2001); A. Ringer, *Arnold Schoenberg. The Composer as Jew* (Oxford: Clarendon, 1990); K. Wörner, "Musik zwischen Theologie und Weltanschauung: Das Oratorium 'Die Jakobsleiter,'" in *Die Musik in der Geistesgeschichte: Studien zur Situation des Jahres um 1910* (Bonn: Bouvier 1970), 171–200.

8. The relation between Schoenberg and Kandinsky is also well documented elsewhere: K. Boehmer, (ed.), *Schoenberg and Kandinsky: An Historic Encounter* (Amsterdam: Harwood, 1997); J. Hahl-Koch, (ed.), *Arnold Schoenberg/ Wassily Kandinsky. Letters, Pictures and Documents*, trans. J. C. Crawford (London: Faber, 1984).

9. Examples in Mahler's music would include the slow movement of the Fourth Symphony, the pastoral interlude in the first movement of the Sixth Symphony, the slow movement of the Sixth Symphony, the passages associated with the Virgin Mary toward the end of the Eighth Symphony, and the closing section of *Das Lied von der Erde* (The Song of the Earth).

10. See J. Johnson, *Webern and the Transformation of Nature* (Cambridge University Press, 1999).

11. See mm. 33–8 of Op. 22, No. 1. Examples in Webern's music include the *Passacaglia*, Op. 1, Five Pieces for String Quartet, Op. 5, Six Pieces for Orchestra, Op. 6, Four Pieces for Violin and Piano, Op. 7. Berg's Violin Concerto may be said to be built on the idea, as its ending underlines. The same ensemble is heard at the end of *Die glückliche Hand* (m. 224ff.).

12. T. W. Adorno, *Mahler. A Musical Physiognomy*, trans. E. Jephcott (University of Chicago Press, 1991), 41.

13. See J. Shaw, "Androgyny and the Eternal Feminine in Schoenberg's Oratorio *Die Jakobsleiter*" in *Political and Religious Ideas in the Works of Arnold Schoenberg*, eds. C. M. Cross and R. A. Berman (New York: Garland, 2000), 61–84.

14. H. de Balzac, *Séraphita*, trans. C. Bell (Sawtry: Dedalus/Hippocrene, 1995), 146.

15. It is clear that this period represented both a personal creative crisis as well as one of artistic language. See J. Auner, "'Heart and Brain in Music': The Genesis of Schoenberg's *Die glückliche Hand*" in *Constructive Dissonance: Arnold Schoenberg and the Transformations of Twentieth-Century*

Culture, eds. J. Brand and C. Hailey (Berkeley: University of California Press, 1997), 112–30.

16. Alexander Ringer points out that the *Moderner Psalm*, Op. 50c, like the two earlier works, also "breaks off with the protagonist in a prayer-stance, manifestly unable to find fulfilment through prayer." See Ringer, *Arnold Schoenberg*, 176.

17. The "death of art" thesis is not explicitly stated by Hegel as such, but has repeatedly been extrapolated from his *Aesthetics*, beginning with commentators such as Croce, Knox, and Heller.

18. One of the sources in the rich genesis of *Die Jakobsleiter* was Strindberg's *Jakob ringt* (Jacob wrestles); the theme of wrestling with God is underlined by Schoenberg himself on several occasions. See his letter to Richard Dehmel of December 13, 1912 in *Arnold Schoenberg Letters*, ed. E. Stein (London: Faber, 1964), 36.

19. See Christensen, "Arnold Schoenberg's Oratorio *Die Jakobsleiter*," Vol.1, 17.

20. In fact, Schoenberg had been considering a setting of *Séraphita* some six months earlier, a dramatic realization that would have taken three evenings to perform. See his letters to Berg (July 27, 1912) and to Kandinsky (August 19, 1912) in Hahl-Koch, *Arnold Schoenberg/Wassily Kandinsky*, 54.

21. The link is explicit in Balzac's novel: "None but the loftier spirits open to faith can discern Jacob's mystical stair." Balzac, *Séraphita*, 123.

22. *Ibid.*, 138–9.

23. *Ibid.*, 143. Gabriel employs the same metaphor in m. 353 of Schoenberg's *Die Jakobsleiter*.

24. See Christensen, "Arnold Schoenberg's Oratorio *Die Jakobsleiter*," Vol.1, 17.

25. Balzac, *Séraphita*, 151.

26. Schoenberg's plans to set the final chapter of *Séraphita* gradually transmuted into ideas for a vast symphony. See Christensen, "Arnold Schoenberg's Oratorio '*Die Jakobsleiter*'"; W. Bailey, *Programmatic Elements in the Works of Schoenberg* (Ann Arbor: UMI Research Press, 1984); J. Johnson, "*Die Jakobsleiter*" in *Arnold Schönberg – Interpretationen seiner Werke*, ed. G. Gruber (Laaber Verlag, 2002), 253–78.

27. *Die Jakobsleiter* makes absolutely clear that the new musical language was shaped by the larger metaphysical project. See, among others, A. Ringer, "Faith and Symbol – Arnold Schoenberg's Last Musical Utterance," *Journal of the Arnold Schoenberg Institute* 6/1 (1982), 87.

28. Ernest Dowson (1867–1900) was associated with W. B. Yeats, Oscar Wilde, Aubrey Beardsley, and Arthur Symons.

29. This idea is discussed in H. H. Eggebrecht, *Die Musik Gustav Mahlers* (Munich: Piper, 1986).

30. Hahl-Koch, *Arnold Schoenberg/Wassily Kandinsky*, 54.

31. In *Die Jakobsleiter* the choruses of "The Indifferent" and "The Quietly Resigned" recall the planned movement of the symphony entitled "The Bourgeois God."

32. This opposition is taken from the text to *Die glückliche Hand*. It recalls a similar one in Mahler's work, between "Das irdische Leben" and "Das himmlische Leben."

33. This view was recently reinscribed in Etter's *From Classicism to Modernism. Western Musical Culture and the Metaphysics of Order*, that takes metaphysics as a central category and Schoenberg as a central character. Although I endorse Etter's view that in order to understand Schoenberg and musical modernism one needs to refer back to philosophical metaphysics, my own conclusions are the opposite of his.

34. W. Worringer, *Abstraction and Empathy: a Contribution to the Psychology of Style*, trans. M. Bullock (Cleveland: World Publishing, 1967).

35. G. W. F. Hegel, *Aesthetics: Lectures on Fine Art*, 2 vols. (Oxford: Clarendon Press, 1975).

36. For an extended discussion of this relationship in the context of Schoenberg's music, and specifically of the category of a "schwebend" (floating) music, see L. Goehr, "Adorno, Schoenberg, and the 'Totentanz der Prinzipien' – in Thirteen Steps," *Journal of the American Musicological Society* 56/3 (2003), 595–636.

37. Hahl-Koch, *Arnold Schoenberg/Wassily Kandinsky*, 54.

Chapter 9 *Pierrot lunaire*

1. The most comprehensive reference on the work is R. Brinkmann, "Pierrot lunaire Op. 21: Kritischer Bericht, Studien zur Genesis, Skizzen, Dokumente," in *Arnold Schönberg Samtliche Werke*, Abteilung VI, Reihe B, Band 24/1 (Mainz and Vienna: Schott and Universal Edition, 1995). Other significant studies include R. Brinkmann, "The Fool as Paradigm: Schönberg's *Pierrot lunaire* and the Modern Artist," in *Schönberg and Kandinsky: An Historic Encounter*, ed. K. Boehmer (Amsterdam: Harwood, 1997), 139–67; J. Dunsby, *Schoenberg: Pierrot lunaire* (Cambridge University Press, 1992); R. Kurth,

"Pierrot's Cave: Representation, Reverberation, Radiance," in *Schoenberg and Words: The Modernist Years*, eds. C. M. Cross and R. A. Berman (New York: Garland, 2000), 203–41.
2. Informative studies of the Pierrot figure include R. F. Storey, *Pierrot: A Critical History of a Mask* (Princeton University Press, 1978); R. F. Storey, *Pierrots on the Stage of Desire: Nineteenth-Century French Literary Artists and the Comic Pantomime* (Princeton University Press, 1985); and M. Green and J. Swan, *The Triumph of Pierrot: The Commedia dell'Arte and the Modern Imagination* (New York: MacMillan, 1986).
3. R. Vilain, "Pierrot lunaire: Cyclic Coherence in Giraud and Schoenberg," in *Pierrot Lunaire: Albert Giraud – Otto Erich Hartleben – Arnold Schoenberg*, eds. M. Delaere and J. Herman (Louvain: Peeters, 2004), 130–1.
4. *Ibid.*, 139–40.
5. For the compositional dating and ordering, see Brinkmann, *Kritischer Bericht*, X–XI, 181, and 212–19.
6. For early reviews, see F. Lesure, *Dossier de Presse Press-Book de Pierrot lunaire d'Arnold Schoenberg* (Geneva: Minkoff, 1985), and Brinkmann, *Kritischer Bericht*, 246–90.
7. S. Youens, "Excavating an Allegory: The Texts of *Pierrot lunaire*," *Journal of the Arnold Schoenberg Institute* 8/2 (1984), 95–115.
8. Brinkmann, "The Fool as Paradigm," 154.
9. S. Weytjens, "Text as a Crutch in Arnold Schoenberg's *Pierrot lunaire* Op. 21?," (Ph.D. Dissertation, Katholieke Universiteit Leuven, 2003), *passim*; and J. Dunsby, "Schoenberg's Pierrot Keeping his *Kopfmotiv*," in *Pierrot Lunaire: Albert Giraud – Otto Erich Hartleben – Arnold Schoenberg*, eds. M. Delaere and J. Herman, 74–5.
10. Brinkmann, "The Fool as Paradigm," 157.
11. See I. Stravinsky, with R. Craft, *Dialogues and a Diary* (London: Faber, 1968), 104–5, and also I. Stravinsky, with R. Craft, *Expositions and Developments* (Garden City: Doubleday, 1962), 67.
12. See H. Keller, "Whose Fault is the Speaking Voice?" *Tempo* 75 (1965–6), 14.
13. Cited from B. R. Simms, *The Atonal Music of Arnold Schoenberg: 1908–1923* (Oxford University Press, 2000), 121.
14. See U. Kramer, "Zur Notation der Sprechstimme bei Schönberg," in *Schönberg und der Sprechgesang*, eds. H.-K. Metzger and R. Riehn, *Musik-Konzepte* 112/113 (July 2001), 6–32.
15. See R. Stephan, "Zur jüngsten Geschichte des Melodrams," *Archiv für Musikwissenschaft* 17 (1960), 183–92; G. Schuller, "A

Conversation with Steuermann," *Perspectives of New Music* 3/1 (1964), 25; J. Goltz, "Pierrot le diseur," *Musical Times*, 147/1894 (Spring 2006), 59–72; M. Schmidt, "Musik ohne Noten: Arnold Schönbergs "'Pierrot lunaire' und Karl Kraus," *Studien zur Musikwissenschaft: Beihefte der Denkmäler der Tonkunst in Österreich* 47 (1999), 365–93; A. Whittall, "*Pierrot in Context: Pierrot as Context*," in *Pierrot Lunaire: Albert Giraud – Otto Erich Hartleben – Arnold Schoenberg*, eds. M. Delaere and J. Herman, 40–1 and 44.
16. A. Schoenberg, "The Relationship to the Text," in *Style and Idea: Selected Writings of Arnold Schoenberg*, ed. L. Stein, trans. L. Black (Berkeley: University of California Press, 1984), 144.
17. Simms, *The Atonal Music of Arnold Schoenberg*, 120.
18. A. Schoenberg, *Berliner Tagebuch*, ed. J. Rufer (Berlin: Propyläen Verlag, 1974), 34. Here and except where indicated below, translations by the author.
19. A. Schoenberg, *Dreimal sieben Gedichte aus Albert Girauds Pierrot lunaire*, Op. 21, "Vorwort" (Vienna: Universal Edition, 1914).
20. See A. Schoenberg, "This is My Fault" (1949), in *Style and Idea*, 145–7.
21. A. Schoenberg, "Pathos" (April 8, 1928) and letter of August 31, 1940 to Erika Stiedry-Wagner; cited in Brinkmann, *Kritischer Bericht*, 301 and 302, respectively.
22. Schoenberg, *Dreimal sieben Gedichte aus Albert Girauds Pierrot lunaire*, "Vorwort."
23. *Ibid.*
24. For instance, see P. Stadlen, "Schoenberg's Speech-Song," *Music and Letters* 62/1 (January 1981), 1–11.
25. See E. Rapoport, "Schoenberg – Hartleben's *Pierrot Lunaire*: Speech – Poem – Melody – Vocal Performance," *Journal of New Music Research* 33/1 (2004), 71–111; and "On the Origins of Schoenberg's *Sprechgesang* in *Pierrot Lunaire*," *Min-Ad: Israeli Studies in Musicology Online* 5 (2006).
26. A. Beaumont (trans. and ed.), *Ferruccio Busoni: Selected Letters* (London: Faber and Faber, 1987), 169.
27. E. Stein, "The Treatment of the Speaking Voice in 'Pierrot Lunaire'," in E. Stein, *Orpheus in New Guises*, trans. H. Keller (London: Rockliff, 1953; original German version published in 1927), 86–9.
28. Quoted from W. K. Wimsatt, Jr. and C. Brooks, *Literary Criticism: A Short History* (New York: Knopf, 1959), 593.
29. For example, see Dunsby, *Schoenberg: Pierrot lunaire*, 28–32. See also E. Haimo,

"Schoenberg's *Pierrot lunaire*: A Cycle?" in *Pierrot lunaire: Albert Giraud – Otto Erich Hartleben – Arnold Schoenberg*, eds. M. Delaere and J. Herman, 147. For a dissenting opinion, see A. Forte, "Sets and Nonsets in Schoenberg's Atonal Music," *Perspectives of New Music* 11/1, 1972, 54.

30. See W. E. Benjamin, "Abstract Polyphonies: The Music of Schoenberg's Nietzschean Moment," in *Political and Religious Ideas in the Works of Arnold Schoenberg*, eds. C. M. Cross and R. A. Berman (New York: Garland, 2000), 1–39; R. Kurth, "Moments of Closure: Thoughts on the Suspension of Tonality in Schoenberg's Fourth Quartet and Trio," in *Music of My Future: The Schoenberg Quartets and Trio*, eds. R. Brinkmann and C. Wolff (Cambridge, MA: Harvard University Department of Music, 2000), 139–60; R. Kurth, "Suspended Tonalities in Schönberg's Twelve-Tone Compositions," *Journal of the Arnold Schönberg Center* 3 (2001), 239–65; and M. Cherlin, "Schoenberg and *das Unheimliche*: Spectres of Tonality," *Journal of Musicology*, 11/3 (1993), 357–73.

31. See A. Schoenberg, *Theory of Harmony*, trans. R. E. Carter (Berkeley and Los Angeles: University of California Press, 1983), 432.

32. Schoenberg, *Theory of Harmony*, 383–4. See also A. Schoenberg, *Structural Functions of Harmony*, ed. L. Stein (New York: W. W. Norton, 1969), 111–13.

33. Beaumont, *Ferruccio Busoni: Selected Letters*, 169.

34. See A. Byron, "The Test Pressings of Schoenberg Conducting *Pierrot lunaire*: *Sprechstimme* Reconsidered," *Music Theory Online* 12/1 (February 2006).

35. For instance, see analyses in Weytjens, "Text as a Crutch," *passim*; and D. Lewin, "Some Notes on *Pierrot lunaire*," in *Music Theory in Concept and Practice*, eds. J. M. Baker, D. W. Beach, and J. W. Bernard (Rochester: University of Rochester Press, 1997), 433–57.

36. Brinkmann, "The Fool as Paradigm," 155.

37. *Ibid.*, 155–7 and *passim*.

38. Dunsby, *Schoenberg: Pierrot lunaire*, 41; Weytjens, "Text as a Crutch," 40–2.

39. For further analysis of the "Entrückung" motive, see Michael Cherlin, *Schoenberg's Musical Imagination* (Cambridge University Press, 2007), 182–5.

40. Brinkmann, "The Fool as Paradigm," 143; compare Haimo, "Schoenberg's *Pierrot lunaire*: A Cycle?" 148 and 152–3.

41. See R. Stephan, "Schoenberg and Bach," trans. W. Frisch, in *Schoenberg and His World*, ed. W. Frisch (Princeton University Press, 1999), 128–30; Brinkmann, "The Fool as Paradigm," 156; and Dunsby, *Schoenberg: Pierrot lunaire*, 42.

42. For instance, Brinkmann, "The Fool as Paradigm," 142.

43. Schoenberg makes this point in an analysis of his own song "Lockung" in *Structural Functions of Harmony*, 111–13; and see Chapter 4.

Chapter 10 Schoenberg as Teacher

I am grateful to Sabine Feisst for her suggestions on an earlier version of this chapter.

1 The Arnold Schönberg Center in Vienna provides extensive information on Schoenberg's teaching activities and pupils; see www.schoenberg.at/default_e.htm. Also see L. Stein, "Schoenberg as Teacher," *The Arnold Schoenberg Companion* ed. W. B. Bailey (Westport: Greenwood Press, 1995), 251–7.

2. *Arnold Schönberg* (Munich: Piper, 1912); English translation by Barbara Z. Schoenberg in *Schoenberg and His World*, ed. W. Frisch (Princeton University Press, 1999), 256.

3. Elisabeth Derow-Turnauer, "Women and the Musical Aesthetics of the Bourgeoisie" in *Vienna: Jews and the City of Music*, eds. L. Botstein and W. Hanak (Hofheim: Wolke, 2004), 123–9; and J. A. Smith, *Schoenberg and His Circle: A Viennese Portrait* (New York: Schirmer Books, 1986), 159–72.

4. R. W. Wason, "*Musica practica*: Music Theory as Pedagogy," in *The Cambridge History of Western Music Theory*, ed. T. Christensen (Cambridge University Press, 2002), 68.

5. J. McBride, "Dem Lehrer Arnold Schönberg," *Journal of the Arnold Schoenberg Institute* 8/1 (1984), 31–8.

6. P. Gradenwitz, *Arnold Schönberg und seine Meisterschüler: Berlin 1925–1933* (Vienna: Paul Zsolnay, 1998); L. Holtmeier, "Arnold Schönberg an der Preußischen Akademie der Künste," in *Wien – Berlin: Stationen einere kulturellen Beziehung*, eds. H. Grimm *et al.* (Saarbrücken: Pfau, 2000), 97–110; and H-K Metzger and R. Riehn, (eds.), *Arnold Schönbergs "Berliner Schule"* (Munich: Edition Text + Kritik, 2002).

7. L. M. Knight, "Classes with Schoenberg January through June 1934," *Journal of the Arnold Schoenberg Institute* 13/2 (1990), 137–62.

8. D. L. Crawford, "Arnold Schoenberg in Los Angeles," *Musical Quarterly* 86/1 (2002), 6–48.

9. S. M. Feisst, "Arnold Schoenberg and the Cinematic Art," *Musical Quarterly* 83/1 (1999), 93–113.

10. See especially D. Newlin, *Schoenberg Remembered: Diaries and Recollections (1938–1976)* (New York: Pendragon, 1980).

11. A. Lessem, "The Emigré Experience: Schoenberg in America," in *Constructive Dissonance: Arnold Schoenberg and the Transformations of Twentieth-Century Culture*, eds. J. Brand and C. Hailey (Berkeley: University of California Press, 1997), 64.

12. Letter from Schoenberg to Emil Hertzka, director of Universal Editions, dated July 23, 1911. Cited in B. R. Simms, "Review of *Theory of Harmony*" in *Music Theory Spectrum* 4 (1982), 157.

13. See the English translation of the latter by C. M. Cross and S. Neff, *Coherence, Counterpoint, Instrumentation, Instruction in Form*, ed. S. Neff (Lincoln: University of Nebraska Press, 1994).

14. R. W. Wason, *Viennese Harmonic Theory from Albrechtsberger to Schenker and Schoenberg* (Ann Arbor: University of Michigan Press, 1985), 136–7; D. W. Bernstein, "Schoenberg contra Riemann: *Stufen*, Regions, *Verwandtschaft*, and the Theory of Tonal Function," *Theoria: Historical Aspects of Music Theory* 6 (1992), 23–53.

15. N. Dudeque, *Music Theory and Analysis in the Writings of Arnold Schoenberg (1874–1951)*, (Burlington: Ashgate, 2005), 15–20.

16. *Ibid.*, 30f.

17. Wason, "Review of *Theory of Harmony*," *Journal of Music Theory* 25/2 (1981), 313–14.

18. Simms, Review of *Theory of Harmony*, 158.

19. R. Hilmar, "Alban Berg's Studies with Schoenberg," *Journal of the Arnold Schoenberg Institute* 8/1 (1984), 7–30. Details of Berg's instruction recounted here are derived from this article.

20. The origins of the text are discussed in the edition and translation by P. Carpenter and S. Neff (New York: Columbia Press, 1995).

21. Crawford, "Arnold Schoenberg in Los Angeles," 28.

22. Stein, "Schoenberg as Teacher," 253–4.

23. Feisst, "Arnold Schoenberg and the Cinematic Art," 103–5.

24. B. R. Simms, "The Society for Private Musical Performances: Resources and Documents in Schoenberg's Legacy," *Journal of the Arnold Schoenberg Institute* 3/2 (1979), 127–49. The "Verein" builds upon an earlier organization he helped found in 1904, "The Society of Creative Musicians."

25. W. B. Bailey, "The Chamber-Ensemble Arrangements of the Orchestral Songs, Opus 8: Realizing Schoenberg's Instructions to his Students," *Journal of the Arnold Schoenberg Institute* 8/1 (1990), 64.

26. *Ibid*, 65; J. McBride, "Orchestral Transcriptions for the Society for Private Musical Performances," *Journal of the Arnold Schoenberg Institute* 7/1 (1983), 113–26.

27. Bailey, "Chamber Ensemble Arrangements," 75–7.

28. *Ibid*, 72–4.

29. Excerpts of a document that probably records Schoenberg's presentation to his pupils can be found in J. Auner, *A Schoenberg Reader: Documents of a Life* (New Haven and London: Yale University Press, 2003), 173–6.

30. Letter from Eisler to Schoenberg dated August 1923. In A. Dümling, "Schönberg und sein Schüler Hanns Eisler: Ein dokumentar-ischer Abriß," in *Arbeitsheft 24: Forum Musik in der DDR* eds. M. Hansen and C. Müller (Berlin: Akademie der Künste der DDR, 1976), 256.

31. R. U. Nelson, "Schoenberg's Variation Seminar," *Musical Quarterly* 50/2 (1964), 141–64.

32. Crawford, "Arnold Schoenberg in Los Angeles," 26–7.

33. See note 2.

34. McBride, "Dem Lehrer Arnold Schönberg." Excerpts from the photo album are reproduced in N. Nono-Schoenberg, (ed.) *Arnold Schönberg 1874–1951: Lebensgeschichte in Begegnungen* (Klagenfurt: Ritter, 1998), 232–5.

35. Evidence of their relationship in corre-spondence and other documents is collected in Dümling, "Schönberg und sein Schüler Hanns Eisler." Also J. Schebera, *Hanns Eisler: eine Biographie in Texten, Bildern und Dokumenten* (Mainz: Schott, 1998), 20–33, 37–47, 176–80, 191–3.

36. Eberhardt Klemm, "'I don't give a Damn about this Spring': Hanns Eisler's Move to Berlin," in *Hanns Eisler: A Miscellany*, ed. D. Blake (New York: Harwood Academic Publishers, 1995), 1–3.

37. O. Dahin and P. Deeg, "Meeting Marianne in Hilversum," *Eisler-Mitteilungen* 42 (October 2006), 12.

38. Letter from Schoenberg to a patron dated August 31, 1922. Dümling, "Schönberg und sein Schüler Hanns Eisler," 254, English translation in *Arnold Schoenberg Letters*, ed. E. Stein, trans. E. Wilkins and E. Kaiser (New York: St. Martin's Press, 1965), 75–6.

39. Letter from Eisler to Schoenberg dated April 13, 1923. Dümling, "Schönberg und sein Schüler Hanns Eisler," 255.

40. Letter from Schoenberg to Anny Winslow dated May 23, 1923. Dümling, "Schönberg und sein Schüler Hanns Eisler," 256.
41. Brecht journal entry dated April 27, 1942. *Journals 1934–1955*, eds. J. Willett and R. Manheim, (London: Routledge, 1993), 224.
42. Brecht journal entry dated July 29, 1942. *Journals*, 251.
43. Eisler, "Notes to Dr. Faustus," trans. K. von Abrams in D. Blake (ed.) *Eisler: A Miscellany*, 252–6.

Chapter 11 Schoenberg, satire, and the *Zeitoper*
1. Schoenberg to Kandinsky, July 20, 1922, *Arnold Schoenberg/Wassily Kandinsky: Letters, Pictures and Documents*: ed. J. Hahl-Koch, trans. J. C. Crawford (London: Faber, 1984), 74.
2. Schoenberg to Fromaigeat, July 22, 1919, *Arnold Schoenberg Letters*, ed. E. Stein, trans. E. Wilkins and E. Kaiser (London: Faber, 1964), 67.
3. Adorno later wrote that in Habsburg Vienna the "constituent traditionalism protested . . . against the tradition itself and revolutionized it with the demand that it take itself seriously," in T. W. Adorno, *Quasi una Fantasia: Essays on Modern Music*, trans. R. Livingstone (London, Verso, 1992), 204. Similarly, René Leibowitz argues, "there is not a *break*, but a *continuity* between [the works composed in the new system and the works which led to the discovery of this system]," in *Schoenberg and His School: The Contemporary Stage of the Language of Music*, trans. D. Newlin (New York: Philosophical Library, 1949), 104.
4. A. Schoenberg, *Theory of Harmony*, trans. R. E. Carter (London: Faber, 1978), 433.
5. The "conservative revolutionary," as Malcolm MacDonald suggests, had become a "revolutionary conservative." M. MacDonald, *Schoenberg* (London: J. M. Dent, 1976), 52. See also J. Auner, "Proclaiming a Mainstream" in *The Cambridge History of Twentieth-Century Music*, N. Cook and A. Pople (eds.), (Cambridge University Press, 2004), 228–59. Carl Dahlhaus writes that it was characteristic of Schoenberg for "musically revolutionary and conservative traits" to cancel each other out. See C. Dahlhaus, *Schoenberg and the New Music*, trans. D. Puffett and A. Clayton (Cambridge University Press, 1987), 102.
6. See, for instance, the *Grotesken-Album* published by Universal Edition, Vienna, in 1920.
7. See Schoenberg, "How One Becomes Lonely" (1937), in *Style and Idea: Selected Writings of Arnold Schoenberg*, ed. L. Stein, trans. L. Black (London: Faber, 1975), 30–53.
8. See H. H. Stuckenschmidt, *Schoenberg: His Life, World, and Work* (New York: Schirmer, 1978), 308–9; Krenek, "Music of Today," Address to the Congress of Music Aesthetics in Karlsruhe, October 19, 1925; trans. S. C. Cook, *Opera for a New Republic: The Zeitopern of Krenek, Weill, and Hindemith* (Ann Arbor: UMI Research Press, 1988), 193–203.
9. Schoenberg to Amadeo de Filippi, May 13, 1949, *Arnold Schoenberg Letters*, 271–2.
10. Krenek may possibly have had his revenge in the opening lines of *Jonny spielt auf*, in which the gloomy composer Max sings of his "Lovely Mountain ["*schöner Berg*"], who attracts me, who compels me to abandon my home, my work."
11. G. Watkins, "The Canon and Stravinsky's Late Style," *Confronting Stravinsky: Man, Musician, and Modernist*, ed. J. Pasler (Berkeley: University of California Press, 1986), 239.
12. Schoenberg, "Criteria for the Evaluation of Music," draft lecture from 1927, revised 1946, republished in *Style and Idea*, 134.
13. Quoted in S. Walsh, *Stravinsky: A Creative Spring* (New York: Alfred A. Knopf, 1999), 421. See also L. Stein, "Schoenberg and 'Kleine Modernsky,'" *Confronting Stravinsky*, 310–11.
14. Schoenberg, "New Music, Outmoded, Music, Style and Idea," lecture, March 22, 1931, revised February 10, 1933, reproduced in *Style and Idea*, 113–23.
15. See A. Goehr, "Schoenberg and Karl Kraus: The Idea behind the Music," *Music Analysis*, 4/1 (1985), 59–71.
16. Schoenberg to Kandinsky, April 19, 1923, Auner, *A Schoenberg Reader*, 168.
17. Schoenberg to Berg, October 1, 1933, J. Brand, C. Hailey, and D. Harris (eds), *The Berg-Schoenberg Correspondence: Selected Letters* (New York: W. W. Norton, 1987), 446; quoted in Auner, *A Schoenberg Reader*, 185.
18. Schoenberg, "How One Becomes Lonely" (1937), *Style and Idea*, 53.
19. H. H. Stuckenschmidt, *Arnold Schoenberg* (New York, Grove Press, 1960), 94.
20. C. Zuckmayer, *Als wär's ein Stück von mir. Horen der Freundschaft* (Frankfurt: S. Fischer Verlag, 1966), 314.
21. Schoenberg to *Deutsche Allgemeine Zeitung* (Berlin), June 18, 1930, in response to a question circulated to prominent national musicians about "musical life and a shift of the centre of gravity from Vienna to Berlin." See *Arnold Schoenberg Letters*, 142.

22. Schoenberg, aphorism published in *Der getreue Eckhart* 2/11 (1921), 512–13. This statement, which appeared in an issue entitled "The meaning of music for German culture," was prefaced by an editorial note that reminded the reader that Schoenberg was an artist who belonged to "the extreme left," who "on the basis of his latest works can be regarded as an outspoken advocate of atonalism and anarchy in music." Even he, it was noted, nevertheless concedes the uniquely valuable aspects of German culture. Trans. adapted from Maja Reid, reproduced in Auner, *A Schoenberg Reader*, 160. In his "National Music (2)" (1931), *Style and Idea*, 172–4, Schoenberg draws attention to the close links he saw between his music and the canonic German composers such as Bach, Mozart, Beethoven, and Wagner.

23. According to documents among the papers of Schoenberg's son-in-law Felix Greissle, it may have been based in part upon the domestic life of the Greissles, although the librettist told Leopoldina Gerhard that noted opera composer (and Schoenberg's close friend) Franz Schreker and his wife were the models. See J. Brand, "Of Authorship and Partnership: The Libretto of *Von heute auf morgen*," *Journal of the Arnold Schoenberg Institute* 14 (1991), 158.

24. See J. Shaw, "The Republic of the Mind," *Music, Theatre, and Politics in Germany: 1848 to the Third Reich*, ed. N. Bacht (Aldershot: Ashgate, 2006), 202–3.

25. Schoenberg, "An Introduction to a Broadcast of *Von heute auf morgen*," in Auner, *A Schoenberg Reader*, 220.

26. Frau: "Ich weiss ja, dass dich zu diesen Frauen nur die Neugier zieht; dass du dir hinter der glänzenden Maske ein phantastisches Wunder erhoffst. Von jeder neuen Erscheinung, die sich modisch gibt, bist du geblendet. Doch ist der Reiz der Neuheit vorbei, blickst du enttäuscht ins Nichts." *Von heute auf morgen*, mm. 224–38.

27. C. Witke, *Latin Satire: The Structure of Persuasion* (Leiden: Brill, 1970), 13.

28. See P. Tregear, "'Stadtluft macht frei': Urban Consciousness in Weimar Opera," *Music, Theatre, and Politics in Germany: 1848 to the Third Reich*, ed. N. Bacht, 237–54.

29. Schoenberg to Steinberg, October 4, 1929, (Rufer/Newlin, 56).

30. L. Rognoni, *Second Vienna School*, trans. R. W. Mann (London: John Calder, 1977), 264.

31. *Ibid.*, 197. J. Rufer, *Composition with Twelve Tones*, trans. H. Searle (London: Rockliff, 1954),

184. R. Gerhard, "Tonality in Twelve-Tone Music," *The Score*, 6 (1952), 23–35.

32. See K. Kalchschmid, "Zwölf Töne gegen die Mode: Zur Music-Dramaturgie in Schönbergs erster Zwölfton-Oper," Von heute auf morgen: *Oper – Musik – Film; Drehbuch und Materialien zum Film von Danièle Huillet & Jean-Marie Straub und zur Oper von Arnold & Gertrud Schönberg*, ed. K. Volkmer, K. Kalchschmid, P. Primavesi (Berlin: Vorwerk-8, 1997), 73–85.

33. D. Puffett, "'Music that Echoes Within One' for a Lifetime: Berg's Reception of Schoenberg's *Pelleas und Melisande*," *Music and Letters* 76 (1995), 209–64.

34. Schoenberg to Wilhelm Steinberg, October 4, 1929, quoted in J. Brand, "A Short History of *Von heute auf morgen* with Letters and Documents," *Journal of the Arnold Schoenberg Institute* 14 (1991), 248–9.

35. T. Adorno, "Arnold Schönberg: *Von heute auf morgen*," *Die Musik* 22 (1930), 446.

36. Rognoni, *Second Vienna School*, 195.

37. See Brand, "A Short History of *Von heute auf morgen*," 252.

38. T. Adorno, *Introduction to the Sociology of Music*, trans. E. B. Ashton (New York: The Seabury Press, 1976), xxx.

39. C. Dahlhaus, *Schoenberg and the New Music*, trans. D. Puffett and A. Clayton (Cambridge University Press, 1987), 102.

40. Schoenberg to Heinrich Jalowetz, in E. Stein (ed.), *Arnold Schoenberg Letters*, trans. E. Wilkins and E. Kaiser (London: Faber, 1964), 148. In 1973 the French film director Jean-Marie Straub produced a film to accompany the music.

41. J. Auner, "Schoenberg and His Public in 1930: The Six Pieces for Male Chorus, Op. 35," *Schoenberg and His World*, ed. W. Frisch (Princeton University Press, 1999), 116.

42. See, for instance, W. J., "Arnold Schoenberg's Idea," *Kölnische Zeitung*, February 11, 1933; quoted in J. Auner, "Arnold Schoenberg Speaks: Newspaper Accounts of His Lectures and Interviews, 1927–1933," in W. Frisch (ed.), *Schoenberg and His World*, 279.

Chapter 12 Schoenberg's row tables

1. See J. Auner, "In Schoenberg's Workshop: Aggregates and Referential Collections in the Composition of *Die glückliche Hand*," *Music Theory Spectrum* 18/1 (1996), 77–105; E. Haimo, *Schoenberg's Serial Odyssey: The Evolution of his Twelve-Tone Method, 1914–1928* (London and New York: Oxford University Press, 1990); B. Simms, *The Atonal*

Music of Arnold Schoenberg 1908–1923 (Oxford and London: Oxford University Press, 2000).

2. A. Schoenberg, "Composition with Twelve Tones," *Style and Idea: Selected Writings of Arnold Schoenberg*, ed. L Stein, trans. L. Black (Berkeley: University of California Press, 1984), 218–45. This essay grew out of lectures given at Princeton (1934), USC (1935), UCLA (1941), and the University of Chicago (1946), see *Style and Idea*, 214. Before coming to the USA in 1933, his most high profile presentation of the twelve-tone method in Europe was his "Radio Lecture on the Variations for Orchestra, Op. 31," broadcast in 1931. See J. Auner, *A Schoenberg Reader: Documents of a Life* (New Haven and London: Yale University Press, 2003), 235–40.

3. See David Headlam's bibliography to the "Twelve-Tone Composition" article in Grove Online which provides an excellent starting point to the literature as well as information about other twelve-tone approaches by Hauer, Roslavets, and others. See also J. Covach, "Twelve-Tone Theory," in *The Cambridge History of Western Music Theory*, ed. T. Christensen (Cambridge University Press, 2002), 603–27.

4. Schoenberg, "Krenek's 'Sprung über den Schatten,'" *Style and Idea*, 479, and see 92 and 386.

5. See, for example, the document he titled "Priority" from 1932 which discusses his concern that Josef Hauer would be given credit for the twelve-tone method. See Auner, *A Schoenberg Reader*, 235–40.

6. A. Ashby, "Schoenberg, Boulez, and Twelve-Tone Composition as 'Ideal Type'," *Journal of the American Musicological Society* 54/3 (2001), 585–625.

7. Cited in W. Reich, *Schoenberg: A Critical Biography*, trans. L. Black (New York: Praeger, 1971), 130.

8. A. Schoenberg, *The Musical Idea and the Logic, Technique, and Art of its Presentation*, trans. and eds. P. Carpenter and S. Neff (New York: Columbia University Press, 1995), 89.

9. Schoenberg, "Composition with Twelve Tones," 218–27.

10. S. Kostka, *Materials and Techniques of Twentieth Century Music* (Englewood Cliffs: Prentice Hall, 1990), 209.

11. www.m-t-software.com/software-matrix.html, accessed April 2009.

12. K. Bailey, "Webern's Row Tables," *Webern Studies*, ed. K. Bailey (Cambridge University Press, 1996), 173.

13. See for example, R. Kurth, "Dis-regarding Schoenberg's Twelve-Tone Rows: An Alternative Approach to Listening and Analysis for Twelve-Tone Music," *Theory and Practice* 21 (1996), 79–122.

14. M. M. Hyde, "The Format and Function of Schoenberg's Twelve-Tone Sketches," *Journal of the American Musicological Society* 36/3 (1983), 453–80. For another useful study that takes Schoenberg's row tables as a starting point, see S. Milstein, *Arnold Schoenberg: Notes, Sets, Forms* (Cambridge University Press, 1992).

15. R. S. Hill, "Schoenberg's Tone-Rows and the Tonal System of the Future," *Musical Quarterly* 22/1 (1936), 14–37; J. Rufer, *Die Komposition mit zwölf Tönen* (Berlin, 1952); E. Stein, "New Formal Principles," in *Orpheus in New Guises* (London: Rockliff, 1953), 57–77.

16. While it is beyond the scope of this chapter, striking evidence of the considerably different trajectories of twelve-tone theory in Germany, as compared to the USA and UK, can be seen in a comparison of the articles on Twelve-Tone Music in the *New Grove Dictionary* and its German counterpart, *Die Musk in Geschichte und Gegenwart*. In contrast to the lack of explicit discussion in the Grove article, MGG deals much more directly with the variety of possible row tables, and reproduces two of Schoenberg's own tables.

17. J. Straus, *Introduction to Post-Tonal Theory* (Englewood Cliffs: Prentice Hall, 1990). See also the similar approach in A. Whittall, *The Cambridge Companion to Serialism* (Cambridge University Press, 2008).

18. E. Krenek, *Studies in Counterpoint* (New York: Schirmer 1940), H. Jelinek, *Anleitung zur Zwölftonkomposition* (Vienna: Universal, 1952).

19. For more on "hexachordal inversional combinatoriality," see Straus, *Introduction to Post-Tonal Theory*, 184–92, and Haimo, *Schoenberg's Serial Odyssey*, 8–15.

20. See sketch page 1594, Arnold Schönberg Center.

21. M. Babbitt, *Words about Music*, eds. S. Dembski and J. Straus (Madison: The University of Wisconsin Press, 1987), 52.

22. R. Lorenz, "Changing Approach to Analysis of 12-Tone Music," in *21st-Century Music* 10/2 (2003), 1–3.

23. C. Neidhöfer, "Composing with Magic Squares," unpublished paper, Annual Meeting of the Society for Music Theory (Los Angeles, 2006). And see G. Nauck, *Musik im Raum-Raum in der Musik: Ein Beitrat zur geschichte der Seriellen Musick* (Stuttgart: Fritz Steiner Verlag, 1997).

24. Anton Webern, *The Path to the New Music*, ed. Willi Reich (Bryn Mawr: Theodore Presser Company, 1963), 56; the text can be

translated as "The sower Arepo holds the wheels with effort." J. Gwyn Griffiths, "The Magic 'Sator' Square," *The Classical Review* 21 (1971), 6–8.

25. Schoenberg, "Composition with Twelve Tones," 220, emphasis in the original.

26. For more on this topic see R. Busch, "On the Horizontal and Vertical Presentation of Musical Ideas and Musical Space," *Tempo* 154 (1985), 2–10.

27. K. Stockhausen, ". . . how time passes . . ." *Die Reihe* 3 (1957; English ed. 1959), 10–40.

28. G. Ligeti, "Decision and Automatism in Structures 1a," *Die Reihe* 4 (1958; English ed. 1960), 38.

29. Schoenberg, "Composition with Twelve Tones," 223.

30. Schoenberg, *The Musical Idea*, 373.

31. *Ibid.*, 18.

32. C. Dahlhaus, "Schoenberg's Aesthetic Theology," in *Schoenberg and the New Music*, trans. D. Puffett and A. Clayton (Cambridge University Press, 1987), 92.

33. A. Schoenberg, "New Music, Outmoded Music, Style and Idea," in *Style and Idea*, 116.

34. A. Schoenberg, "Criteria for the Evaluation of Music," in *Style and Idea*, 132. For a probing study of the Idea from the perspective of temporal unfolding in the Variations for Orchestra, Op. 31, see J. Covach, "Schoenberg's 'Poetics of Music,' The Twelve-Tone Method, and the Musical Idea," *Schoenberg and Words: The Modernist Years*, eds. C. M. Cross and R. A. Berman (New York: Garland, 2000), 309–46.

35. A. Schoenberg, "Breslau Lecture on *Die glückliche Hand* (1928), in *Arnold Schoenberg/Wassily Kandinsky: Letters, Pictures and Documents*, ed. J. Hahl-Koch, trans. J. C. Crawford (London: Faber, 1984), 107.

36. Schoenberg, *The Musical Idea*, 398.

37. Such sketches are the focus of Hyde's "The Format and Function of Schoenberg's Twelve-tone Sketches."

38. See J. Auner, "Schoenberg as Moses and Aron," *Opera Quarterly* 24/1 (2008), 1–12.

39. See J. Auner, "Schoenberg and His Public in 1930: The Six Pieces for Male Chorus, Op. 35," *Schoenberg and His World*, ed. W. Frisch (Princeton University Press, 1999), 85–125.

40. Schoenberg, *The Musical Idea*, 19.

41. *Ibid.*, 18.

Chapter 13 Immanence and transcendence in *Moses und Aron*

1. G. Tomlinson, *Metaphysical Song: An Essay on Opera* (Princeton: Princeton University Press, 1999).

2. *Ibid.*, 78.

3. *Ibid.*, 151.

4. T. Adorno, "Sakrales Fragment: Über Schönbergs *Moses und Aron*," in *Theodor W. Adorno. Gesammelte Schriften*, Band 16, *Musikalische Schriften I–III*, ed. R. Tiedeman (Frankfurt am Main: Suhrkamp, 1978), 454–75. Translations are my own. For alternative English translations, see T. Adorno, "Sacred Fragment: Schoenberg's *Moses und Aron*," in *Quasi una Fantasia: Essays on Modern Music*, trans. R. Livingstone (London: Verso, 1992), 225–48.

5. P. Lacoue-Labarthe, *Musica Ficta (Figures of Wagner)*, trans. F. McCarren (Stanford: Stanford University Press, 1994), 117–45; Tomlinson, *Metaphysical Song*, 147–56.

6. See, for instance, J. Schmidt, "Mephistopheles in Hollywood: Adorno, Mann, and Schoenberg," in *The Cambridge Companion to Adorno*, ed. T. Huhn (Cambridge University Press, 2004), 148–80.

7. Adorno, "Sakrales Fragment," 455.

8. *Ibid.*, 466. On the connection with *Parsifal*, see also G. Steiner, "Schoenberg's *Moses und Aron*," in *Language and Silence* (New York: Atheneum, 1967), 130; Lacoue-Labarthe, *Musica Ficta*, 121, 132, and 134 (using the expression "anti-*Parsifal*"); and Tomlinson, *Metaphysical Song*, 147 and 149.

9. Adorno, "Sakrales Fragment," 456.

10. P. C. White, *Schoenberg and the God-Idea: The Opera Moses und Aron* (Ann Arbor: UMI Research Press, 1985), 8–12 and 91–112. See also P. C. White, "The Genesis of *Moses und Aron*," *Journal of the Arnold Schoenberg Institute* 6/1 (1982), 8–55.

11. See M. Mäckelmann, *Arnold Schönberg und das Judentum, Der Komponist und sein religiöses, nationales und politisches Selbstverständnis nach 1921* (Hamburg: Karl Dieter Wagner, 1984), 119–56 and especially 157–66; see also A. Ringer, *Arnold Schoenberg: The Composer as Jew* (Oxford: Clarendon, 1990), 56–66.

12. On Schoenberg's adaptations to biblical sources, see B. Goldstein, "Schoenberg's *Moses und Aron*: A Vanishing Biblical Nation," in *Political and Religious Ideas in the Works of Arnold Schoenberg*, eds. C. M. Cross and R. A. Berman (New York: Garland, 2000), *passim*.

13. Adorno, "Sakrales Fragment," 456.

14. B. Goldstein, *Reinscribing Moses: Heine, Kafka, Freud, and Schoenberg in a European Wilderness* (Cambridge, MA: Harvard University Press, 1992), 144.

15. Adorno, "Sakrales Fragment," 469.

16. Mäckelmann, *Arnold Schönberg und das Judentum*, 139.

17. Adorno, "Sakrales Fragment," 461.

18. *Ibid.*, 462.

19. *Ibid.*, 465.

20. See also Steiner, "Schoenberg's *Moses und Aron*," 134.

21. Adorno, "Sakrales Fragment," 470. Regarding Schoenberg's engagement with the *Bilderverbot* from 1905 onward, see R. Kurth, "Schönberg and the *Bilderverbot*: Reflections on *Unvorstellbarkeit* and *Verborgenheit*," *Journal of the Arnold Schönberg Center* 5 (2003), 332–72. See also M. Kerling, "*O Wort, du Wort, das mir fehlt*": *Die Gottesfrage in Arnold Schönbergs Oper Moses und Aron* (Mainz: Matthias-Grünewald Verlag, 2004), 102–31.

22. Adorno, "Sakrales Fragment," 458.

23. *Ibid.*, 459.

24. *Ibid.*, 458.

25. *Ibid.*, 469.

26. A. Schoenberg, "The Relationship to the Text," in *Style and Idea: Selected Writings of Arnold Schoenberg*, ed. L. Stein, trans. L. Black (Berkeley: University of California Press, 1984), 141.

27. As David Lewin notes, it is significant that the Divine vocal mass from the Burning Bush combines both speaking and singing, as do many of the choral representations of the *Volk*. See D. Lewin, "*Moses und Aron*: Some General Remarks, and Analytic Notes for Act I, Scene 1," *Perspectives of New Music* 6/1 (1967), 2–3.

28. See Goldstein, "Schoenberg's *Moses und Aron*," 184–5.

29. The sublime is discussed at some length in Lacoue-Labarthe, *Musica Ficta*, 129–32 and 145; see also Tomlinson, *Metaphysical Song*, 151.

30. Schoenberg, "The Relationship to the Text," 145.

31. *Ibid.*, 142, translation slightly adjusted and emphasis added.

32. *Ibid.*, 141–2, translation slightly adjusted and emphasis added.

33. A. Schoenberg, "Aphorismen," *Die Musik* 9/21 (1909), 160. And see J. Auner, *A Schoenberg Reader: Documents of a Life* (New Haven and London: Yale University Press, 2003), 64–5.

34. J. Hahl-Koch (ed.), *Arnold Schoenberg/ Wassily Kandinsky: Letters, Pictures and Documents*, trans. J. C. Crawford (London: Faber, 1984), 54–5, translation slightly adjusted.

35. A. Schoenberg, "My Public," in *Style and Idea*, 96. See also J. Auner, "Schoenberg and His Public in 1930: The Six Pieces for Male Chorus, Op. 35," in *Schoenberg and His World*, ed. W. Frisch (Princeton University Press, 1999), 85–125.

36. See "Art for the Community," in Auner, *A Schoenberg Reader*, 211.

37. A. Schoenberg, "Schopenhauer und Socrates," Arnold Schönberg Center, Vienna, folder T02.09 (my translation).

38. For analytic and interpretive commentary on numerous aspects of the opera's first scene, see Lewin, "*Moses und Aron*," passim; M. Cherlin, "Dramaturgy and Mirror Imagery in Schoenberg's *Moses und Aron*: Two Paradigmatic Interval Palindromes," *Perspectives of New Music* 29/2 (1991), 50–71; M. Shaftel, "Translating for GOD: Arnold Schönberg's *Moses und Aron*," *Journal of the Arnold Schönberg Center* 5 (2003), 311–31. For analytic commentary on the entire opera, see M. Cherlin, *Schoenberg's Musical Imagination* (Cambridge University Press, 2007), 230–98.

39. Relevant properties of this hexachord are discussed in Cherlin, "Dramaturgy and Mirror Imagery," 55–6.

40. See Lewin, "*Moses und Aron*," 6; see also White, *Schoenberg and the God-Idea*, 123, 131, 153–4.

41. Cherlin, "Dramaturgy and Mirror Imagery," especially 53 and 57.

42. M. Cherlin, "Schoenberg's Representation of the Divine in *Moses und Aron*," *Journal of the Arnold Schoenberg Institute* 9/2 (1986), 213–15.

43. Adorno, "Sakrales Fragment," 460.

44. T. Adorno, "Fragment über Musik und Sprache" [1956], in *Musikalische Schriften I–III*, 252. On the theological issues invoked here, and their manifestations elsewhere in the opening scene, see P. Fischer-Appelt, "Die 'göttlichen Stimmen' in Schönbergs Oper *Moses und Aron*," *Journal of the Arnold Schönberg Center* 5 (2003), 373–85.

45. Schoenberg wrote a large exclamation mark on sketch page 2981 (dated Berlin, May 7, 1930) beside his discovery of this solution, immediately following two different attempts.

46. Alexander Ringer observes a similar concealment of the name B-A-C-H in mm. 1–3 and 84–5; see A. Ringer, *Arnold Schönberg: Das Leben im Werk* (Stuttgart: Metzler; and Kassel: Barenreiter, 2002), 257–8.

47. Schoenberg, "The Relationship to the Text," 142.

48. Michael Cherlin examines at length a related phenomenon in Schoenberg's music, dubbed the "time shard," see *Schoenberg's Musical Imagination*, 173–229.

arrangement of the Symphony for two pianos
(Op. 38b) on January 12, 1942 (Rufer, *The
Works of Arnold Schoenberg*, 64).
40. Rufer, *The Works of Arnold Schoenberg*,
65.

Chapter 16 Schoenberg's collaborations
1. Paragraph 10, RdRKK-1 1:4, quoted in
A. E. Steinweis, *Art, Ideology, and Economics in
Nazi Germany: The Reich Chambers of Music,
Theater, and the Visual Arts* (Chapel Hill and
London: University of North Carolina Press,
1993), 107.
2. A. Schoenberg, March 29, 1935 address in
*Style and Idea: Selected Writings of Arnold
Schoenberg*, ed. L. Stein, trans. L. Black
(Berkeley: University of California Press,
1984), 504.
3. Schoenberg, "Finally Alone!" February 4,
1928, J. Auner, *A Schoenberg Reader:
Documents of a Life* (New Haven and London:
Yale University Press, 2003), 209–10.
4. S. Viertel, *The Kindness of Strangers* (New
York: Holt, Rinehart, and Winston, 1969), 208.
5. E. da Costa Meyer and F. Wasserman (eds.),
Schoenberg, Kandinsky, and the Blue Rider
(London, New York, and Paris: Scala, 2004).
6. H. Weber (ed.), *Briefwechsel mit Arnold
Schönberg, Anton Webern, Alban Berg und
Franz Schreker* (Darmstadt: Wissenschaftliche
Buchgesellschaft, 1995), 106–12.
7. See E. L. Keathley, Chapter 6, and "'Die
Frauenfrage' in *Erwartung*: Schoenberg's
Collaboration with Marie Pappenheim,"
Schoenberg and Words: The Modernist Years,
eds. C. M. Cross and R. A. Berman (New York:
Garland, 2000), 156–60.
8. Undated letter from Pappenheim to
Schoenberg (November 1913?), Library of
Congress, trans. Shaw.
9. Postcard from Pappenheim to Schoenberg,
postmarked 1-IV-[1914], Library of Congress,
trans. Shaw.
10. Schoenberg, November 11, 1913 letter to
Alma Mahler: *Arnold Schönberg, 1874–1951:
Lebensgeschichte in Begegnungen*, ed. N. Nono-
Schoenberg (Klagenfurt: Ritter Verlag,
1998), 125.
11. Undated letter from Schoenberg to Emil
Hertzka [February?] 1914, letter 17, Library of
Congress Arnold Schoenberg Collection.
12. See J. Shaw, "Schoenberg's Choral
Symphony, *Die Jakobsleiter*, and Other
Wartime Fragments" (Ph.D. Diss.: State
University of New York at Stony Brook, 2002).
13. *Arnold Schoenberg: Letters*, ed. E. Stein,
trans. E. Wilkins and E. Kaiser (London: Faber,
1964), 106.

14. J. Shaw, "'The Republic of the Mind':
Politics, the Arts and Ideas in Schoenberg's
Post-War Projects," *Music, Theatre and
Politics in Germany: 1848 to the Third Reich*,
ed. N. Bacht (Aldershot: Ashgate, 2006),
200–7.
15. P. Potter, *Most German of the Arts:
Musicology and Society from the Weimar
Republic to the End of Hitler's Reich* (New
Haven and London: Yale University Press,
1998), 19.
16. Schoenberg, July 18, 1930 letter to
Klemperer, trans. P. Heyworth, *Otto
Klemperer: His Life and Times* (Cambridge
University Press, 1983), vol. 1, 333.
17. A. Heuss, "Arnold Schönberg, Preußischer
Kompositionslehrer" (Arnold Schönberg,
Prussian Composition Teacher), *Neue
Zeitschrift für Musik* 92/10 (1925), 583–5.
18. Schoenberg, "National Music," February
24, 1931, *Style and Idea*, 174.
19. Schoenberg, "New Music: My Music,"
(c.1930), *Style and Idea*, 105; see also
Schoenberg's scathing notes on Hans Redlich,
"Die Kompositorische Situation von 1930,"
Anbruch 12/6 (June 1930): 187–8, Arnold
Schönberg Center Archive, T35.37.
20. Schoenberg, "Priority," September 10–11,
1932, Auner, *A Schoenberg Reader*, 236.
21. Schoenberg, "A Text from the Third
Millennium," February 1948, Auner, *A
Schoenberg Reader*, 323.
22. "The Genesis Suite: The Milken Archive
restores an audacious musical work thought to
be lost forever," http://www.milkenarchive.
org/articles/articles.taf?
function=detail&ID=69.
23. Copies of correspondence between
Shilkret and the Schoenbergs, Arnold
Schönberg Center Archive.
24. Schoenberg, *Theory of Harmony* (1911 and
1922 versions), trans. R. E. Carter (Berkeley
and Los Angeles: University of California
Press, 1983), 30.
25. Schoenberg, "Is it Fair?" December 2,
1947, *Style and Idea*, 249–50.

**Chapter 17 Listening to Schoenberg's Piano
Concerto**
1. A. Schoenberg, "Heart and Brain in Music,"
in *Style and Idea: Selected Writings of Arnold
Schoenberg*, ed. L. Stein, trans. L. Black
(Berkeley: University of California Press,
1984), 53–76.
2. *Ibid.*, 69–71.
3. For insight into the Trio's connection to
past styles, see M. Cherlin, "Memory and
Rhetorical Trope in Schoenberg's String Trio,"

Journal of the American Musicological Society 51/3 (Fall 1998), 559–602.

4. Schoenberg, "Heart and Brain in Music," 54.

5. For a discussion of Schoenberg and his audience, see J. Auner, "Schoenberg and His Public in 1930: The Six Pieces for Male Chorus, Op. 35," in *Schoenberg and His World*, ed. W. Frisch (Princeton University Press, 1999), 85–125.

6. The String Trio was commissioned by A. Tillman Merritt of Harvard University for a Symposium on Music Criticism.

7. For information on Levant and the commissioning of the Concerto see W. B. Bailey, *Programmatic Elements in the Works of Schoenberg* (Ann Arbor: University of Michigan Research Press, 1984), 136–51.

8. This sketch, labeled as No. 148, and other sketches for the Piano Concerto are reproduced in Bailey, *Programmatic Elements in the Works of Schoenberg*, 143–9. Facsimiles for all the sketches are available on the website of the Arnold Schönberg Center, Vienna. www.schoenberg.at.

9. Schoenberg, "Composition with Twelve Tones (1) (1941)," in *Style and Idea*, 224.

10. See sketch No. 114 in Bailey, *Programmatic Elements in the Works of Schoenberg*, 145.

11. Schoenberg, "A Self Analysis (1948)," in *Style and Idea*, 78.

12. Schoenberg, "Brahms the Progressive (1947)," in *Style and Idea*, 409.

13. Schoenberg, "Heart and Brain in Music," 61.

14. *Ibid.*, 75.

Chapter 18 Schoenberg reception in America, 1933–51

I would like to acknowledge the generous grant from the Deutsche Forschungsgemeinschaft enabling me to do research on this topic.

1. See for instance: R. Leibowitz, *Schoenberg* (Paris: Editions du Seuil, 1969), 141; and W. Sinkovicz, *Mehr als zwölf Töne. Arnold Schönberg* (Vienna: Paul Zsolnay Verlag, 1998), 254.

2. Leibowitz, *Schoenberg*, 141.

3. E. Krenek, "America's Influence on Its Émigré Composers," *Perspectives of New Music* 8/2 (1970), 117.

4. S. Feisst, "Zur Rezeption von Schönbergs Schaffen in Amerika vor 1933," *Journal of the Arnold Schönberg Center* 4 (2002), 279–91. These performances are documented in royalty statements, concert programs, broadcast schedules, and reviews.

5. Economic pressures and the Federal Music Project (1935–41) creating jobs for innumerable unemployed musicians during the Depression encouraged composers in America, including Schoenberg, to write more conservative music.

6. A. Meyer, "Schoenberg at Last Comes to Symphony Hall," *Boston Evening Transcript*, March 17, 1934.

7. W. Sargeant, "Arnold Schoenberg and the Atonal Style," *Brooklyn Daily Eagle*, October 6, 1935.

8. See, for example, I. Jones, "Schoenberg Music Slated," *Los Angeles Times*, December 12, 1934.

9. These recordings were commercially released in 1950: Alco ALP 1005.

10. Sanromá recorded Opus 19 for RCA Victor, Red Seal M 646 (15862), pre-1940.

11. B. Ussher, "Schoenberg's New Quartet," *New York Times*, January 17, 1937.

12. A. Schoenberg, "Radio Address, 23 August 1949," in: V. Thomson, "Music in Review: Schoenberg Celebrates Seventy-fifth Birthday with Attack on Conductors," *New York Herald Tribune*, September 11, 1949.

13. For positive reviews of the Five Orchestral Pieces and the *Ode to Napoleon* see: V. Thomson, "In Waltz Time," *New York Herald Tribune*, October 22, 1948 and "Beautiful String Music," *New York Herald Tribune*, November 24, 1944. For mixed reviews of the Piano Concerto compare V. Thomson, "Real Modern Music," *New York Herald Tribune*, February 7, 1944 and O. Thompson, "Stokowski Leads Schoenberg Work," *New York Sun*, February 7, 1944. For negative reviews of the Violin Concerto see: E. Schloss, "What's that Awful Din?" *Philadelphia Record*, December 7, 1940; "Schoenberg Critics Chided by Stokowski," *New York Times*, December 8, 1940.

14. O. Downes, "Ormandy Gives His Opening Concert," *New York Times*, October 12, 1949; "Little Orchestra Plays Schoenburg [sic]," *New York Times*, November 4, 1947; "Schoenberg Leads Own Composition," *New York Times*, November 18, 1940.

15. O. Downes, "Ciccolini, Pianist, Heard at Concert," *New York Times*, November 3, 1950; "Stokowski Offers Schoenberg Work," *New York Times*, February 7, 1944.

16. Between the late 1930s and 1951 about twenty Schoenberg works were recorded and released by American labels including Alco, Capitol, Columbia, Dial, Esoteric, and RCA Victor. W. Shoaf, *The Schoenberg Discography* (Berkeley: Fallen Leaf Press, 1994). O. Downes, "Exchange of Views. Distinguished Composer

Discusses Mahler, Himself and Criticism,"
New York Times, December 12, 1948;
A. Schoenberg, "One Always Returns,"
New York Times, December 19, 1948; and
"Protest on Trademark," *New York Times*,
January 15, 1950.
17. O. Downes, "American Composers'
Techniques," *New York Times*, July 22, 1945;
D. G. Mason, "Atonality on Trial," *Musical
Digest* 29/14 (1947), 11 and 15; T. Serly,
"Problems of Style," *New York Times*, January
2, 1949; E. Ansermet, "Music: Expression or
Representation," *Musical America* 69/3 (1949),
6, 140 and 273; W. Sargeant, "Schönberg,"
New Yorker, November 5, 1949, 119–21.
18. R. Leibowitz, "Two Composers: A Letter
from Hollywood," *Partisan Review* 15/3
(1948), 361–65; D. Newlin, "Schoenberg's
Philosophy," *New York Times*, January 16,
1949; R. Sessions, "How a 'Difficult'
Composition Gets that Way," *New York Times*,
January 8, 1950.
19. See note 12 and V. Thomson, "Aaron
Copland Replies to Schoenberg; Conductors
Silent Regarding Attack," *New York Herald
Tribune*, September 25, 1949.
20. E. Wellesz, *Arnold Schoenberg*, trans. by
W. Kerridge (London: J. M. Dent and Sons,
1925); E. Stein, "Schoenberg's Third String
Quartet," *Dominant* 1/5 (1928), 14–16;
"Twelve-Tone Music," *Christian Science
Monitor*, February 16, 1929; "Schoenberg's
New Structural Form," *Modern Music* 7/4
(1930), 3–10; A. Weiss, "The Lyceum of
Schönberg," *Modern Music* 9/3 (1932), 99–107.
21. R. Hill, "Schoenberg's Tone-Rows and the
Tonal System of the Future," *Musical
Quarterly* 22/1 (1936), 31.
22. In the former text, Krenek cautioned
against mistaking a twelve-tone row for a
theme or a motive, yet suggested that motives
could be extrapolated from a row.
23. A. Schoenberg, "Problems of Harmony,"
trans. by A. Weiss, *Modern Music* 11/4 (1934),
167–87, and "Why No Great American Music,"
American Mercury, July 1934.
24. L. Harrison, "Homage to Schoenberg: The
Late Works," *Modern Music* 21/3 (1944),
134–8; M. Brunswick, "Tonality and
Perspective," *Musical Quarterly* 29/4 (1943),
426–37; D. Newlin, "Schoenberg's Variations
on a Recitative for Organ, Op. 40," *Pan Pipes*
40 (1948), 198–201.
25. H. Jalowetz, "On the Spontaneity of
Schoenberg's Music," *Musical Quarterly* 30/4
(1944), 385–408.
26. E. Krenek, "New Developments of the 12-
tone Technique," *Music Review* 4/2 (1943), 81–97.

27. G. Perle, "Evolution of the Twelve-Tone Row:
The Twelve-Tone Modal System," *Music Review*
2 (1942), 273–87 and "Twelve-Tone Tonality,"
Monthly Musical Record 43 (1943), 175–9.
28. Copland, however, declared it to be one of
the ten best books he read in 1949: "'The Best
Books I Read This Year' – Twelve
Distinguished Opinions," *New York Times*,
December 4, 1949.
29. M. Babbitt, "Review: René Leibowitz,
Schoenberg est son école and *Qu'est-ce que la
musique de douze sons?*," *Journal of the
American Musicological Society* 3/1 (1950),
57–60.
30. M. Babbitt, "Review: *Quatrième Cahier
(Polyphonie) – Le système dodécaphonique*,"
Journal of the American Musicological Society
3/3 (1950), 264–7, and G. Perle, "Schönberg's
Late Style," *Music Review* 12/4 (1952), 274–82.
31. A. Schoenberg, "Protest on Trademark,"
New York Times, January 15, 1950.
32. R. Sessions, "Some Notes on Schoenberg
and the 'Method of Composing with Twelve
Tones,'" *Score* 6 (1952), 7.
33. Thanks to Austin Clarkson for invaluable
information on Wolpe.
34. Kurt List to Arnold Schoenberg, letter of
May 20, 1949, Library of Congress,
Washington DC.
35. J. DeLapp, "Copland in the Fifties: Music
and Ideology in the McCarthy Era" (Ph.D.
Dissertation, University of Michigan), 1997,
104–5.

Chapter 19 Schoenberg: dead or alive?
1. See especially M. Kurtz, *Stockhausen*, trans.
R. Toop (London: Faber and Faber, 1992), 34–7.
2. P. Boulez, "Schoenberg is Dead," in
Stocktakings from an Apprenticeship, trans.
S. Walsh (Oxford and New York: Oxford
University Press), 209–14.
3. P. Boulez, "Schoenberg, the Unloved?" in
Orientations, ed. J. J. Nattiez, trans. M. Cooper
(London: Faber and Faber, 1986), 325ff.
4. *Ibid.*, 199.
5. P. Boulez and C. Samuel, *Eclats* (Paris:
Mémoire du Livre, 2002), 24 (my translation).
6. Boulez, *Stocktakings*, 198.
7. *Ibid.*
8. A. Schoenberg, *Arnold Schoenberg Letters*,
ed. E. Stein, trans. E. Wilkins and E. Kaiser
(London: Faber and Faber, 1974), 265.
9. See Kurtz, *Stockhausen*, 34–7 and 86–7.
10. Boulez, "Schoenberg is Dead" (my
translation).
11. *Ibid.*, 210.
12. *Ibid.*, 211.
13. *Ibid.*

14. *Ibid.*, 212f.

15. M. Kagel, *Wörter über Musik* (Munich: Piper, 1991), 85.

16. R. Fearn, *Bruno Maderna* (Chur: Harwood, 1990), 317.

17. L. Berio, *Two Interviews*, trans. and ed. D. Osmond-Smith (New York: M. Boyars, 1985), 103.

18. J. Stenzl (ed.), *Luigi Nono: Texte, Studien Zu Seiner Musik* (Zurich: Atlantis Musikbuchverlag, 1975), 92.

19. Kurtz, *Stockhausen*, 26–7.

20. K. Stockhausen, *Texte, Band 6* (Cologne: DuMont, 1989), 475–6.

21. I. Stravinsky and R. Craft, *Conversations with Igor Stravinsky* (London: Faber and Faber, 1959), 71.

22. Schnebel, "Schönberg's spate tonale Musik als disponierte Geschichte," in *Denkbare Musik* (ed. H. R. Zeller. Köln: Dumont Dokument, 1972), 195.

23. H. Lachenmann, *Musik als existentielle, Erfahrung Schriften 1966–1995*, ed. J. Häusler (Wiesbaden: Breitkopf & Härtel, 1996), 205.

24. *Ibid.*, 71.

25. *Ibid.*, 261.

26. *Ibid.*, 262.

27. *Ibid.*

28. *Ibid.*, 95.

29. B. Ferneyhough, *Collected Writings*, eds. J. Boros and R. Toop (Amsterdam: Harwood, 1995), 204.

30. *Ibid.*, 206.

31. *Ibid.*, 153.

Select bibliography

Adorno, Theodor W. *Gesammelte Schriften*. Band 16 and 18 *Musikalische Schriften I–III*. Ed. Rolf Tiedeman. Frankfurt am Main: Suhrkamp, 1978

    Minima Moralia: Reflections from Damaged Life. Trans. E. F. N. Jephcott. London: Verso, 1978

    "On the Social Situation of Music." In *Essays on Music*. Ed. R. Leppert. Trans. S. Gillespie. Berkeley and Los Angeles: University of California Press, 2002

    Philosophy of Modern Music. Trans. A. G. Mitchell and W. V. Blomster. New York: Continuum, 1973; New York: The Seabury Press, 1980

    Quasi una Fantasia: Essays on Modern Music. Trans. R. Livingstone. London: Verso, 1992

Applegate, Celia and Pamela Potter, (eds.) *Music and German National Identity*. Chicago and London: University of Chicago Press, 2002

Ashby, Arved. "Schoenberg, Boulez, and Twelve-Tone Composition as 'Ideal Type,'" *Journal of the American Musicological Society* 54/3 (2001), 585–625

Auner, Joseph. *A Schoenberg Reader: Documents of a Life*. New Haven and London: Yale University Press, 2003

    "In Schoenberg's Workshop: Aggregates and Referential Collections in the Composition of *Die glückliche Hand*," *Music Theory Spectrum* 18/1 (1996), 77–105

    "Proclaiming a Mainstream." In *The Cambridge History of Twentieth Century Music*. Eds. N. Cook and A. Pople. Cambridge University Press, 2004

    "Schoenberg's Aesthetic Transformations and the Evolution of Form in *Die glückliche Hand*," *Journal of the Arnold Schoenberg Institute* 12/2 (1989), 103–28

    "Schoenberg's Handel Concerto and the Ruins of Tradition," *Journal of the American Musicological Society* 59/2 (1996), 264–313

    "Schoenberg as Moses and Aron," *Opera Quarterly* 24/1 (2008), 1–12

Babbitt, Milton. *Words About Music*. Eds. S. Dembski and J. Straus. Madison: University of Wisconsin Press, 1987

Bacht, Nikolaus, (ed.) *Music, Theatre, and Politics in Germany: 1848 to the Third Reich*. Aldershot: Ashgate, 2006

Bailey, Walter B. "The Chamber-Ensemble Arrangements of the Orchestral Songs, Opus 8: Realizing Schoenberg's Instructions to his Students," *Journal of the Arnold Schoenberg Institute* 8/1 (1990), 63–88

    "Changing Views of Schoenberg." In *The Arnold Schoenberg Companion*, Westport: Greenwood Press, 1998

Programmatic Elements in the Works of Schoenberg. Ann Arbor: University of Michigan Research Press, 1984

Batnitzky, Leora. "Schoenberg's *Moses und Aron* and the Judaic Ban on Images," *Journal for the Study of the Old Testament* 92 (2001), 73–90

Beaumont, Antony (trans. and ed.) *Ferruccio Busoni: Selected Letters*. London: Faber and Faber, 1987; New York: Columbia University Press, 1987

Benson, Mark. "Schoenberg's Private Program for the String Quartet in D Minor, Op. 7," *Journal of Musicology* 11 (1993), 374–94

Bernstein, David Walter. "Schoenberg contra Riemann: *Stufen*, Regions, *Verwandtschaft*, and the Theory of Tonal Function," *Theoria: Historical Aspects of Music Theory* 6 (1992), 23–53

Boehmer, Konrad, (ed.) *Schoenberg and Kandinsky: An Historic Encounter*. Amsterdam: Harwood, 1997

Brand, Juliane. "Of Authorship and Partnership: The Libretto of *Von heute auf morgen*," *Journal of the Arnold Schoenberg Institute* 14 (1991), 153–239
  "A Short History of *Von heute auf morgen* with Letters and Documents," *Journal of the Arnold Schoenberg Institute* 14 (1991), 241–70

Brand, Juliane and Christopher Hailey, (eds.) *Constructive Dissonance: Arnold Schoenberg and the Transformations of Twentieth-Century Culture*. Berkeley: University of California Press, 1997

Brand, Juliane, Christopher Hailey, and Donald Harris, (eds.) *The Berg-Schoenberg Correspondence: Selected Letters*. New York: W. W. Norton, 1987

Brinkmann, Reinhold. *Pierrot lunaire Op. 21: Kritischer Bericht, Studien zur Genesis, Skizzen, Dokumente*. In *Arnold Schönberg Samtliche Werke*, Abteilung VI, Reihe B, Band 24/1. Mainz and Vienna: Schott and Universal Edition, 1995

Brinkmann, Reinhold and Christoph Wolff, (eds.) *Driven into Paradise: The Musical Migration from Nazi Germany to the United States*. Berkeley: University of California, 1999
  Music of My Future: The Schoenberg Quartets and Trio. Cambridge, MA: Harvard University Department of Music (2000), 95–116

Busch, Regina. "On the Horizontal and Vertical Presentation of Musical Ideas and Musical Space," *Tempo* 154 (1985), 2–10

Byron, Avior. "*Pierrot lunaire* in Studio and in Broadcast: *Sprechstimme*, Tempo and Character," *Journal of the Society for Musicology in Ireland* 2 (2006), 69–91
  "The Test Pressings of Schoenberg Conducting *Pierrot lunaire: Sprechstimme* Reconsidered," *Music Theory Online* 12/1 (February 2006)

Cahn, Steven J. "On the Representation of Jewish Identity and Historical Consciousness in Schoenberg's Religious Thought," *Journal of the Arnold Schönberg Center* (2003), 93–108

Cherlin, Michael. "Dialectical Opposition in Schoenberg's Music and Thought," *Music Theory Spectrum* 22/2 (2000), 157–76
  "Dramaturgy and Mirror Imagery in Schoenberg's Moses und Aron: Two Paradigmatic Interval Palindromes," *Perspectives of New Music* 29/2 (1991), 50–71
  "The Formal and Dramatic Organization of Schoenberg's *Moses und Aron*." Ph.D. Dissertation, Yale University, 1983

"Memory and Rhetorical Trope in Schoenberg's String Trio," *Journal of the American Musicological Society* 51/3 (Fall 1998), 559–602

"Schoenberg and *das Unheimliche*: Spectres of Tonality," *Journal of Musicology* 11/3 (1993), 357–73

Schoenberg's Musical Imagination. Cambridge University Press, 2007

"Schoenberg's Representation of the Divine in *Moses und Aron*," *Journal of the Arnold Schoenberg Institute* 9/2 (1986), 210–16

Christensen, Jean Marie. "Arnold Schoenberg's Oratorio *Die Jakobsleiter*," 2 vols. Ph.D. Dissertation, University of California Los Angeles, 1979

Cone, Edward T. "Sound and Syntax: An Introduction to Schoenberg's Harmony," *Perspectives of New Music* 13/1 (1974), 21–40

Cook, Susan C. *Opera for a New Republic: The Zeitopern of Krenek, Weill, and Hindemith*. Ann Arbor: UMI Research Press, 1988

Covach, John. "Twelve-Tone Theory." In *The Cambridge History of Western Music Theory*. Ed. T. Christensen. Cambridge University Press, 2002, 603–27

Crawford, Dorothy Lamb. "Arnold Schoenberg in Los Angeles," *Musical Quarterly* 86/1 (2002), 6–48

Cross, Charlotte M. "Three Levels of 'Idea' in Schoenberg's Thought and Work," *Current Musicology* 30 (1980), 24–36

Cross, Charlotte M. and Russell A. Berman, (eds.) *Political and Religious Ideas in the Works of Arnold Schoenberg*. New York: Garland, 2000

Schoenberg and Words: The Modernist Years. New York: Garland, 2000

Da Costa Meyer, Esther and Fred Wasserman, (eds.) *Schoenberg, Kandinsky, and the Blue Rider*. London, New York, and Paris: Scala, 2004

Dahlhaus, Carl. *Esthetics of Music*. Trans. W. Austin. Cambridge University Press, 1982

Schoenberg and the New Music. Trans. D. Puffet and A. Clayton. Cambridge University Press, 1987

Dale, Catherine. "The 'Skeleton in Schoenberg's Musical Closet': The Chequered Compositional History of Schoenberg's Second Chamber Symphony," *Journal of the Royal Musical Association* 123 (1998), 68–104

Davidson, Stephen. "Of its Time, or Out of Step?: Schoenberg's *Zeitoper, Von heute auf morgen*," *Journal of the Arnold Schoenberg Institute* 14 (1991), 271–98

Delaere, Mark and Jan Herman, (eds.) *Pierrot Lunaire: Albert Giraud – Otto Erich Hartleben – Arnold Schoenberg*. Louvain: Peeters, 2004

Dudeque, Norton. *Music Theory and Analysis in the Writings of Arnold Schoenberg (1874–1951)*. Aldershot: Ashgate, 2005

Dümling, Albrecht. "Schönberg und sein Schüler Hanns Eisler: Ein dokumentarischer Abriß," *Arbeitsheft 24: Forum Musik in der DDR*, eds. M. Hansen and C. Müller Berlin: Akademie der Künste der DDR, 1976, 252–73

Dunsby, Jonathan. *Schoenberg: Pierrot lunaire*. Cambridge University Press, 1992

Feisst, Sabine M. "Arnold Schoenberg and the Cinematic Art," *Musical Quarterly* 83/1 (1999), 93–113

"Zur Rezeption von Schönbergs Schaffen in Amerika vor 1933," *Journal of the Arnold Schönberg Center* 4 (2002), 279–91

Forte, Allen. "Sets and Nonsets in Schoenberg's Atonal Music," *Perspectives of New Music* 11/1 (1972), 43–64

Frisch, Walter. *The Early Works of Arnold Schoenberg, 1893–1908*. Berkeley: University of California Press, 1993

 Schoenberg and His World. Princeton University Press, 1999

Goehr, Alexander. "Schoenberg and Karl Kraus: The Idea Behind the Music," *Music Analysis* 4/1 (1985), 59–71

 "Schoenberg's Late Tonal Works," *The Listener* 17 (1964), 132

Goehr, Lydia. "Adorno, Schoenberg, and the 'Totentanz der Prinzipien' – in Thirteen Steps," *Journal of the American Musicological Society* 56/3 (2003), 595–636

Goldstein, Bluma. *Reinscribing Moses: Heine, Kafka, Freud, and Schoenberg in a European Wilderness*. Cambridge, MA: Harvard University Press, 1992

 "Schoenberg's *Moses und Aron*: A Vanishing Biblical Nation." In *Political and Religious Ideas in the Works of Arnold Schoenberg*, eds. C. M. Cross and R. A. Berman (New York: Garland, 2000)

Goltz, Jennifer. "Pierrot le diseur," *The Musical Times* 147/1894 (Spring 2006), 59–72

Gradenwitz, Peter. *Arnold Schönberg und seine Meisterschüler: Berlin 1925–1933*. Vienna: Paul Zsolnay, 1998

 "The Religious Works of Arnold Schoenberg," *Music Review* 21 (1960), 19–29

Green, Martin Burgess and John C. Swan. *The Triumph of Pierrot: The Commedia dell'Arte and the Modern Imagination*. New York: MacMillan, 1986

Gruber, Gerold, (ed.) *Arnold Schönberg: Interpretationen seiner Werke, 2 vols.* Laaber: Laaber Verlag, 2002

Hahl-Koch, Jelena, (ed.) *Arnold Schoenberg/Wassily Kandinsky: Letters, Pictures and Documents*. Trans. J. C. Crawford. London: Faber, 1984

Haimo, Ethan. *Schoenberg's Serial Odyssey: The Evolution of his Twelve-Tone Method, 1914–1928*. London and New York: Oxford University Press, 1990

 Schoenberg's Transformation of Musical Language. Cambridge University Press, 2006

Hill, Richard S. "Schoenberg's Tone-Rows and the Tonal System of the Future," *Musical Quarterly* 22/1 (1936), 14–37

Hilmar, Rosemary. "Alban Berg's Studies with Schoenberg," *Journal of the Arnold Schoenberg Institute* 8/1 (1984), 7–30

Hyde, Martha Maclean. "The Format and Function of Schoenberg's Twelve-Tone Sketches," *Journal of the American Musicological Society* 36/3 (1983), 453–80

Jacob, Andreas. *Grundbegriffe der Musiktheorie Arnold Schönbergs, 2 vols.* Hildesheim: Georg Olms Verlag, 2005

Jalowetz, Heinrich. "On the Spontaneity of Schoenberg's Music," *Musical Quarterly* 30/4 (1944), 385–408

Kangas, William. "The Ethics and Aesthetics of (Self) Representation: Arnold Schoenberg and Jewish Identity," In *Leo Baeck Institute Year Book* 45 (2000), 135–70

Keathley, Elizabeth Lorraine. "Revisioning Musical Modernism: Arnold Schoenberg, Marie Pappenheim, and *Erwartung's* New Woman." Ph.D. Dissertation, State University of New York at Stony Brook, 1999

Knight, Lovina May. "Classes with Schoenberg January through June 1934," *Journal of the Arnold Schoenberg Institute* 13/2 (1990), 137–62

Kramer, Ulrich. "Zur Notation der Sprechstimme bei Schönberg." In *Schönberg und der Sprechgesang*. Eds. H.-K. Metzger and R. Riehn, *Musik-Konzepte* 112/113 (July 2001), 6–32

Kurth, Richard. "The Art of Cadence in Schoenberg's Fourth Quartet: Metric Discourse or Metric Dialectic?" *Journal of the Arnold Schönberg Center* 4 (2002), 245–70

"Dis-Regarding Schoenberg's Twelve-Tone Rows: An Alternative Approach to Listening and Analysis for Twelve-Tone Music," *Theory and Practice* 21 (1996), 79–122

"Schönberg and the *Bilderverbot*: Reflections on *Unvorstellbarkeit* and *Verborgenheit*," *Journal of the Arnold Schönberg Center* 5 (2003), 332–72

"Suspended Tonalities in Schönberg's Twelve-Tone Compositions," *Journal of the Arnold Schönberg Center* 3 (2001), 239–65

Lazar, Moshe. "Arnold Schoenberg and His Doubles: A Psychodramatic Journey to his Roots," *Journal of the Arnold Schoenberg Institute* 17 (1994) 48–9

Leibowitz, René. *Schoenberg and His School: The Contemporary Stage of the Language of Music*. Trans. D. Newlin. New York: Philosophical Library, 1949

Lessem, Alan Philip. *Music and Text in the Works of Arnold Schoenberg: The Critical Years*, 1908–22. Ann Arbor: University of Michigan Research Press, 1979

Lesure, François. *Dossier de Presse Press-Book de Pierrot lunaire d'Arnold Schoenberg*. Geneva: Minkoff, 1985

Lewin, David. "Inversional Balance as an Organizing Force in Schoenberg's Music and Thought," *Perspectives of New Music* 6/2 (1967–8), 1–21

"*Moses und Aron*: Some General Remarks, and Analytic Notes for Act I, Scene 1," *Perspectives of New Music* 6/1 (1967), 1–17

"Some Notes on *Pierrot lunaire*." In *Music Theory in Concept and Practice*. Eds. J. M. Baker, D. W. Beach, and J. W. Bernard. Rochester: University of Rochester Press, 1997, 433–57

Lewis, Christopher. "Mirrors and Metaphors: Reflections on Schoenberg and Nineteenth-Century Tonality," *19th-Century Music* 11/1 (1987), 26–42

Lindenberger, Herbert. "Arnold Schoenberg's *Der biblische Weg* and *Moses und Aron*: On the Transactions of Aesthetics and Politics," *Modern Judaism* 9 (1989), 55–70

MacDonald, Malcolm. *Schoenberg*. London: J. M. Dent, 1976

McBride, Jerry. "Dem Lehrer Arnold Schönberg," *Journal of the Arnold Schoenberg Institute* 8/1 (1984), 31–8

"Orchestral Transcriptions for the Society for Private Musical Performances," *Journal of the Arnold Schoenberg Institute* 7 (1983), 113–26

Milstein, Silvina. *Arnold Schoenberg: Notes, Sets, Forms*. Cambridge University Press, 1992

Morgan, Robert P. *Twentieth-Century Music: A History of Musical Style in Modern Europe and America*. New York: W. W. Norton, 1991

Namenwirth, Michael Simon. "Twenty Years of Schoenberg Criticism: Changes in the Evaluation of Once Unfamiliar Music." Ph.D. Dissertation, Minneapolis: University of Minnesota, 1965

Neff, Severine, ed. *Arnold Schoenberg: The Second String Quartet in F-sharp minor, Opus 10: Authoritative Score, Background and Analysis, Commentary.* New York and London: Norton, 2006

Nelson, Robert U. "Schoenberg's Variation Seminar," *Musical Quarterly* 50/2 (1964), 141–64.

Newlin, Dika. *Schoenberg Remembered: Diaries and Recollections (1938–1976).* New York: Pendragon, 1980

   "Schoenberg's Variations on a Recitative for Organ, Op. 40," *Pan Pipes* 40 (1948), 198–201

Nono-Schoenberg, Nuria (ed.) *Arnold Schönberg 1874–1951, Lebensgeschichte in Begegnungen.* Klagenfurt: Ritter Klagenfurt, 1998

   Arnold Schoenberg: Self-Portrait. Pacific Palisades, CA: Belmont Music Publishers, 1988

Perle, G. "Schönberg's Late Style," *Music Review* 12/4 (1952), 274–82

Potter, Pamela. *Most German of the Arts: Musicology and Society from the Weimar Republic to the End of Hitler's Reich.* New Haven and London: Yale University Press, 1998

Puffet, Derrick. "'Music that Echoes within One' for a Lifetime: Berg's reception of Schoenberg's *Pelleas und Melisande*," *Music and Letters* 76 (1995), 209–63

Raessler, Daniel M. "Schoenberg and Busoni: Aspects of their Relationship," *Journal of the Arnold Schoenberg Institute* 7/1 (1983), 7–27

Rapoport, Eliezer. "On the Origins of Schoenberg's *Sprechgesang* in *Pierrot Lunaire*," *Min-Ad: Israeli Studies in Musicology Online* 5 (2006)

   "Schoenberg – Hartleben's *Pierrot Lunaire*: Speech – Poem – Melody – Vocal Performance," *Journal of New Music Research* 33/1 (2004), 71–111

Reich, Willi. *Schoenberg: A Critical Biography.* Trans. L. Black. New York: Praeger, 1971

Ringer, Alexander L. *Arnold Schoenberg. The Composer as Jew.* Oxford: Clarendon, 1990

   Arnold Schönberg: Das Leben im Werk. Stuttgart: Metzler; and Kassel: Barenreiter, 2002

Rognoni, Luigi. *The Second Vienna School.* Trans. R. W. Mann. London: John Calder, 1977

Root, Gordon. "Tonal Analogues: The Interaction of Text and Music in the Works of Arnold Schoenberg," Ph.D. Dissertation, University of California at Santa Barbara, 2006

Rufer, Josef. *Composition with Twelve Tones.* Trans. H. Searle. London: Rockliff, 1954

   Die Komposition mit zwölf Tönen. Berlin: Max Hesses Verlag, 1952

   The Works of Arnold Schoenberg: A Catalogue of His Compositions. Trans. D. Newlin. London: Faber & Faber, 1962

Schmidt, James. "Mephistopheles in Hollywood: Adorno, Mann, and Schoenberg." In *The Cambridge Companion to Adorno*, ed. T. Huhn. Cambridge University Press, 2004, 148–80

Schmidt, Matthias. "Musik ohne Noten: Arnold Schönbergs 'Pierrot lunaire' und Karl Kraus," *Studien zur Musikwissenschaft: Beihefte der Denkmäler der Tonkunst in Österreich* 47 (1999), 365–93

Schoenberg, Arnold. "Analysis of the Four Orchestral Songs, Op. 22." Trans. C. Spies,
    Perspectives of New Music 3/2 (1965), 1–21
    Arnold Schönberg – Franz Schreker; Briefwechsel. Ed. F. C. Heller. Tutzing: Hans
    Schneider, 1974
    Arnold Schoenberg Letters. Ed. E. Stein. Trans. E. Wilkins and E. Kaiser. London
    and New York: Faber and St. Martin's Press, 1964–5
    "Attempt at a Diary," trans. A. Luginbühl, *Journal of the Arnold Schoenberg
    Institute* 9/1 (1986), 7–51
    Berliner Tagebuch. Ed. J. Rufer. Berlin: Propyläen Verlag, 1974
    Coherence, Counterpoint, Instrumentation, Instruction in Form. Ed. S. Neff. Trans.
    C. Cross and S. Neff. Lincoln: University of Nebraska Press, 1994
    Der biblische Weg (German/English edition). Trans. Moshe Lazar, *Journal of the
    Arnold Schoenberg Institute* 17 (1994), 162–329
    The Musical Idea and the Logic, Technique, and Art of Its Presentation. Trans. and
    eds. P. Carpenter and S. Neff. New York: Columbia University Press, 1995
    Structural Functions of Harmony. Ed. L. Stein. New York: W. W. Norton, 1969
    Style and Idea: Selected Writings of Arnold Schoenberg. Trans. L. Black. Ed. L. Stein.
    Berkeley: University of California Press, 1975 and 1984
    Theory of Harmony. Trans. R. E. Carter. Berkeley and Los Angeles: University of
    California Press, 1978 and 1983
Schwarzschild, Steven S. "Adorno and Schoenberg As Jews Between Kant and Hegel,"
    Leo Baeck Institute Year Book 35 (1990), 443–78
Sessions, Roger. "Some Notes on Schoenberg and the 'Method of Composing with
    Twelve Tones,'" *Score* 6 (1952)
Shaftel, Matthew R. "Translating for GOD: Arnold Schönberg's *Moses und Aron*,"
    Journal of the Arnold Schönberg Center 5 (2003), 311–31
Shaw, Jennifer. "Schoenberg's Choral Symphony, *Die Jakobsleiter*, and Other
    Wartime Fragments," Ph.D. Dissertation, State University of New York at Stony
    Brook, 2002
Shawn, Allen. *Arnold Schoenberg's Journey*. New York: Farrar, Straus and
    Giroux, 2002
Shoaf, Wayne. *The Schoenberg Discography*. Berkeley: Fallen Leaf Press, 1994
Simms, Bryan R. *The Atonal Music of Arnold Schoenberg: 1908–1923*. Oxford
    University Press, 2000
    "The Society for Private Musical Performances: Resources and Documents in
    Schoenberg's Legacy," *Journal of the Arnold Schoenberg Institute* 3/2 (1979), 127–49
Sinkovicz, Wilhelm. *Mehr als zwölf Töne. Arnold Schönberg*. Vienna: Paul Zsolnay
    Verlag, 1998
Smith, Joan Allen. *Schoenberg and His Circle: A Viennese Portrait*. New York:
    Schirmer Books, 1986
Specht, R. John, "Schoenberg Among the Workers: Choral Conducting in Pre-1900
    Vienna," *Journal of the Arnold Schoenberg Institute* 10/1 (1987), 28–37
Stadlen, Peter. "Schoenberg's Speech-Song," *Music and Letters* 62/1 (January 1981), 1–11
Staudacher, Anne L. *Jüdisch-protestantische Konvertiten in Wien 1782–1914, Teil 2*.
    Frankfurt-am-Main: Peter Lang, 2004

Stein, Erwin. *Orpheus in New Guises*. Trans. H. Keller. London: Rockliff, 1953, 57–77
    "Schoenberg's New Structural Form," *Modern Music* 7/4 (1930), 3–10
    "Schoenberg's Third String Quartet," *Dominant* 1/5 (1928), 14–16
Stein, Leonard. "Foreword: Schoenberg's Jewish Identity (A Chronology of Source
    Material)," *Journal of the Arnold Schoenberg Institute* 3/1 (1979), 3–10
    "Schoenberg and 'Kleine Modernsky.'" In *Confronting Stravinsky: Man, Musician,*
    Modernist. Ed. J. Pasler. Berkeley: 1986
Steiner, George. "Schoenberg's *Moses und Aron*." In *Language and Silence*. New York:
    Atheneum, 1967, 127–39
Stephan, Rudolf. "Zur jüngsten Geschichte des Melodrams," *Archiv für*
    Musikwissenschaft 17 (1960), 183–92
Straus, Joseph. *Introduction to Post-Tonal Theory*. Englewood Cliffs: Prentice Hall,
    1990
    Remaking the Past: Musical Modernism and the Influence of the Tonal Tradition.
    Cambridge, MA, and London: Harvard University Press, 1990
Stuckenschmidt, Hans Heinz. *Schoenberg: His Life, World, and Work*. Trans.
    H. Searle. New York: Schirmer Books, and London: John Calder, 1978
Swift, Richard. "1/XII/99: Tonal Relations in Schoenberg's *Verklärte Nacht*,"
    19th-Century Music 1/1 (1977), 3–14
    "Schoenberg's Second Chamber Symphony," *International Journal of Musicology*
    4 (1997), 169–81
Wason, Robert. W. "Review of *Theory of Harmony*," *Journal of Music Theory* 25/2
    (1981), 307–16
    Viennese harmonic theory from Albrechtsberger to Schenker and Schoenberg. Ann
    Arbor: University of Michigan Press, 1985
Watkins, Holly. "Schoenberg's Interior Designs," *Journal of the American*
    Musicological Society 61/1 (2008), 123–206
Weber, Horst, (ed.) *Briefwechsel mit Arnold Schönberg, Anton Webern, Alban Berg,*
    und Franz Schreker. Darmstadt: Wissenschaftliche Buchgesellschaft, 1995
Weiss, Adolph. "The Lyceum of Schönberg," *Modern Music* 9/3 (1932), 99–107
Wellesz, Egon. *Arnold Schoenberg*. Trans. W. Kerridge. London: J. M. Dent and Sons,
    1925
Weytjens, Stephan. "Text as a Crutch in Arnold Schoenberg's *Pierrot lunaire* Op. 21?"
    Ph.D. Dissertation, Katholieke Universiteit Leuven, 2003
White, Pamela Cooper. "The Genesis of *Moses und Aron*," *Journal of the Arnold*
    Schoenberg Institute 6/1 (1982), 8–55
    Schoenberg and the God-Idea: The Opera Moses und Aron. Ann Arbor: UMI
    Research Press, 1985
Whittall, Arnold. *The Cambridge Companion to Serialism*. Cambridge University
    Press, 2008.
Wörner, Karl. "Musik zwischen Theologie und Weltanschauung. Das Oratorium 'Die
    Jakobsleiter.'" In *Die Musik in der Geistesgeschichte: Studien zur Situation des*
    Jahres um 1910. Bonn: Bouvier, 1970, 171–200
Youens, Susan. "Excavating an Allegory: The Texts of Pierrot lunaire," *Journal of the*
    Arnold Schoenberg Institute 8/2 (1984), 95–115

Index

Cambridge Companions to Music

The Cambridge Companion to Mozart
Edited by Simon P. Keefe

The Cambridge Companion to Ravel
Edited by Deborah Mawer

The Cambridge Companion to Rossini
Edited by Emanuele Senici

The Cambridge Companion to Schoenberg
Edited by Jennifer Shaw and Joseph Auner

The Cambridge Companion to Schubert
Edited by Christopher Gibbs

The Cambridge Companion to Schumann
Edited by Beate Perrey

The Cambridge Companion to Shostakovich
Edited by Pauline Fairclough and David Fanning

The Cambridge Companion to Sibelius
Edited by Daniel M. Grimley

The Cambridge Companion to Verdi
Edited by Scott L. Balthazar

Instruments

The Cambridge Companion to Brass Instruments
Edited by Trevor Herbert and John Wallace

The Cambridge Companion to the Cello
Edited by Robin Stowell

The Cambridge Companion to the Clarinet
Edited by Colin Lawson

The Cambridge Companion to the Guitar
Edited by Victor Coelho

The Cambridge Companion to the Organ
Edited by Nicholas Thistlethwaite and
Geoffrey Webber

The Cambridge Companion to the Piano
Edited by David Rowland

The Cambridge Companion to the Recorder
Edited by John Mansfield Thomson

The Cambridge Companion to the Saxophone
Edited by Richard Ingham

The Cambridge Companion to Singing
Edited by John Potter

The Cambridge Companion to the Violin
Edited by Robin Stowell